Palestine
with Jerusalem

THE BRADT TRAVEL GUIDE

Henry Stedman

Bradt Publications, UK
The Globe Pequot Press Inc, USA

First published in 2000 by Bradt Publications,
19 High Street, Chalfont St Peter, Bucks SL9 9QE, England
web: bradt-travelguides.com
Published in the USA by The Globe Pequot Press Inc, 6 Business Park Road,
PO Box 833, Old Saybrook, Connecticut 06475-0833

British Library Cataloguing in Publication Data
A catalogue record for this book is available from the British Library
ISBN 1 84162 001 7

Library of Congress Cataloging-in-Publication Data
Data applied for

Photographs
Front cover Modern Palestine cross-stitch work (Patricia Aithie/ffotograff)
Text Christine Osborne/MEP (CO), Henry Stedman (HS)
Illustrations Carole Vincer
Maps Steve Munns

Typeset from the author's disc by Wakewing
Printed and bound in Italy by LegoPrint S.p.A., - Trento

Author/Acknowledgements

AUTHOR

Born in Kent, England, Henry Stedman has travelled extensively throughout the Near East, and is the author of Trailblazer's *Istanbul to Cairo Overland*. A full-time travel writer and lecturer, he is also the co-author of the *Rough Guide to Indonesia*, has worked on the *Rough Guide to Europe* and Trailblazer's *Trekking in the Annapurna Region*, and is currently in the process of writing up a trekking guide to the Italian Dolomites while lecturing on a cruise ship in the middle of the Indian Ocean.

ACKNOWLEDGEMENTS

To name everybody who helped me during my trip, either by sharing their knowledge or simply by furnishing me with a glass of *chai*, would make this guidebook stretch to two volumes. Besides, I never caught the names of many of these people, even if their help was vital on many occasions. Please note that the opinions of all those listed below are not necessarily the same as those expressed in this book.

First and foremost, I'd like to thank the new Star of Bethlehem, Dania Darwish of the UN, who helped to set up the opportunity to produce this book in the first place. I'd also like to thank Gemal of the Al-Ahram Hotel (Jerusalem) for proving to be such a reliable and inexhaustible source of information and advice. I'm also extremely grateful to the following, in no particular order: Father Gian-Maria (Bethany); Father Jacob (Beit Jala); Mother Ksenia (Chapel of Ascension, Mount of Olives); Sulaiman Na'eem Abu Kharmeh (Nablus); Yousef Sayegh (Birqeen); Nasser el-Jelda (Gaza); Amro Dagamin (Sumo'a); Khaled F Al Qawasme (Hebron); Ahmed Rejoob (Hebron/Ramallah); Samer Imraish (Nablus); Fawaz al-Sha'arawy, Iyad Gzziwi, Muneep Sultan, Tareq al-Hanini and Tareq Sadeqmoswadee (Hebron); Seth Augustine (USA); Samer Imraish (Nablus); Mamoun (Matt) Shkeir (Jifna); Zahi Slamih (Nablus); Motea Guidaih (Gaza); Ahmed El-Smiry and Esam Abu Amra (Khan Younnis); Tawfik El-Hourani (Gaza Airport); FM Tobail (State Information Service, Gaza Airport); Michael the Swiss photographer (Gaza); Jamal Hussein Hamad (UNRWA); Dr Walid A Abubaker (World Health Organisation), Ahmed Rejoob (Ministry of Culture, Ramallah); Musa Sanad (Artas); Amir Dajani (Telepherique, Jericho).

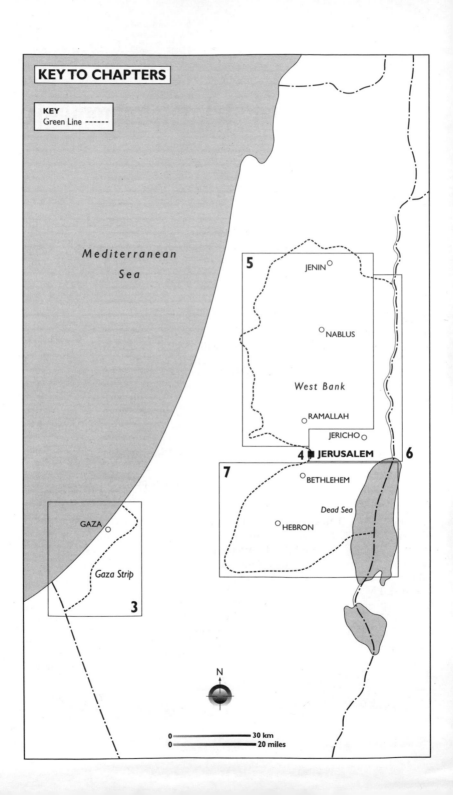

KEY TO CHAPTERS

KEY
Green Line ------

*Mediterranean
Sea*

5
JENIN ○

○ NABLUS

West Bank

○ RAMALLAH

JERICHO ○

4 ■ **JERUSALEM**　　6

7
○ BETHLEHEM

Dead Sea

○ HEBRON

GAZA
○

Gaza Strip

3

N

| 0 |　　　 30 km |
| 0 |　　　 20 miles |

Contents

Introduction

It was during my walk back from Mar Saba, a 4th-century monastery stuck right in the heart of the Judaean Desert, that I received my 'visitation'. The mercury in the monastery's thermometer that day was nudging 42°C; the walk itself, to the nearest village of Obedaiya, is a fairly exacting uphill scramble through honey-coloured sand and shale that takes about an hour and a half to complete. It's arduous but, providing you're adequately prepared, fairly straightforward. Unfortunately, having forgotten to refill my water bottle at the monastery, adequately prepared I most definitely was not. I'd also forgotten to bring a sunhat; and so I did what anybody else with felafal for brains would have done in my position: took off my trousers and wrapped them round my head instead.

Thus, had there been anybody around that day, they would have seen a lonely figure in boxer shorts and an oversized turban marching uphill in the shimmering desert. After a while, they would have noticed this figure's purposeful stride giving way to a Neanderthal-style lope, then a desperate shuffle, and finally a meandering, stop-start crawl on all fours. Walking in the desert that day was like taking a stroll in a furnace. Grit, blowing in the wind, crunched between my teeth, while flies hitched a lift on my forehead. After a while, and with the summit still way off in the distance, I stopped altogether and held an emergency meeting with my brain. Should I continue this forlorn quest to reach the village? Try to roll back down to the monastery and get help? Or simply curl up into a ball and wait for a passing Bedouin tribe to find my desiccated corpse?

It was at that point, as I lay under the blazing sun in the foetal position with a stone for a pillow, that I noticed a small cloud of sand approaching from the distant horizon. My first thought – that the Heavenly Host had come to take me away (I'd obviously been hanging around monks for too long) – was dispelled when, as the cloud grew nearer, I noticed that it was, in fact, wearing a pair of child's flip-flops. A few moments later the cloud came to a halt, the dust settled and there, standing in front of me, was a small boy with a big grin and an even bigger bottle of water.

As the last drop trickled down my throat I began to think of what I could give him to show my gratitude, deciding that my camera, credit cards, travellers' cheques and a written promise to send him half of any future earnings would probably be just about fair. But, in typical Palestinian style, he wanted none of it; seeing a tourist with a pair of trousers wrapped round his head was obviously reward enough. Instead he turned on his heels and, with a wave of the bottle and a big grin, sped off again in the direction from whence he came, leaving a bewildered, ashamed but extremely grateful guidebook writer behind him.

At the beginning of the introduction I described this episode as a 'visitation', simply because that's how many people back in England have interpreted it: the boy was some sort of guardian angel, they say, and I am one very lucky chappy. Either that, or they think I'm just a liar who fabricated the whole story in a vain attempt to liven up my anecdotes. Both of these responses are wrong but both are understandable, for, until you've experienced it for yourself, the Palestinians' extraordinary kindness and genuine concern for foreign visitors does indeed seem either miraculous or fantastical.

When you think just how much suffering the Palestinian people have experienced over the past 100 years — much of it caused by the same Westerners who now parade in their cities and deserts with their expensive cameras, loud shirts and trousers wrapped around their heads – such hospitality seems even more amazing. But then Palestine has a knack of confounding expectations. Most people who've never visited imagine this tiny country to be a land of riots and refugees, Shi'ites and suicide bombers; a sort of Kosovo, only with added hoummus. It's easy to forget that Palestine has so much to offer the tourist, and millions do flock to the country every year – even if, on many occasions, they don't actually realise they're in Palestine when they visit.

Other common misconceptions? Well, despite its Middle Eastern location, Palestine is not all desert. Indeed, much of the country is profoundly fertile: a land where the fruit is so plentiful and cheap you'd think it grew on trees. And even though Israel sits right on its doorstep, Palestine, a modern nation that's just as much at home with computers as with camels, retains a traditional Arab culture that's one of the richest and liveliest in the Near East.

Of course, Palestine's reputation as one of the world's trouble-spots is not entirely undeserved. The antagonism between Arab and Jew in the Holy Land has dragged on for a century now. In that time we've seen two world wars; the rise and demise of Communism and the Soviet Empire; the end of apartheid; independence for India, Africa and a whole commonwealth of other colonies; major conflicts in Indochina, the Balkans and the Gulf; the emergence of a federal Europe; a man on the moon; the development of satellite communications and the computer age; and the irresistible domination of the Spice Girls. Entire countries have disappeared over the past century and dozens of new ones have been established. Yet still the question of Palestine rumbles on, unresolved and intractable.

But please don't let that put you off visiting. You'll notice manifestations of the troubles everywhere you go, from the hypersensitive airport security to the random identity checks at roadblocks and the all-too-visible presence of armed Israeli soldiers parading around Jerusalem's Old City. However, as a tourist you'll be reduced to the status of spectator: you may see a number of mini-dramas played out every day in the Holy Land, but you won't be part of them. And while your government may have been guilty in the past of aggravating the upheavals and compounding the Palestinians' misery, I promise you the locals won't hold you personally responsible.

While this book keeps one eye on safety, we also celebrate the manifold but unsung virtues of this fascinating country that has just about everything you could ask for. Located both at the western end of the Cradle of Civilisation, a fertile arc running from the Mediterranean to Mesopotamia, and at the crossroads of three huge continents, its history is inevitably both long and colourful, and this is evidenced by the wide variety of spectacular ruins dotting the landscape. Along with Israel – the country with which it shares both land and mutual antipathy – Palestine forms part of the Holy Land, with more sites of religious importance than any other region on earth. This is Judaism's Promised Land, Christianity's birthplace and the location of the Islam's oldest mosque. And if that's not enough, Palestine can also boast the earth's oldest city, Jericho; as well as a share in the holiest, Jerusalem. Within its borders you'll find the world's lowest piece of land (the Dead Sea coast), its most over-populated (the Gaza Strip) and, with the ever-controversial and highly addictive Hebron, possibly its most volatile city; not to mention Bethlehem, the focus of the world's millennial celebrations and a vibrant, bustling town in its own right.

If all that history and religion sounds a bit too worthy, you'll be pleased to know that Palestine also has beaches and beer. Its people are wonderful, the food's great, the transport connections are first rate and, by contrast with its expensive neighbour, it's dirt cheap. So don't be put off by what you've read in the press: banish all preconceptions and come to see Palestine for yourself.

Just don't forget your sunhat.

About this guide

Writing a guide to Palestine was always going to be tricky. This is, after all, a nation with no clearly defined border; a country with a government that is able to exercise control over only a fraction of its total territory, and with a flag which, in many areas of the country, its people are not allowed to raise. Furthermore, its population, for the most part, lives abroad.

Yet, whatever the doubts about its borders and status, one thing is for certain: I, and many travellers like me, love being there. But even we recognise that Palestine isn't perfect, and this book is a warts-'n'-all guide to the land. As a guidebook writer it's my prerogative to be opinionated, condemning and critical. That's what I'm paid for.

Nevertheless, when examining the current political situation I have striven to be as non-judgemental as possible. Since I've spent a lot of time with the Palestinians over the past five years, that's where my sympathies tend to lie, but I've tried to prevent my views permeating the text. Besides, I have no grudge against the Israelis. On occasions I may get angry at the treatment they mete out to my Palestinian friends, but they've always treated me with courtesy and politeness. However, I want this book to be about Palestine and the Palestinians; which is why most of the time I've tried to avoid mentioning Israel at all.

Although it was never our aim, by its very nature this guide is still bound to cause offence. Some readers will argue that our definition of what exactly constitutes the nation of Palestine is too small, while others will be horrified that we have even recognised the country. There will also be those who object on the grounds that producing a guide to such a beleaguered nation is at best insensitive, and, at worst, downright crass – as if we are in some way capitalising on the plight of the Palestinians. Then, of course, there will be those who, out of ignorance, accuse me of risking travellers' lives by persuading them to visit such a turbulent country.

We have tried our best to pick our way delicately between all of these accusations, and to avoid being in any way exploitative, prejudiced or irresponsible. My inclusion of the cities of Jerusalem and Hebron, for example, which some may see as a political statement, was not done out of any particular solidarity with the Palestinian cause. Hebron, despite the regular upheaval there, definitely falls within the borders of the West Bank, while Jerusalem is covered simply because it's inconceivable that anybody would tour the Holy Land without visiting the holiest city of them all. Jerusalem is also something of a transport hub – it's almost impossible to travel round Palestine without passing through the city – and many visitors to Palestine will find it a convenient base from which to make day trips to sights on the West Bank. Furthermore, if the Palestinians had their way, Jerusalem would be the capital of their nation, and there can be no doubt that East Jerusalem and the Old City are more Palestinian than Israeli.

As well as these two inclusions, there are two deliberate omissions from this book which may also cause eyebrows to be raised. The first is the monastic town of Latroun, which, though it falls geographically within the borders of the West Bank, was formally annexed by Israel in 1967. It is doubtful that, whatever shape the Palestinian state finally takes, Latroun will ever come under its jurisdiction, and this is why it has been omitted. I have also deliberately left out all the Jewish settlements in the West Bank and Gaza. Though this may be seen as some sort of political statement, to me it's just a matter of common sense: the Palestinians would not thank me for including them, and the settlers themselves would be horrified to find themselves included in a book on Palestine. Besides, there's very little of interest to tourists in these settlements anyway. We have, however, included details of a museum and a tour around a Jewish settlement near Hebron – see page 207 – for the benefit those who wish to find out more about the settlers and their history, lifestyle and ideologies.

Nor do we make any apology for encouraging foreigners to visit Palestine. Far from being exploitative, we feel (and we have the backing of nearly all Palestinians in this regard) that a guidebook can only be beneficial to the region. Palestine has just about everything a tourist could ask for. There is so much to see and do in both the West Bank and the Gaza Strip, and tourism should be a bedrock of the Palestinian economy. But, of course, tourists will only come to Palestine when they finally stop believing that it is a dangerous place. I find myself getting a little annoyed when I hear people, and particularly ignorant journalists trying to create some sort of action-man reputation, bragging about visiting the Gaza Strip or Hebron as if they were war zones where you put your life on the line just by being there.

Quite simply, providing you employ the same amount of common sense and tact that you would when visiting any foreign country, you'll find the whole of Palestine to be very safe. Indeed, as I've already mentioned, despite years of dispersal, defeat and occupation, the Palestinian people have rarely ceased to offer foreign visitors a degree of hospitality that beggars belief. To the inhabitants of the refugee camps of the Gaza Strip or West Bank, the average tourist must appear flash, ignorant, idle, boorish and dissipated – and I include myself in that description. Yet, in all my time in Palestine, I have consistently been treated with a level of kindness, generosity and tolerance that is both overwhelming and humbling. This book may not be perfect but, if it were not for the patient help given to me by so many different people of so many different backgrounds and creeds, there probably wouldn't be a book at all. It is to these people – who made a flash, ignorant, idle, boorish and dissipated Englishman feel so welcome in their country – that I dedicate this guide.

Maps, translations and abbreviations

Palestine has a serious shortage of decent maps and, despite some extensive searching, for a couple of towns we had to resort to drawing the maps by hand, and researching them on foot. As a consequence, the maps are somewhat simplified and the scales offer only a rough approximation. We hope they are still of some use.

Most people in Palestine speak a little English, but to make things easier for you we have also written a phonetic version of the place names in Arabic, with the Arabic script next to it. This should enable you to find your way even in places where nobody speaks English. I have used the term 'Holy Land' as a shorthand phrase to describe the land now occupied by Palestine and Israel.

As you read through this book you'll notice that, when describing a tourist attraction, we've often quoted two entrance fees separated by a '/'. The first is the price for adults, the second for students. Finally, when reviewing hotels we've used the abbreviations sgl/dbl for single/double rooms.

Part One

General Information

PALESTINE FACTS

Location Palestine is split into two parts, and separated by Israel. Gaza lies on the shore of the Eastern Mediterranean, bordering the Sinai desert of Egypt, while the West Bank lies to the west of the Jordan Valley, between Israel and Jordan.

Area 6,210km² West Bank and Gaza Strip (though a large portion remains under Israeli control)

Status Republic (partly occupied by Israel, and with limited powers).

Population 2,250,000 (3–4 million refugees live outside Palestine, it is unclear how many plan to go back to Palestine if they get the opportunity)

Date of Declaration September 13, 1993

President Yasser Arafat

Effective capital Gaza

Major towns Nablus, Ramallah, Jericho, Bethlehem, Hebron, Khan Younnis. East Jerusalem is also widely considered to be Palestinian territory.

Currency Currently using Israeli shekels (NIS). US Dollars, Syrian and Jordanian pounds also widely accepted.

Language Arabic (official), Hebrew (mainly used by settlers in West Bank and Gaza with Israeli citizenship); English widely spoken.

Religion 82% Muslim (predominantly Sunni), 7% are Christians and the remaining 11% largely comprises of Jewish settlers. These figures exclude Jerusalem, which is far more equitably divided.

Background

GEOGRAPHY AND CLIMATE
Geography

Consisting of two separate territories divided by the State of Israel, Palestine is a tiny country, less than half the size of the Netherlands. Of these two territories, it is the **West Bank** – the name given to the disputed lands sandwiched between Israel and Jordan – that is, at 5,860km², by far the larger. Packed within the West Bank are an extraordinary variety of geographic features, from the lofty 1,000m-plus **Samarian Mountains** in the north to the shores of the **Dead Sea** in the south – at 395m below sea level, the lowest point on the earth's surface. The landscape reflects this diverse topography, the agricultural fecundity of the Samarian range being in stark contrast to the barren wastes of the **Judaean Desert**, which in turn presents a different vista from those of the low-lying pastoral hills to the east and south of Jerusalem and the steep, bare gorge of the **Jordan Valley**. This last feature is merely the northern extremity of Africa's Rift Valley, a great crack in the earth's surface where two tectonic plates meet.

While the Jordan River provides a natural border between the West Bank and Jordan, the former has no such convenient geographical feature to separate it from Israel. Instead, the two countries are divided by the so-called '**Green Line**', an arbitrary border drawn up in the aftermath of the 1948 war. Its exact position remains a very contentious issue: there are no posts or fences demarcating the Line, and most maps in Israel refuse to show it altogether. As a rough guide, the northern section of the Green Line runs along the edge of the Jezreel Valley, while to the south the border runs due west from a point almost exactly in the centre of the Dead Sea. On its western side the Green Line runs approximately due north-south, though you'll notice in the map on the inside front cover it suddenly takes a sharp dip eastwards, thereby excluding Jerusalem from the West Bank territories. This anomaly has existed since 1967 and the annexation of East Jerusalem by Israel, and indicates that the Holy City now lies entirely within Israel's borders. The isthmus of Israeli land created to the west of the Holy City by this dip is known as the **Jerusalem Corridor**.

As part of the ongoing war of words between Palestine and Israel, the Israeli authorities refer to the West Bank as **Judaea** and **Samaria** after the ancient Israelite kingdoms (see page 32) that once ruled the area. Samaria refers to the West Bank's northern, hilly region, including Nablus, the largest town in the West Bank, and Ramallah; while Judaea refers to the more barren region to the south, including the Dead Sea, Hebron, Jericho and Bethlehem. To the east of these southerly slopes lies the Judaean Desert.

Much of the West Bank currently remains under Israeli occupation, with only the city centres allowed unrestricted autonomy under the PNA (Palestinian National Authority). The situation is somewhat different with the **Gaza Strip**, a tiny (approximately 360km²) sliver of Mediterranean coastline bordered by Israel to the east and north, and the Egyptian-owned Sinai Desert to the south. The Gaza

Strip owes its existence to the War of 1948 (see pages 15–16) when Egypt stormed in and occupied this narrow stretch of land. Though the Israelis snatched it back in 1967 the territory, with its large population of Palestinian refugees, continued to receive different treatment from the rest of Israel, and with the signing of the Oslo accords was given a degree of autonomy under the PNA in 1994.

Visit Gaza today, and your first impressions may leave you wondering why anybody would bother fighting for such a wilderness. It is a fairly desolate area, though only at the border with the Sinai does it fulfill the official definition of a desert. The plight of the Palestinian refugees seems more visible in the Gaza than on the West Bank, a parlous standard of living exacerbated by overcrowding: though less than a twentieth the size of the West Bank, the Gaza Strip has over half the population (820,000, as opposed to the West Bank's 1,430,000). Nevertheless, it does have a couple of interesting towns and tourist attractions and, for a chance to take advantage of Palestinian hospitality and an insight into the hardships the Palestinians have suffered, a tour of the Gaza Strip is recommended.

Climate

Weather-wise, Palestine is fine to visit all year round. The higher areas of the West Bank do experience a typically wet and cool Mediterranean winter, and Jerusalem occasionally suffers the kind of torrential thunderstorm that would have Noah reaching for his tool kit, but even during these chilly periods it only really gets cold in the low-lying areas at night. Indeed, many people actually prefer to visit at this time in order to avoid the harsh Palestinian sunshine that frazzles the land and its people for much of the year. The summers in these upland areas do tend to be fairly fierce, though the gentle summer breeze provides a welcome accompaniment to the heat.

THE ZONES

To help establish a timetable for implementing the Oslo Peace Accords, the West Bank was divided into three zones: A, B and C. **Zone A**, constituting just 2% of the total West Bank area, covered the major city centres, and these were handed over to the authority of the PNA in 1994–5. **Zone B**, which begins almost as soon as one leaves these city centres (a crossing usually marked by an Israeli checkpoint), remains in Israeli hands at present. This area, 26% of the total area of the West Bank, covers the land immediately outside the main cities and includes a large number of Palestinian villages and smaller towns. While the PNA is responsible for internal administration in these areas, Israel still controls the policing and security of the region. In this way, the Israelis can still 'close the West Bank', preventing movement between Palestinian cities and towns and crippling the economy of the region. The date for handing over Zone B to the PNA has been postponed several times now, although, with the fresh impetus to the peace process provided by the election of Ehud Barak, it is hoped that the handover can take place soon. **Zone C** on the other hand, consisting of the countryside areas, is also under Israeli control, though they should be handed over to Palestine at some indeterminate date in the far-off future. Jewish settlements, and the roads linking them to Israeli territory, are to remain under Israeli jurisdiction for the foreseeable future. While Israelis can pass through Palestinian cities, though few choose to do so, Palestinians cannot pass through Israeli settlements.

The southern half of the West Bank and the whole of the Gaza Strip are pretty warm all year round, with average monthly temperatures rarely, if ever, dipping below 10°C. The heat in Jericho, where average summer temperatures touch 40°C, are particularly fierce to the point of being uncomfortable and dangerous. Avoid the sun in the heat of the day here.

If climate is a major factor in your decision about when to visit, the mild temperatures of spring and autumn are to be recommended, though when visiting the hill regions take an umbrella as protection against the frequent showers.

NATURAL HISTORY
Flora
Though far more barren now than in biblical times – when the slopes were covered with forests, which have since been cleared by the demand for wood for heating and burning sacrificial offerings – with its combination of mountain, desert and coastal scenery, Palestine remains the home of a heterogeneous selection of flora. Native wild flowers include the tulip, iris, hyacinth, cyclamen and buttercup, while in the southern deserts you may find lion's leaf, wild tulips and dandelion. Down the centuries a number of species have been introduced by local farmers, such as citrus fruits, bananas, cherries, tobacco and cereals, and these have taken root and grown alongside the indigenous plants. Though the vast forests of biblical times have largely disappeared now, you can still find cyprus, poplar, willow, lilac, pine and cedar. The palm tree is ubiquitous, thriving particularly well in the sands of the Gaza Strip.

Fauna
Read the Bible and you'd be forgiven for thinking that the Holy Land was one big nature reserve, with creatures ranging from the mundane (sacrificial lambs, lost sheep, lowing cattle etc) to the man-eaters (lions and wolves) and even the mythical (such as the Leviathan, a sort of multi-headed sea monster, and the Behemoth, said to be the first of God's attempts at creating animals) all roaming around the pages of the Good Book.

Unfortunately, thanks to the sharp-shooting Ottomans, the Bible's about the only place you'll find many of these indigenous Palestinian creatures these days. Lions, which crop up regularly in the early religious history of Palestine (Daniel spent a night in a pit full of them, the kingdom of Judaea used a lion as its symbol, and Saint Gerasimos, a 4th-century hermit who founded a monastery near Jericho – see page 175 – kept one as a pet), disappeared during the Crusades.

Despite the loss of so many species, the Holy Land can still boast over 70 **mammals**, including the ibex (mountain goat), wolf, antelope, porcupine and rock hyrax, a sort of foot-long guinea pig whose main claim to fame is that it's the closest living relative to the elephant. Domesticated beasts include donkeys and mules, angora goats, cows and cats – usually Siamese and often rather scruffy and unkempt. Over 80 **reptile** species have also survived into the 20th century, and you're bound to see lizards scurrying from rock to rock if you visit the desert. A number of scorpions, some poisonous, also inhabit the more barren regions of the country. Sightings are, however, very rare.

Palestine lies on the flight-path of many migratory **birds**, and its central position within the habitation boundaries of both northern and southern hemisphere species makes it something of a twitcher's paradise. Wild ducks, herons, cranes, sparrows, finches, starlings, geese, water rails, pigeons, crows, jays, larks, thrushes, swifts, martins, warblers, shrikes, tits, finches, bunting, eagles, kites and sparrowhawks are just some of our feathered friends who touch down in Palestine during the year. There are no major parks or reserves in Palestine where you can see these species (the authorities are in the process of trying to establish their first nature reserve north of Ramallah), but visitors to the Jordan Valley and the Dead Sea, and in particular Jericho, Qumran and Wadi Qelt, will find these places teeming with birdlife.

HISTORY

Thanks largely to geographical proximity, the early histories of Palestine and Israel overlap to such an extent as to be virtually identical. They're like Siamese twins; unfortunately, they're twins who really don't get on. That said, it is almost impossible to find a history of the Holy Land that isn't narrated from an Israeli viewpoint. For example, the Israelites' exile in Egypt, and the 40-year sojourn in the wilderness under Moses that followed, are both given great prominence in a history of Israel and Palestine. Whilst this pro-Zionist slant is perfectly justifiable when discussing the history of Israel – after all, if it weren't for the Exodus there wouldn't even be an Israel – it does make the task of distilling a balanced history of Palestine and the Palestinians more difficult than it should be.

What's more, the early history of the Holy Land tends to rely too heavily on the Jewish Torah (the Old Testament of the Bible) which, though fascinating and inspiring, is unreliable as a source of historical fact. (On page 30 you will find a box, *The Bible as History*, which examines to what extent we can regard the book as a trustworthy historical text.) Therefore, while the following history of Palestine contains many events recounted in the Bible, these have been included only where they are both essential to the integrity of the narrative and corroborated by other, extrabiblical, evidence. The section on Judaism, beginning on page 29, has more details on how the Bible treats the early history of the region.

Early man

Positioned in the fertile crescent that runs around the northern rim of the Arabian desert from the Persian Gulf to Egypt – the so-called **Cradle of Civilisation** – Palestine has been inhabited since the earliest days of mankind's history. Archeologists usually place the arrival of man in the Levant to about 500,000BC, and stone-age sites exist throughout the region, including Tel El-Sultan in Jericho. Initially these early inhabitants would have followed a nomadic existence, wandering along the crescent in search of food; but as new skills such as crop cultivation and animal husbandry were developed, early man began to settle in the region permanently.

The Canaanites

By the third millennium BC the land to the west of the Jordan River was being referred to as **Canaan**. The origins of this term are unclear, though the Bible (virtually the only historical source on the region for this date) gives it a possible genealogical origin, Canaan being the son of Moses' second son Ham. The Bible, however, is confusing when defining who exactly the Canaanites were: sometimes it seems to refer to all the indigenous inhabitants of the region, but occasionally appears to refer to just one specific tribe among the many who lived in Canaan on the Mediterranean coast. Many scholars have identified this tribe as the **Phoenicians**, famed sailors and merchants who migrated from the Red Sea coast in c3500BC and who referred to themselves as Kana'anri. Whatever the truth, the Canaanites were the first settlers in the region to whom we can put a name, and Canaan is accepted as the original name of the land we now know as Israel and Palestine.

These early inhabitants in Palestine were joined in c1900BC by the **Hebrews**. Like the Phoenicians who preceded them and the various Arab tribes who followed later, the Hebrews were just one of a number of nomadic Semitic tribes wandering through the Near East at this time. Under the leadership of Abraham, they had migrated southwest from their homeland in Mesopotamia (now in southeastern Turkey) to the banks of the River Jordan. Though a tiny tribe, their influence on the destiny of the land they knew as Canaan proved to be profound.

The early invaders: Egyptians, Hyskos and Hittites (c2800–1259BC)

While Canaan remained a disunited land peopled by tribes of differing ethnic origin, on either side, in Egypt and Mesopotamia, empires were being formed that would, in the fullness of time, begin to encroach on Canaanite territory. The first to do so were the **Egyptians** in around 2300BC, and though they were ousted for two centuries (2000–1800BC) by the **Hyskos** – a culturally-retarded group of Asiatic warriors whose military successes in the region owed much to their new invention, the horse-drawn chariot – they returned under the New Kingdom pharaoh, Thutmose I, in around 1520BC.

Unfortunately for the Egyptians, while they continued to expand their territory eastwards, reaching as far as modern-day Syria under the command of Pharaoh Seti and his son Ramses II, at home they were riven by a series of political and religious disputes that inevitably weakened their grip on their colonies. This paved the way for the **Hittites**, based in modern-day Turkey, to snatch Syria from them in c1350BC; though whether they ever succeeded in capturing Canaan is uncertain. Their success was short-lived, however, and in 1275BC the resurgent Egyptians, under Pharaoh Ramses II, were squaring up to the Hittites at Kadesh, near Homs in Central Syria. A peace treaty was signed between the two sides in 1259BC, although the overstretched Hittite empire collapsed soon after, leaving Egypt as the unrivalled power in the Near East for the rest of the century.

The Exodus

Drought had forced the Hebrews to move to Egypt from their home in Canaan in c1850BC, but, after centuries of persecution and imprisonment in their adopted home, the Israelites (as the Hebrews were now called), led by Moses, fled Egypt, arriving in Canaan in approximately 1230BC. Upon arriving, the Israelites found their promised land was already occupied. Fortified cities such as Jerusalem and Megiddo had already been established, and the Israelites, weak and weary, were at first forced to settle on unoccupied land in the West Bank, the Negev Desert and, a little later, around Galilee. The West Bank as we now know it was settled by the Israelite tribes of Benjamin, Judaea and Ephraim, leaving the other tribes to head west, south and north in search of land.

The Philistines (1190–597BC)

As other Israelite tribes moved west, however, they encountered a second band of migrants who had also recently moved to the area, and who had made their home on the eastern Mediterranean shoreline, to the immediate west of the Israelites' territory. These were the Philistines, one of the so-called **Peoples of the Sea**, a mysterious, loose federation of tribes whose name surfaces frequently in ancient texts, and who are believed to have been refugees who sailed east from modern-day Greece following the Trojan Wars. Having been repulsed from the Egyptian shore following a monumental naval battle with the forces of Pharaoh Ramses III in c1190BC, the Philistines settled eventually on the Israel/Palestine coast, including the **Gaza Strip**. From there they attempted to expand inland and enjoyed a number of significant military successes, including victories over many of the new Israelite settlements. Indeed, following one victorious campaign, the Philistines snatched the Ark of the Covenant, the wooden chest containing the Ten Commandments, and held it for over forty years.

The kingdom of Israel and the Babylonians (c1000–538BC)

In response, the Israelites organised themselves into a united kingdom. The first king, Saul, was unable to stop the Philistines' progress on to Israelite land but the second king, David, enjoyed greater success, halting the Philistines in their tracks and conquering the rest of Canaan, including the fortified city of Jerusalem (c1000BC). His son and heir, Solomon, prolonged the peace and prosperity of the Israelite kingdom, but after his death (922BC) internal politics split the Israelites into two kingdoms (see page 32), Samaria and Judaea.

For the next few centuries border skirmishes between Philistia and Israel/Judaea were commonplace. Then, in c721BC, a new power in the Near East, the **Assyrians**, marched westwards towards Gaza from their homeland in Mesopotamia. As they did so the northern Kingdom of Israel (Samaria) was destroyed completely. The Philistines, along with the two tribes that made up the Kingdom of Judaea, were allowed to remain in situ and maintained their political identity, though both were forced to swear fealty to their new Assyrian masters.

The Assyrian assault proved to be merely the first in another round of invasions carried out by powerful regional empires. After the fall of the Assyrian Empire in 612BC, Philistia subsequently fell for a third time to the Egyptians. The Egyptian Empire was on the wane by this time, however, and in 597BC both Philistia and Judaea fell to the **Babylonians** under Nebuchadnezzar – an invasion which effectively ended the history of the Philistine people.

Babylonian occupation and Persian rule

According to the sketchy accounts left to us, Nebuchadnezzar's rule was cruel and destructive, but mercifully also brief. Less than 50 years after the conquest of Jerusalem, Babylon itself was sacked in 538BC by the nascent **Persian Empire**,

THE PHILISTINES

The Philistines' occupation of the Palestinian/Israeli coastline and their eventual subsumption by neighbouring empires is relatively unremarkable in a time noted for countless migrations and invasions of one hue or another. Nevertheless, during their tenure the Philistines did leave the region two important and lasting legacies: first the settlement of **Gaza**, which was originally one of the capitals of the five city-states that made up Philistia; and second is the name '**Palestine**', merely the word Philistine corrupted by subsequent Greek and Latin translations. (It seems somewhat ironic that the Philistines should give their name to a piece of land, part of which they lost to the Babylonians and part of which, thanks to the Israelites, they never even occupied!) Interestingly, a number of recent archaeological digs at a number of Philistine settlements have uncovered a wealth of elaborate artefacts, some highly decorated. From these finds, a picture has emerged of a highly developed civilisation, thus giving a lie to the modern term philistine, meaning an uncultured person or materialist.

based in modern-day Iran under the rule of Cyrus II, or Cyrus the Great. He was quick to allow the exiled Judaeans to return home, and even supported their restoration of the temple of Jerusalem (a large but less opulent affair than Solomon's original). It was this enlightened attitude towards his subjects as much as any military prowess which enabled Cyrus to build an empire that stretched from the Volga in Russia to the Hindu Kush in modern-day Pakistan, and as far south as Egypt. Towards the end of the 4th century BC, however, a new power was emerging in Macedonia under the charismatic leadership of one man whose conquests would eventually surpass even Cyrus' efforts.

Alexander the Great, the Hellenistic and Hasmonean Empires (322–63BC)

As the son of a Macedonian prince and a pupil of Aristotle, Alexander the Great was blessed with a most advantageous upbringing, and one that he used to ruthless effect when building an empire that stretched from Macedonia to Egypt and east to India. It isn't so much the size of his empire that is so impressive, however, as the pace at which he constructed it. In just three short years, and still a few months shy of his 25th birthday, Alexander ruled over the biggest empire the world had ever seen. Palestine, of course, was just another part of his empire, a mere stepping stone conquered in 332BC on the way to the ultimate prize, Egypt.

While Palestine meant little to the Hellenistic invaders, their influence on the country was profound. The rich civilisation of Greece with its architects, philosophers, poets, mathematicians and artists introduced a brand and level of culture hitherto unseen in Palestine, providing both an impetus and an influence on the development of the region.

After Alexander's death nine years later in 323BC, his empire was divided up between his former generals, Ptolemy and Seleucus. Palestine, initially ruled by the **Ptolemites**, eventually came under the sway of the **Seleucids** in 198BC. Despite the lasting benefits introduced during the Hellenistic era, the people of Palestine – the **Judaeans** who had returned from exile, the **Samaritans** (possibly people brought in by the Assyrians to replace the Israelites exiled in 721BC), the **Edomites** (who were mainly based to the east of the Jordan) and the **Philistines** – resented their occupation. In particular, the Judaeans detested the Greeks meddling in their religious practices: not only did the Greeks regularly raid the sacred Temple in Jerusalem, but they even tried to re-dedicate it to the Greek god Zeus. This last act, and the accompanying prohibition of many sacred traditions (including such integral Jewish rituals as animal sacrifice and circumcision), caused widespread anger and, under Judas Maccabeus and his brothers Simon and Jonathan, they successfully cast off the Seleucid yoke in the Maccabaean revolt (167–141BC). In its place, the Judaeans established the **Hasmonean Kingdom**, named after the ruling Hasmonean dynasty – the family of Judas Maccabeus.

The Hasmonean era lasted for almost eighty years, during which time the boundaries of their kingdom stretched, under the leadership of John Hyrcanus, to encompass almost all of modern-day Palestine and Israel. The Hasmoneans were powerless, however, in the face of the next power to arrive on these shores.

The Roman occupation (63BC–AD324)

With no united army to oppose his invasion, the Roman general, **Pompey**, found the conquest of the Eastern Mediterranean in 63BC a relatively straightforward affair. The simple tactic of rewarding obedient colonies with lower taxes proved a most effective preventative against rebellion in Provincia Arabia, the Roman name for its Levantine territories. There was only one place that continually caused trouble to the Romans: Palestine.

By the time of the Roman invasion, Palestine was a largely Jewish province (Jew, incidentally, refers to all descendants of the Twelve Tribes of Israel, and not just the people of the Kingdom of Judaea from which the name was derived). Philistia had all but ceased to exist following the Babylonian invasion, and the borders of the Kingdom of Judaea, following a renaissance under the Hasmonean dynasty, now stretched from the Jordan River to the Mediterranean. At first, the Romans were content to place Palestine under the rule of **Herod the Great**, an Edomite whose loyalty to the Roman cause had recommended him to his superiors in Rome. Herod was lenient on the Jews – he was half-Jewish himself – and even helped to finance the restoration and refurbishment of the Temple in Jerusalem. His heirs, however, proved less capable at appeasement, and after a spate of mini-revolts in AD6 the Romans felt compelled to assume complete control.

This did little to quell the anti-Roman hostility, however, and two major rebellions followed, each one succeeding in breaking the Romans' grip for a few years. The first, in AD66, led to a four-year siege of Jerusalem by the Romans, at the end of which they breached the defences and destroyed the rebuilt Temple. A second revolt in AD132, known as the Bar Kochba Rebellion after its leader, lasted for three years before the Romans once again resumed control. Fed up with Jewish insurgency, the Romans decided to teach them a lesson by flattening Jerusalem altogether, building the Roman city **Aelia Capitolina** in its place. Jews were barred from the city. Denied access to the former site of their Temple, they prayed to it from outside the city walls at the foot of the Temple compound – where they still pray today.

By this time, however, a new and radical offshoot of Judaism, **Christianity**, had erupted in Judaea. The Romans responded in typically ferocious fashion, outlawing the religion and feeding transgressors to the local amphitheatre lions. They never succeeded in fully eradicating this new faith, however, and eventually the ideology behind Christianity began to find favour amongst the very highest echelons of Roman society.

The Byzantine Empire (AD324–637)

In AD324 the Roman Empire split in half, with the eastern half based in Byzantium (modern Istanbul), which it renamed Constantinople after its first emperor, Constantine.

This split proved fortuitous for Palestine, for one simple reason: Constantine was a Christian, having been converted by his mother, Helena, a few years previously. Thus, not only did Constantine legalise Christianity in AD331, but the faith now became the official state religion, ending the persecution of its adherents. The Holy Land reaped other benefits. A few years earlier, in AD326, Helena had made a highly publicised pilgrimage to the Holy Land; and as a dictator of fashion her journey encouraged legions of imitators desperate to follow in her wake, with Jerusalem becoming the focus of pilgrimages. After centuries of unwelcome interlopers the Holy Land now received dozens of less aggressive visitors, and the economy of Palestine boomed as a result. The Byzantine emperors also felt duty bound to restore Jerusalem to something approaching its original, pre-Roman splendour (the first Church of the Holy Sepulchre was built at this time) and other important Christian sites such as Bethlehem and Nazareth were beautified as a result.

The Christian Empire was not well received in all quarters, however, with the Jews and Samaritans in particular resenting the restrictions placed on their faith by the Byzantine emperors. The Samaritans held a series of revolts in AD486, and in 614 the invading Persian army found plenty of local support in Palestine for their campaign, particularly as it involved the desecration of many Christian churches and monasteries. But these minor setbacks were as nothing when compared with the threat to the empire that was now brewing south of Palestine in the deserts of Arabia.

Islam and the Islamic dynasties (AD637–1099)

The full story of the Prophet Mohammed and the founding of Islam is recounted on page 36. By the time Mohammed died in AD632 his followers had successfully conquered the Arabian Peninsula. Six years later, the whole of the Levant had fallen to these Arabian armies under Mohammed's successor, Abu Bakr, and his successor, Omar Ibn Al-Khattab. Omar received the surrender of Jerusalem in AD637, a most significant victory when one considers that at the time Islam, like Judaism and Christianity, revered Jerusalem above all other cities (including Mecca).

A succession of Arab dynasties continued the Islamic expansion. The **Ommayad Dynasty** (AD661–750), founded by the Sunni leader Mu'awiya and controlled from his base in Damascus, was the first. It was a short but spectacular reign, during which the empire grew to encompass Spain in the west and the Chinese border in the east. The construction of both the Dome of the Rock and the neighbouring Al-Aqsa Mosque in Jerusalem also date from this period. Filastin (as Palestine and Israel was then known), as a close neighbour, profited from both trade and religious traffic at this time.

Unfortunately, the Ommayad Dynasty proved to be a little too self-serving and, as public opinion turned against the fat cats in Damascus, a more austere dynasty, the **Abbassids** of Baghdad (AD750–968), took control, vowing to return Islam to its original principles. The **Fatimid Dynasty** (AD968–1071) followed them in ruling Palestine and the Levant, establishing a Shi'ite dynasty in Cairo to rival the Abbassids' Sunni Muslim Caliphate .

By the end of the 11th century Islam's campaign for world domination was flagging and, like many other empires before, it began to fracture under a slew of internal disputes. The **Seljuks** (1071–1099), a tribe of Central Asian warriors who'd converted to Islam during their progress through the Near East, briefly revived the impetus of the Islamic movement, filling the vacuum left by the crumbling Byzantine Empire by conquering the Levant – Palestine included – in 1071. The Seljuks were a contradiction. While their capital at Konya in Central Turkey was celebrated for its enlightened, progressive society, tales of their mistreatment of subjugated cities in the Levant filled the rest of the civilised world with horror; one incident in particular, the barring of Christians from Jerusalem, led directly to the First Crusade.

The Christians' revenge: the Crusaders (AD1097–1291)

By 1095 the voracious Seljuks had advanced to within 100 miles of the waning Byzantine Empire's capital at Constantinople. In desperation, the beleaguered Byzantine Emperor Alexius called upon his European neighbour, the Holy Roman Empire, for assistance. The Roman Empire, keen to help an ally and horrified by tales of the Seljuks' mistreatment of Christians in Palestine, responded with the **First Crusade**, a campaign by the armies of Europe to free the Holy Land from the clutches of the infidel.

It proved to be the most successful of all the crusades: Byzantium was saved and in 1099 the Crusaders' ultimate catch – Jerusalem – was landed. Having murdered all the Jewish and Muslim settlers in the city, the Crusaders (or Franks as they were called at the time, due to there being a large number of French nobles in their ranks) established the **Kingdom of Jerusalem**. By building huge defensive fortresses and bribing and cajoling local tribal leaders, the Crusaders had successfully established a feudal system in the Levant, with themselves at the head. By 1124, with the capture of Tyre (in Southern Lebanon) the Crusaders, though heavily outnumbered, had control of the entire Levant.

Although there were seven more crusades, only the next two affected Palestine directly. The **Second Crusade**, dispatched in 1148 to recapture the northernmost Crusader Kingdom, Edessa, back from the Seljuks who'd taken it in 1144, ran out of food and was defeated almost as soon as it arrived. Its conqueror was the Seljuk Nur al-Din (Nureddin), whose nephew, Salah El-Din, defeated the Crusaders in a major battle at the Horns of Hittin in 1187, and went on to take the whole of Palestine, Jerusalem included, that same year. Salah El-Din – or Saladin as he's more commonly known in the West – proved a more enlightened ruler than the Crusaders, allowing Christians the freedom to worship in Jerusalem and restoring the city to a level of religious tolerance last seen two centuries previously during Abbassid rule.

The Christians' defeat at the hands of the Saracen prompted a **Third Crusade** in 1191, under the command of Richard the Lionheart and Philip II of France. They enjoyed several notable successes, including the capture of Acco in 1191 and Jaffa the following year, before retiring, exhausted, three years later. Though the Crusaders held on to Acco for exactly 100 years they never recaptured Jerusalem, and in 1291 the knights relinquished their last remaining stronghold in the Holy Land to the Mamluke sultan, Baybars.

The Ayyubids and Mamlukes

The dynasty that Saladin founded – named the Ayyubids in his honour (Ayyubi being Saladin's surname) – controlled Palestine for over sixty years (1187–1250), though their supremacy in the region depended heavily on the loyalty of their warrior slaves, the Mamlukes, who did much of their fighting for them. The Mamlukes, hailing from Central Asia, had a fearsome reputation and were famed for their skill with the crossbow. Not only had they been instrumental in vanquishing the Crusaders from the Holy Land, but they had also managed to repel the once-invincible Mongol warriors, led by Hulagu Khan, grandson of Genghis Khan, from the Levant in 1260.

By the middle of the 13th century the Mamluke tail had begun to wag the Ayyubid dog. As a procession of weak Ayyubid sultans ascended to the throne the Mamlukes began to wield more and more influence in the court until the last Ayyubid leader, Sultan al-Salih Ayyub, died and left his Mamluke widow in charge.

The **Mamluke Empire** was a truly peculiar one. No matter how high the Mamluke climbed in Mamluke society, he would always be considered a slave; even the sultan was still a slave in name. And being slaves they had no hereditary system where titles and fortunes could be passed down from father to son. This led to bloody battles between potential successors every time a sultan died, and the Mamluke era distinguishes itself as one of the most violent the Near East has ever seen.

Nevertheless, the Mamluke Empire was a successful and enduring one, ruling over Palestine and the Near East for over 250 years (1250–1516) from its base in Cairo. Under its auspices Jerusalem became a centre of learning and, despite the Mamlukes' bloodthirsty reputation, they were keen patrons of the arts whose beautiful buildings still adorn many Palestinian cities.

The Ottoman Empire (1517–1917)

The Ottomans were yet another power that swept down from the plains of Central Asia. They were the descendants and relatives of Othman, a 14th-century 'Turkish Saladin' famed for his chivalry and fighting prowess. Their progress through the Levant in 1516, led by the suitably-named Selim the Grim, was conducted at breakneck speed, the Mamlukes' bows and arrows proving no match for the Ottomans' superior weaponry. Selim's son, the equally aptly-named Suleyman the Magnificent, continued the Ottoman expansion, but also turned his attention to a series of ambitious building projects, including the reconstruction of the splendid walls of Jerusalem.

Subsequent sultans, however, proved to be less than magnificent. Content to collect their taxes and leave the running of their territories to appointed emirs and pashas, the sultans meddled little in Levantine affairs. Palestine (which was now being governed by a pasha in Damascus) became a penniless backwater as a result. These pashas grew increasingly autonomous as their Ottoman overlords became ever more embroiled in political intrigues in their palaces at Constantinople. One such pasha, **Muhammad Ali**, a soldier of Albanian descent who ruled Egypt for the Ottomans, took advantage of their weakening hold on the Near East by conquering the region for himself. Palestine soon fell to this rebellious pasha, until only Constantinople, the capital of his former paymasters, remained unconquered – not, it must be said, because of Ottoman resistance, but because the European powers persuaded him to go no further. The Europeans also prevailed upon Muhammad Ali to relinquish his territory in Palestine and Syria, which was returned to the Ottomans in 1840. (In return, Muhammad Ali was made governor of Egypt for life, a hereditary title.)

As the Ottomans' fortunes continued to slump during the 19th century to a point where they became known as the 'Sick Man of Europe', the European superpowers began to jockey for position in the Levant, waiting for the day when the empire would finally capitulate. For the people of Palestine, Ottoman rule had become a boil that needed to be lanced. As war broke out in Europe at the start of the 20th century, it was the Arab revolutionaries, with assistance from Britain, who performed the operation.

PALESTINE IN THE 20TH CENTURY
Background

The problems that have dogged Palestine and Israel throughout this century actually have their roots in the previous one. It was during the 1880s that the persecution of Jews in Europe (long resented in their adopted countries, as powerful and wealthy minorities so frequently are) reached unprecedented levels, with pogroms throughout Russia and Eastern Europe. This unbridled anti-Semitism pushed many to migrate to the original 'Promised Land' of Moses and the Israelites, an influx that continued into the early years of the 20th century.

As the migrations continued, governments in Europe began looking at a number of places as possible sites for a new Jewish homeland; though it seems absurd now, both Argentina and Uganda were suggested as suitable locations. But the Jews themselves were having none of it. In 1897 Theodore Herzl, an Austro-Hungarian playwright and essayist, created the **World Zionist Organisation** (WZO), a worldwide body dedicated to fulfilling the biggest single dream of the Diaspora: to create, for the first time in nearly two thousand years, an independent Jewish nation in Palestine.

There was, however, one big problem with this scheme: Palestine was already inhabited by a significant population of largely Muslim and Christian Arabs. Yet

the WZO didn't see this as a major obstacle: the first part of the Zionist slogan 'A
land without people for a people without land' shows how, right from the beginning,
they dismissed the rights of the original inhabitants living in the region.

By the end of the first decade of the 20th century, Jews from Europe were
arriving in Palestine in ever-increasing numbers, as much pushed by persecution
in Europe as pulled by the promise of a new Jewish nation. Slow to react at first,
the Arabs in Palestine eventually grew increasingly concerned about this influx,
and in the first decades of the 20th century a number of Arab associations were
formed to counteract the threat of Zionism.

Soon both sides began stockpiling arms as the atmosphere in the Holy Land
became increasingly tense and hostile. But before tensions could come to a head,
in 1914 a far larger conflict began in Europe; it was a war that would soon spread
to the Near East, causing all provincial disputes to be suspended for the next four
years.

World War I and the Arab Revolt (1914–18)

During World War I, the Jewish population in Palestine opted to side with the
Germans and Turks against the allied forces of Britain, France, Russia et al, a
decision that was born out of a desire to exact revenge on Russia for the centuries
of persecution it had suffered rather than any special Turkish or German
affiliation.

The Arabs, however, saw the Allies as their best hope of emancipation from the
Ottomans and sided with them. Though brave and numerous, up until now the
Arabs had always been too fractious to mount a cohesive revolt against Ottoman
rule. But during the Great War, and with the guidance of T E Lawrence and the
British forces based at Suez, the disparate Bedouin tribes united to confront their
Turkish overlords. They attacked the railway that joined the Ottomans' Near
Eastern territories with their capital, Istanbul, and eventually, using guerrilla
warfare, threw off four centuries of Ottoman domination.

The British mandate (1922–1948)

In return for their support against the Turks, the British promised to back the
Arabs in their campaign for independence. Unfortunately, it was a promise that
they had little intention of honouring. While dangling the carrot of independence
in front of the Arabs, the French and British were secretly agreeing to carve up the
Near East for themselves in the **Sykes-Picot Agreement** of 1916. Initially, the
two European allies hoped to treat the region as just another addition to their
respective colonial empires, but under pressure from the newly-formed **League
of Nations** it was agreed that the two countries would have temporary control
only, with Britain mandated to rule over Palestine (including Transjordan –
modern-day Jordan, which was separated from Palestine the same year).

With the Great War finally at an end, Jewish immigrants began to flood into
Palestine once more, prompting further calls from the Arab world for the British
to intervene. The British government, however, though unwilling to upset the
Arab lobby, were beginning to see the merits of the Zionists' arguments. The
Balfour Declaration of 1917 stated: 'His Majesty's Government view with
favour the establishment in Palestine of a national home for the Jewish people, it
being clearly understood that nothing shall be done which may prejudice the civil
and religious rights of the existing non-Jewish communities in Palestine....'. At the
time, with only 60,000 Jews in a total Palestinian population of 600,000, this
declaration, though containing two conflicting aims, may have seemed both
achievable and even-handed. But a secret memo addressed by Balfour to his

cabinet colleagues in 1919 reveals a more pro-Zionist and arrogant viewpoint: 'In Palestine, we do not propose even to go through the form of consulting the wishes of the present inhabitants of the country'.

This clandestine support for the establishment of a Jewish homeland in Palestine was born not of any impartial assessment of the rights and wrongs of the Zionist cause, but merely out of self-serving common sense. After all, if a Jewish homeland in Palestine was established with the help of British backing, Britain would have introduced a loyal ally into the heart of a strategically vital region.

Whatever their secret hopes, publicly the British would, throughout their mandate, procrastinate in announcing any decisions on the fate of the region, a frustrating policy that served only to increase the tension. As anti-Semitism once again gripped Central Europe during the 1930s with the rise of the **Nazis**, the Jewish population in Palestine continued to increase, until by 1936 it stood at 29% of the population as a whole. This increase prompted the **Palestinian Revolt** of 1937, a series of strikes that paralysed much of the country. Entire Jewish communities in Hebron and Jerusalem were wiped out in some of the bloodiest incidents seen in the dispute thus far. To quash the revolt, the British drafted in 20,000 troops to restore order, which they achieved, with some difficulty and a little help from the Jewish auxiliary police, late that same year.

If nothing else, the Palestinian Revolt at least proved to the British that the Balfour declaration was simply impossible: you cannot have a Jewish homeland in Palestine without prejudicing the existing rights of the non-Jewish communities there. But the British continued to prevaricate over announcing a decision. Instead, their attention now turned towards developments in Central Europe, and Palestine, the tiny strip of land on the western edge of Asia, was once more left to its own devices.

Yet again, a world war had postponed any solution to the Palestinian question. But though the fighting never reached the Holy Land, World War II was to have a dramatic influence on the outcome of the Palestinian dispute. The atrocities committed in the **Holocaust** against the Jewish populations of Europe polarised world opinion in favour of the establishment of a Jewish state, and brought the Palestinian problem to the forefront of the international agenda. As the war finished, over 100,000 Jewish survivors from the Nazi concentration camps attempted to gain entry into Palestine. The British, mindful of the antagonistic effect this would have on Palestine's Arab population, tried to limit the numbers entering the country, but their action smacked of anti-Semitism and aroused widespread condemnation.

The war of 1948

The problem in Palestine was clearly becoming too great for the British to handle. Criticised on the one side for their lack of compassion towards the survivors of the Holocaust, and on the other by the Arabs who saw their land being appropriated by these new immigrants, they were finding their Palestinian mandate unworkable. In 1947 they handed responsibility over to the UN, though they continued to police the territory.

The **United Nations Special Committee on Palestine** (UNSCOP) proposed **partition** as a possible solution. By dividing the territory into two halves, one for the Zionists and one for the Palestinians, they hoped to appease both sides. Under this proposal, the Palestinians would retain control over the West Bank, Gaza Strip and certain other areas that had an Arab majority, while the Jewish immigrants would receive the Negev Desert, Galilee and the coast from Haifa to Tel Aviv/Jaffa and beyond. Jerusalem, too important a city for either side to relinquish, would become an **international city** under the UN plan, belonging to neither side.

Though the partition proposal fell short of the wishes of both Arabs and Jews, the two sides reacted differently to the UNSCOP suggestion. The Zionists, disappointed that they would have to share Palestine but consoled by the thought that their dreams of a Jewish State were to receive international sanction for the first time, accepted the plan. The Palestinians, however, shot themselves in the foot somewhat by later rejecting the proposal outright, and refusing to attend the subsequent UN negotiations, thereby foregoing the chance to have their views heard by the international community.

To be fair to the Palestinians, the partition plan, though it seemed a just solution on the surface, was weighted in favour of the Zionists. The new Jewish state as proposed by UNSCOP would cover over half the land of Palestine, even though only a third of the population at this time was Jewish. As David McDowall points out in his excellent book, *The Palestinians, The Road to Nationhood*: 'It was manifestly unjust (and arguably absurd) in its demographic division, since it proposed a Jewish state that would be virtually 50% Arab, yet an Arab state that would be no less than 98.7% Arab.'

Thanks to the energies and policies of the new Zionists, however, this imbalance of population was soon redressed as Jewish settlers began forcibly to remove Palestinians from the land which, under the UNSCOP proposal, would become theirs when the British finally withdrew. This inevitably led to further violence, though once again the Palestinians proved to be no match for the *Haganah*, the Jewish army, many of whom had fought alongside the British in World War II.

So successful was the Jewish onslaught against Palestinians living inside Israeli territory that when the British did finally leave, on May 15 1948, 300,000 Palestinians had been rendered homeless already, and the new state of Israel, as proposed by UNSCOP, had a considerable Jewish majority.

Needless to say, the British withdrawal, far from leading to the peaceful emergence of two states as had been hoped, only triggered an escalation in the fighting as the neighbouring states of Egypt and Jordan, under the pretext of helping their fellow Arabs, moved into the Holy Land in the hope of snatching some territory for themselves. By the time an armistice had been agreed, one year on from the British withdrawal in 1949, the map of the Holy Land looked very different from the one drawn up in the UN partition plan. Egypt had snatched the Gaza Strip, Jordan the West Bank and most of Jerusalem, and Israel, the biggest winner of them all, now held 73% of the territory formerly known as Palestine under the British mandate. In just a few short years, the Palestinians had seen their entire country snatched away from them by a combination of ambitious neighbours and Zionist settlers.

The aftermath of 1948 – the Palestinians in exile

Over 700,000 Palestinians found themselves homeless in the wake of the 1948 war. Some had been driven from their land by the new Jewish settlers, keen to purge their new state of any non-Jewish elements. Many more had fled in panic and fear as stories of anti-Arab atrocities committed by the Zionists filtered through to the villages of rural Palestine.

As early as 1948 the UN reaffirmed the right of these refugees to return to their homes, though their edicts fell on deaf ears in Israel, whose leaders refused to countenance the return of Palestinians to what was now Israeli territory. Thus the Palestinians now faced the prospect of a lengthy exile from their old home towns, and an extended stay in their new homes in Egypt (including the new Egyptian-controlled territory of the Gaza Strip), Jordan (including the newly acquired West Bank), Syria and Lebanon. To the international community, these exiled Palestinians were unanimously lumped together under the collective name **refugee**; the experiences of these Palestinians, however, varied widely depending on where they'd been exiled to.

In the **Gaza Strip**, now under Egyptian control, the sudden influx of 200,000 refugees into such a small territory which already had a population of 80,000 only exacerbated the problems of poverty, malnutrition, sanitation and lack of shelter that had affected most of the Holy Land since 1948.

Though the problems of overcrowding in the **West Bank** were minor compared with those of Gaza, King Abdullah's annexation of the region in 1950 created its own problems. The population of the Hashemite kingdom now trebled almost overnight; it was a population, moreover, where the majority were disgruntled refugees who suspected Abdullah of colluding with Israel in order to further his own ambitions. His subsequent neglect of the West Bank, which became an economic backwater under his rule, and his decision to remove the word Palestine from all Jordanian-produced maps, only fuelled their disaffection, leading eventually to Abdullah's assassination in Jerusalem's Al-Aqsa Mosque in 1951.

Amongst the Arab states that received refugees, **Syria** proved by far the most sympathetic to the Palestinians' cause. Where Abdullah had attempted to integrate the Palestinians into Jordanian society, offering all refugees Jordanian citizenship, the Syrians gave the Palestinians the same rights as its own citizens while allowing them to retain their national identity.

Lebanon, however, which at the time was undergoing a crisis of its own, was worried by the influx of Palestinian refugees, fearing (and rightly so, as it transpired) that the delicate religious balance of the country's constitution could easily become upset. The Lebanese dithered for a while over the appropriate status to confer on the refugees, before finally creating a special category that defined them neither as citizens nor as foreigners – an awkward limbo that served neither side particularly well.

The birth of the PLO

Ironically, it was only post-1948, when so many of their people had been forced from their land and sent into exile, that the Palestinians finally began to forge a proper national identity. The essentially disparate mix of Bedouins, city workers, farmers, Christians and Muslims that constituted the Palestinian population during the British Mandate were now united by a common suffering and grief, developing a strong bond with each other that had never really existed before.

The **Palestinian Liberation Army** (PLA), formed in 1960, and the **Palestine Liberation Organisation** (PLO), established in 1964, were the most obvious manifestations of this national awakening. Initially, the PLO were merely a political organisation, attempting to win back by peaceable means the land now occupied by Israel, Jordan and Egypt; terrorism played no part in their early strategy, and military force, if deployed at all, was only to be used in a conventional war. Unfortunately, that conventional war arrived just three years after the PLO's inception – too early for the PLO to have much of an impact.

Infiltration and the Six-Day War

The years between the wars of 1948 and 1967 were characterised by persistent attempts by Palestinian refugees in exile in Jordan or Egypt to visit their former homeland in Israel. These visits were conducted at great personal risk: those caught at the border were usually summarily shot by Israeli guards. Their reasons for attempting such a dangerous mission were two-fold: some were intent on revenge against the state that had dispossessed them, and a number of terrorist attacks took place over these two decades. Others, however, merely wished to visit their ancestral home – a conclusive refutation, if one were needed, of the charge made by Zionists that the Palestinians held no attachment to their land.

The terrorist attacks served only to increase the tension in the region, with Israel (rightly) accusing its Arab neighbours – Jordan and Egypt in particular – of complicity in these atrocities. In response, the Arab states began to indulge in ever more stirring speeches against Israel, though often these were little more than a sop to the Palestinians who lived within their borders as refugees. However, as the speeches continued to grow increasingly inflammatory, the Arab states soon felt compelled to back up their rhetoric with action.

Once again, however, Israel proved to be one step ahead of its enemies. When Egypt closed the Straits of Tiran – the northeastern arm of the Red Sea between the Sinai Peninsula and Saudi Arabia – in May 1967, it provided Israel with just the excuse it needed to launch an all-out attack, beginning on June 5, on its neighbours Egypt, Jordan and Syria. Though the Arab states had been preparing for just such a war, the Israelis' pre-emptive strike caught them all unawares. Egyptian planes were bombed as they stood idle on the ground and Israeli troops stormed into Arab territories largely unopposed. After just six days, Israel had snatched East Jerusalem from Jordan, thrown Egypt out of the Gaza Strip and pushed them all the way back to the Suez Canal – appropriating the Sinai as they did so – and taken the Golan Heights from Syria.

However, as in 1948, it was the Palestinians who suffered the most. Over 800,000 new refugees were created as a result of the Six Day War of 1967, as Palestinians fled from villages and refugee camps now under Israeli control. In the West Bank alone, 355,000 Palestinians, petrified of what the Israelis would do to them, fled across the river into Jordan.

Once again, Israeli might had proved too much for its Arab opponents. A call by the UN, enshrined in Resolution 242, urged Israel to 'withdraw … from territories of recent conflict', and to have 'respect for and acknowledgement of the sovereignty, territorial integrity and political independence of every state in the area and their right to live in peace within secure and recognised boundaries...'. But the Israelis, not for the first time, ignored the request and within weeks East Jerusalem and the Old City, the greatest prize of the 1967 War, had been officially incorporated into the State of Israel.

The Palestinian response

If nothing else, the war of 1967 at least taught the PLO one simple lesson: if they were going to win back their homeland, it would have to be they who did it, rather than their more-powerful but less-motivated, disunited Arab friends.

While the PLO continued to favour a peaceful approach to solving the Palestinian question, other groups, such as **Fatah** (a reverse acronym of its full title, Harakat Tahrir Filastin, or Palestinian Liberation Movement), founded in 1959 by a young engineer called **Yasser Arafat**, favoured more violent methods. Initially, Fatah enjoyed a minority following only, but after heroics by some of its members in the '67 War recruits flooded to join the ranks of this radical party. In the elections of 1969 Fatah swept the old guard of the PLO out of power, Yasser Arafat becoming the Chairman of the PLO's Executive Committee. Recognition by the UN of the PLO as the official representatives of the Palestinian people came in 1974.

However, Arafat found his power as the head of the largest Palestinian organisation was not as absolute as he had hoped. Numerous smaller Palestinian parties, including the **Popular Front for the Liberation of Palestine** (PFLP) and its various splinter groups – such as the **PFLP General Command** (PFLP-GC) and **Democratic Front for the Liberation of Palestine** (DFLP) – all had their own views on how to win back their native lands. The PLO thus became, at times, little more than a mediator between the various factions, and Arafat spent as much of his time uniting the PLO as he did fighting for the Palestinian cause.

The PLO exile from Jordan

As if this political in-fighting, combined with the continued stubbornness of the Israelis in refusing to allow the return of the Palestinians to their homeland, wasn't enough for the refugees, they then watched as the relationships between the PLO and the Jordanians began to fray. The Jordanian monarchy, with **King Hussein** at its head, was alarmed by the majority Palestinian population in their country and the perceived threat to their authority that the PLO posed. They were also worried by the increasingly militant attitude of the PLO, which had begun to launch guerrilla attacks into Israel from their bases in Jordan. The inevitable Israeli reprisals that these attacks incurred alarmed the Jordanian monarchy, and it came as little surprise when, in 1970, the Jordanians decided to attack the PLO themselves. In the month now known as **Black September**, the Jordanian Army, under orders from King Hussein, launched an all-out attack on Palestinian bases, driving the PLO out of Amman. What was surprising, however, was the severity of the putsch. Over 3,000 Palestinians, many just civilians, were killed in the fighting. Those in the PLO who survived this ordeal fled to Lebanon to regroup there.

The PLO and the war in Lebanon

Unfortunately, Lebanon was in no position to take them. When they first arrived, in the wake of the 1948 war, the exiled Palestinians were largely made to feel welcome by their hosts, particularly by Lebanon's Shia Muslims who, as a fellow downtrodden Muslim minority, felt a great deal of empathy for the Palestinian cause. Post-1970, however, as the PLO began to launch attacks in Israel from their new Lebanese bases, and as Israel responded in kind by bombing targets in southern Lebanon, popular opinion in Lebanon turned against the PLO and their cause.

> ### THE WAR OF YOM KIPPUR AND THE CAMP DAVID ACCORDS
>
> In October 1973 the combined forces of the Syrians and Egyptians caught the Israelis totally unawares by invading Israel during the national Jewish holiday of Yom Kippur. Though Israel managed to scramble its forces and retaliate, driving Egypt back towards the Suez Canal and Syria beyond the borders established in 1967, it proved for the first time that Israel was not infallible. It also made the Israelis more amenable to negotiations and, following a shock visit to the Knesset, the Israeli parliament, by **Anwar Sadat** in 1977, Israel agreed to negotiations. These produced the Camp David accords, in which Israel agreed to withdraw from the Sinai, though proposals in the accords for Palestinian autonomy bore no fruit.

The Lebanese government had another reason for resenting the PLO's presence in their country. As the Palestinians flooded into Lebanon from 1948 onwards, the Muslim population swelled to an extent where they now outnumbered the Christians by three to one. The Muslim population in Lebanon therefore began to call for greater political representation in parliament, the Christians in power refused, and the seeds were sown for a 19-year conflict in which the Palestinians, as so often before, emerged as both aggressors and, eventually, victims.

Israel, having lost the veneer of invincibility following the war of 1973 (see box on page 19), and having made peace with Egypt in the Camp David accords of 1978, invaded Lebanon on June 6 1982. Their motives included a desire to drive the PLO out of their bases in Lebanon; with the help of their Christian Phalangist allies, this proved fairly simple. Within one week they had stormed through southern Lebanon to the capital, Beirut, where they issued an ultimatum: either the PLO leave immediately, or the Israelis invade. Shorn of options, the PLO acquiesced, boarding a boat bound for **Cyprus** in August 1982.

The Israelis, however, failed to keep their side of the bargain. Instead, less than a month after the PLO withdrawal, on September 16, they stood by and watched the senseless slaughter of over a thousand defenceless Palestinians – men, women and children – living in two refugee camps, **Sabra** and **Shatila**, in West Beirut. The massacre was carried out by the Israelis' allies, the Phalangists, but, though the extent of the Israelis' culpability has never fully been established, their failure to stop the carnage earned them worldwide condemnation. Subsequent pressure by the international community forced the Israeli army to leave Beirut but, instead of an absolute withdrawal back to their homeland as they had promised, the Israeli forces decided to retreat only as far as **southern Lebanon** – where they remain an occupying force to this day.

Terrorist activity

From being the most enduring *cause célèbre* of the Arab world, the Palestinians now found themselves treated like pariahs, ostracised by their Arab brethren. Shunted from one Arab country to another since 1967, the PLO finally wound up in **Tunis** in 1982 following their enforced withdrawal from Lebanon. This eviction, though humiliating at the time, was not without its blessings: the PLO, enmeshed in wars in Jordan and Lebanon, had lost sight somewhat of their original aim of winning back the Holy Land for the Palestinians. The enforced retreat from Lebanon facilitated their extraction from a war which, from the outset, didn't really concern them, and enabled them to refocus once more.

Throughout the seventies and eighties the PLO perpetrated a number of terrorist atrocities. Initially these attacks at least brought the Palestinians' plight to the attention of the international community; but as time passed and they grew increasingly horrific, they did little except besmirch the reputation of both the PLO and the Palestinian community in general. The hijacking and subsequent destruction of three airlines in 1970, the killing of eleven Israeli athletes at the 1972 Olympics in Munich by a Fatah splinter group and the Achille Lauro affair in 1985, where a disabled American Jew on board a cruise ship was shot and dumped in the sea, all helped to fix in the minds of people the idea that to be a Palestinian was to be a terrorist. It also gave the Israelis an excuse to exact revenge on the Palestinians living within their territory.

The Intifada

The PLO's campaign was running out of steam. Guerrilla attacks had failed to dislodge the Israelis from Palestine, and the PLO's attempts to win back their land by negotiation had borne little fruit. Their refusal to accept UN Resolution 242 (see page 18 – a resolution also ignored by Israel) because it would have meant recognising the State of Israel, and their refusal of a similar resolution (number 338) following the war of 1973 for similar reasons, only weakened the PLO's bargaining position in the UN.

The PLO also began splitting into various factions as their campaign faltered. Some hardliners remained true to the original ideals of the party (ie: the reclamation of the whole of Palestine and the destruction of Israel), whereas others preferred, initially at least, to limit their ambitions to the recovery of the lands captured by Israel in 1967.

It was this lack of confidence in the PLO that prompted the Palestinians living in the so-called **Occupied Territories** (ie: the West Bank and Gaza, captured by Israel in 1967) to begin a popular rebellion against their Israeli oppressors. Beginning on December 8 1987 after an Israeli truck driver had accidentally run over and killed four Palestinians in Gaza, this uprising, known as the *Intifada* (literally, 'shaking'), took a number of different forms, including the **boycott** of Israeli goods, large-scale **demonstrations** against the Israelis and blanket **strikes**. Initially a peaceful uprising, the Intifada grew more violent as time went on. Attacks against Jewish settlers in the West Bank and rock throwing by Palestinian youths against Israeli soldiers became popular and enduring pastimes. The Israelis, predictably, were ruthless in their response. Armed patrols, the indiscriminate use of rubber bullets, curfews, torture and the appropriation of goods and land in retaliation for non-payment of taxes were just some of the measures taken

Nevertheless, the Intifada did much to further the Palestinian cause. For the first time the people of the Occupied Territories stood shoulder to shoulder in defiance of the Israeli soldiers. Footage of the heavy-handed Israeli response was shown throughout the world, turning popular opinion against the Israelis for possibly the first time since 1948. Even many Israelis were horrified by its ruthlessness. The exorbitant cost to the Israelis in terms of the extra policing required, the loss of output in Israel (which relies on Palestinian labour to perform many of its more menial tasks) and other indirect economic costs now made them more willing to negotiate with the Palestinians. The Palestinians' refusal to pay taxes also hit the Israeli coffers hard, and soon the Occupied Territories began recording an annual loss. The Israelis could never again look upon the West Bank or Gaza as an economic asset. To add pressure to the Israelis, in 1988 the PLO accepted Resolution 242, thus implicitly accepting the State of Israel, which now stood alone in rejecting the resolution, inviting opprobrium from the international community.

The Israelis were also frightened by the emergence of a new enemy at this time. **Hamas** (Arabic for zeal) was a scion of the Al-Mujamma Al-Islami, or **Muslim Brotherhood**, a zealously Islamic group based in the Gaza Strip that had been active since the early seventies. It is widely believed that in the early days Hamas had actually received funding from Israel, which saw them as a useful tool in undermining the authority of the PLO. Nobody could have predicted, however, just how popular Hamas, which favoured military action against Israel and viewed peace processes and negotiations as a waste of time, would become. But Hamas' call for a **Holy War**, or *Jihad*, against their oppressors met with a great deal of popular support, particularly in the Occupied Territories. After all, it was religious extremism that had underpinned the achievements of the Zionists a century before, so why couldn't it work for the new *diaspora*, the Palestinians?

The Gulf War and the Oslo accords

If the Intifada made Israel more amenable towards the idea of negotiating a settlement, the Gulf War of 1991 provided it with the opportunity of doing so. Iraq's invasion of tiny, oil-rich Kuwait in December 1990 brought the entire Middle East, and the relations between the countries, to the attention of the world. The Near East played a vital part in the success of the UN offensive that followed. Israel's role was to do nothing, thus ensuring that the Arab alliance against Iraq did not fracture (for no self-respecting Arab soldier would fight on the same side as Israel against a fellow Arab). But many Palestinians, tired of America's sponsorship of Israel and livid that Iraq's Saddam Hussein was being forced by might to obey the UN, while Israel had flagrantly flouted their resolutions for years, supported Iraq, and demonstrations of support were held on the streets of Amman by Palestinian refugees living there. The PLO, desperately trying to win back some popular support amongst its own people, also declared allegiance to Saddam.

The Gulf War served to bring the Palestinian question to the forefront of the international agenda, and in October 1991 in **Madrid** a peace summit between Israel and the PLO was held. Many Palestinians treated the summit with scepticism, especially as they had lost so much faith in the PLO. Were the PLO attending the summit to negotiate the best deal for the Palestinians, or merely to re-establish themselves as the rightful representatives of the Palestinian people, even if that meant selling their people short?

As it transpired, the PLO acquitted themselves well in Madrid, and the dignity, skill and common sense of their negotiators earned high praise. Unfortunately, little progress was actually made, and this stalemate would continue for the next two years, during which time the Israelis continued with their policy of filling the Occupied Territories with Jewish settlers. Allegations of torture and human rights abuses were also widespread at this time. While the Israelis were willing to talk peace and return the Occupied Territories appropriated in 1967, their actions gave the lie to their words.

The fighting between the Palestinians and the Israelis actually intensified following the Madrid summit. Many new Jewish settlements in the West Bank and Gaza came under attack from Palestinians and the Israeli premier, Yitzhak Rabin, responded by having over 400 members of Hamas arrested and then, bizarrely, dumped at the Lebanese border. The Lebanese refused to accept them and the four hundred found themselves in no-man's land with nowhere to go. The Israeli government's action backfired badly. The predicament of these exiled Palestinians attracted international attention, and the dignity of their behaviour garnered further support for both Hamas and the Palestinian cause.

The Oslo Accords

The stalemate between the PLO and Israeli negotiators was broken in 1993 in Oslo. The settlement reached, though not to everyone's satisfaction, was probably as good as the Palestinians could have hoped for at this stage. The treaty allowed for the establishment of an interim Palestinian National Authority (PNA) to oversee the creation of a Palestinian nation based on UN Resolution 242 (ie: covering the areas of the West Bank and Gaza Strip). The PNA would rule for a 'transitional' period of five years, beginning as soon as Israel withdrew from Jericho and the Gaza Strip (which they did in 1994). The rest of the West Bank would gradually be turned over to PNA control during this transitional period, at the end of which elections would be held to determine who would govern the country after that. Jerusalem, it should be noted, would remain in Israeli hands.

Of course, after everything the Palestinians had lost over the last 50 years, this accord was of meagre comfort. But it was at least a first and crucial step on the road to nationhood, and a launch pad for further possible concessions from the Israelis later on. However, the peace deal did little to stem the violence on the streets of the Occupied Territories. On February 24 1994 a Jewish settler opened fire with a machine gun in a mosque; 29 worshippers were killed that day. Hamas (who looked upon the signing of the Oslo accords as a betrayal by Yasser Arafat) took out their own bloody revenge, killing 12 people in separate bombing incidents within Israel the following week.

Netanyahu and the Wye Agreement

Following the heady days of 1993, the peace process lurched from one disaster to the next. Over the next few years the two sides were called together time and again by the UN, usually with considerable US backing, in an attempt to get the process back on track. The biggest single blow to the hopes of those who wish for peace came in 1995 with the assassination of Yitzhak Rabin by a Jewish extremist who felt Rabin had betrayed the State of Israel. Though there was nationwide grief over Rabin's death, many in Israel also felt that Israel had paid too high a price for peace, and in May 1996 the hardliner Binyamin Netanyahu swept to power after promising to adopt a tougher approach in the peace process.

Netanyahu's term in office was punctuated by a series of Israeli-Palestinian clashes. In October 1996 over 70 people died in riots in Jerusalem following the opening of the Western Wall Tunnel (see page 108). Further clashes in Hebron over the building of new Jewish settlements stretched the goodwill between the two sides to breaking point. Though a new deal, the Wye Accords (named after a river in America near to where the negotiations were conducted), was signed in 1998, it quickly floundered as each side accused the other of reneging on their part of the bargain. Netanyahu felt that the Palestinian authorities weren't doing enough to combat terrorist atrocities perpetrated against Israelis by Palestinians. Meanwhile, Yasser Arafat, fed up with the delaying tactics employed by the Israelis, threatened in June 1999 to announce the inception of a Palestinian state, regardless of the current progress of the peace process. To cap it all, King Hussein of Jordan, the man who did so much to get the peace process off the ground and a major mediator between the two sides, passed away in January 1999. Many felt at the time that his death would be the final, fatal blow to the accords.

The Wye II Agreement

Just as many were predicting the demise of the peace process, fresh impetus arrived in the form of a new and dovish Israeli prime minister, Ehud Barak, whose election victory over Binyamin Netanyahu owed much to his enthusiasm for getting the peace process back on track. Fulfilling promises made during his campaign, Barak re-opened negotiations with two of Israel's oldest adversaries, President Assad of Syria, and Palestine's Yasser Arafat.

Talks with the latter culminated in the signing of the Wye II Agreement, a deal that aimed to re-implement the proposals of the original Wye Agreement. Suspended by Netanyahu since December of the previous year, Wye I had brought little in the way of tangible benefits to the Palestinians. Of the withdrawal from 13% of the West Bank, only 2% had actually been vacated, while of the 750 Palestinian prisoners that Israel had promised to release as part of the deal, only a third had so far been set free. Furthermore, of those 250, over 60% were said to be common criminals, and not the political prisoners that the Palestinian negotiators had been hoping for and expecting.

REFUGEES AND UNRWA

Of the 2.3 million Palestinians who still live in Palestine, over half – approximately 1.38 million – are UNRWA-registered refugees who lost their original homes in Israel in the wars of '48 and '67. Just under half of these refugees, about 578,000 in total, live in refugee camps, of which there are 27 dotted throughout the West Bank and Gaza Strip. The figures for Gaza alone are even more depressing. Of the 785,500 refugees registered with UNRWA (United Nations Relief and Works Agency for Palestine Refugees in the Near East) in the Gaza – which is over 90% of the total Gazan population – 428,000 live in refugee camps.

Yet these figures pale into insignificance when compared with those of the Palestinian population that fled the Holy Land altogether to live in neighbouring countries, hoping to return to their original homes and villages when the fighting stopped. They are still waiting today. Over 367,000 fled to **Lebanon**, where over 200,000 are still forced to endure the hardships of life in a refugee camp. Approximately the same number fled to **Syria** (though only 108,000 are still in the camps), while an incredible 1,487,500 Palestinians now live in **Jordan** – over half of the entire Jordanian population – with 272,000 in camps. As a result, over half of the Palestinian people don't even live within the country's borders.

Though grim, the refugee camps of today are a considerable step up from the original canvas slums of a few decades ago. The buildings are now concrete, and most are linked up to the electricity and water supplies. However, life in these camps remains incredibly bleak. Overcrowding is a serious problem, with the camps of the Gaza Strip amongst the most populated areas in the world. Lack of a decent sewage system, an intermittent power supply and inadequate health and education facilities compound the hardship. In the camps of southern Gaza, wastewater and sewage flow into paths and alleyways, endangering the health of those who live nearby and the underground freshwater supply.

Under Wye II, signed on September 5 1999 at the Sinai resort of Sharm El-Sheikh, it was agreed that a further 350 Palestinian prisoners should be released, and that the Israelis withdraw from a further 11% of the West Bank, to be conducted in three stages, the first withdrawal beginning within ten days of the agreement. The deal also provided for the opening of safe passage routes across Israel to allow Palestinians to travel between the West Bank and Gaza. In addition, the Palestinians have been given the go-ahead to build a new seaport in Gaza.

Perhaps most importantly of all, the deal also paves the way for the so-called 'final-status negotiations' which will determine once and for all the final size, shape and status of Palestine. And while chief Israeli negotiator Gilead Sher's one year deadline for the conclusion of these final status negotiations is rather optimistic, given the trouble the two sides have had in even reaching this agreement, it does at least signal the intention of both sides to work quickly towards a final solution.

Whither the peace process?

Throughout the last six years, since that first historic agreement in 1993 in Oslo between the Palestinian authorities and Israel, those who wish for peace in the Holy Land have had their hopes and expectations raised and then dashed with tiresome regularity. As I write this, following the signing of Wye II and the withdrawal of Israeli troops from parts of the West Bank, expectations are once more running high. Much of the credit for this must go to Ehud Barak who, in

UNRWA is the main organisation charged with improving the lot of these refugees, providing health centres and schools – and people to staff them – as well as attempting to give the camps a better infrastructure. Their work is not without controversy. Many argue that the solution to the refugee situation lies not in improving the living conditions within the camps, but in persuading the Israelis to accept **Resolution 242** which calls for all land appropriated during war to be returned to its original owners, thereby allowing the Palestinians to return to their old homes. Improving living conditions within the camps, therefore, is seen by some as almost pro-Israeli, a tacit acceptance of the status quo and acknowledgement that Israel will never abide by Resolution 242.

Still, it's not difficult to see how important UNRWA is to the survival of so many of the camps' inhabitants. As part of their duties, they used to arrange tours around a camp, including interviews with camp residents. Unfortunately, these days they tend to open their tours to journalists only, following criticisms that too many ghoulish tourists were signing up and taking photos of the misfortunes of others. However, if you have a valid reason for wanting to visit a camp, the UNRWA tour is the best way to do so, and you may be able to persuade them to let you join a trip by calling in at their offices in Jerusalem (see page 91) or Gaza City (page 78). Alternatively, there are camps near most of the major cities in the West Bank and Gaza, many within walking distance of the town centre, which you can amble through. Please be sensitive when visiting, and don't go around thrusting your camera everywhere or showing off your wealth.

Though UNRWA is financed by governments (the budget for the Gaza alone in 1998 was US$98,800,000) there are also a number of private charities and agencies attempting to provide relief for camp inhabitants. One of them, the **Palestinian Children's Relief Fund**, receives a percentage of the royalties from this book; to find out more, see page 37.

spite of the (perfectly justifiable) cynicism from both his own countrymen and the Palestinian people, does appear both sincere and determined in his quest for peace. The Palestinian authorities are also to be praised for their patience, particularly during the years of delay and obfuscation by the Netanyahu government.

However, it is worth remembering that Wye II, like its predecessor, is a mere 'stepping stone' (to use Bill Clinton's description) on the road to a comprehensive peace process. The agreement is both broader in scope than the original deal, in that it specifies a schedule for reaching a final agreement, and carries more weight than the original Wye accord, if only because Barak is more committed to finding peace than Netanyahu ever was, but the more contentious and emotional issues have yet to be solved. The final status of both the West Bank and Gaza Strip, the arguments over water supply, the rights of the two million Palestinian refugees still living in camps across the Middle East, the future of Jewish settlements on Palestinian land and, perhaps toughest of all, the future of Jerusalem, are the main problems facing both sides when they begin the final-status negotiations next year. And, while Yasser Arafat and Ehud Barak appear to have built a level of trust and confidence in each other (Arafat even went so far as to call Barak his 'new partner' in the peace process), both parties face considerable opposition at home. Ariel Sharon, the new leader of Israel's right-wing Likud party, has already criticised the release of 350 political prisoners as 'moral bankruptcy'. On the Palestinian side, the PFLP and the DFLP also condemned the deal, saying that the Israelis had extracted too many Palestinian concessions from Arafat.

Meanwhile, the leader of the extreme Hamas group, Sheikh Ahmed Yassin, described the deal as a sell out, and said his supporters reserved the right to resist Israeli occupation.

Undoubtedly, Wye II is a positive move forward, and the peace process is looking healthier now than it has done for a number of years. The mutual trust between the two leaders is perhaps more encouraging than the actual agreement, and can only bode well for the future. But it has to be said that a final and lasting peace in the Holy Land still seems a mighty long way off. As Madeleine Albright said in a news conference following the signing of Wye II: 'A great task has been completed. An even larger one remains.'

ECONOMY

The economic development in Palestine over the past decade has been considerably hampered by the Intifada and the heavy-handed Israeli response to it, both of which have discouraged investors from the territories. The lack of employment opportunities in Palestine is the country's major economic concern, with unemployment rates currently running at 35% in the West Bank and 45% in the Gaza Strip. If the country is ever to become economically viable, this problem must be addressed soon. With unemployment so high, many Palestinians have returned to **agriculture**: olives, citrus fruits, vegetables, beef and dairy products are the mainstay of the primary economy. Because of poor soil and insufficient rainfall, agriculture is limited on the West Bank to the hills and oases. Palestine does have some **mineral resources**, particularly salt and potash which can be found in large quantities in the Dead Sea, though these have yet to be exploited. Other industries are very small-scale, usually family run concerns producing soap, olive-wood carvings and other souvenirs. The country's **$6 billion GDP** ($4 billion contributed by the West Bank) is supplemented by remittances from Palestinians in Israel and the Gulf states, though these were dramatically reduced in the early nineties after the PLO declared its support for Iraq during the Gulf War. **International aid**, amounting to approximately $500 million in 1998, is also a major contributor to the economy of Palestine.

PEOPLE

The uncertain ethnic origins of the Palestinian people lie behind much of the current troubles. Zionists maintain that the Arabs in the Holy Land are descendants of the **Bedouin tribes** who conquered the region for Islam in the 7th century. It therefore follows, so the argument goes, that the Jews (who, according to the Bible, have lived in the region since the arrival of the Israelites in c1250BC, following their exodus from Egypt) have a more valid claim to the land according to the I-saw-it-first law of possession.

In response, the Palestinians claim that they are something of an ethnic mishmash, being descendants of many of the races and tribes (the Hebrews, or Israelites, amongst them) who lived in the area at one time or another, including the **Canaanites** and **Philistines** who preceded the Israelites in the Holy Land. It therefore follows that the Palestinians have as much right to be in the Holy Land as the Jews. It is, of course, unlikely that either argument will ever be proved; though, judging by the diverse variations of skin, hair and eye colour that one finds amongst the Palestinians today, their mixed-race theory would seem to hold water.

Whatever the truth, today the Palestinian Arabs are by far the largest ethnic group in Palestine. In the West Bank they constitute 83% of the total population of approximately 1.5 million, and in the Gaza Strip the figure is officially 99.4% –

PALESTINIAN DRESS

One of the most distinguishing characteristics of the Palestinian people is the traditional dress, which is not only the most flamboyant in the Arab world, but, almost uniquely, is still worn as everyday clothing, particularly by elderly female villagers. The dresses are full length, but vary in style and design according to region. The *qabbeh*, the embroidered chest-piece of gold and variegated silk threads, is the most exquisite part of the dress. Simpler designs decorate the sleeves. The dress is often gathered in at the waist and tied round with a belt or sometimes a woollen shawl. If it is cold the women wear a *taksireh*, a short jacket embroidered simply with silk thread (for everyday use) or with silver and golden thread (for special occasions). On their head they wear a veil; the elaborate, multi-layered hat decorated with coral beads and coins worn by married women is a rare sight these days. Finally, in winter, a black- and red-striped woollen overcoat is worn over the dress, to complete the outfit and keep the wearer warm.

Occasionally, you may come across an elderly woman with her face, particularly around the lips, tattooed. This is an ancient Bedouin tradition and is a mark of ownership, showing that she is married; it is a practice that has all but died out.

about 820,000 Palestinians. The remaining population consists almost entirely of Jewish settlers, mainly from Europe, who live in closely guarded camps that dot the West Bank (about 122,000 settlers in total) and Gaza Strip (5,000).

Palestine has a fairly young population, with those in the under-14 age bracket making up almost half of the population. Only 3% of the entire population is over 65. In terms of religious divisions, about 82% are Muslims (predominantly Sunni), 7% are Christians and the remaining 11% are Jews. By comparison, Jerusalem is far more equitably divided between Jews and Arabs. There are also a considerable number of minority populations including Syrians, Ethiopians, Armenians and Greeks, all of whom are associated with the monastic orders that have lived in the Old City for centuries.

Palestinian identity and Palestinian society

Palestinian society has proved remarkably resilient in the face of an influx of cultural influences brought over from the West by European Jews. But it's not really correct to talk about just one Palestinian society, when the Palestinian population is made up of so many factions and faiths, from the urbane city dweller of Ramallah to the Bedouin shepherd of the southern deserts, and from the Muslim who looks to the east for his cultural and religious inspiration to the Christian who, perhaps unwittingly, is influenced by and assimilates into his or her lifestyle the fads and fashions of the West.

To witness traditional Palestinian society at its most rudimentary and ancient, it is necessary to get away from the big cities to the villages, the traditional settlements of Palestine, where Palestinian society evolved and where life continues today pretty much as it has done for thousands of years.

Palestinian society is largely **patriarchal**. While women in the city are, by the standards of the Arab world, fairly empowered, and many hold down vital strategic jobs of real power and importance, in the villages their role is still mainly that of homemaker and child-bearer. Men rule the villages and one man, the *Mukhtar*, rules the men as the village chief. Although this kind of social stratification is becoming less common as the traditional village hierarchy is disrupted by changes in the modern world outside, it still exists in some of the smaller Palestinian villages lying off the beaten track. If you find yourself in one, it pays to visit the local chief before anyone else.

The *Mukhtar* used to have a special room put aside for guests visiting his village, or at least male guests; you can see a recreation of just such a guestroom at the In'Ash Al-Osra Folklore Museum in Al-Bireh. This penchant for hospitality, combined with an innate conservatism and a certain religious devotion, still runs through every sector of Palestinian society today, having survived the destruction of many hundreds of villages in 1948 and the gradual village-to-town migration that's taken place over the past 50 years.

Though indubitably part of the Arab world, Palestinians are also quite separate from it, thanks to differences in their history, their status as an **oppressed minority** and even their regional accent. As such, their attitude towards the rest of the Arab world is somewhat ambivalent, cherishing them as bigger brothers but despising them for their failure to do more to help them against the Israelis. This ambivalence manifested itself most clearly during the years 1948–67 when the Jordanians assumed control of the West Bank. Many Palestinians have gone on record as saying that this occupation was even more unwelcome than the subsequent Israeli one: living under a largely occidental regime is one thing, for at least you can hate your oppressor without feeling uneasy or guilty; living under the rule of your neighbour and close relative, however, is quite another.

Similarly, Palestinians in the West Bank and Gaza Strip are ambivalent towards those who decided to stay in Israel – though to be honest, few Palestinians were given the choice – taking Israeli citizenship and enjoying all the benefits that it confers. Though exactly the same race of people, from the same background and with the same genealogy, the Israeli Arabs are seen as traitors to the Palestinian cause. Many consider that, by not opposing the Israeli regime, the Israeli Arabs have given the Jewish nation their tacit approval. In other words, many Palestinians feel the Israeli Arabs have sold out. This is a little unfair, as the Israeli Arabs have gained little by remaining in their native villages, have had to endure half a century of state-sponsored oppression and are often treated as second-class citizens in Israeli society.

Language

Arabic, particularly the quasi-Syrian dialect of Arabic spoken in Palestine, is an incredibly difficult language to learn and almost impossible for the Western tongue to pronounce – at least not without firing phlegm all over the shirt of the listener. Mercifully, English is fairly widely spoken, and visitors to Palestine can get by with little more than the two common forms of greeting – *Marhaba* ('hi') and the more formal and Islamic *Salaam Aleikhoom* (literally 'peace be upon you') – along with 'goodbye' (*Masalama*) and 'Thank you' (*Shokran*). Other phrases I find useful include *Fish mushkele* ('no problem'), *bikam* ('how much does it cost?'), and *ghaali* ('expensive'), which often proves invaluable in Jerusalem's Old City.

If you can, it's also worthwhile getting to grips with the **Arabic numbering system**, both written and spoken; a familiarity with, and fluency in, Arabic numbers could prove very useful when it comes to haggling. A more complete list of Arabic words and phrases can be found on page 217.

Though most Arabs are fluent in Hebrew, whether you should bother learning any, or using that which you already know, is not entirely clear. On the one hand, it may help you to communicate with a Palestinian if his or her English and your Arabic are not good; attempting any Hebrew, however falteringly, will also make you extremely popular amongst the inhabitants of the Jewish settlements. On the other hand, it's bound to raise suspicions amongst Palestinian locals if you suddenly break out into fluent Hebrew, and speaking it in the Gaza Strip or Hebron is just asking for trouble. To be honest, I've never learnt – or had to use – any Hebrew apart from the greeting 'shalom'.

RELIGION

The religious intolerance that so bedevils Palestine starts to take on an aspect of absurdity when you realise just how inter-related the three major religions are. Simply put, Christianity was originally just a radical branch of Judaism, and all of the early figures in Christianity (including Christ Himself) were Jewish, while Islam can be seen as an extension of both religions. The bottom line is these faiths are all monotheistic (ie: worship one God only) and all worship the same deity, whether they call him Yahweh, God or Allah.

Though Islam is by far and away the most popular faith in Palestine, and Christianity second, the following descriptions of the three religions have been put in chronological order. Thus Judaism, as the oldest faith, is first, followed by Christianity and then Islam.

Judaism

Possibly the world's oldest religion still widely practised today, Judaism is the cornerstone of all major monotheistic faiths, and both Islam and Christianity's views on the Creation, the origins of Man and his relationship with God borrow heavily from Judaism.

Historical background

In about 1900BC a group of nomads under the leadership of Abram (later called **Abraham**) headed west from Mesopotamia to the land of Canaan (modern-day Israel, Palestine and southern Lebanon). Abraham had rejected the idolatrous pagan religion of his village of Ur, preferring instead to worship one god only, whom he called **Jehovah**. God rewarded Abraham for this show of loyalty by promising that his descendants would receive the land of Canaan. Abraham's son Isaac and grandson Jacob received similar promises, and this triumvirate became known as the **Patriarchs**, the forefathers of Judaism.

Jacob (also known as Israel) went on to have twelve sons, the descendants of whom would become the **Twelve Tribes of Israel**. Drought eventually forced the Israelites to leave Canaan for Egypt (c1750BC), though under the leadership of **Moses** they returned in about 1250BC following years of persecution by the Egyptian pharaohs. It was during this hike from Egypt to the 'Promised Land', a forty-year trek known as the Exodus, that Moses received the **Ten Commandments**, an event that Jews look upon as the birth of the nation of Israel (albeit a few hundred miles to the west of their eventual homeland).

Moses, who by this time was approaching his 121st birthday, never did reach the land of Canaan; instead, after he'd died on the border on Mount Nebo (now in Jordan), it was left to his appointed successor, **Joshua**, to lead the Israelites to the Promised Land. They wasted little time in conquering it for themselves.

With no worthy successor to Joshua following his demise, the Israelites soon became disunited and a number of feudal military leaders, called **Judges**, took charge, the best-known of these being **Samuel**. It was a fractious and largely unsuccessful period in Israelite history, and for the sake of unity amongst the tribes

PROVING THE BIBLE – THE ARCHAEOLOGICAL EVIDENCE

By the early 20th century, scholars had consigned much of the Old Testament to the realms of fantasy. Many of the biblical stories simply didn't tie in with what we knew at that time of the history of the region which had been compiled using only extra-biblical sources. Furthermore, as much of the **Hebrew** Bible (ie: the Old Testament) had been written a few centuries after the events were supposed to have taken place, biblical scholars decided that many of the stories were simply the product of the author's over-fertile imagination.

The archaeological evidence discovered since **William Matthew Flinders Petrie** conducted the first excavation in the Holy Land, at Tel El-Hesi in 1890, has therefore proved quite enlightening. True, the lack of expected archaeological finds has, in some cases, backed up the claims of those who feel that the Bible is largely a work of fiction. However, just occasionally, archaeological evidence has gone some way to refuting the scepticism surrounding the early biblical stories. Of course archaeology can't prove the Bible: though we have evidence of Herod's existence, for example, we can't prove that the events surrounding his life as described in the Bible actually occurred. But archaeology can go some way towards increasing our understanding of why, how, when and if certain events took place, and, by helping us to recreate the buildings and cities of yesteryear, can provide a backdrop on which our imaginations can paint the biblical episodes. The following brief run through the major episodes in the Bible explores the evidence, or lack of it, discovered during excavations held throughout the Near East.

Though much of **Genesis** is impossible to prove or disprove, archaeologists at various locations have discovered water-stained strata deep in the earth, seeming to confirm that a vast flood once swamped the land as described in the story of **Noah** (Genesis 6-10). However, the dating of these saturated strata varies from 4000 to 2700BC. So while there seems to be a history of flooding in the region, there doesn't appear to have been one Great Flood. As for Noah's Ark, it is claimed that there's a boat-shaped land formation on Mount Ararat in Armenia, where the Bible says the Ark came to rest. Archaeological digs, however, failed to find any evidence of such a mammoth wooden vessel.

The rest of the Pentateuch, including the stories of the patriarchs, the Israelites' exile in Egypt and the **Exodus**, suffers from a lack of archaeological evidence. The discovery of 25,000 written tablets at the ruined palace at Mari, on the Euphrates, does at least prove that names in Abraham's genealogy existed at around 2000BC, when many scholars say that he lived. What's more, there's evidence that his wife Sarah's provision of a handmaid, with whom he could have a child, was common practice at this time. There's also an 18th-century BC papyrus, now in the Brooklyn Museum, that lists foreigners sold as slaves to Egypt, and talks of a Semitic man sold by his companions into slavery – just as **Joseph** had been by his brothers in Genesis 37.

Evidence for the Israelites' arrival, conquest, and the establishment of their monarchy in Canaan is also rather patchy. Extensive excavations at **Tel El-Sultan** in Jericho by Kathleen Kenyon revealed stone walls that appeared to have tumbled down the glacis (banks), thus seeming to confirm the story of Joshua's most famous victory. Unfortunately, the demolition of these walls has been dated to 1550BC, 350 years before the accepted date of Joshua's conquest in c1200BC. And while the excavations by Kathleen Kenyon in Jerusalem have uncovered the **City of David**, there's no trace of his son Solomon's First Temple.

Indeed, the first clear and unequivocal evidence of any biblical event occurs only after the split in the Israeli and the fall of the northern Kingdom of Israel to the Assyrians in 721 BC, an event recorded on obelisks and stelae from the Assyrians' homeland in northeastern Iraq. Typical Israelite names crop up on documents from various parts of Assyria at this time, providing evidence that the Israelites were indeed scattered throughout the empire after their defeat. Similarly, Jerusalem's demolition at the hands of **Nebuchadnezzar** is also backed up by documents of the time, as is the subsequent conquest of Babylon by the Persians.

Jumping forward, New Testament buildings abound thanks to the architectural excesses of Herod and his Roman paymasters, though written evidence of New Testament events is scant. One of the most interesting discoveries was that of the **Praetorium**, or **Antonia Fortress**, where Jesus was said to have been tried and imprisoned, to the north of the Temple. Evidence of **crucifixion** – including an ossuary where the forearm and heel bones had been pierced by nails – and tombs closed by a rolling stone have also been found outside the city walls, which could date from the time of Christ.

Re-dating the Bible
Much of the trouble with trying to find archaeological evidence for the Bible is that the dates given to ruins simply don't correlate with the accepted dates of biblical events. So, for example, as we have seen above, though Kathleen Kenyon did find collapsed walls in Jericho, they appear to pre-date the time of Joshua by 350 years. Attempts to reconcile the two have tended to concentrate on re-examining the way we date biblical events, which, with its dependence on unreliable biblical sources, appears to be shaky at best. One archaeologist, however, **David Rohl**, has attempted a reconciliation between the two by examining the methods scholars have used to date the ruins themselves.

Ancient Palestinian ruins are usually dated by comparing the **pottery pieces** found on the site with similar pottery shards discovered in Egypt. So, for example, a piece of Palestinian pottery may resemble a shard from the New Kingdom era in Egypt, which, thanks to the Egyptians' more extensive records – in the form of papyrus scrolls and hieroglyphs – can be dated with a fair degree of accuracy. So once we know the date for an Egyptian pottery shard, we can deduce that a similar shard from Palestine has a similar date, and from this we can guess at the approximate date of the entire ruin.

But is it right to rely on these Egyptian records and our interpretation of them? No, according to Rohl, who argues in his book *A Test of Time – From Myth to History* that our entire understanding of Egyptian history, and in particular the accepted chronology of the Pharaohs, is inaccurate. Simply put, he believes that a couple of pharaohs ruled concurrently, rather than one after the other as we've always believed. This compresses the time span for certain Egyptian eras, shifting the accepted dates for Egyptian history forward by approximately 350 years, which has profound implications for archaeology in Palestine. It means that the walls of Jericho found by Kenyon really did collapse in around 1200 BC, which ties in with the accepted date for Joshua's conquest. Other anomalies, such as the dating of the temple at Shechem near Nablus (see page 145), also appear to tie in with Rohl's new dating system. As Rohl himself admits, his theories are controversial, but they do open up a whole new forum of debate, and encourage archaeologists to review the way they will conduct their researches in future.

it was decided that a monarchy should be established: **Saul**, priestly prophet and judge, was chosen by God and the people to be the first king.

With a united Israel behind him, **David**, Saul's son and heir, went on to expand his kingdom up to the Euphrates (now in Iraq), including the capture of the city of Jerusalem (c1000BC) which he made his capital. His son, **Solomon**, continued the good work, and his reign is often called the Golden Age of Judaism, a time when art, commerce and theology reached their apogee. The **First Temple**, built to house the **Ark of the Covenant** (a wooden chest containing the Ten Commandments as received by Moses on Mount Sinai), was erected under his supervision on Mount Moriah, a small hill to the north of David's capital at Jerusalem.

Unfortunately for the Israelites, subsequent monarchs proved less able and, following Solomon's death (c922BC), the Kingdom of Israel split into two: ten of the Twelve Tribes broke away to form **Israel**, a land to the north of Jerusalem. (To prevent confusion between this kingdom and the united Israeli kingdom of David and Solomon, in this book we call this breakaway kingdom Samaria, or, more commonly, the **northern Israelite kingdom**.) The remaining two tribes (the Judaeans and the tribe of Benjamin) formed the **Kingdom of Judaea** (including Jerusalem) to the south. The northern Israelite kingdom was obliterated from history by the Assyrians in 721BC; its people, scattered in mass deportations, became known as the **Ten Lost Tribes**. The Judaeans, meanwhile, stayed put until 586BC, when they were exiled to Babylonia by Nebuchadnezzar. Solomon's Temple was flattened at this time. Only after Cyrus of Persia had conquered Babylon nearly 50 years later (538BC) were the Judaeans (now called **Jews**) allowed to return home to rebuild Jerusalem and the Temple; they lived in (relative) peace until the Greeks of Alexander the Great arrived in the 4th century BC.

A Jewish revolt under **Judas Maccabeus** in 166BC re-established Jewish independence for the next century, though the arrival of the Romans in 63BC under General Pompey once more subjected the Jewish Kingdom to foreign rule. Two further rebellions, in AD66 and 132 (the latter called the **Bar Kochba Revolt**), proved less successful, the Jews incurring the severe wrath of Rome each time. Following the Bar Kochba Rebellion the Temple was flattened and the Jews were barred from Jerusalem altogether.

With no Temple and no homeland, the Jews were forced to split up and find new homes elsewhere, but even this enforced exile and subsequent dispersal could not crush Judaism. Instead, by adhering to the common set of laws, beliefs and sacred rituals, the **Diaspora** (Hebrew for 'Scattered'), as they called themselves, were able to maintain a common bond with each other and keep their Jewish identity wherever they went. This exile from the Holy Land continued for almost two thousand years, until the Zionists of the last century began their campaign for a Jewish homeland.

As with all the major religions, over time Judaism developed different branches, foremost being the **Sephardic** community, which traces its cultural roots to Babylonia, and the **Ashkenazic** community whose ancestral affiliations are with Palestine. Much later, in the 17th century, the mystic Jewish sects of **Hassidism** and **Kabbala** emerged, which place more emphasis on prayer and piety than study. The last major development in Judaism was the emergence of a reformist movement in the 19th century, which attempted to update the religion by demanding full equality for women, changing many of the sacred rituals, and even holding services in languages other than Hebrew. Needless to say, many Jews find these modern adaptations offensive.

Sacred texts

The most holy Jewish scripture is the **Torah**, consisting of the first five books of the Old Testament (Genesis, Exodus, Leviticus, Numbers and Deuteronomy), known as the **Pentateuch**, on which the entire Jewish faith is founded. These books deal with the Creation, Abraham's migration to Canaan, the years in Egypt and the Exodus under Moses; more importantly, they also contain God's guidance for mankind as revealed to Moses, including the divine laws on which Jewish society should be ordered (called the **Mosaic Law** after Moses). The Torah, combined with the books of the Prophets and the Sacred Writings, forms the Jewish Bible, the **Tenakh**, which is identical to the Old Testament apart from the order in which some of the books are placed.

Completed in the 5th century AD, the **Mishnah** is the earliest known codification of Jewish law: a written interpretation of the Mosaic Law that had governed Jewish society since its formation. It can be viewed as a sort of instruction manual for Jewish society, containing regulations regarding daily prayer, the conduct of religious ceremonies and festivals, the design of temples, the foundations for criminal law and so on. Intensive, separate studies of the Mishnah in Babylon and Palestine in the fourth century AD resulted in two interpretations that together form the second sacred Jewish text, the **Talmud**.

Beliefs

The Jews believe it is man's ability to choose between right and wrong that distinguishes us from all the other creatures on the earth, and that the Jews themselves are the **high priests** chosen by God to teach and guide the Gentiles (non-Jews). By contacting Abraham, the founder of Judaism, God made the Jews his **chosen people**, and the Torah is God's recipe for a just and Godly society.

The laws enshrined in the Torah and interpreted in the Talmud are constantly being added to and adapted to cope with the advances of the modern age. Some of these regulations, such as the proscription of pork and other non-kosher food, are well known. But, with the exception of the laws regarding **Shabbat**, the Jewish Sabbath that runs from Friday dusk to Saturday dusk, during which time everything closes down, few of these regulations will impinge on your trip to Palestine.

Christianity

Christianity grew out of the turmoil into which Judaism had plunged during the Roman occupancy of Palestine. Many of the faithful had become dissatisfied with the way the religion was being run by self-serving leaders creating, as they saw it, ever-more ridiculous laws. Essentially, Christianity can be seen as a movement away from the letter of Jewish law and towards its spirit, as exemplified by Jesus' Sermon on the Mount, a distillation of all His teachings.

Historical background

Historians are now fairly satisfied that there was a man called Jesus, who was born circa 5BC and lived for about 35 years, mostly in Nazareth. Beyond that, things are less certain. According to the Gospels, Jesus was born in Bethlehem to the Virgin Mary but spent much of his infancy in Egypt, where his family had fled to escape the massacre of children by Herod. On his return Jesus was baptised by his cousin John the Baptist and settled down in Galilee as a teacher. He became just one of many reactionaries who toured the land at this time. His outspoken views and crowd-pleasing miracles with the blind and lame soon earned him a small following. Unfortunately, they brought him many enemies too.

THE CHRISTIAN EXODUS

For the past few centuries Christianity has been in decline in the Holy Land as its adherents flee the Arab-Israeli troubles. This exodus from the church has accelerated over the last 100 years. Caught in the middle of a power struggle between two religious heavyweights, the Christian community in Palestine is being squeezed out. It is a pattern that has been repeated throughout the Near East, but seems particularly poignant in Palestine, the birthplace of the faith. Few monasteries now hold more than a dozen monks where once they used to house up to 5,000. **Mar Saba**, for example, now has 14 monks, while nearby **Mar Theodosius** is the home of just one. William Dalrymple's excellent book *From the Holy Mountain*, which charts the decline of Christianity in the Near East, quotes a Palestinian writer who states that the entire Christian population in Jerusalem could be flown out of the city in just nine jumbo jets. There are now more Palestinian Christians living in Sydney than in Palestine and, of the major Palestinian cities, only Bethlehem and Jericho have Christian populations that equal their Muslim counterparts. As Christians seem able to secure residency abroad with a greater degree of ease than their Muslim countrymen, and with little incentive to hang around, the prospect of a further exodus from the Holy Land seems inevitable.

In around AD30 he went to Jerusalem to celebrate the Jewish festival of the Passover. He must have known his life was in danger, having criticised the Jewish governors in many of his sermons. He further angered them by upsetting the tables of the moneylenders in Herod's Temple, and was eventually arrested in the Garden of Gethsemane. He was tried for blasphemy (since his people called him the 'Messiah', the Hebrew word for 'anointed' or 'blessed'; Christ is the Greek translation of 'Messiah'), and was crucified on the Jewish leaders' insistence by the Roman Governor Pontius Pilate. But of course the story doesn't end there. Three days later he was rising from the dead and the rest, as they say, is history.

Unfortunately, the only detailed records of Jesus' life are the **Gospels**, written by Christians for Christians. They were also written long after Jesus had died (the first is attributed to Mark, cAD62). But however uncertain its beginnings, there is no doubt that Christianity would never have become the world religion it is today if it were not for the efforts of the **Apostles** (Greek for 'Messengers'), the followers of Jesus charged with spreading the Christian message and establishing the church throughout the civilised world. Eleven of the twelve apostles were the original disciples ('followers') who followed Jesus during his ministry; the twelfth disciple, Judas, hanged himself after betraying Christ. He was replaced by Paul, the most zealous and successful of the apostles who travelled for ten years around the Mediterranean, establishing Christian communities wherever he went. Paul's most valuable contribution to Christianity, however, was to persuade the apostles' leader, Peter, in the Council of Jerusalem of cAD50, that Christianity should be an inclusive religion: that is to say Gentiles as well as Jews should be allowed to join.

The apostles continued to preach Christianity, despite widespread persecution from the Romans, particularly following the burning of Rome under Emperor Nero in AD64. The Romans' destruction of Jerusalem in AD70, following the Bar Kochba Rebellion, forced the Christians to remove their capital and find a new base from which to spread the Christian message: their choice of Rome, the centre of the empire and hub of the civilised world's communications, proved to be a masterstroke. From being a persecuted minority, by the middle of the 4th century Christianity had become the official state religion of the all-powerful Byzantine Empire, and continued to hold sway in Palestine for the next three hundred years.

During the Byzantine period the church split down a number of theological lines, which eventually led over the years to the establishment of three major churches: **Eastern Orthodox**, based in Constantinople, **Roman Catholic**, and **Oriental Orthodox**, formed from the Syrian and Egyptian Coptic churches. Most of the Christians in Palestine today follow the Eastern Orthodox faith. Much later, in the 16th century, a second split took place in the European church with the establishment of the **Protestant** faith, a reaction to the wealth and corruption in Rome.

Travellers brought up in the Western church are often surprised by how much of an imbalance there appears to be between the denominations. The world's largest denomination, for instance, Roman Catholicism, owns very few of Christianity's sacred sites, whereas smaller denominations – the tiny Armenian church, the Greek Orthodox and the Egyptian and Syrian Copts – maintain a far more visible presence in the Holy Land. The Protestants, so dominant in Northern Europe, barely get a look-in in Palestine.

The most disturbing aspect of Christianity in Palestine today is the friction that exists between the various churches, which spend a great deal of time and effort arguing with each other over who owns what in the Holy Land. Visit the Holy Sepulchre in Jerusalem or Bethlehem's Church of the Nativity and you'll see what I mean. The majority of sacred Christian sites in Palestine are now owned by the Greek Orthodox, followed by the Armenians (who own over 30%), while the Roman Catholics own less than 20%.

Sacred texts

The **Bible** is more of a library than a single text, containing within its covers a total of 66 books arranged in a loose chronological order. The first 39 books are collectively known as the **Old Testament**, and are borrowed wholesale from the Jewish Tenakh (see page 33).

The **New Testament**, which starts with the four **Gospels** detailing the life of Jesus, begins around 500 years after the Old Testament ends. After the gospels the works of the **Apostles** are described, followed by their open letters to various towns and cities in the Near East. The Bible finishes with the **Book of Revelations**, a prophecy revealed in a series of visions that predicts the final victory of God over his enemies.

Beliefs

Christianity began as little more than a schism, albeit a heretical one, from Judaism. The Christian beliefs about the origins of man, his place on earth and his relationship to God are virtually identical to Jewish beliefs. Where Christianity splits from Judaism is in its treatment of Christ. Simply put, the Jewish tradition has it that a **Messiah** will visit the earth, and that this Messiah, a descendant of King David, will deliver the faithful from their tormenters. Matthew, the writer of the first gospel, is keen to establish Jesus' credentials as the Messiah and provides a detailed ancestry of Jesus and His direct lineage from King David. But the Jews rejected Jesus as the Messiah, whereas Christians, of course, view Him as both the Messiah and the Son of God.

Islam

The West's perception of Islam is usually a negative one. To many it is a religion followed by extremists, governed by antiquated laws enforced through barbaric punishments, and populated by misogynists who reduce the role of women to virtual slavery; whereas in fact it is not so far removed from Christianity and Judaism. Indeed, many of the **prophets** in the **Koran**, including Adam, Noah, Abraham, Jesus and others, will be familiar to both Jews and Christians, and many Islamic practices (such as prostrating oneself during prayer, which is based on the old Christian method of praying, or sacrificing animals, which has its root in Judaic practices) have been lifted wholesale from the other two faiths.

Historical background

Mohammed was born in Medina in AD570. His father died before he was born, so little Mohammed was raised by first his grandfather, Abd al-Muttalib, the head of the powerful Hashem clan (which is why Jordan, whose monarchy claims descent from the grandfather, is known as the Hashemite Kingdom), and then his uncle, Abu Talib.

On reaching 40, Mohammed began to receive messages from Allah (God) via the angel Gabriel. On these revelations he built a new religion, **Islam**, or 'Submission' (to Allah's will). Having failed to convert most of the citizens of Mecca, in AD622 Mohammed and his followers the **Muslims** – Arabic for 'Surrendered', as they have surrendered themselves to God – fled to Medina where they received a far warmer reception. The Islamic calendar dates from this flight, and is known as the **Hejira** – 'flight' – calendar. Whilst there they built a massive following and returned in triumph to conquer Mecca in AD630. Two years later Mohammed died. By this time, his forces had conquered all of Arabia with an unstoppable mixture of persuasion and force. Mohammed's successor, Ibn Bakr, continued the Islamic expansion, until by AD638 the whole of the Levant was under Islamic control.

Soon after Mohammed's death Islam split into two. Originally the argument was one of succession: the fourth successor to Mohammed was his son-in-law Ali, who had been implicated in the assassination of the previous successor, Caliph Othman, under whose rule the collected teachings of Mohammed had been published in a book called the **Koran**. In revenge Mu'awiya, one of Othman's relatives and the founder of the Ommayad Dynasty, had Ali killed (maybe) and established himself as the new Caliph (meaning 'successor'). The followers of Mu'awiya became the **Sunni Muslims**, who maintain that the Caliphate should be an elected position. The followers of the descendants of Ali (the only true descendants of Mohammed) believe that the Caliphate should be hereditary, and they became known as the **Shi'a Muslims**. Of these two main branches of Islam, it is the Sunnis who are more widespread in Palestine today.

Sacred texts

The Koran, or **Qur'an** (Arabic for 'Reading' or ''Recitation'), the holy book of Islam, is the collected words of God as revealed to Mohammed and dictated to his followers. It is roughly the same size as the New Testament, and is divided into 114 chapters, called suras, which have been arranged into approximate length order, with the longest first.

Beliefs

Though Muslims view many figures from the Bible, including Christ, as prophets, they do not consider Christ as the son of God, and look upon Mohammed as the only prophet to whom God revealed everything. From the divine messages he received, Mohammed began to establish a religion built on **five pillars** – the essential tenets on which Muslims should base their lives. The first of these pillars is to profess one's faith in God (Allah) by the phrase 'There is no God but Allah

THE PALESTINE CHILDREN'S RELIEF FUND

The Palestine Children's Relief Fund (PCRF) is a non-profit, non-political, humanitarian organisation committed to initiating and supporting medical projects in Palestine and, to a lesser degree, other parts of the Middle East too. The charity not only sends Palestinian children for free medical care in North America, but also supports other projects, sending teams of surgeons to the region to treat patients and train professionals there. They also send shipments of medical supplies and equipment and support training programs for Arab doctors in the US. These medical projects are designed to fill voids in the quality of health care for Arab children and are designed to provide a long-term solution to their medical needs.

The PCRF was founded in 1991 by Stephen Sosebee, the current director, who at that time was working as a freelance writer in Jerusalem, covering the daily tragedies of the Intifada. Whilst there, he heard how a passing patrol of Israeli soldiers had thrown a bomb at a family as they ate lunch near their home in Hebron; as a result, their 11-year-old son had lost both of his legs, an eye and a hand. Inspired by the boy's courage and determination, Steve Sosebee returned to his native Ohio and found prosthetic specialists, doctors and others who were willing to provide the child with the kind of first-rate specialist medical care that he could never hope to receive in Palestine. The boy and his sister, who also needed extensive surgery following the bombing, became the first of over 70 children treated by the PCRF. Most of the children are Palestinians living in the West Bank and Gaza Strip, though more recently a number of seriously wounded children from Lebanon and other parts of the Near East have also been helped by the PCRF.

Currently, the PCRF is running a 'Healing Hearts' campaign in an attempt to tackle the serious problem of congenital heart disease that kills hundreds of children in the Middle East every year. The campaign's aim is to build the first and only paediatric cardiac surgery in Palestine, and to train local doctors and nurses in order to staff the unit.

As well as financial support, the PCRF relies on volunteers from the medical profession, and people to act as host families for children flown to the West to receive medical treatment. More details about the PCRF's work can be found by visiting their website at www.wolfenet.com/-pcrf/. A percentage of the royalties from this book will be going to the charity.

and Mohammed is his prophet'. Five times a day you will hear this phrase spoken by the Muezzin when calling the faithful to prayer.

The act of **praying** is the second pillar. The faithful can pray anywhere, as long as they pray towards Mecca. The head must be covered, and a set of ritual ablutions should be carried out before praying. A fountain is usually set in the courtyards of the mosques for this purpose. The third pillar is to give a proportion of one's **income to charity**, whilst the fourth is to observe the fasting month of **Ramadan**. The final tenet is that all Muslims must make a **pilgrimage to Mecca** at least once in their lives. Other rules that were added later include the proscribing of alcohol, pork, gambling and fraud.

In many regards, Islam's beliefs and traditions have more in common with Judaism than with Christianity. Both are strictly **monotheistic** (whereas Christianity, with its beliefs regarding the Holy Trinity, seems less so), and rigidly

iconoclastic, Islam forbidding the depiction of any living creature. Many of their rituals (circumcision, animal sacrifices and the ritual preparation and proscribing of certain foods) are also very similar. The main conflict occurs over Mohammed's claim to be the last prophet (or the 'seal' to use the Koranic term), the culmination of a prophetic tradition stretching all the way back to Abraham. According to Islam, Mohammed was chosen by Allah to restore the purity of God's religion on earth – a purity that became corrupted by Judaism and Christianity.

EDUCATION

Palestinians set great store by education, more so than any other nation in the Arab world. The Israeli occupation may have something to do with this: if you live in an uncertain world where all of your material possessions could be taken from you overnight, as the Palestinians undoubtedly do, education is one of the few assets of great value that cannot be taken away. Educational qualifications can also be seen as a passport out of the country and away from the troubles and poverty. This is why the Gulf States, at least before Iraq's invasion of Kuwait, were so keen to employ Palestinians to work on their oil bases as engineers, doctors and chemists. As a result of the emphasis placed on education, Palestine has no fewer than 21 universities, a massive number for a country so small.

Palestinians are obliged to take a minimum of nine years compulsory education, despite a massive shortage of schools and equipment in some parts of the country. Gazan schools follow an Egyptian curriculum, while those on the West Bank adhere to the Jordanian format. Schools are operated and funded by either the government, religious foundations such as churches or mosques (a school attached to a mosque is known as a *madrassa*) or a charitable organisation such as UNRWA. After the nine years are up, pupils can opt for a further three years, after which they take the *tawjihi* examination; pass this, and they're ready for university. The number one university in Palestine, the country's equivalent of Oxford or Harvard, is Bir Zeit University, north of Ramallah, though you'll find nearly every big city has at least one university. As well as offering the traditional, academic subjects for study, some universities run courses that reflect the flavour of the town. Bethlehem, for example, has a course in pilgrim tour guiding, tourism and travel agency management and religious education.

Practical Information

BEFORE YOU GO
Visas
With so much of Palestine still under Israeli control, it's hardly surprising that the visa laws for Palestine are identical to those of Israel. That is to say, most nationalities require **no visa**, just a valid passport. On arrival at either Ben Gurion or Gaza Airport, visitors are given a **stamp** in their passport (or on a piece of paper – see page 40) allowing them to stay for three months in Palestine and Israel. This stamps allows for travel throughout Israel and Palestine: the only border separating the two runs between Israel and Gaza, though there are checkpoints everywhere. Carrying your passport everywhere is a **legal requirement**, and makes things easier at these checkpoints.

The rules and regulations for **work visas** are the same in Palestine as in Israel. That is to say, it's illegal to work on a tourist visa, though many people do so in Israel and Jerusalem. The only way you can work legally in Israel is on a **moshav** or **kibbutz**, of which there are none in Palestine.

Embassies and consulates
Palestinian representation abroad
Australia General Palestinian Delegation, 19 Carnegie Cres, Narrabundah (tel: 62950222)
Canada 45 Country Club Drive, Ottowa, Ontario KI V9 (tel: 7360053)
Egypt 33 El-Nahdah St, El-Doki, Cairo (tel: 3602998)
France 14 Rue du Commandant, Léandri, 75015 Paris (tel: 48286600)
Germany PLO Office, August-Bier-Str, 335300 Bonn (tel: 8212035)
Jordan PO Box 995757, Amman (tel: 663813)
Lebanon Kurnish EL-Mazra'ah, Beirut (tel: 300819)
Netherlands General Delegation of Palestine, 73 in Copes Van Cattenburch 2585, the Hague (tel: 3617045)
Syria Morshed Khater St, PO Box 2289 (tel: 443525)
Turkey PLO Office, Filistin, Sok 45/006700/GOP, Ankara (tel: 4360824)
United Kingdom PLO Office, 4 Clareville Grove, London SW7 5AR (tel: 020 7563 0008)
United States PLO Office 818–18 St, NW 620, Washington (tel: 202 7858391)

Foreign representation in Palestine/Israel
As with everything else in the Holy Land, the location of a country's embassy here is, in itself, a political statement. Most countries which refuse to recognise Jerusalem as the capital of Israel have their embassies in Tel Aviv, and run two consulates in Jerusalem: one in East Jerusalem for Palestine and one in the West for Israel. To further complicate matters, there are also consulates in Ramallah and Gaza, and a couple each in Eilat and Haifa in Israel.

If you're planning to obtain a visa from any of these embassies or consulates, please read the box about Israeli passport stamps on page 40. A visa issued in

AVOIDING AN ISRAELI STAMP: WHY AND HOW

While it's tempting to add to the collection of stamps in your passport, by acquiring an Israeli one you could be letting yourself in for a whole host of problems on subsequent trips, particularly to the Middle East and North Africa. Syria, Lebanon, Iraq, Sudan, Libya and Iran are among the countries that refuse entry to anyone who has previously visited Israel, or intends to go there at some time in the future. An Israeli stamp in your passport will thus disqualify you from these countries automatically, as does a stamp issued by the Jordanian or Egyptian authorities at the border with Israel, or a foreign visa issued in Israel that clearly states where it was issued. (If you're flying into Gaza, note that Syria currently considers a **Palestinian stamp** as bad as an Israeli one, believing that anyone visiting Palestine will inevitably visit Israel too.)

This rule is particularly unfortunate for visitors to Palestine. They may have no desire to visit Israel, but until Palestine finally separates itself from its neighbour it still comes under the authority of Israel, and still has to use Israeli passport stamps. There are, however, ways around this particular problem.

The Israelis and Palestinians fully recognise the troubles their stamps cause, and as a result customs officials in both countries are willing, if you ask, to stamp your **immigration card** rather than your passport. This solves the problem of unwanted Israeli stamps, but still leaves those travelling overland with the problem of how to avoid a stamp from Egyptian or Jordanian officials at the border with Israel and Palestine. (See the *Overland* section on page 48 for details of the various crossing points.) While the **Jordanians** are cooperative and will also stamp your immigration card if you ask them, the **Egyptians** are unfortunately unwilling to do the same. There are tales of travellers who've managed to bribe them into stamping something other than their passport, though this is a risky (and illegal) practice at the best of times. Thus, if you intend to cross overland from Egypt to Palestine via Rafah in the Gaza Strip, or into Israel at the Taba/Eilat border, you will almost definitely receive an Egyptian stamp which will bar you from all anti-Israeli nations. The only way round this is to **catch the ferry from Egypt** (from Hurghada, Sharm el-Sheikh or Nuweiba) to Aqaba in Jordan, and enter Palestine via the West Bank as outlined above.

Israel/Palestine will clearly state that it was issued in Israel, and this will be enough to bar you from Syria, Lebanon and all other other countries listed in the box.

In East Jerusalem

Belgium Sheikh Jarrah (tel: 02 5828644)
France Sheikh Jarrah (tel: 02 6259481)
Greece Sheikh Jarrah (tel: 02 5619583)
Italy Sheikh Jarrah (tel: 02 5618966)
Spain Sheikh Jarrah (tel: 02 5828006)
Sweden Sheikh Jarrah (tel: 02 5828117)
Turkey Sheikh Jarrah (tel: 02 5323310)
UK 19 Nashashibi Street, Sheikh Jarrah (tel: 02 582 8281)
USA 27 Nablus Road (tel: 02 622 7230)

In Gaza
Egypt PO Box 1234 (tel: 07 2824290)
Jordan (tel: 07 2825134)
Norway (tel: 07 2824615)

In Ramallah and Al-Bireh
Austria Ras El-Tahuneh (tel: 02 2958477)
Canada PO Box 2286 (tel: 02 2958604)
Denmark Trust Bldg, 5th Floor, 48 Othman Ben Affan St, PO Box 2444
(tel: 02 2961331)
Germany (tel: 02 2984786)
Netherlands (tel: 02 2987639)
South Africa (tel: 02 2987355)

Insurance
Taking out insurance is essential. The chances of anything bad befalling you are very slim, but we both know that if you don't take out insurance, those odds are increased dramatically. Cover falls into two basic categories: **health** and **luggage**. If you're not too bothered about losing your luggage, you can usually buy health cover only, which saves you about 25% of the total premium. Premiums vary widely from company to company. Remember to check these details before plumping for one:

- How much is the deductible (the amount the insurers charge when you make a claim)?
- When you're making a claim, can the insurers compensate you immediately, while you're still in Palestine, or do you have to wait until you get home before receiving any money? This is important as Palestinian hospitals, as a rule, insist on cash up-front.
- How long after the event do you have in which to claim, and what proof (receipts, police statements and so on) is required?
- If you plan any dangerous activities, such as rock climbing or diving, are these covered?

Be careful of the free travel insurance offered by credit card companies when you book your flight on their card. More often than not, their cover extends only to the goods that you actually bought with the card – ie: the flight – and not the holiday itself. Some insurers, such as Endsleigh (available through STA), treat all countries bordering the Mediterranean as part of Europe, and consequently charge a lower premium. Expect to pay about £37 for one month's cover. Premiums for the elderly – usually those above 65 – are normally double. In Britain, Columbus (020 7375 0011), Backpackers (0800 163518) and STA (020 7361 6160) all provide comprehensive policies.

Finally, remember to leave a copy of your policy, or at least the details and a contact number, with a friend or relative at home.

Inoculations
No vaccinations are legally required to enter Palestine, but to be on the safe side make sure you're inoculated against typhoid, tetanus, polio and hepatitis. There has been the odd case of malaria reported in Palestine, but the chances of you contracting the disease are so slim that it's not worth taking prophylactics which, after all, have their own risks attached to them.

Travel clinics
UK
British Airways Travel Clinic and Immunisation Service 156 Regent St W1, tel: 020 7439 9584. This place also sells travellers' supplies and has a branch of Stanford's travel book and map shop. There are now BA clinics all around Britain and three in South Africa. To find your nearest one, phone 01276 685040.
Nomad Travel Pharmacy and Vaccination Centre 3–4, Wellington Terrace, Turnpike Lane, London N8 0PX; tel: 020 8889 7014.
Thames Medical 157 Waterloo Rd, London SE1 8US; tel: 020 7902 9000. Competitively priced, one-stop travel health service. All profits go to their affiliated company InterHealth which provides health care for overseas workers on Christian projects.
Trailfinders Immunisation Centre 194 Kensington High St, London W8 7RG; tel: 020 7938 3999. Also 254–284 Sauchiehall St, Glasgow G2 3EH; tel: 0141 353 0066.
MASTA (Medical Advisory Service for Travellers Abroad) Keppel St, London WC1 7HT; tel: 09068 224100. This is a premium-line number, charged at 50p per minute.

USA
Centers for Disease Control The Atlanta-based organisation is the central source of travel information in the USA with a touch-tone phone line and fax service: Traveler's Hot Line, (404) 332 4559. Each summer they publish the invaluable Health Information for International Travel which is available from Center for Prevention Services, Division of Quarantine, Atlanta, GA 30333.
Connaught Laboratories PO Box 187, Swiftwater, PA 18370; tel: 800 822 2463. They will send a free list of specialist tropical-medicine physicians in your state.
IAMAT (International Association for Medical Assistance to Travelers) 736 Center St, Lewiston, NY 14092. A non-profit organisation which provides lists of English-speaking doctors abroad.

Australia
TMVC Tel: 1300 65 88 44; website: www.tmvc.com.au. TMVC has 20 clinics in Australia, New Zealand and Thailand, including:
Brisbane Dr Deborah Mills, Qantas Domestic Building, 6th floor, 247 Adelaide St, Brisbane, QLD 4000; tel: 7 3221 9066; fax: 7 3321 7076
Melbourne Dr Sonny Lau, 393 Little Bourke St, 2nd floor, Melbourne, VIC 3000; tel: 3 9602 5788; fax: 3 9670 8394.
Sydney Dr Mandy Hu, Dymocks Building, 7th floor, 428 George St, Sydney, NSW 2000; tel: 2 221 7133; fax: 2 221 8401.

South Africa
There are four **British Airways travel clinics** in South Africa: *Johannesburg*, tel: (011) 807 3132; *Cape Town*, tel: (021) 419 3172; *Knysna*, tel: (044) 382 6366; *East London*, tel: (0431) 43 2359.

WHAT TO TAKE
Documents and money
Documents should include your **passport, travellers' cheques, ATM** and **credit cards** and **cash**, insurance details and any student or youth hostel cards you may have. Take a money belt to carry these in while you're away. Make photocopies of the above – and of your air tickets – and keep them separately elsewhere in your luggage; they can be useful if anything is lost or stolen. It's also a good idea to leave your insurance policy details, travellers' cheque numbers, credit card details etc with somebody at home, so you always have at least one copy.

Bring a mixture of US$ cash and either **travellers' cheques** or an **ATM/credit card**. Thomas Cook and American Express travellers' cheques are the most common and popular. There are no restrictions on taking money into the country, though if you're changing more than US$500-worth of shekels back at the end of your trip, you'll need to provide a bank receipt as proof of the original exchange.

Clothing

What you will be wearing in Palestine depends on where you're going and in which season. A **coat, jumper, thermal socks, woolly hat** and **gloves** are important winterwear, and are vital if you plan to head to the mountains. As well as day-to-day **boots** or **trainers**, in summer a pair of **sandals** is recommended. A smart set of clothes is also worth bringing; if you can't fit it in, then at least try to make sure one of your outfits remains relatively unsoiled, in case, as is likely, you get invited to somebody's house. Army surplus gear, while popular with travellers the world over, is not such a good idea in Palestine where looking like an off-duty Israeli soldier is less a fashion statement than a political one. Though the clothes you bring in summer will obviously be a lot skimpier, remember that it is vital not to offend the locals. Men shouldn't wear shorts or sleeveless shirts (vests) unless they wish to be stared at. Women travellers should exercise particular caution: a glimpse of bare leg will either offend or cause a frenzy of arousal. Neither reaction is welcome, so cover up. At mosques and other holy places, it is vital that all bare limbs be hidden from public gaze, unless you wish to become public enemy number one.

Toiletries

Your rucksack or suitcase should also contain a washbag (complete with soap/shampoo, toothbrush/paste, razors, tampons, deodorant, toilet roll (in a plastic bag so that it remains dry). You'll also need a towel of course. A medical kit is a good idea, containing plasters, antiseptic cream, paracetamol, contact lens equipment, sun cream, insect repellent and a couple of sterilised syringes and needles. Some people also take along vitamin tablets to counterbalance the lack of nutrition available in a felafel and shwaarma diet. If you're worried about the tap water, iodine or purification tablets should allay your fears.

Photography

Another piece of essential travelling kit, at least amongst most travellers and tourists, is a camera. Though film is widely available throughout Palestine, it's probably safer to bring your own from home; that way, you know you're getting the film you want from a stockist you trust. I'd also take some sort of camera cleaning kit, or at least a soft cloth, to wipe away all the bits of grit and dust that attach themselves to your lens and appear on your photos, or infiltrate your camera and clog the whole thing up.

Miscellaneous

Other essential bits and bobs to pack include a sheet or sarong (a multi-purpose garment beloved by travellers) for sleeping on, a day pack, a torch and, of course, this guidebook. Non-essential items you may consider include an umbrella, penknife, washing line and/or string, a water bottle, sleeping bag and other camping gear (though opportunities for camping are rare in Palestine) and books.

Highlights

Though a tiny country, it's surprising how much there is to see, and how difficult it is to see everything you want in just one trip. Careful planning is therefore required if you're going to make the most of your holiday in Palestine. The following list has been compiled as an aid to planning, helping you decide which attractions you'd like to visit on your holiday and which you'd rather avoid.

Religious sites
Where do we begin here? Obviously Jerusalem takes priority in this section, for apart from the **Holy Sepulchre**, **Temple Mount** and **Wailing Wall**, the town is also convenient for the **Mount of Olives** and the neighbouring villages of **Bethany** and **Bethphage**, both of which feature prominently in the gospels. Only slightly less essential than Jerusalem is **Bethlehem**, site of the Nativity and home to one of the oldest churches in Christendom. In my opinion, no trip to Palestine would be complete without calling in on a monastery or two, and in the vicinity of Bethlehem there are a couple, **Mar Theodosius** and **Mar Saba**, near the village of Obedaiya, that are both rather captivating in their own way. For my money, however, the **Mar George of Koziba** monastery in the Wadi Qelt is the most fascinating.

Away from Christianity, the **Haram Al-Khalil** in Hebron ranks as one of the holiest shrines in both Judaism and Islam, and is quite fascinating. I'm also rather keen on the **Nabi Musa**, or Tomb of Moses, though this is due to its desert setting as much as its spiritual importance. Finally, for something a little different, a trip to the Samaritans' hilltop base on **Mount Gerizim**, overlooking Nablus, is definitely worth the effort it takes to get there, and there's a museum and a number of ruined temples to help you understand the complex differences between the Samaritans and their Jewish cousins.

Historical ruins and old cities
Most Palestinian towns are historical sites in their own right. Jericho, in particular, stands out in this category thanks to its reputation as the oldest continually inhabited city in the world. However, the proof of this, the archaeological excavations at **Tel El-Sultan**, are something of a disappointment; whereas the nearby ruins at **Hisham's Palace** are anything but, especially the stupendous mosaic that justifies the entrance fee in its own right. Similarly spectacular ruins can be seen at the **Herodion**, Herod's hilltop palace that plays host to a lengthy, labyrinthine series of tunnels running right through the hill, and **Sebastiye**, the capital of the ancient Samarian Kingdom, 13km north of Nablus. **Nablus** itself has a number of ruins within its city limits, including Roman theatres, hippodromes and the excavations of ancient **Shechem**.

The biggest draw in Nablus, however, is the restored **Casbah**, or Old City, something that Palestine rather specialises in. Nablus' Casbah is rather quaint where **Hebron's** is rough and ready; it's worth mentioning **Gaza** here too, whose Daraj and Zeitoun quarters are home to some beautiful old mosques and churches. But of course, nothing can beat the **Old City of Jerusalem**: yes, it's over-run with tourists, and of course it's hot, noisy and rather unfriendly, but take a walk along the ramparts and you'll appreciate just what a beautiful and endlessly fascinating place it is.

Outdoor activities
Quite by chance, **Jericho** appears to have become the outdoor pursuits capital of Palestine. Not only is this the only city where you can hire **bicycles**, which is a great way to see the sights, but Jericho is also just a short taxi ride away from the salt-choked waters of the **Dead Sea**. Swimming is all but impossible in the Dead Sea, but floating most definitely isn't, and it's meant to be good for the skin too. For landlubbers, the hills surrounding the Dead Sea are great for exploring,

particularly near the **Ein Feshka Nature Reserve**; but for unparalleled hiking scenery you're better off visiting the **Wadi Qelt**, a 40km valley running westwards from Jericho towards Jerusalem that's now a national park. A second hike, running from Solomon's Pools all the way to the Herodion, is currently being established.

The state of the nation today

Those trying to get to grips with Palestinian life today will see both ends of the spectrum in the **Gaza Strip**, from the splendour of the legislative council to the squalor of the refugee camps. A trip to Hebron – where the tension between Arab and Jew is at its most profound – and a trip to both sides of the Green Line in **Jerusalem** could prove enlightening, especially for gauging the current state of the relationship between the two sides. For Palestine at its brashest and most modern, I'd also recommend an excursion to **Ramallah**, a busy, bustling town with bars and shops aplenty.

TOUR OPERATORS AND TRAVEL AGENTS
Tour operators specialising in the Holy Land

There is, as yet, no overseas company dedicated to providing tours round Palestine only: despite some extensive ringing around, all of the operators we contacted offer some sort of Holy Land package combining Palestine with Israel. Thus, if you wish to take a guided tour around Palestine only, you'll be much better off signing up with one of the local Palestinian companies. Try the **Palestinian Association for Cultural Exchange** (see page 133) in Ramallah, or **Alternative Tours**, run from the Jerusalem Hotel in East Jerusalem (see page 92).

Palestinian workcamps

Though financially unrewarding, Palestinian **workcamps** offer the chance for volunteers to participate in projects designed to improve the lot of the Palestinians. Basic manual tasks, such as rubbish clearing, road laying and painting, are the most common chores of the volunteers. These workcamps usually take place in summer only. You have to sort out and pay for your own travel arrangements, insurance and pocket money, while they contribute accommodation (usually with a local family or in a public building such as a school or town hall). Contact the Palestinian representatives in your country to find out which programmes are currently running.

Travel agents

Getting a flight that lets you feel as if you've got a good deal is becoming more daunting as local flight specialists fight with global flight consolidators. Put everybody on the internet and the competition just gets hotter. Below is a list of travel agents and flight operators who give good service at a reasonable price. Getting the cheapest price will require several calls and may result in some rather complicated rerouting of the plane.

In the UK

Bridge the World targets the independent traveller. Their offices are at 47 Chalk Farm Rd, Camden Town, London, NW1 8AJ; tel: 020 7911 0900; fax: 020 7813 3350; email: sales@bridge-the-world.co.uk; web: www.b-t-w.co.uk.
Flight Centre is an independent flight provider with over 450 outlets worldwide. In the UK head office is at Level 3, Broadway House, Wimbledon, SW19 1RL; tel: 0990 666677; fax: 020 8541 5120. They also have offices in Australia, New Zealand, South Africa and Canada.

Quest Worldwide 4/10 Richmond Rd, Kingston-upon-Thames, Surrey, KT2 5HL; tel: 020 8547 3322; fax: 020 8547 3320. An independent agent that has been in operation for nine years offering competitive prices and specialising in long-haul flights.

STA Travel 6 Wrights Lane, London W8 6TA; tel: 020 7361 6262; fax: 0207 937 9570; email: enquiries@statravel.co.uk; web: www.statravel.co.uk. STA has 12 branches in London and 25 or so around the country and at a different university sites. STA also has several branches and associate organisations around the world.

Trailfinders has several offices around the UK. The main office is in London at 194 Kensington High St, London, W8 7RG; tel: 020 7938 3939; fax: 020 7938 3305; web: www.trailfinders.com. With origins in the discount flight market, Trailfinders now provides a one-stop travel service including visa and passport service, travel clinic and foreign exchange.

ARRIVING AT TEL AVIV'S BEN GURION AIRPORT

Israel's Ben Gurion Airport is a surprisingly twee little airport. The security, however, is tighter than a pair of cellophane hotpants, but providing you manage to remain calm and avoid attracting suspicion you should negotiate the various trials without coming to any harm.

After touching down you're faced by a bank of passport control counters. The procedure here is usually fairly simple but don't forget to ask officials to **stamp a separate piece of paper** rather than your passport if you plan to visit certain Arab nations at a later date (see the box on page 40). Occasionally, however, if the guards are suspicious (or bored) you may be whisked off to somewhere private for a more intimate examination of both mind and body. This is usually pretty straightforward too, the severity of the inquisition depending on the amount of suspicion you've raised. Asking passport control not to stamp your passport should earn you a light grilling, while those with a Syrian visa – or indeed any Arab stamp in the passport – can expect at least a 20-minute roasting. After that you're free to collect your luggage, pass through customs and enter the unexciting **arrivals hall**. Please note that though there are some money-changers in the arrivals hall, the rates are uniformly bad; if it will accept your card, the **cash machine** in the baggage reclamation hall gives a fairer rate.

From the airport you have two main ways of getting to Jerusalem. The first is by the 45-minute **public buses** (numbers 423, 428, 945 and 947) which leave from the airport forecourt: from Gate 8 turn left and walk for 50 metres. The advantage with the bus is that it's the cheapest way to get to Jerusalem (NIS19.30/17.40). The disadvantage is that it drops you off at the Egged Bus Station, at the western end of Jaffa Road in West Jerusalem, so you'll need to catch a second bus (number 6 to the Old City's Jaffa Gate and number 20 to the eastern end of Jaffa Road are the most popular) to your destination within Jerusalem.

Alternatively, after walking through airport customs you can turn right at Gate 8 and catch a **sherut**, or shared taxi (see page 53); these depart when they're full. They cost almost twice as much as the buses (NIS 37), but do drop you off at your desired destination in Jerusalem.

Those going straight to Gaza from the airport will have to take a bus to Tel Aviv and try to catch a *servis* to the Erez checkpoint from there.

Travel Bag provide tailor-made flight schedules and holidays for destinations throughout the world. Their main office is at 12 High St, Alton, Hampshire, GU34 1BN; tel: 01420 541441; email: freequote3@travelbag.co.uk; web: www.travelbag-adventures.co.uk.

Travel Mood provide flights and tailor-made holidays. 214 Edgware Rd, London, W2 1DS; tel: 020 7258 0280; fax: 020 7258 0180.

USIT Campus Travel Head office is at 52 Grosvenor Gardens, London, SW1W 0AG; tel: 020 7730 8111; fax: 020 7730 6893; web: www.usitcampus.co.uk. 40 branches around the country focusing on students and people under 26.

WEXAS is more of a club than a travel agent. Membership is around £40 a year but for frequent fliers the benefits are many. 45-49 Brompton Rd, Knightsbridge, London SW3 1DE; tel: 020 7589 3315; fax: 020 75898418; email: mship@wexas.com; web: www.wexas.com.

In the USA

Airtech 584 Broadway, Suite 1007, New York, NY 10012; tel: 800 575 TEC or 212 219 7000; email: fly@airtech.com; web: www.airtech.com. Standby seat broker that also deals in consolidator fares, courier flights and a host of other travel related services.

Around the World Travel provides fares for destinations throughout the world. 411 4th Av, Suite 430, Seattle, WA 98101; tel: 877 327 3638; fax: 206 223 1865; email: travel@netfare.net; web: www.netfare.net.

Council on International Educational Exchange is at 205 East 42nd St, New York, NY 10017-5706; tel: 212 822 2600; fax: 212 822 2699; email: info@ciee.org; web: www.ciee.org. Although Council focus on work exchange trips they also have a large travel department. Council Travel sells cheap tickets at over 60 offices around the US. The New York office is at 205 East 42nd St, New York, NY 10017-5706; tel: 212 822 2700; web: www.counciltravel.com.

National Centre for Educational Travel has been providing cheap travel services for over 30 years. They are at 438 N Frances St, Madison, WI 53703; tel: 800 747 5551 or 608 256 5551; fax: 301 384 9289; email: ncet@idt.net; web: www2.ios.com/~ncet/.

STA Travel has several branches around the country. Freephone on 800 777 0112. A selection of city branches include: 120 Broadway #108, Santa Monica, Los Angeles, CA 90401; tel: 310 394 5126; fax: 310 394 4041; 10 Downing St (6th Av and Bleecker), New York, NY 10014; tel: 212 627 3111; fax: 212 627 3387; 4341 University Way NE, Seattle, WA 98105; tel: 206 633 5000; fax: 206 633 5027.

Ticket Planet 59 Grant Av, 3rd Floor, San Francisco, CA 94108; tel: 800 799 8888; fax: 415 288 9839; email: info@ticketplanet.com; web: www.ticketplanet.com

Worldtek Travel operates a network of rapidly growing travel agencies. For your nearest office contact 111 Water St, New Haven, CT 06511; tel: 800 243 1723 or 203 777 1483; email: dave.smith@worldtek.com; web: www.worldtek.com.

In Canada

Flight Centre is at 604-1200 West Pender, Vancouver, V6E 2S9; tel: 604 606 9000 or freephone: 188 WORLD31; fax: 604 664 0334.

Travel CUTS is a Canadian student travel organisation with 60 offices throughout Canada. Based in Toronto at 187 College St, Toronto, M5T 1P7; tel 416 979 2406; fax: 416 979 8167. Call the telephone sales centre toll free on 800 667 2887 for your nearest branch or visit the website at www.travelcuts.com.

In Australia

Flight Centre has over 200 stores in Australia. Head office is at 157 Ann St, Brisbane, Queensland 4000; freephone: 133 133.

AusTravel's head office in Australia is at 7 Macquarte Place, Sydney, NSW 2000; tel 2 92 47 48 33; fax: 2 92 51 35 41; email: ausops@oze.mail.com.au. web: www.austravel.com. They also have several offices in Europe and the US. STA Travel is at Shop 10, The Village Centre, 24-30 Springfield, Kings Cross, Sydney NSW 2011; tel: 2 9368 1111; fax: 2 9368 1609.

In New Zealand
A good starting point for cheap airfares is **Flight Centre** Level 7, 48 Emily Place, Auckland, New Zealand; tel: 0800 FLIGHTS; fax: 9 379 8798.

In South Africa
Flight Centre Shop L3, Eastgate Centre, Bradford Rd, Bedfordview, Johannesburg 2008; tel: 11 622 5634; fax: 11 622 5642.
Student Travel Centre is linked to the STA network. The Arcade, 62 Mutual Gardens, Corner of Oxford Road & Tyrwhitt Av, Rosebank, Johannesburg 2196; tel: 11 447 5551; fax: 11 447 5775.

GETTING THERE AND AWAY
Getting to Palestine
By air
Via Gaza
At the beginning of 1999 in Gaza the Palestinian authorities opened Palestine's first international airport to a huge fanfare and an explosion of publicity from the world's media. The first scheduled carrier to the airport, **Royal Air Jordanian**, has now been joined by six other international carriers: Cyprusair, Air Qatar, Turkish Air, Egyptair, Palestinian Airlines and Air Morocco.

Via Israel
The obvious alternative is to fly into Israel's Ben Gurion airport, situated halfway between Jerusalem and Tel Aviv, or Eilat airport in the south of the country. There are plenty of chartered and scheduled flights to both destinations, and fares are pretty cheap. (One word of warning, however: those intending to visit Syria and Lebanon during their trip are advised not to fly into Israel or Palestine. To avoid evidence that you've been to Israel you'll have to fly to Egypt or Jordan instead: see the box on page 40 for details).

Flights to Israel tend to be cheaper than those to either Amman or Gaza. However, if you do decide to fly to Israel, bear in mind that what you gain in terms of a lower price you forfeit in terms of a greater amount of hassle; the security checks when you leave, particularly at Tel Aviv, are an absolute nightmare (see below).

Flights during the main Christian or Jewish holidays need to be booked well in advance, and you should expect to pay a premium at these times.

Overland
Palestine has border crossings between the West Bank and **Jordan** at the Allenby Bridge, and between the Gaza Strip and **Egypt** at Rafah. There is also the quasi-border post between Israel and the Gaza at Erez, details of which can be found on page 71. (The border between Israel and the West Bank is marked by checkpoints rather than any border posts, and crossing between the two is not a problem.) Please read the box on Israeli passport stamps on page 40 before attempting any crossing.

From Egypt

This border crossing (open daily from 09.00 to 17.00; tel: 07 6734205) between the Gaza and Egypt at **Rafah**, home of a large refugee camp and the international airport, is still controlled by the Israelis, even though Rafah is part of Palestinian territory. The border post lies by the airport, a couple of kilometres out of town (NIS1.5 from Rafah town centre).

There are no public buses from Egypt to this border, though there are **servis taxis** leaving from the bus terminal on Sharia Orabi in Cairo to Rafah, a journey of around five or six hours (with other services from Qantara and El-Arish). Set out early, as you'll need to make the onward connection to Gaza (see page 83) because there is no accommodation at Rafah. Some tourist buses from Cairo to Tel Aviv also use this crossing, and it's possible, if you arrange it beforehand, to get dropped off in either Rafah or Gaza City. However, don't expect much of a reduction, if any, on the price of your ticket, and you may not get dropped off in the centre of Gaza City, depending on the mood of the driver. **Tickets** can be bought from the agencies on Sharia Talaat Harb. Having crossed the border, if you need to change money you can do so at the **bank** at the **international airport**, or wait until Gaza where the rates are better. At the border there are also direct buses to Tel Aviv (one a day), Ashqelon (two daily) and Beersheba (one a day).

The Israelis also have a border crossing with the Sinai at **Taba**, near Eilat, which is more convenient for those coming from the seaside resorts of Dahab and Sharm El-Sheikh.

From Jordan

There is only one bridge between Jordan and its former territory of the West Bank: the **Allenby Bridge** (02 9943358), or the **King Hussein Bridge** as it's known by the Jordanians and most Palestinians (which is not to be confused with the Sheikh Hussein Bridge to the north of the West Bank). Though Jordan renounced its claim over the West Bank in 1988, this remains the only border where you can enter Palestine without officially leaving Jordan. In other words, your original Jordanian visa is still valid, should you decide to return to Jordan after Palestine, whereas at border crossings leading directly into Israel you will be stamped out by the Jordanian border guards and will have to buy a new visa if you wish to re-enter Jordan. (I hope that's clear!) As at Gaza, the Israelis control the border crossing. The border is open from Sunday to Thursday, 08.00–midnight, and Friday and Saturday 08.00–15.00. Both the Israelis and the Jordanians will stamp a separate piece of paper rather than your passport if you ask.

Coming from Amman, **JETT buses** leave from their office on Sharia Al-Malik Hussein at 06.30 and deliver you right at the Israeli checkpoint. The cost is JD6. The driver will collect your passport to give to the Jordanian border guards; make sure you tell him that you don't want it stamped, or keep hold of it and visit passport control yourself. **Servis taxis** from Amman charge just JD2 for the 45-minute trip to the foreigners' terminal at the border, though you'll have to negotiate the border formalities yourself, and then take a bus (JD1.5) to cross the Allenby Bridge into the West Bank. **Public buses** running from Amman to the local people's terminal are cheaper still, though you'll have to walk from there to the foreigners' terminal.

Having crossed into the West Bank, you'll find a number of money-changers offering truly terrible rates of exchange. My advice is to wait until you get to Jericho or Jerusalem, as Jordanian dinars are accepted in many places on the West Bank. At the border, there are buses (NIS6) to Jericho, from where you can catch connections to Jerusalem via Bethany (NIS8 in total) and Ramallah (NIS10).

By sea

There is currently no international shipping company serving the Gaza Strip, or indeed a major port in the territory, though as Palestine becomes more autonomous and breaks away from Israel it's conceivable that we may see one in the years ahead. **Haifa** in northern Israel has a twice-weekly ferry service from **Piraeus** in Greece, which takes two-and-a-half days, costs about US$160 and calls in at Rhodes and Limassol en route. **Aqaba** in Jordan has a twice-daily ferry service to and from **Hurghada** in Egypt that calls in at Nuweiba and Sharm el-Sheikh in the Sinai. Fares from Nuweiba to Aqaba are approximately US$32 for the three-hour crossing on the *Santa Catherina*, or US$42 by the faster (50-minute) catamaran. Thanks to differences in tax regulations between the two countries, fares from Aqaba to Nuweiba are approximately US$10 cheaper.

Leaving Palestine

The procedure for leaving Palestine overland via the Rafah or Allenby Bridge checkpoints, or from Gaza Airport, is dealt with in the relevant chapters on Gaza and Jericho. Please remember that there is a **departure tax** of about NIS100 to pay when you leave the country (though not at the Erez border between Israel and Gaza) and, for travellers heading to Egypt, a small **Egyptian arrival tax** too.

Leaving from Ben Gurion and Eilat airports

If you thought the grilling you received upon arrival at Ben Gurion was bad, it's nothing compared with the ordeal you'll receive when you leave. Everybody, from sweet little old ladies clasping zimmer frames to children clutching teddy bears, will have to answer a barrage of questions fired from one and sometimes two security officers before they've even checked in. As a result, it's not unheard of for people to miss their flight because, though they may have turned up two hours before departure, the queue for security was such that they didn't check in on time. Furthermore, those who don't get on board are not compensated in any way, and have to find their own accommodation for the night, at their own expense. So for your own sake please turn up at least **two-and-a-half hours prior to departure**, or three if you want to be on the safe side. This may sound excessive, but it's the only way to guarantee you'll catch your flight.

The security guards are there to make sure nobody is carrying a bomb on to the plane, nothing more. However, if you have any very inflammatory **anti-Israeli material**, it may be confiscated. At the security point, there are two essential rules that must be obeyed if you want to make it easy on yourself. The first is: **don't lie**. Some people try to pretend that they didn't go to the Gaza or other Palestinian territories because – quite rightly – they feel that the guards give those tourists who did visit Palestine a harder time; but, if you've been to Gaza, they will know this already: your passport number was entered on to their database when you crossed over the Erez checkpoint. So lying will only add to their suspicions, and increase the grief for you. Furthermore, by making up some story about where you've been, you're increasing the chances that you'll contradict yourself later on – which isn't advisable.

Secondly, **do not lose your temper**. Everytime I go to Ben Gurion Airport I see somebody throwing a wobbly. The result is always the same: they look stupid, and the guards are even more suspicious that they've something to hide. So don't get flustered, and don't start losing your temper just because they keep on asking the same questions (it's part of their tactics). Instead, be as helpful as possible, smile at them, and work out what you're going to say while you're waiting in the queue.

And if you were in Palestine on business and have business cards from the people you met to show to the security guards, so much the better.

However, I'm afraid that it's almost certain that, if you've spent some time in Palestine, your bag is going to be searched – thoroughly. You'll be whisked off to a room in one corner of the airport where every item of your luggage, and the bag itself, will be examined closely. Although this whole ordeal can be humiliating – especially when they're holding your unwashed undergarments up to the light, in full view of all the other tourists undergoing the same ordeal – if you've built up a rapport with the security guard (which you should have done by now) it shouldn't be too painful. You may also be searched, even strip-searched if they're very suspicious, and in the most extreme cases you may hear the snap of a rubber glove behind you, followed by a request to bend over the back of a chair. What they're looking for is anyone's guess; but all you can do in this situation is smile – or at least grit your teeth and grimace.

After the security check comes the **airline check-in**, followed by **passport control** upstairs; beyond is the **departure** and **duty-free** lounge.

HEALTH AND SAFETY
Health
Palestine is a fairly hygienic country, and it's highly unlikely that you'll suffer anything more than a bout of the runs or, if you're careless, a touch of **sunstroke**. To protect against the latter wear a high-factor suntan lotion and a hat, and drink a lot of fluids. Maintaining a reasonable salt intake should prevent dehydration.

Diarrhoea is often symptomatic of a change of diet rather than any malignant bacteria. So if you get a vicious dose of the runs and your sphincter feels like a cat flap in the Hoover Dam, don't panic and assume you've got food poisoning. Even the **tap water** is safe to drink in most places, though for rural areas you're probably better off sticking to bottled water. Washing fruit, vegetables, and your hands and ensuring food is thoroughly cooked can all help to prevent food poisoning – things you would do at home anyway. An **insect repellent**, to prevent you from being eaten alive by the biblical plagues of insects that swarm over the Holy Land annually, is also a good idea.

If you do become ill in Palestine, don't panic. A visit to the local *sadaliya* (pharmacist) or *tabeeb* (doctor, sometimes called *doktor*) should suffice. The listings magazine *This week in Palestine* and the *Jerusalem Post* carry a list of late-opening pharmacies. For more serious problems the hospitals in Palestine are first rate, though be warned: doctors and hospitals in Palestine expect to be paid immediately, in cash. If you require an ambulance, the number is different in Jerusalem (tel: 101) from the rest of Palestine (tel: 02 741161/162/163).

Safety
First of all, let me reiterate one more time: travelling in Palestine is **safe**. The Palestinians have no quarrel with tourists. Indeed they love tourists. The more tourists who come to Palestine, the sooner they can rid themselves of this absurd reputation for hostility. Tourists are interested in their culture. Tourists bring in money too, and they're funny: they wear stupid clothes and they can't pronounce Arabic.

So the only way you're going to become embroiled in any trouble is if you're an innocent bystander who becomes an unfortunate victim of the Arab-Israeli hostilities, or you suffer from the kind of misfortunes, such as theft, that aren't specifically Palestinian, but could happen anywhere in the world. In response to

---

SAFETY FOR WOMEN TRAVELLERS

Women, particularly blonde women, could find themselves subjected to a fair bit of unwanted attention in the Near East, although women I've spoken to say that the attention is far worse in Israel, where the men are apparently more persistent and aggressive. Please do not let the reputation of Arab men deter you from visiting Palestine. Most of their approaches are harmless, and a quick '*imshi!*' ('Go away!' in Arabic) usually does the trick. Some women even prefer to travel through Palestine on their own, and the advice they give to other female travellers is always the same: provided you do not draw attention to yourself with skimpy clothes or outrageous behaviour, you will be treated with respect by everyone, whatever their nationality. If somebody is being a little over-aggressive in his approaches, don't hesitate to humiliate him by shouting. Embarrassment is a most effective weapon in cooling Eastern ardour.

---

the first scenario, it's worth noting that physical violence against tourists in Palestine is extremely rare. The stone-throwing days of the Intifada, when anybody who looked more Israeli than Arab was considered fair game, are long over. The only instance of stone-throwing I've ever been subjected to occurred in a place no tourists go to, was perpetrated by very small children throwing pieces of gravel rather than stones, and they were quickly and brutally reprimanded by their parents who then invited me in for tea. This episode was typical in that it was because I was mistaken for an Israeli that I became a victim. So, to reduce the chance of becoming a victim yourself, take the following precautions. First, always carry your passport with you wherever you go. Not only will this help to convince locals that you're a tourist and not an Israeli, but it is also a legal requirement. Secondly, by keeping your ear to the ground and listening for news of any impending trouble, you can avoid potential hotspots (Hebron and, less occasionally, the Old City of Jerusalem are the most likely venues for trouble). Thirdly, it does pay to look as non-Jewish as possible, perhaps by wearing a crucifix. I also make a point, in places that receive next to no tourists, of speaking to people; walking with your head down through a crowded area will look as if you've got something to hide, whereas by talking to them you build up trust. However, if all else fails and you do find yourself threatened by trouble – though I must emphasise again, this is very rare, and has never happened to me – the phrase *Mish Jehud* ('not Jewish') could prove a lifesaver.

As for reducing the chances of theft, this is simply a matter of common sense. Don't leave valuables in your room but hand them in to reception for safekeeping; don't display your wealth ostentatiously, particularly when touring the poorer areas of Palestine such as the refugee camps; keep your passport, credit cards and cash in a money belt or pouch worn next to the skin; and be particularly wary when walking through crowded areas (Jerusalem's souqs and the Damascus Gate are especially notorious). Once again, don't worry too much: in all my time in Palestine I have never lost anything.

MONEY AND BANKING

The US dollar (US$), Jordanian dinar (JD) and **New Israeli shekel** (NIS) are all widely used in Palestine, though only the NIS has universal acceptance. The NIS is divided into 100 **agorot**. There are 20, 50, 100 and 200 NIS notes, 1, 5 and 10 NIS coins and 5, 10 and 50 agorot coins. The 5 and 10 agorot coins are of little use these days, and you'll find many people refusing to take them. Keep hold of them, however, as occasionally they come in useful, particularly on Israeli buses which operate a weird fare system.

A mix of US dollars and shekels seems the most useful combination of currencies: use your shekels for small transactions (bus fares, food etc), and keep your dollars to pay for hotel bills or when haggling (Palestinian shopkeepers tend to regard the US dollar as a more attractive currency than the shekel).

For most of your time in Palestine you'll be relying on money-changers or banks. There are very, very few cashpoints in Palestine, and almost without exception the ones that do exist do not accept foreign cards. The **BBME** (British Bank of the Middle East) has offices in Ramallah where you can withdraw money from the cash machine using a switch card. There are also plenty of cashpoints in West Jerusalem. **Money-changers**, fortunately, are everywhere in Palestine. The rates are usually very good, they rarely charge commission (though ask first to make sure) and they're open longer hours than the banks. It's worth shopping around before changing anything, however: rates vary widely, especially for non-dollar currency, and you'll always find one money-changer who'll quote a ridiculously low rate in the hope that you know no better.

As well as the office-based money-changers, you'll also find the odd **independent trader** sitting on a stool by a busy junction clutching a bundle of foreign notes. These guys are more used to dealing with other Arab currencies (the Jordanian dinar or Syrian pound for example) than dollars or sterling. They are also more likely to rip you off, so make sure you're *au fait* with Israeli currency before attempting to change with them. That said, most are scrupulously fair and continue to operate after the banks and money-changers have closed for the night. For money-changers, I've always found Jerusalem offers the highest rates, though the difference is marginal.

Haggling

Whatever your budget, there is one way you can save money: Bargain! Westerners always feel awkward at first about haggling for things, but bargaining in Palestine is the norm, at least in the souqs, and when looking for hotel rooms or private taxis. When you do haggle, remember to smile, keep it friendly – charm is a very potent weapon in Palestine – and treat the whole thing as a game, not a life-or-death argument. What's more, having agreed a price, don't go back on your word, and don't regard it as a slight on your ego if you don't get the price you want – lighten up and remember you're on holiday.

GETTING AROUND
Servis taxis or sheruts

The shared taxi (known as the **sherut** in Israel and Jerusalem, and the **servis taxi** in Palestine), is the speediest, most frequent, most comfortable and best value form of public transport in Palestine, and the one you'll be using most often. The procedure for catching a servis taxi is the same everywhere: simply find out where the servis taxi to your destination leaves from, then grab a seat (the passenger seat by the driver is the roomiest and most comfortable, though make sure the seat belt works). You then have to wait until the car is full, at which point it will depart. You pay the driver as soon as the car sets off; fares are only a fraction more than on the buses. If you're planning to jump out before the final destination, tell the driver at the beginning, though the fare is the same no matter how far you travel.

It's also possible to pick up a servis taxi somewhere along its route. Just stand by the side of the road and flag down one that's heading in your direction. Be careful, however, that you don't unwittingly hire a private taxi instead. The new flashy yellow Opel Astras are often private, or special taxis, while the older, squarer Mercedes 240D or 3000 and the Ford Transit vans are usually servis taxis. To be certain that you're climbing into a servis, and not a private taxi, simply ask the driver. Again, handing over the fare at the beginning of the trip will avoid any arguments later on.

Buses

Palestine's bus network has never really recovered from the restrictions imposed on it during the years of the Intifada, and some services (such as the number 23 between Jerusalem and Jericho) seem to have stopped running altogether. Buses are slow, lumbering beasts in Palestine, often taking a circuitous route to their destination that adds hours to the journey time. The bus between Hebron and Jerusalem, for example, goes via Bet Sahour and takes twice as long as the servis. To add to the disadvantages, **many buses don't run on Friday**. They are better, however, if you are trying to save every last shekel (they're usually NIS1 or 2 cheaper) or if you have a lot of luggage: Palestinian buses rarely fill up, so you'll have plenty of room for your bags, and bus drivers rarely, if ever, ask for extra money for taking them. Keep hold of your ticket, particularly on longer journeys, as sometimes they are collected halfway through the journey.

Private taxis or 'specials'

This is simply a taxi as a Westerner would know it, called a 'special' in the Holy Land to distinguish it from a servis taxi. These are expensive, but come into their own when you're trying to reach a tourist attraction not served by public transport. The most important rule when arranging a trip by private taxi is to sort out all the details, including the fare, beforehand, and remember to haggle. The cost of the trip should reflect the length of the journey and the amount of waiting time at the site. If you can get a group together, hiring a private taxi needn't be too much of a burden on your wallet. The most common journey by private taxi is the trip to the Mar Saba monastery from Bethlehem.

Car hire

While the big international companies – Hertz (tel: 03 9711165), Avis (tel: 03 9711979), Budget (tel: 03 9711504), Eurodollar (tel: 03 9731271) and Europcar (tel: 03 9721097) – all have offices at Ben Gurion Airport and elsewhere in Israel, it is unwise in the extreme to drive your **Israeli-based hire car** over the Green Line and into **Palestine**: the Palestinians will take one look at your yellow number plates, assume you're an Israeli, and could start stoning your vehicle. Actually, instances of stoning are rare now, but it is still advisable to rent your vehicle from a Palestinian outfit, of which there are a number in the big cities: try **Orabi** in al-Bireh, near Ramallah (tel: 02 9953521 or 9955601; fax 02 9953521). Though much smaller than Hertz *et al*, these companies are all pretty reliable, and have the magical green Palestinian plates that should guarantee your safety. Note that almost every company insists that the driver is over 24, and most insist you hold an international driver's licence too.

Bicycle

Cycling can be a little hazardous in Palestine: some of the roads could do with an extra (or, indeed, initial) layer of tarmac, much of the northern half of the West Bank is extremely hilly, and when cycling you do run the risk of being mistaken for a Jewish settler, and could be the target of a few insults (and missiles) hurled in your direction. It's a wee bit scary cycling through some of the big cities too. Confirmation

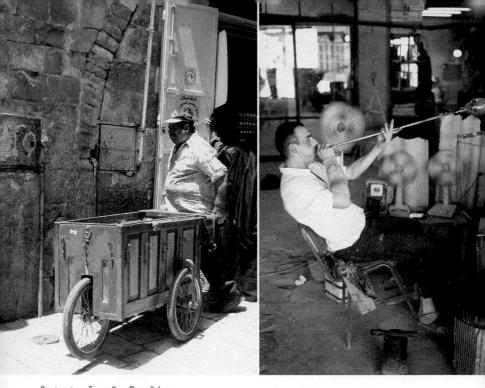

Previous page Sus seller, Ramallah (HS)
Above left Barrow man, Jerusalem (HS)
Above right Glass blower, Hebron (HS)
Below Melon seller, Souq Al-Fraj, Gaza City (HS)

Above left Children in the Old City, Nablus (HS)

Above right Shepherd, Bethel (HS)

Left Palestinian woman in traditional dress, Old City, Nablus (HS)

Below Poster seller, Hebron (HS)

Next page Town centre, Ramallah (HS)

of the fact that Palestine isn't really set up for bicycles is provided by the Palestinians themselves, very few of whom own bikes. On the other hand, some cyclists maintain that Palestine is a rewarding place to cycle around, being both compact and full of interesting sights en route. Bicycles also allow you to visit villages and areas not covered by public transport. They do have a point: the one place in Palestine where you can hire bicycles is Jericho, and it's enormous fun cycling around the sites.

Local tour operators
Some companies offer tours around the towns or cities in which they are based; these are mentioned in the relevant chapters. **Alternative Tours** (tel: 052 864205) run from the Jerusalem Hotel in Jerusalem, does day trips to Hebron, Ramallah and Nablus, and the Gaza Strip, but the best of the bunch by far is **PACE** (Palestinian Association for Cultural Exchange) based in Ramallah; see box on page 133.

ACCOMMODATION
Palestine's accommodation infrastructure, at least outside of Jerusalem, is still very much in its infancy. While almost every big town has one hotel or hostel, you won't have much choice about the quality. For this reason, most travellers in Palestine stay in Jerusalem and take day trips out from there (and if they go to Gaza, they use the capital, whose accommodation situation is improving all the time, as their base). I'm inclined to disagree with this tactic. It's true that Jerusalem's hotel options are second to none, with accommodation ranging from the no-frills bargain basement to the sort of plush pile where you have to check your pillow before bedtime, lest you wind up with a complimentary executive chocolate lodged in your ear. But **Jericho** and **Bethlehem** both have enough sights in their vicinity to warrant staying a couple of nights in each, while **Nablus** is a perfect base for exploring northern Palestine. And as for **Ramallah**, while it lies only 30 minutes from Jerusalem, its main attraction is its bars and plentiful supply of alcohol – and you'll be glad you took a hotel in the city after you've had your share, rather than face the journey back to the Holy City. Some people complain about the lack of budget accommodation, but that's only really the case in Ramallah (where the cheapest hotel charges US$25 per night), Hebron (which has one hotel only, charging US$35) and Bethlehem (which does have hospice accommodation at only US$13 per night). You also get the chance of savouring more of the real Palestine by staying outside Jerusalem, which is, after all, half Israeli.

Many of the better hotels quote their prices in dollars; shekels are acceptable, but they often use a terrible rate to convert one to the other. Breakfast is also included in the price of nearly all hotels above budget level.

Finally, when outside Jerusalem remember to haggle, and if you're coming at Christmas or Easter time, don't forget to book well in advance (at least six months in advance for hotels and hospices in Bethlehem).

EATING AND DRINKING
Palestinian food is Arabic food, and delicious it is too. But, while your tour through the country could turn into a gourmet extravaganza, if you're on a tight budget it will be the same few, cheap staple meals that you'll be gnawing on day after day.

Religious standards are as important as hygienic ones in the kitchens of Palestine. For Muslims, all meat must be *halal*. **Halal** meat has been drained of blood, comes from animals that have been slaughtered according to certain rules, and is not the flesh of a carnivorous animal or a pig. Though Christian chefs don't have to labour under the same regulations, many of them choose to do so for sound, practical business reasons, and you'll rarely find pork on a menu in Palestine. Jewish *kosher* laws are similar to the halal restrictions: once again piggies are proscribed and blood must be drained first. Any defects – scars or injuries for example – would also render the animal non-kosher.

Snacks

The number-one Arab staple is **felafal**, a deep-fried golf ball of mashed chick peas. These balls are squashed into a salad-filled pitta bread, which is then covered with tahini and/or chilli sauce and occasionally more exotic dressings. This is also called a felafal. The style of felafals varies from town to town. In Ramallah and the Gaza the balls are often cigar-shaped, while in Nablus they have DIY felafals: you're handed a pitta bread and a couple of felafal balls, and you do the rest by filling the bread from the communal bowls of salad and sauces on the counter.

The **shwaarma** or **kebab** is a felafal for carnivores, where meat is used instead of chick peas. Everywhere you go you'll see large cone-shaped slabs of unidentifiable meat (usually lamb or chicken) being roasted slowly on a skewer. Ask for a shwaarma and the chef will carve thin strips off this skewer and place it in pitta bread. The shwaarma is the meat; once in the pitta, the dish is called a **sandweech**. They are lovely, if a little greasy. Occasionally, instead of a thick piece of pitta, the chef will use a larger, thinner, circular piece which he will then wrap around the filling.

Outside the Arab world, these shwaarmas are usually known as kebabs, but in the Arab world kebab, or **shashlik** as it's more commonly known, refers to the small roasted chunks of meat grilled over hot coals (which we would probably call shish kebab). **Kofta**, or minced lamb-meat balls served on a plate with finely chopped onions or in a sandweech, are also cooked over hot coals. Occasionally, kofta is cooked with onions, encased in cracked wheat and called a **kubbeh**.

On both felafals and shwaarmas, various sauces are used to spice things up a little. **Hoummus** is a creamy chick-pea paste, while **tahini** is its sesame seed equivalent that's often flavoured with garlic, onion or lemons. Both may be served on their own, usually swimming in olive oil and with pitta bread on a side plate. Tahini is also an essential ingredient in another Arab speciality, **baba ghanoush**, where it's combined with mashed eggplant, and often lemon or garlic.

Mezze

In the better Arabian restaurants, felafal balls are often served as part of **mezze**, a selection of salads, nuts, and snacks that is often eaten as an accompaniment to beer or araq. Other mezze dishes include **fuul** (stewed fava beans mashed with a fork and served warm with lemon, garlic or oil), **salata Turkiya** (a spiced Turkish salad of tomato paste, hot pepper puree, parsley and onion) and **labanah** (a sort of cream cheese made from salted yoghurt that's often served with olive oil or cucumber). Less common mezze dishes include **sambousek**, a semi-circular or three-cornered pie stuffed with spinach, cheese or mincemeat, and **sfeeha**, a type of pizza with a mincemeat topping containing chopped tomatoes, peppers, onions and parsley, that's similar to the Turkish/Armenian *hors d'oeuvre* of **lahmacun**.

Main course

Palestinian main courses often take a long time to prepare. For this reason, it is often better to call in at the restaurant during the day and tell them what you will be eating that evening, to give them time to prepare it for you. **Masakhan**, grilled chicken served on bread over a bed of sauteed onions and sumac, is one of the more popular Arabian dishes, though I personally prefer **farrouj mahshi**, which is chicken stuffed with spicy rice and meat, roasted in an oven and served with yoghurt and vegetables. As you can imagine, this dish is extremely filling, and quite expensive by Palestinian standards. Other meat and vegetables can also be served 'mahshi-style', including courgettes, eggplants and peppers that can be adapted to suit vegetarian requirements. Other vegetarian dishes include **mujadra** – rice cooked with lentils and onions, often served on bread – and **waraq dawali**, which are vine leaves, normally stuffed with meat and rice, though onions, garlic, tomatoes and parsley can replace the meat.

For carnivores, the menu is that much more extensive. **Kidra** is lamb meat served with saffron rice, all smothered with spices and cardamom and served with garlic. This is quite rare; far more common (and, I reckon, delicious too) is **mansaf**, boiled lamb on top of rice on top of shrak (a sort of flat, round wheat crust), with hot yoghurt and pine nuts sprinkled over the result. Another favourite is **maqlubeh**, layers of rice, fried meat and vegetables (aubergine and cauliflower) cooked in a pan and served upside down. Mansaf is also famous as the traditional dish of a Bedouin feast. If you're invited along to one, it is inevitable that you'll be asked, as the honoured guest, to eat the greatest delicacy of the meal, the **eyeballs** of the sheep. This offer is made partly out of tradition, and partly to see if you can swallow them without retching.

Desserts

Probably the biggest single cause of tooth decay in the Arab world, **baklawa** comes in all sorts of varieties, but the basic format is always the same: layers of pastry dripping in honey, syrup and nuts. You'll see baklawa shops throughout Palestine, though the two on Souq Khan El-Zeit in Jerusalem's Old City are the most renowned.

On sale alongside the baklawa, **qatayef** are pancakes stuffed with chopped walnuts or cheese that are particularly ubiquitous during Ramadan, and **kenafeh** is soft cheese cooked between layers of orange-flavoured pastry and served with syrup, for which the town of Nablus is famous. **Hilmah** (a flat dough of semolina, olive oil and fenugreek seeds, often stuffed with nuts) and **mamul** (semolina pastry prepared with different fillings) are also readily available. Just writing about these sweets makes my teeth itch; don't forget to pack a large tube of toothpaste before you arrive in Palestine.

For the less adventurous, a trip to the local sweetshop will show you just how much the Palestinians love **ice-cream**. Much of the locally produced, pre-packaged stuff costs as little as NIS1, and is a real pick-me-up on hot days. Gaza is famous for its ice-cream, though there seem to be only a couple of places where you can actually buy it.

Drinks

Chai (tea) is the number-one drink in the Arab world, a position challenged only by Arabic coffee. Both drinks look and taste nothing like their Occidental equivalents. Chai is served in small glasses and is incredibly sweet – two parts liquid to one part sugar – with occasionally a touch of mint added too, which improves its taste tenfold. **Coffee** also comes in small glasses, and is black, sweet and often mixed with cardamom, a concoction known as **qahwa**. It tastes sensational. The secret of enjoying Arabic coffee is to learn the art of drinking as much of the liquid as possible, without asphyxiating yourself on the silty powder at the bottom of the glass. A glass of water is often served as an accompaniment, to wash it down with afterwards.

Another drink, served by extrovert vendors in scarlet livery at major road junctions in every city, is **tamar hindi**. It's a dark, sweet liquid made of boiling tamarind juice that's meant to be a pretty potent aphrodisiac.

Contrary to popular belief, Palestine is not a dry country. Not only are there the **wines** of the monasteries (the Cremisan monastery, to the south of Jerusalem, has the best reputation) but there's now **Taybeh beer**, the product of Palestine's only brewery, based in Ramallah. It's really delicious. And no survey of Arab drinks would be complete without mentioning **araq**, a generic term that covers a multitude of alcoholic firewaters. Usually aniseed based, araq tastes like the illegitimate offspring of Bertie Bassett and the devil himself. It runs down your throat like volcanic lava. Do try some.

TOURIST INFORMATION
Apart from the Israeli-run information centres in Jerusalem, the Christian Information Centre opposite the Tower of David in the Old City and a newly-opened kiosk in Nablus, Palestine does not as yet have any information centres. However, help is at hand in the form of the offices of the **Ministry of Tourism and Antiquities** which you'll find in all the big cities. You may feel a bit of a pratt when you first walk into these places, as they clearly aren't designed to receive visitors' enquiries, but they're usually very helpful, and you'll probably get a cup of coffee out of them if nothing else. In East Jerusalem, the English-language **Educational Bookshop** at 22 Salah El-Din has a good selection of books and periodicals about Palestine.

PUBLIC HOLIDAYS AND FESTIVALS
Muslims follow a **lunar calendar**, so the dates on which their holidays fall vary from year to year. Years are counted from the escape by Mohammed from Mecca to Medina in 622, and the calendar is known as the **Hejira** ('flight') calendar; the year 2000 will be 1418AH in the Muslim calendar, and not 1378 as you might expect, because the lunar year is about eleven days shorter than the solar year.

The most important festival in the Muslim year is **Ramadan**, a period of self-denial and fasting that lasts a whole month. During Ramadan, Muslims are forbidden to allow anything to pass their lips during daylight hours, be it food, drink or even cigarettes, and may only eat after the sun has gone down. Because of this, shops close early during Ramadan to allow people to prepare their evening meal, while cafés may close throughout the day but open in the evening. Tourists are often advised not to visit Palestine during this month; but while it's true that a few things close down altogether, and it's very difficult to find food during the day, travelling around Palestine during Ramadan is not quite the ordeal it's often made out to be. At the end of the month there follow three days of festivities and gorging, called **Eid al-Fitr**, that's quite something to behold.

The second most important festival is the Muslim New Year, or **Al-Hejira**, which commemorates Mohammed's flight to Medina. Another major festival, **Eid Al-Adha**, celebrates Abraham's attempt to sacrifice his son to God. This holiday is traditionally the time when Muslims attempt to complete the fifth pillar of their faith, the pilgrimage to Mecca. Two other Muslim festivals which, though celebrated throughout the land, aren't actually public holidays in Palestine, are **Moulid Al-Nabi**, the Prophet Mohammed's birthday, and **Leilat Al-Miraj**, which marks the date on which the Koran was revealed to Mohammed.

To confuse matters further, Christians hold their own holidays throughout the year, based on the Western, **solar calendar**, but each denomination has its own date for the celebrations. Christmas, for example, is held on December 25 by the Latin and Western churches, on January 7 by the Eastern Orthodox faith and on January 19 by the Armenians. **Palm Sunday**, celebrating Jesus' triumphal march into Jerusalem, **Easter**, the time of Jesus' resurrection, and **Ascension Day**, which marks Jesus' departure to Heaven five-and-a-half weeks later, are all important festivals in the Christian calendar. Christian festivals in Palestine tend to be far more religious and sober affairs than their equivalents in the west, so don't expect all-night drunken parties. None of these festivals are national holidays in Palestine, though Christian-owned shops and schools will close over these days. Remember, too, that the **Christian Sabbath** is on a Sunday. Monasteries and other Christian places sometimes close on Sundays, though some close on Saturdays instead. As many of these sights (particularly the monasteries) take a lot of effort to get to, make sure they're open before you head off.

If you're basing yourself in Jerusalem, it would be an idea to keep one eye on the Israeli calendar too, and watch out for their holidays. The **Israeli Sabbath**, or *Shabbat*, runs from Friday dusk to Saturday dusk. It, too, is strictly observed, and certain quarters of Jerusalem close down altogether. A brief rundown of Jewish holidays is listed below; as the Jews also use a lunar calendar, the dates on which their festivals fall also change from one year to the next; only the dates up to the year 2002 are given.

Muslim, Jewish and Israeli holidays

All of the following are approximate dates only, depending on the first sighting of the new moon.

Muslim holidays	*2000*	*2001*	*2002*
Eid Al-Adha	17 Mar	6 Mar	23 Feb
Al-Hejira	5 Apr	24 Mar	13 Mar
Moulid Al-Nabi	14 June	3 June	23 May
1st of Ramadan	27 Nov	16 Nov	5 Nov
Eid Al-Fitr	8 Jan & 27 Dec	16 Dec	5 Dec

Jewish and Israeli holidays (only the festivals involving major shutdowns are listed here)

Passover	20 Apr	8 Apr	28 Mar
Shevuot	9 Jun	28 May	17 May
New Year	30 Sept	18 Sept	7 Sept
Yom Kippur	9 Oct	27 Sept	16 Sept
Succot	14 Oct	2 Oct	21 Sept
Simhat Torah	21 Oct	9 Oct	28 Sept

Palestinian holidays

In addition to the religious festivals, Palestine has a number of official, secular holidays. Two of these – **Fatah Day** (January 1), marking the founding of Fatah in 1965, and **Independence Day** on November 15 each year, which celebrates the declaration of an independent State of Palestine by the Palestinian National Council in 1988 – are official public holidays. Two weeks after Independence Day, **UN Palestinian Day** marks the UN's solidarity with the Palestinian people. A third national day in November, **Balfour Day**, is rather a curious one, for it commemorates the 1917 Balfour declaration in which the British Foreign Secretary promised Jews a homeland in Palestine – a declaration that one would have thought the Palestinians were keen to forget.

Other national days mark events in the troubled history of the Palestinians this century. **Jerusalem Day** on February 22 is a day of mourning throughout the Muslim world to mark the loss of the Holy City to the Israelis in 1967, while **Land Day** on March 30 recalls an incident in 1976 when six Israeli Arabs lost their life defending their land. A far larger massacre, that of the village of Deir Yassin near Jerusalem, in which over 200 men, women and children were slaughtered by Israeli troops in 1948, is commemorated with **Deir Yassin Day** on April 10. Black September, when the PLO was forced out of Jordan by the armed forces under King Hussein, is also commemorated each year with **Black September Day**, on the 18th of that month.

BUSINESS HOURS

Most Palestinian businesses have an afternoon **siesta**: standard shopping hours tend to be Monday–Thursday 08.00–13.00 and 16.00–19.00, though many shops stay open beyond this time.

The Islamic holy day, or **Sabbath**, is Friday. It is pretty rigidly observed in most Palestinian towns, where you'll find shops closed, buses refusing to run and tourist attractions locked up for the day. On Fridays, you may like to base yourself in Bethlehem or Jerusalem, both of which have significant non-Muslim populations. The Christian holy day is Sunday: most Christian-owned sights and businesses close down on this day, but the Christians aren't numerous enough to paralyse entire cities.

The Jewish Sabbath, called Shabbat, begins at dusk on Friday and continues until dusk on Saturday. This is strictly observed in Israel, and you will find that all cafés, restaurants, tourist attractions (with the exception of a couple in Jerusalem) and transport shuts down for 24 hours. If you're touring around the entire Holy Land, it's a good idea to plan your schedule so that you're in Palestine rather than Israel during Shabbat.

TIME

Palestine is two hours ahead of GMT, so, excluding for the moment any daylight saving schemes, when it's midday in Palestine, it's 01.00 on the North American West Coast (PST), 05.00 on the east coast of America (EST), 10.00 in the UK, 18.00 in West Australia, 20.00 in Eastern Australia and 22.00 in New Zealand. Palestine has adopted Daylight Saving Time (DST), so the clocks go forward by one hour in March, and back in September. Be warned, however: the dates when the Palestinians switch over to DST and back usually differ from Israel's. To confuse matters further, many Palestinians, particularly those who work in Israel, choose to operate according to Israel's DST scheme.

COMMUNICATIONS
Post

To the delight of philatelists everywhere, Palestine has its own **stamps**. Just remember that if you stamp your letters with Palestinian stamps, you have to put them in a Palestinian post box. If you post a letter in East Jerusalem or any other area outside PNA jurisdiction, it will go through the Israeli postal system. Letters posted to Europe take three to four days to arrive, though America- and Australia-bound letters can take over a week. Note that Arab countries that refuse to accept mail sent from Israel will accept Palestinian-stamped letters.

When writing to Palestine, it's probably safest to write '**Palestine, via Israel**' on the letters, to avoid offending anyone. The letters take a little longer to arrive than those sent to Israel only. Palestine has a sketchy **poste restante** service. If you have an email address, use this instead. Poste restante addresses should be written as follows:

Henry STEDMAN (note capitals and underlining for surname)
Poste Restante
Main Post Office
Bethlehem (or other big city),
Palestine
Via Israel

You'll need to take along your passport when collecting your mail. Palestinian post offices are open from Saturday to Thursday, 08.00–14.00.

Telephone

There's currently a touch of confusion surrounding the phone systems of Palestine and Israel. While the Palestinian telephone company are busy setting up phone boxes everywhere which accept Palestinian phone cards only (the post office and newsagents usually stock them), they are still heavily reliant on Bezeq, the Israeli phone company, who maintain and control the phone line. Nearly all call boxes operate using **phonecards**, though there is still the odd public phone, usually owned and operated by local shops, that accepts **coins**. These are fine for making local calls, but are said to be a tad expensive when dialling overseas. Palestinian cards come in values of NIS10, 20, 40 and 50.

Phone boxes can be used to phone abroad. Not too long ago, callers from Israel and Palestine dialled the international access code of 00 when calling overseas. Nowadays, however, 00 is just one of four possible access codes, the others being 014, 013 and 012, which all charge different rates. Which one you should use, and when, depends on when and where you're calling, though as a general rule 00 is now the most expensive access code and should usually be avoided. Currently, it is unknown whether this rule will also apply to the Palestinian phone network. Having dialled the access code you follow it with the country code, then the area code (minus the first zero) and finally the number. Calls are 25% cheaper between 22.00 and 01.00 and throughout Saturday and Sunday, and 50% cheaper between 01.00 and 08.00 throughout the week.

To confuse matters still further, numbers in Israel are changing. Soon, all numbers in the West Bank and Gaza Strip will have seven digits, not six. If the number has changed, you should hear a message (usually, but not always, in English) telling you the new number. Unfortunately, Palestine is rather neglected by Bezeq, and you shouldn't be surprised to find that the phone line is out of order. As a result, trying to ring Palestine from abroad can be fraught with difficulties. The international code for Palestine is the same as that for Israel, namely **0972**. There are only three **area codes**: 02 for Jerusalem, Ramallah, and the southern and eastern parts of the West Bank; 09 for Nablus and the northern West Bank, and 07 for the Gaza Strip. Dialling codes 050, 052 and so on are for mobile phones.

Remember to drop the initial 0 from area codes when ringing from abroad.

The media
Newspapers

The weekly *Jerusalem Times* is Palestine's only English-language newspaper. While its coverage of local issues provides an essential counterbalance to the right-wing Israeli daily *Jerusalem Post*, it cannot compete with the latter when it comes to covering international news, sports and so on. It has to be said that, at NIS4 for a mere 16 pages, it's somewhat overpriced too. The top-selling Arab newspaper, Al-Ahram, can also be picked up in Palestine.

Though the full implementation of the Oslo Accords seems as far off as ever, the peace process has at least brought about an unprecedented degree of freedom for the Palestinian press, resulting in an explosion in the number of Palestinian periodicals documenting the current political situation. Of these, two in particular are worthy of your attention. The first, the *Palestine Report* (NIS4), published weekly by the non-profit organisation the Jerusalem Media and Communications Centre, is the oldest and most popular of all the Palestinian periodicals, providing the reader with excellent reports, summaries, interviews and analyses on the very latest issues in Palestinian society. The second publication, the monthly *News from Within,* is the organ of the politically active, Jerusalem-based Alternative Information Centre and, though it's more of an anti-Zionist polemic than a newspaper, the passionate and well-informed articles often make for compelling reading. Both of these publications, and many others, can be found in the Educational Bookshop in East Jerusalem (see page 99).

Finally, *This Week in Palestine* is an entertaining listings booklet which, despite its title, comes out every fortnight (the proprietors hope to publish weekly soon). As well as news of events and entertainments in Palestine, they also run small features on Palestinian tourist attractions, recipes, useful information, telephone numbers and so forth. The bigger hotels in East Jerusalem usually have some in stock by reception.

TV and radio

Palestine does have its own television station, broadcasting from Ramallah and Gaza. Most West Bank households have access to Jordanian and Syrian television, while those in the Gaza can sample the delights of Egyptian TV. Israeli television can also be picked up in Palestine.

The internet
Internet cafés

Palestine is now fully on-line, and every major town with the exception of Hebron and Jericho has at least one internet café (and often more; Nablus has no fewer than ten). Prices are much lower than in Israel – about NIS7 for 30 minutes – with discounts for regular customers. You rarely have to wait for a machine either, and the machines are surprisingly speedy.

SHOPPING

It's an unusual traveller who returns from Palestine without a souvenir of some description. The relentless hectoring from local shopkeepers, particularly in Jerusalem, will wear down even the most resilient of tight-fisted tourists. And besides, many of the locally made products are really quite charming; so the secret to successful shopping is not to buy nothing, but to buy carefully.

Most of the regions in Palestine have a reputation for specialising in some local craft. Bethlehem, for example, is famous for its **olivewood carvings**. It is said that the art of carving was brought over by monks as early as the 4th century, following the construction of the Church of the Nativity. Because of the tree's association with Christianity, it's hardly surprising that so many olivewood carvings have a religious theme. One of the earliest olivewood products to be made were rosary beads, and these days olivewood crosses, nativity scenes, prayer beads and statuettes abound in the souvenir shops of Bethlehem and Jerusalem. While the large pieces probably seem a little naff for Western tastes, the tiny crucifixes are rather endearing and it's hard not to admire the work and craftsmanship that's gone into producing many of the items.

The most striking feature about traditional Palestinian dresses is the highly decorative front panels, known as the qabbeh. The **embroidery** work on these chest panels takes the breath away; and while few tourists will get much wear out of such a dress, the local embroiderers have branched out, turning their talents to all manner of items from tablecloths to napkins, cushion covers and handkerchiefs. Some of the best-quality work can be found in the folklore museums, of which there are a number in Palestine, or in the **Palestinian Needlework Shop** in the Sheikh Jarrah district of Jerusalem. The work here, made by refugee women in the camps of Gaza, is of exceptionally high quality.

Working with **mother-of -pearl** is another craft thought to have been brought over by friars, this time during the 14th and 15th centuries by Franciscan friars from Damascus, who hired craftsmen from Genova in Italy to teach the locals the secrets of their trade. Initially, mother-of-pearl collected from the Red Sea was used, though today the abalone shells come from as far afield as Australia, New Zealand, Mexico and California. The jewellery is inexpensive and quite attractive, particularly the tiny crucifixes. Unfortunately, plastic imitation mother-of-pearl is now being used with alarming frequency to mass-produce cheaper copies of the real stuff, and many are predicting the eventual death of the industry due to the skill and diligence required to produce genuine mother-of-pearl items. Still, there are over 50 mother-of-pearl factories in the Bethlehem district alone, so its demise, if it ever happens, shouldn't be too imminent.

One of the most popular exports, appealing to the tastes of the Occidental traveller, is the local **glassware**, despite the obvious problems of exporting the item back home without smashing it into a million pieces. Hebron is the centre for glass manufacture, and no trip to this fascinating city would be complete without a trip to a local factory, where you can see glass being blown and shaped using the traditional methods. The prices are reasonable and the work often admirable. Most of these glass manufacturers also use their kilns to blast pieces of **pottery**, from tiles to vases to ashtrays and mugs, which you can buy on site, or at any number of souvenir shops in Jerusalem's Old City. Further south, the villages around Sammu are famed for their **carpets**, which are woven at dozens of little cottage factories. The traditional green, black and red colours of the Palestinian flag feature prominently. Prices aren't cheap but again the quality is often exceptional; see page 216 for details.

The Gaza Strip is famous for its ability with **cane**, which is made into all sorts of furniture pieces. For most visitors, however, furniture is simply too bulky for the backpack, and they prefer instead to choose something from the **PLO Flag Shop** (see page 77), the home of Palestinian paraphernalia.

ARTS AND ENTERTAINMENTS
Music
The tragedies suffered in the *nakba* (the Palestinians' word for the tragedy of 1948) awoke Palestine's moribund artistic world from the torpor into which it had slipped, giving its artists both a fresh impetus and new subject matter. Nowhere was this seismic change in artistic direction more discernable than in the world of Palestinian music. Pre-1948 the musical scene in Palestine was dominated by the **folksongs** of the *fellahin*, or rural worker. These were simple ditties sung in the fields by farmers to accompany their daily labours such as coffee-grinding, sheep-herding or fishing. Down the centuries these folksongs evolved into a number of classifiable forms, depending on the style of the singing

or the tune or subject matter. Most of these musical forms were for men only, such as the **ataba**, comprising four verses of sung poetry. The women had their own musical forms, such as the **zaghareet**, which is recognisable by the long piercing shriek at the beginning. These folksongs are still widely sung today, particularly at weddings where they're accompanied by an entire Palestinian orchestra consisting of the **shababi** and **ney** (both flutes), the **tabla, oud** and **drums**. Clearing away the plates and dishes from the feast, the guests could then indulge in the **dakba**, or dance (literally, 'foot-tapping'). The wedding is also the most likely place to catch a performance of the **sahja**. This is where the guests stand in two rows facing each other, with one row repeating the verse of the other. Professional singers, or **qawaali**, are also a feature of many weddings. Skilled lyricists as well as singers, two qawaali are usually paid to engage in a sort of improvised musical debate, with each singing the praises, literally, of the family they represent.

In addition to these folksongs, the **Koranic incantations** of the *Mawaali* and the epic songs of the itinerant **storytellers**, or *Hakawati*, who wove epic tales of ancient heroes while playing a soft tune on the **rababah** (a one-stringed violin-like instrument), both added features to the musical map of the country.

But after 1948 the scenario changed: while the folksong format survived, the subject matter lost its romantic, poetic inclinations. Instead, artists began to sing about the tragedies of '48 (and, later, '67) and the dream of nationhood. Gone were the mythical heroes of traditional folksongs, in favour of national heroes and freedom fighters whose deeds in the Palestinians' struggle against the Israelis were lauded in song. The first Palestinian artist to enjoy popular success in the aftermath of the nakba was Mustafa Al-Kurd, whose early 1970s cassette 'Kullee Amal' ('Full of Hope') became a local best-seller, despite Israeli attempts to ban its sale.

By the late seventies other bands were following in Al-Kurd's wake, though again most of their output had to be sold under the counter for fear of reprisals by the Israeli authorities. A limited access to decent recording facilities also stifled the growth of a viable music industry in Palestine throughout the seventies and eighties, though bands such as Al-Ishiqeen ('The Lovers') and Bassam Bashara – whose album *Children of the Stones* (about the Intifada) was such a big hit – both managed to forge lasting success in the eighties.

Today, the Palestinian music industry, while still tiny, is looking more robust than ever before. The opening of the **Jerusalem Centre for Arab Music** and Ramallah's **National Music Conservatory**, and the emergence of bands dedicated to the revival of traditional songs such as the Popular Palestinian Arts Band in Ramallah, Ghassan Kanafani's Band for Dabka at Bethlehem University and the JuThoor Band of Bir Zeit, all bode well for the survival and development of Palestinian music. As yet, however, recorded Palestinian music remains incredibly difficult to buy outside Palestine, and all of the few cassettes by Palestinian artists that I've managed to unearth back in England were recorded outside Palestine. The tiny London-based record company Venture's *Palestine – Music of the Intifada* is a good introduction to Palestinian music, and remains the most readily available cassette; most decent record shops should be able to track down a copy for you.

Theatre and literature
With Palestine's music industry successfully suppressed by the Israelis during the Intifada, the Palestinians looked for a new artistic avenue in which to vent their feelings. The result was the emergence of a highly politicised movement in

Palestinian theatre, centred on the **Hakawati Theatre** in East Jerusalem. To avoid censorship, playwrights were forced to use allegories, metaphors and highly symbolic language to convey their frustration and anger at the Israelis' regime. Despite these precautions, the theatres were still subjected to routine closures by the Israeli authorities, as they are to this day. Yet the prodigious output of the various Palestinian theatrical companies shows no sign of abating, and new theatres, particularly in Ramallah and Gaza, are an indication of just how popular this medium is in Palestine. Unfortunately, nearly every play is written and performed in Arabic, though some of the larger theatres, including the Hakawati, thoughtfully provide English-language summaries in the programmes.

Palestinian **literature** developed alongside the radical theatre movement in the seventies and eighties. The most famous Palestinian writer, and probably the only one to enjoy true international success, is the poet Mahmoud Darwish. Born in Galilee in 1942, his unwavering opposition to the Israeli occupation has brought him to the attention of the Israeli authorities on several occasions, and to avoid arrest and persecution Darwish was forced to live in exile for 25 years, returning only in 1996. He has had over 30 works of both poetry and prose published, and his books have been translated into 35 languages. His more popular works include *Memory of Forgetfulness*, and his collection of poetry, *Psalms*, published in 1995. Currently, he is the editor of the prestigious literary review *Al-Karmel*, which resumed publication in 1997.

CULTURAL DOS AND DON'TS

There are a few gestures and actions that are commonplace in the West, but which would cause offence in Palestine. **Pointing** to somebody, for example, is considered very bad form, and pointing at someone with your foot is downright offensive. Don't use your **left hand** when eating either, particularly when taking food from a communal bowl. The Arabs come up with all sorts of stories about how this tradition came about; some say that the devil sits on your left shoulder, others insist it is because Mohammed always ate with his right hand. But the simple fact of the matter is that, in the Arab world, the left hand is traditionally the toilet-paper substitute.

Most of the other forbiddens are simple courtesies common to most of the world: avoid canoodling with your partner(s) in public, don't blow your nose in public or make a great display of picking your teeth in restaurants (cover your mouth with your other hand), dress conservatively in towns and cities and avoid eating, drinking and smoking in public during Ramadan.

Further to these constraints, there is a special code of etiquette that should be followed when visiting mosques. First, always remove your shoes and make sure you are modestly dressed, with arms and legs fully covered. Don't come on Fridays or during the five-times-a-day prayers (when you'll doubtless be refused entry anyway). Once inside, keep quiet and don't use flash photography; people use the mosque to pray in all day, not just during the official prayer times, so don't distract them. And if a mosque is closed to non-Muslims, it means just that, so don't try to flout the laws by sneaking in: it only gives tourists a bad name.

Interacting with local people

At first, it's all too easy to regard with deep suspicion every Palestinian who tries to start up a conversation with you, simply because we in the West are unused to people being so friendly, and so open, without harbouring some ulterior motive. This suspicion is only heightened in Jerusalem, where 90% of the time those who start talking to us really do have an alternative agenda, one that usually involves a relative's souvenir shop and your money. Of course, you can swan around Palestine ignoring everybody for your entire trip, but you'll be so much the poorer if you do, so it is of paramount importance that you learn to interact with the locals as soon as possible – and just as importantly, learn which locals are worth interacting with, and which should be avoided. Palestine has its good and bad guys like everywhere else, so learn to distinguish between the two as quickly as possible. Unfortunately, there's no hard and fast rule; it's a case of developing your instinct, and working out who is interested in you, and who is interested in your money. Women travellers, of course, should be extra alert. But in general, if somebody invites you to sit with them and have some coffee, play chess or simply chew the fat, and it feels right, go with it.

Part Two

The Country

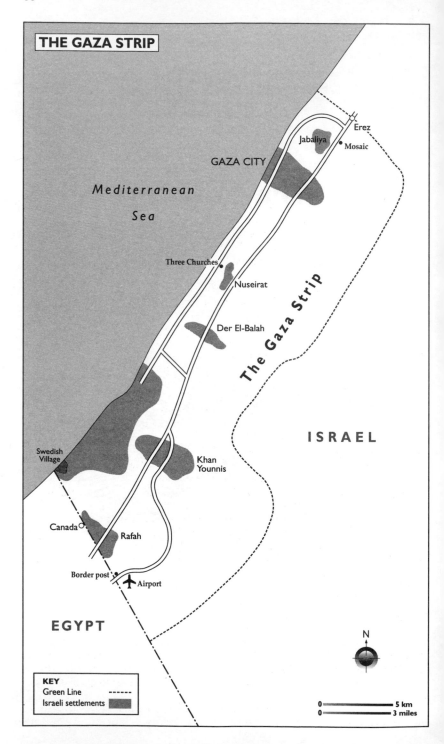

THE GAZA STRIP

Erez
Jabaliya
• Mosaic
GAZA CITY

Mediterranean

Sea

Three Churches •
Nuseirat

Der El-Balah

The Gaza Strip

ISRAEL

Swedish
Village

Khan
Younnis

Canada ○
Rafah

Border post •
✈ Airport

EGYPT

N

KEY
Green Line   ----
Israeli settlements

0   5 km
0   3 miles

The Gaza Strip

Just 42km long and 10km wide at its narrowest point, the sliver of sandy Mediterranean shoreline known as the Gaza Strip is one of the most densely populated areas on earth. Over one million Palestinians, including 785,000 refugees living in the shanty-town squalor of the refugee camps, inhabit this artificial geographical entity, a by-product of the 1948 nakba. Though the Strip is 14 times smaller in surface area than the West Bank, its population is only 400,000, or 30% fewer, working out at an incredible 2,773 people per km^2 for the whole of the Strip.

The semi-barren Strip simply doesn't have the resources to cope with its huge population, a fact borne out by the statistics. Over 40% of the local population – about 314,000 people – is unemployed, and 90% live below the poverty line. Of those who do work, 25% of the refugees are forced to seek employment over the border in Israel, where they receive wages that are, on average, 40% below those of their Israeli counterparts. To prevent complete economic meltdown, the Strip relies on some US$250 million in aid, including US$98 million from UNRWA. Yet despite this vital injection of cash, the Strip *still* suffers from a chronic shortage of drinking water, over 30% of houses *still* aren't connected to the main sewage system, and the local kids *still* have to take it in turns to go to school, because there simply aren't enough facilities to teach them all at the same time. Meanwhile the local, largely agrarian economy limps on – an economy underpinned by the growing of olives, citrus fruits, beef and dairy products – with donkeys still providing the backbone, as they have done for centuries. Gaza's cause isn't helped by the Jewish settlers who appropriated much of the best arable land for themselves following 1967, and who live in complete isolation from the rest of Gaza's population in the 18 settlements dotting the Strip.

These figures make for some pretty grim reading, as I'm sure you'll agree, and you'd be forgiven for thinking that Gaza is out of bounds for tourists. Cross into the Strip, and your first impressions will do little to dispel this conclusion: everything, from the cars to the roads, the buildings to the donkeys and even some of the people, looks knackered.

What's more, with all the upheavals of the past 50 years, the tourist trade has had to take a back seat in the Gaza. There's no real tourist infrastructure, few official attractions and very little in the way of evening entertainment. In addition, transport to the Gaza is infrequent, the accommodation, with one or two exceptions, is expensive and confined to the capital, and unlike the rest of Palestine – which permanently basks under a halo of holiness – the Gaza Strip doesn't even have any major biblical associations to redeem it. (It receives just 15 biblical mentions altogether, most famously as a place where Samson tangled with a prostitute.)

Nevertheless, those serious about getting to know Palestine simply must pay a visit to Gaza. If you make the effort, I'm sure that you will be as pleasantly surprised as I was. The venue for many of Palestine's greatest tribulations, the Gaza Strip is now enjoying, more than any other part of the country, the benefits derived from the 1993 Oslo Accords and the establishment of a Palestinian state. This is the seat of the Palestinian government and the home of both its international airport and its biggest cultural centre. Furthermore, thanks to a huge amount of foreign and local investment, the centre of Gaza City around Midan Jundi must now rank as one of the tidiest and most modern parts of the entire country, while gleaming buildings are sprouting up almost overnight along the seafront. And OK, so there aren't many tourist attractions here, but Gaza makes up for it in other ways. Despite their inherent conservatism, the people are just wonderful. Their reputation as the friendliest people in Palestine is deserved (though you'll need to learn a little Arabic to appreciate it fully). The food is occasionally great too, and the markets, particularly the weekly bazaar at Khan Younnis, are real spectacles, providing a glimpse of Palestine at its rawest and most compelling. In a nutshell, Gaza is Palestine at its most exotic, oriental, and untrammeled. And it's fascinating.

HISTORY

The history of the Gaza Strip really begins in 1948. Before then, the territory was a quiet backwater that derived most of its income from the local port. It managed to steer clear of the worst of the hostilities engulfing the Holy Land during the first half of the 20th century, though in 1929 the British were forced to evacuate Gaza City's tiny Jewish population for fear of trouble. By the time the British withdrew in 1948 there was only one Jewish settlement, and this was abandoned soon after the fighting started.

Under the UNSCOP-brokered partition plan, the Gaza Strip was due to fall under Palestinian jurisdiction. After the dust had settled in 1948, however, **Egypt** had taken control. It proved to be an acquisition of dubious worth. Over 250,000 refugees flooded into the Strip as a result of the fighting and the destruction of Palestinian villages in Israel, creating enormous pressure on the local resources and trouble for the Egyptian government. They responded by ruling Gaza with an iron rod, a repressive rule that continued until 1956 and the **Suez Crisis**, when control was transferred to the Israelis. The Israelis were forced by the international community to hand the territory back four months later, and the Egyptian president **Nasser** decided to reward the unstinting support shown by the Gazans throughout this period with a programme to revitalise the Strip: Palestinians were given a degree of autonomy over the territory, and a legislative body – a precursor to the PLO – was formed. More importantly, Nasser became a vociferous and powerful supporter of Palestinian rights, and began measures to achieve the liberation of the Holy Land from Israeli occupation by force, including compulsory military training for all Gazan school students.

All these preparations proved to be in vain, however, when, during the Six-Day War of 1967, Egypt lost their grip on the Strip and control was transferred to **Israel**. Their repressive regime and the desperate economic plight of the Gazans led to the establishment of the **Muslim Brotherhood**, essentially a peaceful organisation dedicated to improving the lot of Gazans by building schools, hospitals and other public buildings. Initially the Israelis supported the Brotherhood, which they saw as a more pliable rival to the aggressive PLO. However, during the eighties a radical schism of the Brotherhood, the **Islamic Jihad**, was founded. The Jihad was far more violent and hostile to the Israelis than anything seen previously. Israel responded, belatedly, by raising its military presence in the Strip and clamping down on political activism.

While all this went on, the economic conditions of the Strip deteriorated still further, and as the situation grew more desperate the Palestinians responded with sporadic demonstrations and terrorism. Eventually, on December 8 1987, the Gazans' frustration exploded into full-scale riots, boycotts and strikes; the **Intifada** was born. The PLO established the United National Leadership of the Uprising (UNLU) as a means of coordinating the demonstrations to maximise their effectiveness. In response, the Muslim Brotherhood founded **Hamas**, a rival organisation to UNLU with its own agenda.

By the early 1990s Gaza was considered ungovernable by the Israeli authorities. The Intifada had now raged on for over five years with no let up, pushing the Strip to the very edge of economic collapse; the Gulf War pushed it over the precipice. The Palestinians' decision to back Iraq saw the expulsion of Palestinians from Kuwait, aid from Saudi Arabia halted and remittances from ex-pat Palestinians working in the Gulf dry up as a result. Exports also fell sharply, and the decision by Israeli Prime Minister Yitzhak Rabin to close the Green Line prevented Gazans from travelling to Israel to work. The situation was desperate. But secret negotiations between Yasser Arafat and Rabin gave some cause for hope, and in September 1993 the **Oslo Accords** were signed, giving the PLO authority over the Gaza Strip. Following the **Cairo Agreement** on May 17 1994, the PNA took control of the Strip, and made Gaza City their provisional capital.

But the accords did not enjoy unanimous support, and many Gazans considered that Arafat had sold out. After all, the Israelis still occupied over 40% of the Strip in the form of **Jewish settlements**, the 'feeder' roads to these settlements and various military compounds. Fundamentalist organisations such as Hamas and Islamic Jihad enjoyed resurgence in support, with one in every three Palestinians declaring their dissatisfaction with the PNA. Matters reached a head in November 1994 when a pitched battle between the fundamentalists and PNA left sixteen dead. Soon after, Arafat rounded up the fundamentalist leaders and imprisoned them.

Today, the situation has improved inside the Gaza Strip. Services are better, and the economy is enjoying its first upturn for decades. But not everything is rosy. As with the rest of the country, the PNA stand accused of widespread corruption and a regime every bit as oppressive as the Israeli one that it replaced. Many Gazans still have to cross into Israel to find work, and the frequent and arbitrary closing of the border by the Israeli military causes economic hardships for many. The future may look more promising now than it has done at almost any time over the last fifty years, but a myriad of problems remain; and barring a miracle they will continue to blight the Strip for decades to come.

CROSSING INTO AND FROM THE GAZA STRIP
Getting to the border
There are servis taxis from Jerusalem to Gaza. There are also fairies at the bottom of your garden and abominable snowmen roaming the Himalayas, but your chances of seeing any of them, let alone catching one, are extremely slight. There are usually one or two **servis taxis** to Gaza, leaving every morning from outside Damascus Gate, but judging their departure time is tricky. My advice is to turn up as early as possible – by 08.00 at least. Sometimes the servis will fill up immediately and you won't have to wait – NIS25 is the normal fare here – while on other occasions you could be sitting there for hours. Usually, if the car is only half-full and the prospect of further passengers materialising seems slim, you can strike a deal where each passenger pays a bit more (usually NIS40) to leave at once, thus

WHAT'S IN A NAME?
Nobody's very sure where the name 'Gaza' comes from. Some attribute it to the original settlers, the Canaanites, and believe the word means 'strength', though there is little evidence to substantiate this. A second theory suggests that the name is derived from the Persians, who knew the city and port as Hazatote, or 'treasure'. There's also a school of thought that believes that it's named after the prophet Mohammed's great grandfather, Gazet Hashem, who died here during one of his annual commercial trips to the city.

compensating the driver for the empty seats. If you're really having no joy, consider travelling to **Tel Aviv** and trying from there.

The border حاجز مرور/Erez حاجز ايريز

Providing you're not of Palestinian origin, the border crossing between Israel and Gaza at **Erez** (tel: 07 6741672) is reasonably straightforward, if a little long-winded. Coming from Israel or the West Bank, you'll be dropped off in a massive car park, where the flow of people heading into Gaza decants into two streams: foreigners, VIPS and UN workers on one side, Palestinians on the other. Unless you splashed out on a *special* to get you here, expect to be dropped on the Palestinian side, 200m from the foreigners' channel.

There are **three Israeli checkpoints** on the foreigners' side. The first will give your passport a quick once-over before ushering you through. At the second, a little white kiosk, your passport is re-examined and, rarely, your bags are searched. Be nice to the baby-faced Israeli guards here: remember, they'd probably rather be somewhere else too. And besides, they've each got a gun big enough to blow a gaping hole in your forehead.

Pass this examination and you'll be handed a little slip of paper, which you then take with you to the third and final Israeli post. The next stop after this is the Palestinian checkpoint where, amid much *marhaba*ing and waving and smiling, you'll be ushered through – to be met by a tide of desperate taxi drivers eager to make you NIS40 poorer for a journey that, by servis taxi, should cost only NIS2. Be cool, be patient, and unless you arrived at a very strange hour you should eventually be able to gather enough people together to fill a servis.

The return

Again, this crossing is much simpler in the mornings, when transport is easier to come by. Servis taxis from Gaza to Erez leave from Midan Al-Shujaya (NIS2) frequently.

The exit procedure at the border is much the same as that given above (but in reverse, of course), though with one small exception: at the white kiosk you'll be given a slip of paper again, which you should then take with you to customs. Any bags you're be carrying will be x-rayed, and any vehicles searched thoroughly. Assuming everything's OK, the customs officials will stamp your piece of paper, which you should then take back with you to the kiosk to hand in. In return you'll be given another slip of paper, which gives you clearance through the third and final checkpoint.

For onward transport, head back round to the Palestinian queue where servis taxis await to take you to Jerusalem (often), Ramallah (occasionally) and destinations in Israel (very frequently, especially in the morning). There are also three **buses** daily (the number 37) to Ashqelon in Israel.

ON THE WAY TO GAZA CITY

The main road from Erez to Gaza is a short but diverting one. Right by the border, the **Paz petrol station** witnessed the incident that sparked off the Intifada. On December 8 1987, an Israeli army truck ploughed into two vehicles full of residents from the local Jabaliya refugee camp. Four of the refugees were killed. Despite Israeli protests that it had been an accident, the people of Jabaliya went on the rampage, looting and rioting; the Intifada had begun.

The **Jabaliya camp**, one of the more wretched and depressing of the refugee camps, is still home to more than 95,000 people today, making it the largest in Palestine. Most of it lies between the highway and the sea, about 4km on from the border, hidden from the road by a chain of low hills. Yet even in such a desperate place as this one finds, situated just by the side of the road to the right, a sight of quite inordinate beauty. The remains of a 4th-century **Byzantine church**, said by local experts to be the fourth oldest in the world, lie to your right as you head south, just across the road from a little blue petrol station. Little has survived of this church save for its **mosaic floor**, which is currently covered with a protective layer of sand. The Gazan authorities hope to have the entire site open and ready for tourists by the year 2000; if they succeed, don't miss the chance to visit, for the mosaic is fabulous: a pair of scantily-clad lovers eye each other across a stream, a hare tries to shake the fruit from a palm tree, a deer grazes on the upper leaves, and all around leaping lions, lowing cattle and assorted wildfowl fill any remaining spaces. The artists themselves must have been rather proud of their work, for they've 'signed' the mosaic using little black tesserae. Quite how the Byzantines could have concentrated on their prayers with all that going on beneath their feet, however, is a complete mystery. Over the road, next to the petrol station, is a **cemetery** with graves dating back to Roman times, including some family tombs in which pottery has been found.

GAZA CITY   مدينة غزة

The current capital of Palestine (I say current, because the majority of Palestinians still regard Jerusalem as their rightful capital), Gaza, like most large cities, is a bit of a jumble. While certain quarters of the city are desperately impoverished, the recent influx of investment is having a huge impact on both the beachside Remal district and the area around the Parliament building, which is now an orderly array

---

NUMBER PLATES

The combinations of colours used on Gazan number plates may appear to be completely random, but they do follow a logic of sorts. The most common colour scheme is **green figures on white plates**, which denote that the vehicle was registered on Palestinian soil. Conversely, plates with a **green background and white figures** indicate that the car is a taxi. Then there are plates with **red numbers on a white background**, which are used by those working for the Palestinian authorities. Finally, there are plates with a **white background and black figures**. I have yet to find out what exactly this combination means, but according to a couple of sources it denotes cars that were originally registered in Israel, where they were given a yellow number plate, but now belong to Palestine as one of the agreements of the Oslo accords.

By the way, note that even the humble donkey cart has its own set of number plates in Gaza..

of gleaming new high-rises, wide, painted boulevards and neatly manicured lawns. Those expecting only poverty and unrest, therefore, will be quite surprised by just how normal Gaza really is. As it's the only place with accommodation in the Strip, you'll inevitably use Gaza as a base, and the city is worth exploring in its own right, with enough sights to merit a couple of days' stay at least.

History

For centuries a prosperous trade centre lying on the caravan route between Egypt and Syria, Gaza began life as a humble Canaanite village in about 2000BC. Under the Egyptians (circa 15th century BC) the city became the administrative centre for its area, and when the Philistines took over in about 1200BC, it grew to become their largest port and a member of the Pentapolis, one of the five city-states of the Philistine empire. The wealth the city generated attracted the attention of the major regional powers, and for the next 600 years the Pharaohs of Egypt, the Babylonians, the Assyrians and the Hittites fought each other for the right to exploit its money-earning potential – until eventually Gaza lay in ruins and there was nothing left to fight for. The town managed to rise from its ashes and by the 4th century BC it could boast a population of 10,000. Unfortunately, the unstoppable force of Alexander the Great laid waste to the city once more, selling every one of these 10,000 people into slavery in 332BC.

As the location of a famous school of rhetoric and philosophy during Roman times, and later as an important town under the Ommayad caliphs, Gaza continued to enjoy a moderate amount of success. The Mamlukes prolonged and increased the city's prosperity by undertaking a massive rebuilding programme, much of which has survived to this day, and by 1483 the town was, according to contemporary accounts, twice the size of Jerusalem. The good fortune didn't last, however. The Ottomans neglected the city throughout their 400-year reign (a rule broken only by the Egyptian ruler Muhammad Ali for nine years, and Napoleon Bonaparte for one) and the British under General Allenby bombed much of it to smithereens during their victory over the Ottomans in 1917. They held it until 1948 when the Egyptians took over, anointing it the capital of their Palestinian territories, before they in turn lost it to the Israelis. Whether the events of 1994, when the city became the capital of the whole of Palestine, will lead to a revival in fortunes and a more stable future, remains to be seen.

Orientation and practicalities

Servis taxis from the Erez checkpoint drop passengers off at the Shujayyah junction at the eastern end of **Sharia Omar Al-Mukhtar**. Named after a Libyan revolutionary, this street runs due west all the way from the junction to the beach through the heart of the city. Nearly everything of interest to the visitor lies within a few hundred metres of the road, including **Midan Filasteen**, the transport hub and commercial centre of town, and **Midan Jundi**, a small square outside the parliament building. A servis anywhere in town costs NIS1; in Gaza, the chances are that if you flag down a car that's going in your direction, it'll probably be a servis. Alternatively, you can hire your own transport: **Yafa** (07 2865907) on El-Mukhtar Street just below the Al-Amal hotel, have Opel Corsas for US$40 per 24 hours.

As you may expect, there's no official **tourist office**, though the Ministry of Tourism and Antiquities have just opened a regional office in the Shriteh Building, about 1.5km south of Sharia Omar Al-Mukhtar near the coast (look for the high rise surmounted by a red 'bobble'). They may be able to help with your enquiries, though they're not really used to receiving tourists and may get a little flustered. If it's just a map of the city you're after, call in at the **municipality** (closes at 15.00) by Midan Filasteen. Further west along Sharia Omar Al-Mukhtar is Gaza's first **internet centre**, the Cyber Internet Café, on the 5th floor of the Kazem Abu-Shaban Building (aka the Islamic Bank Building). It's NIS4 for 15 minutes, NIS12 per hour. Continuing west along Al-Mukhtar, the main **post office** is the brilliant white building next to the city park.

Banks are reluctant to accept foreign currency, at least not without charging a hefty fee, while official money-changers are scarce. There are a couple near Midan Al-Jundi, however, and dozens of unofficial changers in the gold souq next to the Grand Mosque, who often offer the best rates. Rates vary widely, so shop around.

Accommodation

There is a widely held belief that all accommodation in Gaza is expensive, a myth perpetuated by the large hotels who want as much custom as possible, and the lazy authors of inferior guidebooks (!). This book will prove otherwise. To start with, there's the **Beit Hashem Sarraj** (tel: 07 286904), near the British Council, the cheapest in the classy Remal district with rooms for US$15 per night, or less if you're staying longer. The owner, Hekmat Sarraj, has twice tried to open a proper hostel, but without success. His house, however, where the rooms are meticulously clean and the breakfast hearty, is ample compensation.

Not cheap enough? Then visit the **El-Mohatah** (no phone) on Midan Shujayyah, the hotel with the lowest prices in Gaza. OK, so you wouldn't want to spend your honeymoon here, but at NIS20 for a bed in a four-bed room you can't complain, and it's very convenient for the old city. The manager, Mohamed, seems a friendly, affable sort, and the place is growing popular amongst those journalists not on expenses.

Still not cheap enough? Then consider sleeping on the beach. To the south of Gaza a number of camps have been set up that charge only NIS12 for a night in one of their tents. Not advisable for those with valuables or an allergy to sand, they're perfect for those whose budgets and standards are both low. The camps are not permanent, and often close altogether at certain times of the year (and in particular, winter), though there's usually at least one open.

Most of the upmarket hotels line the beach, or sit at the western end of Sharia Omar Al-Mukhtar. Haggling is possible in all of them. The cheapest is the **UN Beach Club**, though you have to put up with the rude and unhelpful staff if you want to take advantage of their reasonably priced rooms (US$25 plus membership fee). The **Al-Amal** (tel: 07 2841317), a deathly quiet pile on Omar Al-Mukhtar, is not far behind, with large rooms and shared bathrooms. Prices (approximately US$35/40 sgl/dbl per night) include a decent breakfast; ask for a room with a balcony overlooking the road.

Of the others along the seafront, the **Cliff** (tel: 07 2861353; fax: 07 2820742), with its gaudy red interior, has rooms (US$50 per night) with satellite TV, a (non-alcoholic) minibar and a direct-dial phone. Nearby, the **Beach Hotel** (tel: 07 2828800) is the most luxurious on the seafront, a four-star place with rooms for US$77/110. Palestinian television uses it when they want a backdrop that suggests class and affluence.

Just back from the seafront and providing sturdy opposition to the Beach Hotel, the **Al-Quds** (tel: 07 2825181) on Sharia Omar El-Mukhtar is one of Gaza's fanciest, a harmonious mixture of Islamic decor and Western-style luxury – the kind of place where they put a 'Sterilised' sash over the toilet bowl and have a prayer room on every floor. Other touches include a non-alcoholic mini-bar in every room, as well as satellite TV and air-conditioning. At US$59/79 sgl/dbl it's

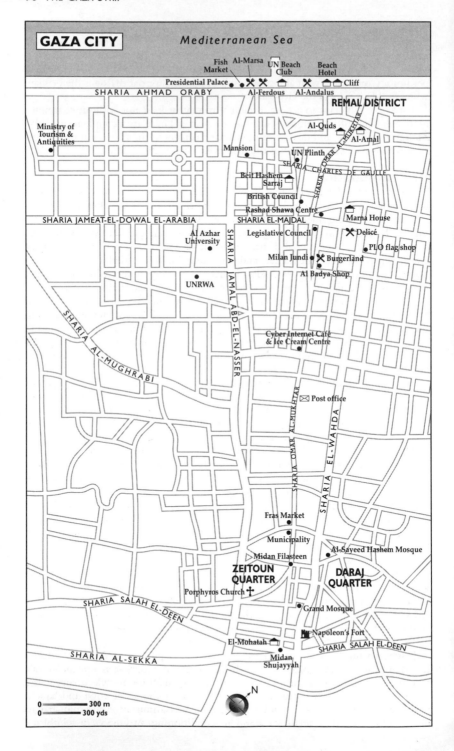

GAZA CITY

Mediterranean Sea

Fish Market
Al-Marsa
UN Beach Club
Beach Hotel
Presidential Palace
Al-Ferdous
Al-Andalus
Cliff

SHARIA AHMAD ORABY

REMAL DISTRICT

Ministry of Tourism & Antiquities

Al-Quds
Al-Amal

Mansion
UN Plinth

SHARIA CHARLES DE GAULLE

Beit Hashem
Sarraj

British Council
Rashad Shawa Centre
Marna House

SHARIA JAMEAT-EL-DOWAL EL-ARABIA
SHARIA EL-MAJDAL

Al Azhar University
Legislative Council
Delicé

Milan Jundi
Burgerland

PLO flag shop

Al Badya Shop

UNRWA

SHARIA AMAL ABD-EL-NASSER

SHARIA AL-MUGHRABI

Cyber Internet Café & Ice Cream Centre

Post office

SHARIA OMAR AL-MUKHTAR

SHARIA EL-WAHDA

Fras Market

Municipality

Midan Filasteen
Al-Sayeed Hashem Mosque

ZEITOUN QUARTER
DARAJ QUARTER

Porphyros Church ✝

SHARIA SALAH EL-DEEN

Grand Mosque

Napoleon's Fort

El-Mohatah
SHARIA SALAH EL-DEEN

SHARIA AL-SEKKA

Midan Shujayyah

N

0 ——— 300 m
0 ——— 300 yds

probably the best value in Remal, though I advise you pay an extra US$20 for a balcony room with sea view.

Even further away from the beach, **Marna House**, 25 Ahmad Abd-Al Aziz Street (tel: 07 2822624; fax: 07 2823322), is quite homely, and though the prices ($60/70 sgl/dbl) are a little outrageous, the rooms are big, and the shady front lawn is wonderful. The friendly, homely atmosphere and the hotel's proximity to the Legislative Council make this another favourite with foreign journalists.

Food

If you plan on having just one slap-up meal in Palestine, the capital is the best place to do it. Some of the **street stalls** in Gaza are less hygienic than their counterparts on the West Bank, though you should try **Abu Kamal's** at 154 Al-Mukhtar (daytime only) and the shwaarma stall just to the south of Rue Charles de Gaulle. At the upper end of the scale, however, the variety is greater, the hygiene standards are superior, and the menus are excellent value.

No trip to the Strip would be complete without a visit to **Delicé** on Sharia Ez-El-Deen-El Qassam. Founded by a Palestinian who returned to Gaza after spending a number of years in France, this pâtisscrie feels like a slice of the Left Bank that's been lifted up and dumped in the eastern Mediterranean. The coffee here is gorgeous, the croissants are great, the chocolate cakes mouthwatering and the cream horns simply incredible. If all this luxury, situated right in the heart of so much deprivation, induces guilt, visit one of the more down-to-earth **fast food shacks** on Midan Jundi, such as the **Pizzaland** or **Burgerland**. They aren't special, but the food's OK and the square is a nice place in which to sit in the evening. Gaza's favourite junk food outlet, however, is undoubtedly the anonymous **ice-cream parlour**, about 2km to the east of Midan Jundi by the entrance to the Islamic Bank building (the home of the internet café). Cones are only NIS1, a paltry price that has locals queuing for miles on really hot days.

For more up-market fare, your best bet is to head down to the coast where, in between all the fancy hotels, are some equally fancy restaurants. The following is just the briefest of selections. The **Al-Andalus** is my favourite; with main courses starting at NIS20 (though for their fish, which you should really try, expect to pay NIS40–60,) this place is extremely reasonably priced, and the service is excellent. The **Al-Ferdous** and, right by the fish market, the **Al-Marsa**, also specialise in fish dishes, with the exact menu depending on what's been caught that day. Finally, probably the most popular eatery on the coast is the **Al-Sammak**, another fish restaurant with the best and most extensive seafood menu in the city.

Shopping

Gaza is thankfully free of the welter of overpriced junk that passes for souvenirs in the West Bank. Indeed, the souvenirs in Gaza are both cheap and tasteful – well, apart from the stuff on offer at the wonderful **PLO Flag Shop** on Sharia Al-Wihda. As its name suggests, the shop deals in all manner of PLO mementos, from PLO T-shirts to flags and even inflatable Yasser Arafats (I kid you not). The presence of such unique souvenirs in your luggage will both amaze fellow travellers, and ensure you have to get your kit off during the security check at Tel Aviv airport.

The **Al-Badya Shop for Palestinian Heritage** on the northern side of Midan Al-Jundi is a charitable organisation that sells locally made goods. Apart from some first-class embroidered blankets, cloths etc, they also have carved wooden souvenirs, some jewellery and other mementos. Everything smacks of real quality and the prices are very reasonable too. But if Gaza is famous for one product, it's pottery, and on Sharia Hawakat Al-Fawakheer there's a whole string of pottery and earthenware shops, one or two of which make their wares on site.

Entertainment
It's not surprising the locals always grumble about the lack of things to do in the evening. The town's three cinemas have all closed, and there are no pubs, clubs or bars and only two places where you can buy alcohol. The first is the **UN Beach Club**, where you can spend an evening being bored rigid in the company of the foreign press corps. Alternatively, there's a guy called Mario who sells cans and bottles from his house near the British Council on Sharia Al-Nassera. A beer here will set you back about NIS7.

Other ways to fill your evening include playing on the internet (see page 75), playing pool in the hall about 50m up from the **Al-Amal** hotel, or watching the sun go down on Midan Al-Jundi. If you're lucky, the cultural centre might have something going on, but don't bet on it. Or you can take the locals' lead, sit on the pavements and chat the night away.

What to see
The following account has been split into two 'walking tours', designed to cover all the major sights of the city. You can do both in one day, though it'll be a very long, sweaty and exhausting one. If you've got the time, take a couple of days at least.

Remal and the Midan al-Jundi
This walk begins at the western end of Sharia Omar El-Mukhtar by the beach. This area, Gaza's 'Riviera', is known as the Remal ('sandy') district for obvious reasons. It's a relatively new quarter, developed after World War I, and is currently enjoying an unprecedented economic boom. As I write, two more hotels are being erected, closing off another section of the beach to the public, and all along the coastal road one's view of the sea is impeded by an ever-increasing number of large hotels and fancy restaurants.

Walking south along the coastal road from Omar El-Mukhtar, after 600m or so your progress will be halted by the presence of a roadblock and a number of armed guards. They're here to watch over the stately **Presidential Palace** by the sea. Those determined to continue south could, providing they hand over their passport, walk for a little way along the beach below the palace, a sandy wasteland that has become a sort of retirement home for old tractors, which spend their dotage rusting silently in the sea air. Looking back to the north you'll see **Gaza port**, full with fishing boats. The port was once poetically known as 'Anthedon', or the white flower, though it was changed during the Byzantine era to Constantina (after the first emperor), and then to **Tida**, its current name.

Much to the chagrin of Yasser Arafat's wife, the President himself rarely uses his seaside palace, preferring instead a modest flat just up the hill from the **fish market**. Nowadays the palace itself is used more as a guesthouse for visiting dignitaries, as is another grand mansion at the top of the hill facing on to **Rue Charles de Gaulle**. This road was built in 1996, and commemorates Palestine's friendship with the French, their closest ally in Western Europe. Facing east away from the palace, **Al-Azhar University** lies to the southeast across a large, empty patch of ground on which they hope to build an exhibition and entertainment centre. The study of Islam is compulsory at Al-Azhar, and in many ways the university is like an overgrown *madrassa*, the traditional Islamic school that places a strong emphasis on religious education. Opposite the university to the east is the **headquarters of UNRWA** (open Sun–Thurs 07.30–15.00). This is still the place to come if you fancy joining a tour around a refugee camp, although, as I said in the introductory chapter, they're somewhat reluctant to take tourists. Ring 07 867044 if you want to try to persuade them to let you tag along. They also have information, brochures and maps related to their activities.

The work done by UNRWA and the UN over the past fifty years is commemorated by a **plinth** on Rue Charles de Gaulle, 350m northwest of the university. Continuing north from here, we soon arrive back at Sharia Omar Al-Mukhtar. About 300m up the hill to your right is the political centre of town. The first building of note that you come to, however, has nothing to do with politics, but is in fact the **Rashad Shawa Centre**. Built over eleven years (1974–85), this is Gaza's foremost cultural and exhibition centre. It's named after a former mayor of the city who commissioned its construction. Originally chosen by the Israelis as a suitably pliable, amenable candidate for the post, Rashad Shawa resigned his commission after just two years following heavy criticism from locals who believed he had become an Israeli pawn. He was reappointed in 1975, but then sacked for voicing his opposition to the Camp David Accords and his overt support of the PLO. Though not much to look at on the outside, the highlight of the centre's interior is the **Diana Tamari Sabbagh library** containing 90,000 books, many in English (though, surprisingly, few that deal with Palestine). Unfortunately, a lack of demand for all things cultural has forced the centre to diversify in order to survive, and these days its three halls are used mainly for business seminars, workshops, conferences and 'expos'. Even the weekly cinema evening has been forced to close through lack of interest. Nevertheless, if there is a concert, play or festival going on in Gaza, the chances are it's going on here. Call in or ring (07 864599) for details of forthcoming events

Tucked immediately behind the centre, the gold-domed **Legislative Council** is Palestine's parliament building. Built by the British during their Mandate, it used to be known as **Mansion House**, a name that's still used occasionally today. Opposite is **Midan Al-Jundi**, Soldier Square, a pretty and fastidiously maintained square named after an anonymous freedom fighter from the '48 war who is buried in the ground underneath here. A statue of a soldier used to stand on top of the plinth in the centre of the square, until the Israelis pulled it down in '67.

The Daraj and Zeitoun quarters

These two quarters, 3km east of the coast, form the oldest part of the city, and contain most of its ancient sights. Begin by catching a servis to **Midan Filasteen** (NIS1–1.5). Below the **municipality**, immediately to the west of the square, is the **Fras Market**, a fruit and vegetable bazaar that's always worth a couple of photographs. For Zeitoun, however, continue east from the midan along Sharia Omar El-Mukhtar, and take the first right. Many of the houses in Zeitoun (which means 'olives', after the olive trees that still grow here) look dull and plain on the outside, but are quite exquisite on the inside. The **florist's**, 200m along the street, is a classic example, its tiled living room full of Ottoman stucco decorations. Ask politely and you may be allowed to view.

Just a few metres further on, the minaret of the tiny **Kaleb Welayat Mosque** signals the presence of the Orthodox **Porphyros Church** that lies immediately behind it. The entrance is through the courtyard to the left of the church; there should be somebody around to let you in. Saint Porphyros (or Berferjos) was born in AD347, and spent much of his time as a recluse near the Jordan River before taking up the post of priest in Gaza City. At the time, Gaza was still largely pagan, and Porphyros' arrival was greeted with a hail of stones and abuse. Such was the locals' intolerance towards Porphyros and his faith that for a number of years he

> **WARNING**
>
> Please note that no matter how tempting, **swimming** in the sea off Gaza is a particularly hazardous activity. Vicious undertows drag a number of unsuspecting bathers to their doom each year. Take good care if paddling, and don't go in above your waist unless you're certain the sea is safe where you are.

was barred from the city altogether, living instead outside the city walls. Following the intervention of his Byzantine superiors in Constantinople, who forced the closure of the temples and prohibited the use of pagan idols in the town, Porphyros was allowed back in and Gaza was converted to Christianity. The church was built in celebration and opened its doors for the first time in AD407, making it one of the oldest churches in the Holy Land (though most of what you see today is a Crusader reconstruction). Porphyros died in 420, and his body, save for his forearm which is in a silver **reliquary** next to the iconostasis, lies buried in the church grounds. The winding streets and alleys around Porphyros Church play host to Gaza's minuscule **Christian community**. The dilapidated house next door to the church to the north, with the cross in the brickwork under the eaves, is typical of the interesting architecture you can see in the vicinity.

Heading back to Omar Al-Mukhtar Street and down the hill to Midan Shujayyah, just across the road lies the **Shujayyah district** (named after a soldier killed in battle against the Crusaders in 1239) and another market, the home of Gaza's Friday bazaar. Turning left and heading back up the hill on Sharia Al-Widha, you find yourself in the **Daraj**, or 'stairs' quarter, so-called because from a distance the quarter looks like a staircase running up the hill. **Napoleon's Fort** or Qasr Al-Basha, once a house for the ruling Radwan family during the Ottoman period and now the home of the Al-Zahra girls' secondary school, lies just 100m up the hill. Many believe that Napoleon used the building as his headquarters during the siege of Acre in 1799, though in all probability he only spent a few nights here on his way through the town. Next door is a small **fountain**, believed to be a monument to Samson. Built in the 16th century, it was renovated by Sultan Abdulhamid in 1893.

Five hundred metres further west along Al-Widha, a road on the right leads down to the **Mosque of Al-Sayeed Hashem**. This 19th-century mosque is named after the Prophet Mohammed's great grandfather, a trader who used to visit Gaza every year and is supposedly buried in the grounds. A mosque, school and hostel for itinerant traders has stood here since the 12th century, though the white-domed structure seen today dates from 1850 and was built upon the orders of the Ottoman sultan Abdul Majid. Other than Fridays and during prayer times there shouldn't be any problem looking around, but for a better view of the mosque and the octagonal minaret – a feature that it shares with the Grand Mosque (see below) – ask if you can climb up to the roof of one of the houses opposite.

From the mosque head back to Sharia Al-Widha, cross over and continue straight on back towards Midan Filasteen. Just before the square, on your left, is a narrow market street that leads down to Gaza's **Great Mosque**.

Al-Jami' Al-Omari Al-Kabir, the Grand Mosque   المسجد العمري الكبير
Closed Friday and during prayers; free
Take your shoes off and leave them in the pigeonholes inside the main door if you want to have a nose around this mosque, the number-one sight in Gaza and a great

source of pride to the people of the city. The sewing machine operators who work in the market opposite the entrance will tell you that the mosque was built between 3,000 and 4,500 years ago. Of course this is something of an exaggeration – the earliest part of the building dates from the early 12th century – though certainly the history of the site is a lengthy one. Indeed, there may well have been a temple on this site dedicated to Marnas about 3,000 years ago, and before that one dedicated to Dagon which, famously, Samson toppled to end both his life and that of his Philistine tormentors. More recently, a 5th-century Byzantine church stood here, then a Norman-style Crusader church, and this forms the bulk of the building today: note the round window above the entrance, and the basilica-style layout. It was converted into a mosque following Saladin's victory in 1187, the minaret, mihrab and minbar replacing the Christian cross and altar. The Mamlukes added the prestigious library, which now contains more than 20,000 books; the Ottomans renovated and extended the site; and the High Islamic Council carried out further work in 1926, largely to repair damage caused by British bombing during World War I. Other renovations are recorded on the massive front doors.

The mosque, like so many others in Palestine, is named after the man who conquered Palestine for the Muslims in 637, **Omar Ibn Al-Khattab**. Its interior is a rather drab white, the only splash of colour provided by the sunlight shining through the stained-glass window above the entrance. The minbar and mihrab lie in the gloomy southeastern corner. Look out too for the Jewish **menorah** (seven-pronged candelabrum) scratched into one of the pillars, a detail which had the Israelis whooping with joy in the mistaken belief that this mosque was originally a synagogue. Scholars have dismissed this claim, however, arguing that the pillar was probably shipped over from Alexandria with its decoration already etched on. Next door to the mosque is a dark, atmospheric **souq** devoted almost entirely to gold jewellery, providing a neat juxtaposition of the commercial with the spiritual.

Transport from Gaza City

Buses to Khan Younnis (NIS2) leave every hour from Midan Filasteen, or you can take a servis from the same place for NIS3, many of which continue on to Rafah (NIS4). There are no buses to the Erez border, but you can catch a servis from Midan Shujayyah for NIS2; the taxis are frequent in the morning, but peter out by mid-afternoon.

SOUTH OF GAZA CITY

The two major roads heading south pass by a number of refugee camps, olive groves and, if you take the coastal road for some of the way, miles and miles of palm-fringed **beaches**. Twelve kilometres south of Gaza, and set a little way back from the coast near the refugee camp of **Nuseirat**, the remains of **three churches** dating from the 5th to the 8th centuries have been found, each built over the ruins of the last. Discovered during the Israeli occupation, the churches were once part of a large **monastic complex**, traces of which have only recently been found. It is estimated that the monastery grounds stretch for over 9,000m², of which only 5,000m² has so far been excavated.

Nobody knows for certain what caused the destruction of the three churches, though it's not unreasonable to assume that an earthquake destroyed the oldest some time in the late 5th century, while the demise of the second can probably be attributed to Islamic invasion in the 7th. At the moment the site is only partly excavated, and officially closed to the public. Turn up, however, and one of the on-site archaeologists will be glad to show you around. Don't expect to be astounded, but there are a couple of mosaics which, while no competition for those near Jabaliya, are worth a close inspection. Ask to be shown the cross-shaped baptismal font too, and the monastery's wine press, and take a close look at some of the pillars: they're made of granite that's come all the way from Aswan.

If you're on the coastal road you'll continue past the prettiest stretch of coastline in Gaza and on to **Der El-Balah**, the smallest of Gaza's refugee camps with only 16,000 people. The coastal route ends here: though the road continues, it runs into the Jewish settlement of **Nahal Qatif**, and is therefore closed off. The main inland road continues, however, to the market town of Khan Younnis.

KHAN YOUNNIS خان يونس

Gaza's second city is probably the most conservative in Palestine. Burqa-clad women are the norm rather than the exception here, and most of the men sport wiry black beards. (How ironic, then, that it lies on the eastern edge of Gaza's largest Jewish settlement, Neve Deqalim.) The city derives its name from the 14th-century **khan** that still stands in its centre, and which in turn was named after a local Mamluke official. With locals more concerned about their Jewish settler neighbours and where their next meal is coming from than preserving ancient monuments, the khan has been allowed to fall into ruin, and little survives save for part of its facade that today lines one side of the town square.

But the few tourists who venture this far south of Gaza City don't come to look at the khan. Nor indeed do they come to look over the small **museum** in the **Nasser Red Cross Hospital**, a 15-minute walk west of the khan on the way to the beach, which examines the plight of the refugees, the traditional Palestinian way of life and the work of the hospital. It's worthy but, though it pains me to say it, a tad dull too.

No, the only reason to come to Khan Younnis is to visit the **Wednesday market**. Simply put, if it's not a Wednesday morning, don't bother coming to Khan Younnis; if it is, however, don't miss it. Sure, you can see many of the same traders in the Friday market in Gaza and in Rafah on a Saturday; but in Khan Younnis, the number of traders seems to double, the characters become more colourful and their wares more exotic. Locals will warn you that the market is dangerous, and I have heard stories of items going missing in the crush of people; so bring as little as possible and keep what you have close to you. The locals are a little camera-shy too, so ask before taking photos. The **livestock section**, filled with bunny rabbits, chickens, geese, pigeons, the odd camel or two and, of course, the long-suffering donkey, is the most fascinating part – though be prepared for the jostling crowds.

Orientation

It's easiest to think of Khan Younnis as a square. From Gaza, most servis taxis drop passengers off by the main roundabout on the northeastern corner of this square, while servis taxis to and from Rafah call in at the southwestern corner. Joining the two is the market, which runs along the eastern and southern sides of this square (and beyond), while the khan lies on the western side of the square.

Tour guides

If you'd like to explore the town in greater detail, there is an Egyptian-based tour company just to the north of the Khan called **Quick Trade and Tourism Development**, who can guide you around for about US$15 per day.

RAFAH رفح

At the very southern end of Gaza, the barren dusty landscape becomes even more barren and dusty as it approaches the Sinai, finally fulfilling the official description of 'desert'. It is here that you'll find the dusty town of Rafah, a small, pleasant but sweltering oasis nestling right against the Egyptian border.

To the west of town lies one of the more absurd and tragic results of the Israeli-Arab conflict. As part of the Camp David Accords, Israel agreed to return the Sinai to Egypt. For convenience, the two sides decided to use as their border the one that had existed before 1948, forgetting that since then a huge **refugee camp** had grown up near Rafah – a camp which, following the war of '67, sprawled over both sides of the border. Thus, overnight, Rafah's refugee camp was split completely in half, with houses, offices and roads that lay on the new border cleft in two. Most tragically, many families were also divided by the border so that, though they lived but a few yards from each other, they no longer lived in the same country, and were prevented by the new border from seeing each other.

Despite promises by all the relevant authorities to end this farcical situation, the camp remains divided to this day, with 3,000 or so of Rafah's total refugee population still living in Egypt (in a village dubbed **Canada** after the country of origin of the UN troops stationed there during the 1950s). The situation has given rise to Gaza's answer to the Wailing Wall, the so-called **Shouting Fence**. Every morning members of these divided families meet at the border to shout their messages across to each other – a situation that would almost be funny if it wasn't so sad.

Another strange geographical anomaly lies on the coast near Rafah. The **Swedish Village** is a fishing port for refugees, constructed for them by the Swedish government in the 1950s, that lies right in the heart of the Jewish settlements, cut off from the rest of town by Israeli military posts. You can visit, though make sure you're not mistaken for a settler.

In keeping with the semi-surreal nature of Rafah, the PNA, for reasons best known to themselves, have decided that this town would make an ideal base for their **international airport**, which lies about 2km to the east of town. Servis taxis from Rafah leave from the junction of Othman Ebn Affan Street and Abu Badwa Al Sidiq Street, one block south of the town's main square (identifiable by the star in the middle of it).

Gaza Airport مطار دولي

Palestine's international airport is small but perfectly formed, providing a little drop of jet-setting glamour in an area that sorely needs it. It was designed, as you can probably tell by the profusion of patterned tiles and elegant arches, by a Moroccan who based his design closely on the international airport at Casablanca. Opened on November 24 1998, its first flights arrived in the New Year, and seven international carriers now operate a regular service to Rafah.

Facilities in the airport remain basic. There's one **bank**, the Arabland, and no tourist office, though one is promised soon. There's only one **taxi company**, too, called **EMAD**. It closes for business at 20.00, but that shouldn't be a problem as most flights have arrived well before then. The approximate taxi tariff is: Gaza, NIS50; Khan Younnis, NIS30; Rafah, NIS15; Erez border NIS70. There are, however, cheaper ways to get into town. You can hail a cab from the road to Rafah (NIS1.5), then catch a servis from there, or, if you turn up at the right time, you can catch the daily bus to Gaza. This bus is meant to be for airport workers only, but they usually have room and for NIS2 you can join them. (Incidentally, if you're travelling to the airport, the bus leaves Gaza's Midan Filasteen or Midan

Shujayyah at 07.30. If you're going straight to Egypt, a road runs directly from the airport to the border.

Leaving Palestine at Rafah

It's important, if travelling to the border from Gaza City by taxi, to tell the driver that you want to go to Rafah border (*Masr*, Arabic for 'Egypt'), and not Rafah town (*Rafah balad*) which lies 2km away. Those travelling by servis taxi or bus will go via the town anyway, then catch a second taxi (NIS1.5) to the border from there. At the border there's a **departure tax** of NIS108.5, and an **Egyptian entry tax** (currently E£10). On the other side, servis taxis leave for El Arish, Qantara and Cairo; if the last Cairo taxi has left, travel to one of the other two and catch a servis to the Egyptian capital from there.

Jerusalem

4

'Jerusalem is a festival and a lamentation. Its song is a sigh across the ages, a delicate, robust, mournful psalm at the great junction of spiritual cultures. Here among the constant ruins and rebuilding of civilizations lies the coexistence of diversity and intolerance.'
David K Shipler, Arab and Jew – Wounded Spirits in a Promised Land

'....Jerusalem was a squalid town, which every Semitic religion had made holy. Christians and Mohammedans came there on pilgrimages to the shrines of its past, and some Jews looked to it for the political future of their race. These united forces of the past and the future were so strong that the city almost failed to have a present.'
Lawrence of Arabia, Seven Pillars of Wisdom

Derived from the Hebrew Yerushalayim, the name Jerusalem translates approximately as 'City of Peace'. We can only assume this is a very early example of that famous Jewish sense of humour, for it is difficult to think of another city that has been besieged, conquered, pillaged and plundered as often as the Holy City, its inhabitants persecuted and slaughtered, its buildings defaced and destroyed.

A clue as to why this should be the case can be gleaned from the Arabic name for the city: Al-Quds – 'The Holy'. As a city sacred to the three major forms of monotheism, it has become the spiritual centre for over a third of the planet's population. For Jews, it is the location of Solomon's famous **temple**, built to house the Ark of the Covenant. Jerusalem is mentioned no fewer than 660 times in the Old Testament alone; Zion, a name synonymous with Jerusalem, occurs another 154 times. For Christians it was the venue of **Jesus' crucifixion** and subsequent resurrection. When the earth was still considered flat, the Christian cartographers of the Byzantine era drew Jerusalem as the middle of the world, every other city, no matter how big or important, was reduced to a mere satellite. For Muslims, this is the so-called 'furthest place' mentioned in the Koran, the earthly destination of the famous **Night Flight** taken by Mohammed. Before Mecca and Medina assumed greater importance, Mohammed's followers, on his orders, used to pray towards Jerusalem, and it remains the third most sacred city in Islam.

It comes as little surprise, therefore, that for the last couple of millennia all of these faiths have fought to wrest control of Jerusalem from their rivals, committing inhuman atrocities in the name of their God as they did so.

Things are a little quieter for the 600,000 souls who call Jerusalem home today, but that's only because the two main rivals have cleft the city completely into two, West Jerusalem for the Israelis and East Jerusalem for the Arabs. (For simplicity, I've ignored for the moment the manifold minority populations: the Armenians,

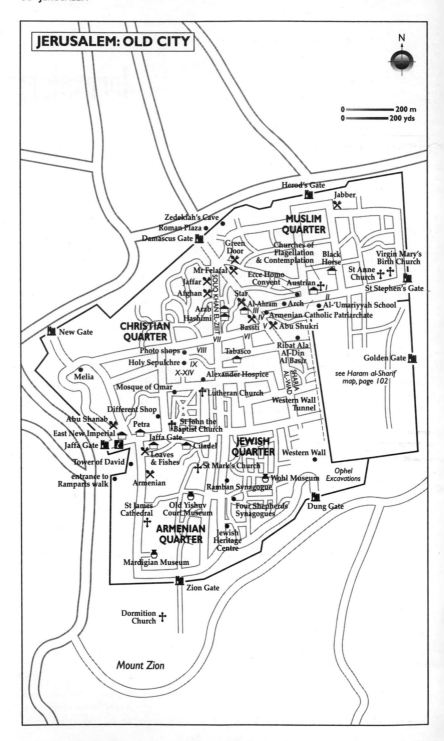

JERUSALEM: OLD CITY

N

0 — 200 m
0 — 200 yds

Herod's Gate

Jabber

MUSLIM QUARTER

Zedekiah's Cave

Roman Plaza

Damascus Gate

Green Door

Churches of Flagellation & Contemplation

Black Horse

Virgin Mary's Birth Church

St Anne Church

Mr Felafal

Ecce Homo Convent

Austrian

St Stephen's Gate

Jaffar

Afghan

Star

Al-Ahram

Arch

Al-'Umariyyah School

Arab Hashimi

Bassti

Abu Shukri

Armenian Catholic Patriarchate

CHRISTIAN QUARTER

New Gate

Ribat Ala Al-Din Al Basir

Golden Gate

Photo shops

Tabasco

Holy Sepulchre

Alexander Hospice

see Haram al-Sharif map, page 102

Melia

Mosque of Omar

Lutheran Church

Western Wall Tunnel

Different Shop

Petra

St John the Baptist Church

Abu Shanab

East New Imperial

Jaffa Gate

Citadel

JEWISH QUARTER

Western Wall

Jaffa Gate

Loaves & Fishes

Tower of David

St Mark's Church

Wohl Museum

Ophel Excavations

entrance to Ramparts walk

Armenian

Ramban Synagogue

St James Cathedral

Old Yishuv Court Museum

Four Shepherds Synagogues

Dung Gate

ARMENIAN QUARTER

Jewish Heritage Centre

Mardigian Museum

Zion Gate

Dormition Church

Mount Zion

Syrians, Ethiopians, Greeks, Russians and so forth.) There's no border to demarcate the two sides, but the dividing line between the two – the so-called **Green Line** first established as a border between Jordan and Israel in 1948 – is obvious. **West Jerusalem** has the air of an affluent European city, albeit one with Hebrew signs and a proliferation of kosher restaurants. **East Jerusalem**, on the other hand, is a slice of unrestrained Arabia.

Despite the increasing presence of fanatical Israeli settlers encroaching into East Jerusalem, and the large numbers of Arab workers employed by their Jewish neighbours in West Jerusalem, the two sides pretty much keep themselves to themselves. But there's one part of the city whose ownership they simply cannot agree upon, and probably never will: the **Old City**. Formerly part of East Jerusalem, and still containing a massive Palestinian majority, the Old City, home to the holiest sites in Judaism and Christianity and the third most sacred shrine in Islam, is the most beautiful, controversial and fascinating part of this beautiful, fascinating and controversial city. This part of the metropolis is not so much steeped in history as suffocating under it. Every road, every alley, every smooth-surfaced flagstone and rough-hewn brick is ingrained and scarred with the events of the past two thousand years.

However, the Old City is most definitely not a museum; it's a living, breathing, sweating self-contained city where the ancient and holy sites form a mere backdrop to the voluble and passionate lives of the people who live and work here. And in spite of its rampant, tourist-oriented commercialism, the ubiquitous presence of boyish Israeli soldiers with very big guns and the constant simmering tension that always threatens to spill over into violence, it remains an endlessly absorbing place that you'll want to return to again and again.

This being a comprehensive guidebook, we cover both sides of Jerusalem, West and East. However, as it's a guidebook to Palestine, we make no apologies for concentrating more on those areas with a Palestinian majority, East Jerusalem and the Old City, particularly as regards hotels and restaurants. But don't worry, for you will miss out on nothing: apart from the Israel and Holocaust Museums, a couple of minor sights and the city's nightclubs (all of which we describe), everything of interest to the tourist lies in the Old City and East Jerusalem and is covered in considerable depth in this book.

HISTORY
David's Jerusalem

It could be argued that the tempestuous 3,000 years suffered by the Holy City were caused by one single act· the installation of the **Ark of the Covenant** following David's capture of the city from the Jebusites (relatives of the Canaanites) in 1000BC. Before that moment, Jerusalem (whose name incidentally, originally meant 'The Foundation of the God Shalem' and had nothing to do with 'peace' at all) was just an unremarkable city founded in 2600BC by the Jebusites. True, the city was large enough to merit a mention in the Egyptian execration texts of the 18th century BC, and again in the Egyptian Amarna texts of the 14th century BC (see page 179). Jerusalem also crops up in Genesis, where it is ruled by a king named Melchizedek and is called simply Salem. However, lying away from major trade routes, Jerusalem never had the opportunity to expand as much as other cities at this time.

David's choice of capital was probably a sound one: though part of the territory conquered by the Israelite tribe of Benjamin, the city, with its population of Amorites, Hittites and Jebusites, was left alone. It thus served David's need for a centrally located city independent of the twelve tribes. To ensure all the tribes recognised this city as the capital he moved the Ark, to which all tribes gave allegiance, to a threshing floor just north of the city. David's son, Solomon, gave the ark the home it deserved by building a huge **temple** over the threshing floor and linking it to the rest of the city by a palace, thus doubling the size of Jerusalem and unwittingly advertising the city's wealth to would-be invaders at the same time.

Those invaders did indeed pour in for much of the next thousand years. Now the capital of the Kingdom of Judaea following the division in the old Israelite kingdom, Jerusalem survived the Assyrian invasion that destroyed the northern kingdom of Israel in 721BC, but only after a four-year siege. King Hezekiah built an extra wall to protect the Israeli refugees who had settled by the existing walls outside the city, but even these extra fortifications proved useless against the **Babylonian conquest** of 586BC, an invasion that led to the destruction of Solomon's Temple and much else. The Israelites who returned from exile under Persian rule in 538BC rebuilt the temple under the direction of Zerubbabel and the walls under Nehemiah. The dimensions of the rebuilt city were probably no bigger than those of the city of David and Solomon, large enough for a few thousand people only, and the temple was a simpler, more modest imitation of Solomon's masterpiece. A proper refortification of the city began during the hiatus in the Hellenistic period caused by the Maccabean Revolt (160–134BC), and was carried out by Jonathan Maccabeus.

It was left to the builder king himself, Herod, to restore the glory of the Holy City fully. Amongst his architectural achievements were a fortress called **Antonia** (after his boss Mark Anthony) by the Temple's northwestern corner, an amphitheatre (not located), a theatre, a hippodrome and a palace in the upper city protected by three great towers, one of which, the **Tower of Phasaelis** (now part of the Citadel), surpassed in height the Pharos of Alexandria (a lighthouse and one of the Seven Wonders of the Ancient World). His crowning achievement was the rebuilding of the Temple which, if anything, outdid Solomon's majestic efforts of 900 years before. Water for Herod's capital was brought into the city along great aqueducts: one that ran from Arrub via Birket El-Sultan to the city was over 67km in length. Yet in spite of all this building, Herod didn't expand the city walls, and much of today's Old City would have lain outside of the city of Herod's day. This includes the area around the Holy Sepulchre, which most experts agree was at that time a disused quarry known as **Golgotha** – thus corresponding perfectly with the description of Jesus' crucifixion and burial given in John 19: 17–42.

Without the diplomatic skills of Herod the Jews found it difficult to abide Roman rule, and after his death they rebelled twice, in AD66 and 132; Jerusalem was left in ruins both times. After the second uprising, known as the Bar Kochba rebellion, the Romans banned the Jews from their holy city altogether, razed the city (temple included, but excluding the Tower of Phasaelis) and rebuilt a pagan town in its stead, which they called **Aelia Capitolina**.

Byzantine Jerusalem and the Islamic invasion

For three hundred years Aelia Capitolina remained a medium-sized city in an obscure province of an empire in trouble. When that empire finally split into two and the eastern half, the Byzantine Empire, converted to Christianity, Jerusalem, as the epicentre of the religion, enjoyed a new lease of life. It became a major place of pilgrimage after Constantine's mother, the sprightly septuagenarian Helena, toured around the Holy Land building churches on a number of important sites, including that of the Holy Sepulchre over the supposed site of Christ's crucifixion and resurrection. A bloodless invasion by the Muslims in AD637 – the conqueror, Omar Ibn Al-Khattab, recognised Christians as fellow 'Peoples of the Book' and promised their safety if they handed over the keys to the city – introduced the graceful lines of Islamic architecture into the cramped confines of the Old City, beginning with the two mosques on the Temple Mount. The harmony between the three religions was disrupted by the mad Fatimid Caliph, Al-Hakim (966–1013), who revived the ancient art of religious persecution, ordering the Christians to wear heavy wooden crosses. The **Seljuk Turks** (1071) were similarly prejudiced, barring Christians from the Holy City altogether.

News of these atrocities filtered steadily back to Europe's predominantly Christian population. In response, they organised a Crusade to win back the Holy Land from the Infidel, and on June 7 1099 the knights of the **First Crusade** gathered at the Gates of Jerusalem. Legend has it that one of the priests who accompanied them dreamt that if they all marched round the city walls barefoot three times, the city would be theirs. This they did, and just five days later the walls were breached and the European Christians entered the city (presumably with their shoes back on). After only two days they had put 40,000 Muslim men, women, and children to the sword; the Jews were burnt to death. Godfrey de Bouillon was pronounced ruler of the Kingdom of Jerusalem, and one year later on Christmas day his brother, Baldwin, was crowned King of Jerusalem (a title his brother had always refused out of piety).

The Crusaders were to last 87 years before the Muslims, under the guiding influence of Saladin, returned the city to Muslim rule once more. Saladin also reintroduced the city to a level of religious tolerance last seen two centuries before, allowing Christians and Jews the freedom to worship (though at the cost of greater taxes). The **Mamlukes** who followed him into power enhanced the beauty of the city with their own, distinctive style of architecture. They lost out to the **Ottomans** in 1516. Apart from a brief frenzy of building under Suleyman, including the construction of the walls of the city that you see today, the Ottomans allowed Jerusalem to fall into disrepair.

World War I

Following the Arab Revolt of 1917, General Allenby arrived at Jaffa Gate on December 11 1917 to liberate the city from 400 years of Ottoman-inspired doldrums. The tension between Arabs and the Jewish immigrants flooding into the Holy Land was already running high by this stage, and the ownership of Jerusalem – which was by now growing way beyond the confines of Suleyman's walls – was at the forefront of their arguments. In the short term it became part of the British Mandate of Palestine, though this proved to be a temporary solution only.

As neither side, Arab or Jew, could stomach the possibility of a future without Jerusalem, the UN, as part of its partition plan, decided to turn Jerusalem into an **international city** belonging to neither one side nor the other. Ideal on paper, this plan failed in practice as both sides jostled for greater control. Whereas previously the two communities lived together, now entire neighbourhoods became polarised – either wholly Jewish or wholly Palestine – with the minority community in a neighbourhood forced out by the majority. Soon after the British pulled out in May 1948, Jerusalem was divided, with the Israelis to the west and the Jordanian army to the east (including the Old City). The **Green Line** and a whole trough of **No-Man's Land** ran between the two sides. The Palestinians got nothing, and still had nothing after the Israelis had seized control of the whole city in 1967.

Today, the city remains a major bone of contention, and probably the single most important obstacle to a final solution to the troubles. Israelis see Jerusalem as their 'eternal, united capital', and have the powerful support of the Americans. Palestinians regard the city as their capital too, while the international community as a whole, refusing to recognise Israel's rule over East Jerusalem, maintains consulates in both East Jerusalem (for the Palestinians) and West Jerusalem/ Tel Aviv (for the Israelis). To strengthen their hold, however, the Israelis have expanded their territory via Jewish settlements right up to the municipal boundaries of Ramallah and Bethlehem, and have encircled East Jerusalem with three rings of settlements, encouraged by the policies of former Prime Minister Binyamin Netanyahu. The Oslo Accords have proved ineffective in stopping them. One can only hope, for the sake of peace if nothing else, that Ehud Barak takes a more enlightened line.

ORIENTATION AND PRACTICALITIES
Orientation
The city is divided into Palestinian East and Israeli West Jerusalem by the **Green Line**, an invisible border that hugs the western and northern walls of the Old City as far as the Damascus Gate Servis park, where it heads north along the main four-lane highway that the Israelis call Hel HaHandasa, and the Palestinians call simply Road Number One. (You'll find many road and place names in Jerusalem have at least two names to reflect its divided status.) The **Old City** lies in the southeastern corner of metropolitan Jerusalem entirely within the Palestinian part of the city. Apart from Road Number One, three other major roads radiate north from the city walls. Running from Jaffa Gate is Jaffa Road, the main thoroughfare through Israeli **West Jerusalem**. At the road's northwestern extremity, 3km from the Old City, is the **inter-city bus station**. If you're arriving by bus from Ben Gurion airport, or anywhere else in Israel, this is where you'll be dropped off. Bus number 6 travels along Jaffa Road to the Old City's Jaffa Gate, number 27 to the Damascus Gate.

The other two major roads heading north from the Old City, Sharia Nablus and Sharia Salah El-Din, run roughly parallel to each other through Palestinian **East Jerusalem**. Between the two lies the **Central Bus Station**, terminal of buses serving the West Bank, while to the west of Sharia Nablus, opposite the Old City's Damascus Gate, is the city's main **servis station** (servis taxis are more commonly-called 'sheruts' in Jerusalem). A second terminus, the **Nablus Road Bus Station** opposite the Garden Tomb on Sharia Nablus, is useful for buses to Ramallah.

Maps
The Arab Hotel Association's free map of Bethlehem and Jerusalem, available from East Jerusalem's larger hotels, has the best map of the Old City and is very user friendly, though is a little sketchy on West Jerusalem; conversely, the Israeli tourist office's map rather ignores East Jerusalem. The jewellers H Stern inside Jaffa Gate also produce maps of the Old City.

Public transport
Except for a few sights in the outer suburbs, you'll rarely need to use public transport to get around. Details of bus services are given where necessary in the chapter. For Israeli buses, fares are a standard NIS4.50; for Palestinian buses, which leave from the Central Bus Station (CBS), fares vary but are no more than NIS2.

Practicalities

The Palestinian authorities have yet to set up a tourist office in Jerusalem, probably because of the furore such a move would cause. Because of this, the best place to glean information about sights in Jerusalem (and the West Bank) is from the ever-helpful **Christian Information Centre** (Mon–Sat 09.00–13.00) on Omar Ibn Al-Khattab Square. The staff's knowledge of the Holy Land is first rate, and they have plenty of useful leaflets on sights and local transport. On the other side of the square by the Jaffa Gate is an **Israeli Tourist Office**, and there's a larger one in West Jerusalem by the municipality (Sun–Thurs 09.00–16.00; Friday 09.00–13.00. Sat closed). A little further up the road lies West Jerusalem's **general post office**, with an **exchange booth** that offers the best rates I could find in the city. East Jerusalem's post office (Sun–Thurs 08.00–18.00, Fri 08.00–12.00, Sat 08.00–14.00) at the southern end of Salah El-Din also has an exchange counter, but it seems to be always closed. (A third post office, with no exchange facilities, lies opposite the Tower of David.) Private exchange counters can be found further up Salah El-Din, including the reliable Aladdin; most, if not all, charge no commission these days, and nearly all of them offer the same rate too, though do shop around a little just to make sure. For **cash machines** you'll have to visit the shopping centre in West Jerusalem (there are none on the Palestinian side); the HaPaolim Bank, 200m north of the post office on Jaffa Road, seems to accept most major cards.

At 74 Christian Quarter Street in the Old City, the Different Shop (daily, 08.00–20.00, closed Sunday) has two **internet** terminals and charges a standard NIS6 for 15 minutes. This place stands out on two counts: not only is it the only internet centre in the Old City, it's also the only one with a 'frequent surfer scheme': if you plan on staying in Jerusalem a while, you can register with the manager, Ghassan Kattou'a, and after every ten sessions you get one free. Outside of the Old City, Strudels (Sun–Fri 10.00 to late, Sat 15.00 to late), at 11 Monbaz Street in the Russian compound, was the city's first internet bar and remains the most popular. They charge NIS6 for 15 minutes; during happy hour you can get a beer and 15 minutes on the computer for NIS14. Also in the Russian Compound, 150m down the hill, the Netcafé at 9 Helene Hamalka (daily, 10.00 until late) boasts the fastest connection in town and live music on Wednesdays, Thursdays and Saturdays.

There are a couple of decent **photographic shops** in the Old City, Studio Varouj at 36 Al-Khanka Road and Elia Studios 100m above them. However, I find the most reliable and best value store to be Klik Photo, on the Jaffa Road in West Jerusalem.

Finally, many countries have their own cultural centres; ask at your embassy for details. The **British Council** (Mon–Thurs 07.30–15.30, Fri 07.30–13.30) just a few steps west of Orient House in East Jerusalem, is one of the best, and has internet facilities: at just NS2.5 for 15 minutes it's the cheapest in town.

The **UNRWA office** in Jerusalem lies almost exactly on the Green Line on Karl Netter Street in Sheikh Jarrah (tel: 02 589400). Like the offices in Gaza, they have plenty of information, brochures and maps detailing the success of their work, though again they are reluctant to allow sightseers on to their tours of the refugee camps.

Tour guides

There are a number of independent operators offering guided walking tours around the sights of Jerusalem. Two of the best are **Alternative Tours** (see page 92) and **Zion Tours**, which offer a variety of different excursions exploring various parts of the city. If you just want an overview of the Old City, their thrice-daily walk around the four quarters (US$10 for 3 hours) is one of the most interesting. Visit their offices opposite the Tower of David (tel: 02 287866). **Archaeological Seminars** (tel: 02 6273515) are an Israeli company specialising in the excavations of the Old City and beyond. As well as offering the chance to join one of the archaeological digs, they also organise walking tours at US$16 a time, including trips through the **Western Wall Tunnel** (Sun, Tues and Wed at 09.30). The **city council** organises free walking tours every Saturday at 10.00, leaving from the City Hall Complex at 32 Jaffa Road. They cover a different area of the city every week – ask at the tourist office for details, or just turn up on the Saturday.

For an alternative view of the Old City, however, try to track down **Ali Jiddah**. Born in Chad and a former resident of the Old City's African Quarter, Ali Jiddah has a history that's almost as interesting as the city in which he now works. Ali is a former member of the political and terrorist organisation, the PFLP. As part of a gang responsible for a bomb that injured nine people, Ali was sentenced to almost twenty years in jail. Having served his time, he now offers alternative tours of the city where he grew up, concentrating less on the history and religion and more on the current political situation. In the mornings he tends to hang around by the Jaffa Gate, or you can call him on 052 438109.

Finally, if you wish to explore the part of Jerusalem that lies outside of the Old City, consider buying a ticket on **Egged bus 99**. This bus travels throughout the new city from the Knesset, Israel's parliament, to Mount Scopus in East Jerusalem and back again in a big loop that takes in most of the sights of the new city. There's on-board commentary of the sights en route (though if the majority of passengers are Israeli I'm afraid it will be in Hebrew), and you can get out and rejoin the bus wherever and whenever you want. Tickets cost NIS20 for one day, NIS30 for two; buses leave from Mamilla Street near Jaffa Gate every hour; ring 02 5304422 for reservations and timetables.

Tours to Palestine

Very, very few companies specialise in visiting towns and cities in the West Bank, though a number of companies combine a trip to the Israeli archaeological site of Masada with a trip to Jericho and surrounding sights, a lightning tour that's really for masochists only. For other Palestinian towns, there are only a couple of tour companies to choose from: **PACE** in Ramallah (see page 133) and **Alternative Tours** (tel: 052 864205), run from the Jerusalem Hotel near the Garden Tomb. As well as a three-hour walking tour around the Old City, they offer twice-weekly one-day tours of **Hebron** (NIS60) a weekly day trip of **Ramallah and Nablus** (NIS90) and, perhaps best of all, the first regular tour of the **Gaza Strip** (twice weekly, NIS130). Unfortunately, they require a minimum of five people to make

---

HOSPITALS AND EMERGENCY SERVICES

For minor ailments, read the advice given on page 51. The *Jerusalem Post* usually contain a list of late-opening pharmacies. There are a number of hospitals in Jerusalem, the best of which is probably the Hadassah (tel: 02 6776040) or the Augusta Victoria (tel: 02 6287122), both on Mount Scopus.

Important Jerusalem telephone numbers

Information	144	Police	100
Ambulance	101	Fire Service	102 or 02 6282222

it worth their while, so you may have to wait if you wish to join one of their less popular trips. They also offer half-day tours around the **refugee camps** of the West Bank (NIS35), which I've heard are fascinating.

ACCOMMODATION

I know I'm biased, but I reckon that the Palestinian part of Jerusalem – that's to say, the Old City and East Jerusalem – has the best hotels. At the budget end, the Old City hostels are cheaper and more popular than those in West Jerusalem, whilst in the luxury bracket, at the very top of the scale, the **American Colony Hotel** and its rival, the **Christmas**, are stylish where West Jerusalem's David Hotel is merely flash.

Most hostels have a kitchen and free lockers for guests to use, and some have free tea and coffee too. Student cards may get you an extra few shekels off. Hotels include breakfast in the price. Outside the main holiday periods (Christmas, Easter) there shouldn't be any need to book ahead except for the more popular places.

The Old City

I have it on good authority (ie: the manager) that the **Tabasco Hostel**, just off Souk Khan el-Zeit at Akabat Tekieh 8 (tel: 02 6281101) is the only Palestinian-owned hotel in the Old City. Coincidentally (or maybe not), this is also the most popular place within the city walls. Staying in the roof dorm (NIS12) is, to be honest, little short of purgatory: 24 people, two toilets, one shower and cats – lots and lots of cats – all contained within the same 150 square yards. There is a good atmosphere up there, however: I guess you could compare it to wartime Britain, where the squalid conditions engendered a kind of solidarity between those forced to live in them. For those with standards, however, the dorms downstairs are smaller, cleaner, brighter and more habitable. Free lockers, information, tours and a great bar/café in the basement keep the punters more than happy.

A few steps down the souq yet quite a way up the quality scale, the **Hashimi** at Suq Khan El-Zeit 73 (tel: 02 6284410), is unrecognisable from its former incarnation as a hovel for budget travellers. It still caters for the same clientele, but its recent and thorough renovation has made it positively charming now. It charges a wee bit more than the other hostels – the equivalent of US$5 (currently NIS20) for a night in a ten-bed dorm, NIS100–150 for the en suite private rooms – but the extra is worth it: as well as the usual facilities (free use of the kitchen, free tea, a safe for valuables and so on) the Hashimi's upstairs lounge affords a great view across to the Dome of the Rock. For a glimpse of how the Hashimi used to look before the facelift, check out the creaking **Al-Arab**, just down the road at number (tel: 02 6283537). To be honest it's not too bad, has all the mod cons (kitchen, safe, free tea) and is in a prime position. Unfortunately, I've always found it a little grimy and soulless too. However, if every last agorot is vital, the roof dorm here is, at 12NIS, the cheapest in town.

At first you may find the **Al-Ahram** (tel: 02 6280926) a bit of a curiosity. Located in a prime spot on the Via Dolorosa, with a friendly manager, Gebal, and rooms, though a little scruffy, very cheap (NIS15/12 for a bed in the covered-roof dorm, NIS25/20 inside, and private rooms between NIS65–85), and with a kitchen and safe for residents to use, you may ask yourself why it's so empty here. Then the call to prayer from the abutting minaret starts to holler (the beds on the roof are less than five metres from the speakers), and it all makes sense. Pre-dawn wailing apart, it's a great place.

There's another cluster of hotels and hostels by Jaffa Gate. The **Hotel East New Imperial** (tel: 02 6282261), up an alley off Omar Ibn Al-Khattab Square, is a charming, rambling old place with some delightfully eccentric members of staff, but is unfortunately let down by some slightly tatty rooms. If you're going to stay here, try to get a room overlooking David's Tower. The ramshackle **Petra Hostel** at 1 David Street (tel: 02 6286618) is the city's oldest, having been around in one incarnation or another since the mid-19th century. The place is extremely popular with rooftop sleepers (NIS15), some of whom have their own tent up here. Rooms (NIS120 for a double) are a little tired, but overall it's OK.

Probably the best-value hostel in this area, however, is the **Jaffa Gate Hostel** (tel: 02 6276402), tucked away in an alley behind the Christian Information Centre. The rooms are kept very clean, the staff are friendly and the view from the roof over the Christian Quarter is excellent (private rooms NIS120–150, haggling allowed; try to get a room upstairs). My only grumble is the breakfast, which at NIS30 is way overpriced, though you have the option not to take it. The **Citadel** (tel: 02 6274375), a little further back at 20 Mark's Street, has some wonderful refurbished rooms (NIS100–140), and offers free use of the kitchen and free tea and coffee. It's let down a little, however, by some of the unfriendliest staff I've ever encountered.

Back down in the Muslim quarter, the **Black Horse** (tel: 02 6276011) at Aqabat Darwish 28 lies in my favourite part of the Old City, the subdued residential district. The dorms are huge (22 beds) and dank, the atmosphere is a little miserable (though they do have a safe and free use of the kitchen, as well as free tea and coffee), and the price is fair (NIS20/18 in the dorm; NIS70/80 sgl/dbl). To the west, back on the Via Dolorosa at number 37, the **Austrian** (tel: 02 6274636) is the oldest (established 1863) and my favourite of the Christian-run **hospices** in the Old City. The building has the austere presence of a consulate, is as clean as a hospital and as tranquil as a convent; not surprising, really, as it has been all of these at some stage in its history. The view from its roof will make your jaw drop. The rooms are clean and comfortable (US$15/50 dorm/dbl) and, though doors close at 22.00, keys are available to residents.

East Jerusalem

There are a couple more hostels outside the Old City that are worth a mention. The **Cairo** (tel: 02 6277216) at 21 Sharia Nablus has recently re-opened under new management. It's a bit spartan and bare, but is in a great spot just up from the Nablus Road Bus Station, and good value too at just NIS20 for a dorm bed, NIS15 for a spot on the roof. Opposite the Damascus Gate by the servis station there's the **Faisal** (tel: 02 6287502), which I've always found rather empty and dull but which has a ferociously loyal following amongst hardened backpackers. Dorms are NIS20, including free tea and coffee, and there's a satellite TV in the lounge. A little further up, **Palms** (tel: 02 6273189) is a long-established favourite with dorms (NIS25/20) and private rooms (NIS100/130).

A lot of the hotels near the southern end of Salah El-Din are much of a muchness, though a few stand out. On Sharia Al-Zahra at number 13, the **Azzahra** is a very friendly, smart little place (tel: 02 6282447) where the bow-tied staff will bend over backwards to help. The rooms are a tad plain compared with the stone-clad reception, though they're clean and comfortable enough and all have en-suite bathrooms (US$60/80 sgl/dbl). The staff at the **Capitol** (tel: 02 6282561) at 17 Salah El-Din are also a welcoming bunch, but the rooms, though comfortable, could do with a makeover: entering a bedroom here (US$70/95 sgl/dbl) is like stepping back to the seventies. Opposite the Azzahra, the **National**

Palace at number 4 (tel: 02 6273273) is one of the larger, grander hotels in the area, and the rooftop restaurant is recommended by many. Rooms, all en suite, cost US$50/80 including breakfast.

Back on Sharia Nablus, it seems strange to find a hotel as pretty and relaxing as the **Jerusalem Hotel** (tel: 02 6283282) right next to the noise of the bus station. Originally built by a feudal warlord, the hotel has retained the original shape and layout of the house, while filling it with suitably Arabesque furniture. Each of the rooms is individually furnished and has remote control satellite TV and direct dial phone, and many come with private balconies. As you can probably tell, I love this place as a cheaper but equally atmospheric rival to the American Colony (see below). Prices start at US$68/85 sgl/dbl including breakfast. Further up the hill, the **Pilgrim Guest House** (02 6283302) is part of St George's Cathedral. The best part about this place is the wonderful garden, a most peaceful place to sit and sip tea. The rooms themselves, now modernised to include a TV and phone, are pretty nice too, and were once part of the choir school. Prices, including breakfast, start at US$47/70 sgl/dbl.

For pure, unadulterated splendour, visit the **American Colony**, 150m past St George's Cathedral on the Nablus Road (tel: 02 6279777; email reserv@ amcol.co.il). For over a hundred years now, the American Colony has been immersing discerning travellers in a level of luxury almost unequalled in the Holy Land. The history of how the hotel was founded is a fascinating one. Anna Spafford's early marriage to her lawyer husband was blighted by tragedy. Having lost four daughters in a shipwreck in which she survived, Anna then watched her fifth child, and her only son, die of scarlet fever at the age of four. Instead of being sympathetic, however, the Christian community in which they lived in Chicago, and which Anne's husband had helped to found, blamed their misfortunes as God's way of punishing them for their sins, and decided to excommunicate them. With nowhere else to go, the Spaffords and their two surviving children, along with 12 other members of the community who disagreed with their excommunication, moved to Jerusalem in 1881 in an attempt to find peace. There they bought a large house that had once belonged to a local Muslim dignitary, Huseini Effendi, who had built it for himself and his four wives. By 1902, the house was first used as a hotel when Baron Ustinov, owner of the Park Hotel in Jaffa and grandfather of Peter, asked the American Colony (as they had become known) if he could house his American and European guests there. Community members doubled up while guests slept in their bedrooms, and it was from this humble beginning that the splendid hotel you see today was born.

The descendants of the Spaffords still own and run the hotel. Famous guests who have stayed there down the years include Lawrence of Arabia (and Peter O'Toole, who played him in the film), General Allenby, Malcolm Muggeridge, Graham Greene, Alec Guinness and many, many others, all taking advantage of the salubrious surroundings and the luxurious rooms complete with minibar, cable TV and so on. Of course, you pay for such refinement: standard rooms cost US$140/185 sgl/dbl +15% service charge, while the original rooms of Husseini Effendi and his wives cost US$230/275 +15%.

Opposite the American Colony, the shiny marble **Addar** at 53 Nablus Road (tel: 02 6263111; fax: 02 6260791) is only slightly less luxurious (US$150/175 sgl/dbl), though currently it's surrounded by two massive building sites where two new hotels are being erected. Stiffer opposition to the American Colony is provided by the excellent **Christmas Hotel** (tel: 02 6282588) at 1 Sharia Ali Ibn Abi Taleb, a polished palace of pristine perfection with a beautiful garden. Rooms, at US$78/98 sgl/dbl including TV, minibar, shower and breakfast, are excellent value.

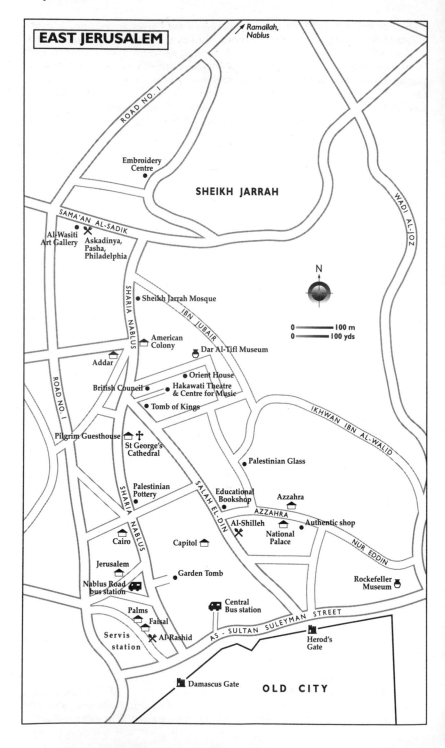

EAST JERUSALEM

↗ Ramallah,
Nablus

ROAD NO. 1

WADI AL-JOZ

SHEIKH JARRAH

Embroidery
Centre

SAMA'AN AL-SADIK

Al-Wasiti
Art Gallery
Askadinya,
Pasha,
Philadelphia

N

SHARIA NABLUS

● Sheikh Jarrah Mosque

IBN JUBAIR

American
Colony

Dar Al-Tifl Museum

Addar

● Orient House

British Council ●

Hakawati Theatre
& Centre for Music

0 ——— 100 m
0 ——— 100 yds

ROAD NO. 1

● Tomb of Kings

IKHWAN IBN AL-WALID

Pilgrim Guesthouse

St George's
Cathedral

● Palestinian Glass

SHARIA NABLUS

Palestinian
Pottery

SALAH EL-DIN

Educational
Bookshop

Azzahra

AZZAHRA

Al-Shilleh

National
Palace

Authentic shop

NUR EDDIN

Cairo

Capitol

Jerusalem

Rockefeller
Museum

Nablus Road
bus station

● Garden Tomb

Palms

Central
Bus station

Faisal

AS - SULTAN SULEYMAN STREET

Servis
station

Al-Rashid

Herod's
Gate

Damascus Gate

OLD CITY

Finally, way to the east and south on the Mount of Olives, at number 53 Mount of Olives Road, is the appropriately named **Mount of Olives** (tel: 02 6284877; fax: 02 5894427). This so-so hotel charges US$42/62 sgl/dbl for B&B, though apart from the excellent view the soulless establishment has little else to recommend it, and is included here for its location more than anything else.

FOOD
There is all 'manna' of different cuisines in Jerusalem, and finding something to suit your taste and budget should be no problem. Though food is somewhat more expensive here than elsewhere in Palestine, it's still cheap, and the quality and variety makes up for this price differential. The tourist offices hold copies of *Jerusalem's Best Menus*, a guide to the best restaurants in the Holy City that's fairly useful. The following account concentrates on the Old City and East Jerusalem, where a number of new restaurants have opened that are just delightful.

The Old City
The anonymous **felafal stall** and coffee shop at 5 Sharia Al-Wad serves the best-value felafals in town, no question. The moustachioed fellow behind the counter (who calls himself Mr Felafal, though his real name's Mahmoud) acts as if he's new to the job, so enthusiastically does he bounce around the place. For NIS3 you get the yummiest felafals in the city; another NIS3 and you can get a cup of orange or carrot juice too. Round the corner to the east, the **Green Door Bakery** (07.00–midnight) is something of an institution amongst travellers, a 200-year-old Ottoman bakery that serves delicious seven-inch pizzas (NIS6), complete with onions, egg, cream cheese and tomato (and meat for a shekel more). Further in the Muslim Quarter, the **Jabber Café**, on the bend of El-Qadiseh 100m south of Herod's Gate, is a large coffee house and the best of its type in the Old City. Their *chai* (NIS3), improved with the addition of mint leaves, is the most refreshing brew in the Old City, and their porch is a great place to people-watch. Opposite is **Uncle Moustache**, with fair to middling felafals.

Of the restaurants on Al-Wad, the **Star Restaurant** is a little overpriced, while the **Pizzaria** (*sic*) **Bassti** is hugely popular with tourists, though their food is overpriced and the staff are often surly. Further down, **Abu Shukri** specialises in producing the Holy Land's tastiest hoummus. It's expensive, but well worth it. Over on Souq khan El-Zeit, the **Afghani Bakery**, just north of Aqabat el-Tuteh, serves egg-bread that makes a filling, if rather bland breakfast. Just up the hill there are a couple of glittery restaurants serving *baklava*, the teeth-rotting, sickly-sweet desserts and sweets that are something of an Arab institution. **Jaffar Sweets** at number 42 is probably the best. Just to the north, the Mauristan area is full of restaurants, most with outdoor seating, that get really busy during the day. The **Fountain Coffeeshop** at 62 Al-Daghbati is one of the cheapest in this tourist ghetto, while **Papa Andrea's** at number 64, though its Arab menu is way overpriced, has excellent views from its rooftop dining area.

By the Tower of David there are a plethora of restaurants and cafés catering specifically to the tourist droves, though sadly most are bland, overpriced affairs. The **Loaves and Fishes** is the exception, a smart, Christian-run café in a prime spot that serves mainly vegetarian meals. Unfortunately, when I visited the food was merely adequate, and the coffee cold. The **Armenian Tavern**, just 100m south at 75 Armenian Patriarchate Road, does good salads and *lahmacun*, a sort of minced meat pizza that's tastier than it sounds.

But for the best gustatory experience in the Old City, you must visit **Abu Shanab's** (Arabic for Father's Moustache), just up from the Tower of David at 35

Latin Patriarchate Road. This excellent pizzeria is way ahead of the rest of the field in terms of delicious food, good service and value for money, with pizzas beginning at only NIS10. They have also recently started serving alcohol. My only gripe is the hard-backed chairs, which can be excruciating after a while.

East Jerusalem

The **Al-Rashid** is the best value and friendliest of the string of felafal restaurants to the north of Damascus Gate by the servis station. They also, uniquely, use eggplant as an ingredient. On Sharia Salah El-Din, the **Al-Shilleh** is another Shwaarma and felafel joint, where the profits seem to have been ploughed back into the decor which is clean, airy and pleasant. Alas, the other eateries on the street are unexceptional.

Thankfully, however, three new restaurants have opened to the north on Sama'an Al-Sadik to rescue East Jerusalem's culinary reputation. Each can boast exquisite food served in pleasant surroundings with al-fresco seating, and though a touch pricier than other restaurants in East Jerusalem (about NIS30–45 for a main course), they are well worth the money. **Pasha's**, at number 13, round the back of the Al-Wasiti Art Centre, does a fantastic *kufta be tehninieh*, (mince meat, sesame oil and potatoes). Alcohol is served, and afterwards you can sit back and enjoy a hubbly-bubbly pipe. Next door to the east is **Philadelphia's**, which also has a branch on Sharia Al-Zahra; this is a rather classy joint serving traditional Arab food, including excellent tahini and hoummus. Finally, there's the **Askadinya** at number 11. With Jews and Muslims both proscribing the consumption of pork, it's easier for a camel to pass through the eye of the needle than it is to get a decent pork chop in the Holy Land; which is why the Askadinya, with its delightful pork chops in apple sauce, is a welcome addition to Jerusalem's restaurant scene. Though a little inconveniently located, Pasha's offers a free shuttle service to your hotel, and the others may well follow suit.

NIGHTLIFE

Israelis tend to look upon Jerusalem's nightlife scene as something of a joke, but if they think it's a little quiet in West Jerusalem, they should try crossing over to the east side. There's little in Palestinian East Jerusalem in the way of bars and clubs; you'll have to cross the Green Line for those. One thing East Jerusalem does have, however, is the **Hakawati Folk Theatre** (tel: 02 6288189), Palestine's oldest and most controversial theatre company, established in 1984. Plays considered too political for the Israeli authorities are regularly closed down, and during the Intifada many of the actors were arrested. As you may expect, the plays are conducted in Arabic, but an English-language summary of the plot is often provided in the programme. They also hold exhibitions, one-off folklore evenings and other events, for which a knowledge of Arabic isn't such a necessity. A second company, the **Al-Qasabah Theatre** (tel: 02 6280957) in Obeid Ibn Jarrah Street, offers similar fare. Also in East Jerusalem, and right next to the Hakawati Theatre, is the **Jerusalem Centre for Arabic Music**, which occasionally holds live performances. Ring 02 6274774 for details of forthcoming events.

There are a couple of bars in the Old City, including the rowdy **Tabasco Bar**, in the basement of the hostel of the same name. This place has stolen a march on bars in West Jerusalem by offering two happy hours every evening, an all-you-can-drink punch party on a Friday, and cheap beer throughout the day and night. It's a bit, well, *young*, for some tastes, but it's always lively.

In West Jerusalem, the **Underground** has a Happy Twenty Minutes where it's all-you-can-drink for FREE, though it costs NIS5 to enter; at midnight, this place turns into a sweaty nightclub-cum-meat-market. Just round the corner on Jaffa Street, the **Arizona** always seems dead quiet whenever I visit, though some people rave about the place, and in particular the draught Taybeh, one of over thirty beers on tap. The Russian Compound, home to bars such as **Cannabis** (no, you can't legally smoke it here), **Galliano** and the funky internet café **Strudels**, lies over the road and up the hill.

SHOPPING

The first place to look for souvenirs is, of course, the Old City. David Street, Christian Quarter Road and the Via Dolorosa are lined with shops selling all sorts of keepsakes. Some of the shops, particularly around the northern end of the Via Dolorosa, are quite exclusive, but most of the stalls in the rest of the city sell the same mass-produced gear. Look out too for **Melia**, a Palestinian women's cooperative on Freres Street in the Christian Quarter. Wherever you shop, the number-one rule remains the same: always haggle.

For more specialist outlets, an amble around the shops of East Jerusalem could prove very rewarding. The English-language **Educational Bookshop** at 22 Salah El-Din is something of an institution, stocking a comprehensive selection of books and periodicals about Palestine. If you're serious about getting to know the country, a trip here could prove extremely rewarding. Back down the road a little, the picture framer at number 19 has stocks of the very popular black-and-orange **posters** of Palestine produced during the British Mandate. Round the corner from the Educational Bookshop, on Sharia Al-Zahra, is the wonderful **Authentic Shop**. Most of their stock consists of designer tableware and home furnishings, but upstairs is a permanent gallery of wonderful black-and-white photos of Palestine from the thirties to the fifties, all taken by the father of the shop's owner. You can buy copies of the photos for NIS75.

Over on Sharia Nablus, the **Palestinian Pottery Company** (Mon–Sat 09.00–16.00), at number 14 opposite the American Council, sells hand-painted, traditional-style pottery tiles, pots, vases and ashtrays at very reasonable prices. The company has been making wares on site since 1922, and can make goods to order, or personalise them for just NIS10 extra.

Jordan Souvenirs, part of the Ritz Hotel, has a fine collection of Hebron glass on the first floor, and a number of Palestinian brass lamps and coffee pots on the ground floor. Though the whole place is in need of a good spring clean, the elderly manager is refreshingly unaggressive, allowing you to wander at will around his store, and the prices are fixed.

The Mennonites are a Catholic order that organises and sponsors a number of worthwhile and effective projects for refugees in the West Bank and Gaza Strip. Their needlework programme is one of the most successful of these ventures. Begun in 1950, the programme's aims are threefold: to preserve the traditional Palestinian embroidery, to offer refugee women a chance to supplement the family income, and to enhance their self-reliance through employment. Now a 300-member cooperative, the programme's beautiful results are on sale at the **Palestinian Needlework Shop**, 79 Nablus Road, opposite the Ambassador Hotel in the district of Sheikh Jarrah. The products, which range from embroidered tablecloths to place mats, and napkins to cushion covers, as well as a small selection of olive wood carvings from a similar scheme, aren't cheap, but they are of the highest quality and you can take comfort in the fact that your money is going to a good cause.

WHAT TO SEE AND DO IN THE OLD CITY

If Jerusalem is a simmering cauldron of religious and racial tension, a melting pot of cultures, ideas and beliefs, then the Old City is the flame that keeps those tensions percolating. With over 25,000 people of almost every religious persuasion crammed into an area no bigger than one square mile, it's no wonder the atmosphere can get a little intense at times.

The Old City walls, built by Suleyman the Magnificent in the 16th century to keep the invaders at bay, now serve only to keep the seething tension bottled up inside, the **seven city gates** that puncture them thus acting like valves on a pressure cooker. Inside the walls, and excluding the Temple Mount, the city is divided loosely into four quarters. The largest, the **Muslim Quarter**, takes up most of one side of the Old City, from Souq Khan El-Zeit eastwards. It's a largely residential area, though you'll also find here the Via Dolorosa. Filling the Old City's northwestern corner is the **Christian Quarter** which, like the **Armenian Quarter** in the southwest, is more ecclesiastical than residential, the buildings being largely monasteries, churches, hospices and shops rather than houses.

Vying with that of the Armenians as the smallest quarter is the **Jewish Quarter**, immediately west of the Temple Mount. This is the only quarter that belongs wholly to one community, following the expulsion of non-Jewish residents in 1967. In the other quarters the different ethnic and religious communities live side by side, though to say they mingle is not entirely accurate: many Jewish settlers in the Muslim Quarter, for example, are not welcomed by the locals, who view them (correctly, in most cases) as political extremists hell-bent on securing the entire Old City for the Jews. As a result, their houses tend to be shrouded in a morass of high security, and contact with their neighbours is minimal.

Apart from these four main communities, you'll also find significant pockets of Syrians, Ethiopians, Egyptians, Greeks and Russians, many attached to a church or monastery, and a small Black Community who settled here during Jordanian rule.

The Old City is built on a number of hills and, as you'll notice when walking around, the ground is rarely level. There is no one main street, though **Sharia Al-Wad**, running from the Damascus Gate to the Temple Mount along the course of the dip between hills known as the **Tyropoeon** ('Cheesemakers') **Valley**, is a useful thoroughfare, particularly as it's a lot emptier than the other main road running north-south, the **Souq Khan El-Zeit**. This is possibly the most constipated street in the Middle East, and one of the most exotic too. With the noise of the barrow boys, traders, shoppers and the hymn-singing pilgrims, and the pungent bouquet of cardamom, coffee, saffron, sandalwood, incense, putrefying meat, mint, donkey poo and freshly baked bread, the souq will linger in memory for longer than any of the Old City's 'official' tourist sights. As a means of getting from A to B, however, the Souq is the world's worst thoroughfare; if you plan to reach the other end of the city before your visa expires, take a less congested path.

Ramparts Walk

Sat–Thu 09.00–16.00, Fri 09.00–14.00; NIS12/6 for a two-day ticket allowing one-time entry to both sections

I love the Ramparts Walk. It enables you to enjoy the hustle and bustle of the Old City, without all the jostling, shoving and general hassle that a walk within the city usually entails. On parts of the 4km-long ramparts you can even hear birds singing as you go, and the views, as you can imagine, are quite breathtaking.

The walls were built by the greatest Ottoman sultan of them all, Suleyman the Magnificent, between the years 1537 and 1542, starting with the north wall and continuing with the western and eastern sections. Work on the final, southern section was delayed due to a dispute over funds. Unwilling to pay the extra cost required to enclose Mount Zion and the Coenaculum, the architects insisted that the Franciscans, who owned the mount, should pay for it; but the Franciscans, penniless, couldn't afford to meet the extra costs involved. The architects therefore excluded Mount Zion from their walled city; Suleyman, angry that his original specifications had been altered and that one of the city's holy sights now lay outside the walls, beheaded the architects.

For security reasons, that part of the wall surrounding the Temple Mount is closed to the public. The rest of the wall is split into two halves; note that, though you can join the Ramparts Walk only at the following points, you can leave at any gate. The first half of the walk runs from the Jaffa Gate to St Stephen's Gate along the northern and eastern walls. Access to this section of the wall can be gained either at the **Jaffa Gate**, behind the jewellers H Stern, or at the Roman Plaza (see page 119) by **Damascus Gate**. For the best photo opportunities, try to visit the wall Ramparts around the Damascus Gate after Friday prayers (about 14.00), when the Islamic faithful head back from the Temple Mount in their thousands, creating a carpet of keffiyah-covered heads that's wonderful to behold. Other features of the wall include the **machioulis holes** for pouring boiling oil on to the heads of the invaders, and the occasional Jordanian **lookout-post**, one of the few remaining legacies of their 19-year tenure of the city.

The second section of the Ramparts Walk is shorter and less exciting. Entrance is behind the **Tower of David**. This section looks over Mount Zion to the south, and the Armenian and Jewish Quarters within the walls, both of which are filled with a lot of car parks, waste ground and unexcavated ruins. The Dome of the Rock is only visible at the end of the walk, on a section of the ramparts that's free to enter anyway.

Haram Al-Sharif – The Temple Mount

Sat–Thurs 07.30–11.30; 13.00–14.30; 08.00–10.00 only during Ramadan; free entry into sanctuary; NIS36/24 for entry into the mosques and museum

The contrast between the hullabaloo of the Old City and the refreshing tranquillity of the Haram Al-Sharif, or Noble Sanctuary, is striking. This reverential hush is hardly surprising given that its location, on the summit of **Mount Moriah**, is of great significance to each of the big three monotheistic faiths.

According to Jewish tradition, Mount Moriah is the spot where Abraham prepared his son Isaac for sacrifice (Genesis 22; in Islam it was his elder brother Ishmael who was prepared). A couple of millennia later, King David bought the hill, then just a threshing floor, for six hundred shekels of gold as the location for a temple to house the Ark of the Covenant, a temple eventually built by his son, Solomon, in c960BC. The temple formed the focal point of the Jewish faith until demolished along with the rest of the city by Nebuchadnezzar's forces in 587BC.

THE COMBINATION TICKET

Useful to non-students who wish to study the Old City in some detail, the combination ticket costs NIS30 and allows entry into the Ramparts Walk and five (minor) sights: the Ophel Archeological Garden (page 109), the City of David (page 127), the Spring of Gihon (page 127), Roman Plaza (page 119) and Zedekiah's Cave (page 119). The ticket is valid for five days, though you are only allowed to enter into each attraction once.

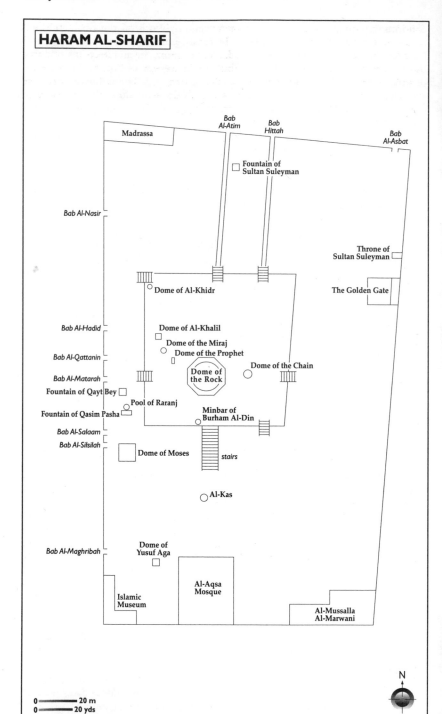

HARAM AL-SHARIF

Madrassa

Bab Al-Atim

Bab Hittah

Bab Al-Asbat

Fountain of Sultan Suleyman

Bab Al-Nasir

Throne of Sultan Suleyman

The Golden Gate

Dome of Al-Khidr

Dome of Al-Khalil

Bab Al-Hadid

Dome of the Miraj

Bab Al-Qattanin

Dome of the Prophet

Dome of the Chain

Bab Al-Matarah

Dome of the Rock

Fountain of Qayt Bey

Pool of Raranj

Fountain of Qasim Pasha

Minbar of Burham Al-Din

Bab Al-Salaam

Bab Al-Silsilah

Dome of Moses

stairs

Al-Kas

Bab Al-Maghribah

Dome of Yusuf Aga

Islamic Museum

Al-Aqsa Mosque

Al-Mussalla Al-Marwani

N

0 ▬▬ 20 m
0 ▬▬ 20 yds

The Jews who returned from exile rebuilt the temple under Zerubbabel in 535BC. Though similar in size, it lacked the luxuriance and ostentation of Solomon's original. Five hundred years later Herod, seeking approval from his Jewish subjects (not to mention his Jewish wife), refurbished Zerubbabel's efforts in an attempt to match the original glory of Solomon's masterpiece. Priests were used as masons and carpenters in the sacred areas considered off-limits to those of a lesser calling. Herod also enlarged the temple platform, moving the Tyropoeon Valley west and the Kidron Valley east by filling parts of them in, until the sanctuary measured approximately 300m across by 450m long. The temple at this time was really a city within a city, employing thousands of priests, scribes, guards and maintenance men, and every day within the gigantic sacrificial enclosure, countless cattle were ritually slaughtered.

It is Herod's Temple that appears frequently in the life of Jesus, and for this reason the Temple Mount has considerable significance for Christians too. His parents found Him praying here as a young boy (Luke 2:41–51), the Devil set Him upon the highest point of the Temple to show Him the world and tempt Him with earthly goods (Matthew 4: 5), and it was in this temple that He upset the tables of the moneylenders (Matthew 21: 12–17). According to Mark's Gospel (15: 38), at the hour of His crucifixion the Babylonian veil separating the Temple's nave from the Holy of Holies was mysteriously rent completely in two.

Before He died, Jesus predicted the destruction of the Temple so that 'there shall not be left one stone upon another, that shall not be thrown down', a prophecy fulfilled to the letter by the Romans in AD70. A Roman temple may have been erected on the site in AD135, but thereafter the Temple Mount remained in ruins until 637 and the Islamic invasion. The Muslims' reverence for the site is derived from the 17th Sure (chapter) of the Koran, which concerns Mohammed's **Night Flight**. Having fallen asleep while praying to God in his hometown of Mecca, Mohammed was woken by the archangel Gabriel and, mounting a winged beast called Al-Buraq, was taken to the 'furthestmost place'. Once there, he ascended to Heaven to pray with Abraham, Moses, Jesus and other prophets, and received the instructions that form the five pillars of Islam. For whatever reason, Muslims have identified this furthestmost place as Jerusalem, and the Temple Mount as the place from where he ascended to Heaven. Accordingly, you'll often hear Muslims referring to the entire site as the **Haram Al-Aqsa**, or the 'Furthestmost Sanctuary'.

The second Muslim Caliph, Omar Ibn Al-Khattab, who conquered Jerusalem in AD637, four years after Mohammed's death and 17 years after the night flight, cleared away the debris and built a wooden **mosque** that held 3,000 worshippers. His efforts were followed in AD685 by the Ommayad Caliph Abdul Malik Ibn Marwan, who began work on the Dome of the Rock. So pleased was he with the result that, according to legend, the Dome was washed before every prayer time with saffron, musk and ambergris in rosewater. A few years later Al-Khattab's wooden mosque was replaced by a more permanent structure, capable of holding over 5,000 worshippers. Save from an interim of 88 years during the Crusader era, the Muslims have occupied the mount ever since, thanks in part to their greater numbers and in part to the Jewish reluctance to set foot on the Temple Mount again (see the Western Wall, below).

Touring around the Haram
The paved Haram covers almost a fifth of the Old City, some 35 acres in total, and is dotted with shrines, mastabas, mihrabs, fountains and plenty of shaded, leafy areas where one can hide from the sun. Though visitors can exit by any of

THE JEWISH QUARTER

Though the Israelis only regained this quarter in 1967, the area had been a stronghold for the city's Jewish community since the 12th century when they were allowed back into the city by Saladin, following an absence of 88 years while the **Crusaders** held the city. The city's Jewish citizens lived in relative peace in the quarter for most of the next nine centuries, until, in 1948, the area fell to the **Jordanians** and the residents were evicted. Before they fled 19 years later, the Jordanian army systematically destroyed many of the buildings.

The Israeli government have invested heavily in the area since then, and it now contains many of the Old City's newest buildings. The architecture is pretty and fits in nicely with earlier buildings, but the quarter as a whole is rather anaemic when compared with the noise and passion of the rest of the Old City. It's a very wealthy area now, with some of the highest real-estate prices in the city, though it's mainly extremist Jews who choose to live here.

Among the excavations carried out while redeveloping the quarter, the **Cardo** is perhaps the most interesting. The old colonnaded Roman High Street today lies some way below ground level to the south of the Souq Khan El-Zeit. Lying at its southern end are remains of earlier eras, including **Hasmonean walls** and even, so they say, buildings from the First Temple period. At the Cardo's northern end, shops have begun to move back in, trading in the same spot as their Byzantine forefathers over 1,500 years ago.

As you would expect, the quarter is dotted with synagogues. The oldest is the **Ramban Synagogue**, built by the man who led a mass Jewish immigration back into the quarter in 1267 following Saladin's victory over the Crusaders the previous century. The original mosque of Ramban (whose real name, incidentally, was Rabbi Moshe Ben Nahman) was destroyed by heavy rain, but was rebuilt during the Mamluke period. Over on HaKehuna Street, **Four Sephardi Synagogues** dating from the 17th century lie deep underground, in accordance with an Ottoman ruling forbidding them from being higher than surrounding buildings. They remain the centre of the Sephardic community today. It is possible to visit all four (Sun–Thurs, 09.30–16.00, Fri 09.30–12.30; NIS3).

Among the museums in the quarter are the **Old Yishuv Court Museum** (open Sun–Thurs 09.00–14.00; NIS6) at 6 HaHayim Street, which explores life in the Jewish Quarter under the Ottomans, and the **Jewish Heritage Centre** at 1 Jewish Quarter Road. This small centre offers a 35-minute **multimedia** tour of the Jewish Quarter throughout history (in English, Sun–Thurs, 11.00, 14.00 and 17.00). Best of the lot, however, is the **Wohl Archaeological Museum** (Sun–Thurs 09.00–17.00, Fri 09.00–12.00; NIS7) where the remains of six priests' houses from the Herodian era are preserved. Next door, and included in the ticket to the Wohl Museum, is the **Burnt House**, a priestly house destroyed in AD70 by fire, which, perversely, has preserved it rather well. An audiovisual show provides an explanation of the excavations.

Just a few metres south lies the compound of **St Mary's of the Germans**, a 12th-century Crusader construction. Stairs to its south lead to the Western Wall, above which you can see the Golden Dome of the Rock glistening in the sunlight.

the **ten gates** leading into the 35-acre Haram, non-Muslims can enter only via the **Bab Al-Maghribah**, the Moors' Gate, to the east (right) of the Western Wall. Muslims view the entire compound as one giant mosque; consequently, modest dress and undemonstrative behaviour are of the utmost importance throughout the Haram, and when wandering around the grounds, don't stray too far: the authorities are very jumpy and will apprehend anybody who meanders into a prohibited area. The best time to arrive is in the early morning, for after 09.30 the tourist herds start trickling through; a trickle that, by 10.30, is a torrent.

Entry into the Sanctuary is free, though you'll have to buy a ticket to enter into either of the mosques, or the small **museum** in the Haram's southwestern corner. The ticket office is a small kiosk to the west of the Al-Aqsa Mosque. It has a stock of small but useful guidebooks, but officials seem strangely reluctant to dish them out. Ask for one: after all, they're free.

Dome of the Rock

The summit of Mount Moriah has for the last 1300 years sheltered beneath the 20m-diameter golden roof of the so-called Dome of the Rock, the oldest mosque in the world. The Dome itself, the apex of which sits 35m above the floor, is sadly no longer made of solid gold but of oxidised aluminium; an Ottoman sultan, short of funds, melted it down to pay off his creditors. The five-daily washes in rosewater are a thing of the past too. However, the mosque probably looks much the same now as it did over 1,300 years ago, the only significant addition being the dazzling **blue tilework** of the exterior, inscribed with Koranic verses, flowers and geometric patterns and commissioned by Suleyman the Magnificent in the 16th century.

Inside, the exquisite, 8th-century **Syrian mosaics** (Syrian Christians being the best mosaicists in the world at that time) of green and gold and the plush red carpets of the interior provide a neat juxtaposition with the simplicity of the **rock** itself, which emerges as a single grey lump from the centre of the floor, partitioned off from the rest of the mosque by a wooden balustrade. The **footprint** left by Mohammed as he ascended to Heaven marks the rock, and this is also supposed to be the exact spot where Abraham tried to sacrifice his son. The tall, carved cabinet surmounted by a clock in the southwestern corner of the balustrade contains hairs from the beard of Mohammed, though it's only opened once a year. On the southern side of the rock steps lead down to a small **grotto**. On either side of these steps are two prayer niches, marking shrines to **Abraham** and **El-Khader** (see page 199).

Al-Aqsa

Shaken to its very foundations by earthquakes, greatly reduced in size since the 11th century and almost burnt to the ground in 1969, few mosques have suffered so much abuse in the Holy Land as the Al-Aqsa. It is quite surprising that it's survived at all, and positively incredible that it still looks as good as it does.

Entering the mosque, one of the first things you notice is its asymmetry. Standing in the wide central aisle, you'll see that the roof covering the eastern half of the mosque (to your left) is flat and held aloft by marble **columns** topped with **Byzantine capitals**, whereas the roof on the western wing is vaulted and has, to support it, a series of immense **rectangular pillars** made of stone. These differences in architectural detail are symptomatic of the mosque's chequered history. Believed to be the spot where Mohammed tethered Al-Burak (his winged steed) before ascending to Heaven, this was the site of the sanctuary's (and the city's) first mosque. Caliph Al-

JERUSALEM'S GATES

Suleyman built **six gates** into his city walls. Though all have been restored at some point down the years, three of the gates – Zion, Damascus and Jaffa – still maintain their original L-shape, designed to break the momentum of enemy invaders trying to storm in. The **Damascus Gate**, so-called because the main road to Damascus once ran northeast from here, is the liveliest and, from a historical point of view at least, by far and away the most interesting gate of the seven. It is also the most attractive, with its unique rounded crenellations designed to mimic Ottoman helmets. The gate is known as **Bab Al-Amud**, 'Gate of the Column', in Arabic, after a column bearing Hadrian's statue that used to stand inside the gate during the Roman era (and which you can see, in hologram form, in the Roman Plaza excavations; see page 119).

Continuing clockwise from Damascus Gate, the next portal we come to is **Herod's Gate**, the smallest of Suleyman's entrances, which provides a convenient conduit between the Old City and East Jerusalem. The **Lions' Gate** in the eastern wall, so-called because of the two lions carved into the stone, is also known as **St Stephen's Gate** (after the martyred disciple who was believed to have been stoned to death here), **Bab Al-Ghor**, or 'Jordan Valley Gate', as it faces east towards the Jordan Valley, and **Bab Sittna Maryam**, or 'Gate of our Lady Mary', as it lies near the traditional site of her birth. The unfortunately-named **Dung Gate**, on the other, southern side of the Temple Mount, is so-called because, in days gone by, rubbish was taken through here before being dumped in the Kidron Valley. The Arabs refer to this gate as **Bab Harat Al-Magharba**, or **Moors' Gate**, after the large north African community that used to live in the area now occupied by the giant esplanade. Still on the southern wall, the **Zion Gate**, running between the Armenian Quarter and Mount Zion, is followed to the north by the **Jaffa Gate**. The Arabs call this entrance **Bab Al-Khalil** as the road south to Al-Khalil (Hebron) once started here. General Allenby marched through this gate in 1917 when recapturing the city from the Ottomans. Finally there's the **New Gate**, not one of Suleyman's entrances but a late 19th-century addition by Sultan Abdul Hamed II. Unlike most of the other gates, this one is undecorated, and is merely a hole that's been punched into the north wall.

As well as these seven, in the southeastern corner of the wall by the Temple Mount you can see two more gates, both now bricked up. In the southern wall there are the **Hulda Gates**, that once provided an alternative entrance into the Temple Mount, while in the eastern wall are the so-called **Golden Gates**, originally Herodian but blocked off by the Ommayads who restored them in the eighth century. The Jewish messiah is supposed to enter the city through these gates, as Jesus did at the end of His triumphal procession to the Holy City.

Walid replaced this timber structure with one in stone in AD715, though this was rebuilt in AD787 by Mohammed Al-Mahdi on a much grander scale, with 15 doorways and 20 aisles. Two earthquakes, in 1016 and 1033, convinced the architects under Caliph Al-Dharir that it needed to be reduced in size to make it more quake-proof, hence the reduction in width to the current seven aisles. Converted into a church during the Crusader era, it was re-converted by Saladin who decorated the

ARMENIAN QUARTER

There's been an Armenian quarter in the Old City since at least the 5th century, and Armenians have been living in the city for nigh on 2,000 years. The first state in the world to accept Christianity as its national religion, the country has suffered terribly at the hands of its larger and more aggressive neighbours, the Russians and, in particular, the Turks, culminating in the genocide of 1915 when over two thirds of the Armenian population were killed or incarcerated in concentration camps. Unsurprisingly, the holocaust still haunts the community today, with posters throughout the quarter detailing the massacre.

Many of the community's 2,000-strong population are the descendants of refugees who fled the massacre. The Armenian quarter, once a huge pilgrim's hospice, became a residential quarter for this Armenian diaspora almost overnight. Stretched between the Zion and Jaffa Gates, most of the Armenian quarter lies behind the high stone walls of this former hospice and is closed to the public. A couple of places within the compound are open to the general public, however, and provide a revealing insight into the life and history of the city's Armenian population. See page 117 for details.

milırab and brought in the famous **minbar** from the northern Syrian town of Aleppo; a minbar that was burnt, along with many other wooden furnishings, in a fire started deliberately by an Australian Christian fanatic in 1969.

The other thing that hits you as you enter the mosque is the sense of space and simplicity: where the Dome of the Rock is crammed with relics and decorations, the Al-Aqsa is remarkably uncluttered. Even the stained-glass windows (of which the mosque has 121), the only major decorative frill in the nave, are obscured by the pillars and wooden beams that run below the ceiling. Indeed, the only visible decorative flourishes lie directly above your head – the ceiling was painted courtesy of Egypt's King Farouk – and under your feet, with the patterned Persian carpets. This, clearly, is a mosque designed for silent contemplation rather than garrulous ostentation.

The **qibla wall** stands at the opposite end to the entrance. This, too, is fairly plain, and the modern **minbar**, a simple affair with green railings, is a bit of a disappointment. Indeed the only detail of note on this wall – one of the few Ommayad structures in the mosque to have survived – is the **mihrab** itself, a wonderfully intricate confection of stone, mosaic and mother-of-pearl. This craftsmanship is matched by the mosaics lining the interior of the dome above your head, part of the decorations introduced by Saladin.

While putting your shoes back on, you may notice a set of steps leading down under the mosque. These steps (closed to visitors) lead down to **Solomon's Stables**, a cave which once possibly held sacrificial animals during the Second Temple Period, and which was used by the Crusaders as a place to stable their horses.

The Islamic Museum

This museum first opened in 1922, making it the oldest in Jerusalem. It's housed in two rooms, both of which originally formed a **Crusader armoury** built by Godfrey de Bouillon (the Al-Aqsa mosque was converted into a church at this time), and both of which served as mosques. The northern hall, where you enter, was used as a mosque by the large African community that arrived in the wake of Saladin's conquest of the city in 1187; the mihrab from this mosque has been opened to provide access to the southern room, which served as a **women's mosque** in the Mamluke and Ottoman periods.

The opening display is dedicated to the 17 who lost their lives in 1990, when Jewish extremists attempted to position a foundation stone for a new temple in the sanctuary. As Israeli police opened fire to try to protect them from outraged Palestinians, 19 people were killed and 300 injured – none of them Israeli. Beyond this room, the museum contains relics collected down the centuries from the Dome of the Rock and Al-Aqsa. These include a number of **Korans** (the eldest dating back to the 9th century), wooden panels from the ceiling of Al-Aqsa, part of the **aluminium roof** fitted to the Dome of the Rock in the 1960s and a number of crescents which once surmounted the Dome.

The Western Wall
No smoking, and no taking of photgraphs during the Shabbat
Originally part of the Temple's retaining wall – a wall so big that, though its construction was started by Herod in c35BC, it wasn't actually completed until AD64 under Herod Agrippa II – this is the largest part of Herod's Temple renovations to have survived the Roman demolition in AD70. The Jews, barred from the city as a result of the Bar Kochba Revolt, congregated at the Western Wall (then outside the city) to cry and bemoan the loss of their Temple. It was for this reason that the wall earned its gentile nickname, the **Wailing Wall**.

Though they were allowed back into the city during the Byzantine era, the Jews refused to visit the ruins of their temple, and still refuse to visit the Haram today. The reason for this is simple: by walking on the mount, they may unwittingly set foot on the **Holy of Holies**, the sacred shrine that's off-limits to all except the high priests. This religious law was given secular backing following the troubles of 1990, when the Israeli government introduced a statute forbidding Jews from praying on the Mount.

Thus, the Jews still pray to the Temple Mount 'by proxy' via the Western Wall. The Wall is organised like a traditional synagogue, with men on the left, and women (since 1928) on the right. Prayers are written on paper and inserted into the Wall, and throughout the day and night you'll see the devout praying, their heads bobbing rhythmically up and down as they recite the traditional prayer, or **daven**: 'Hear O Israel, the Lord our God, the Lord is one.' Try to visit on Monday and Thursday mornings when **Barmitzvahs** – the coming-of-age ceremonies that celebrate the first time a Jewish boy is allowed to read from the Torah – are celebrated, or for the weekly Shabbat prayers when the wall is crowded with worshippers.

Curiously, as part of the Temple Mount, both the wall and the synagogue are owned by the city's Muslims, with Jewish jurisdiction beginning only at the **esplanade** immediately to the west. This large esplanade was, until 1967, the **Marghaba Quarter**, with the houses extending right down to the wall itself. Within one month of their victory, the Israelis had razed the quarter to the ground. With the harsh sun reflecting off the bright concrete floor it can be a painfully dazzling esplanade, particularly during the middle of the day, so do bring sunglasses.

Men are allowed to visit the left-hand side of the Wall, providing they cover their head (yarmulkas are provided). Women can visit the female side, though their arms and legs as well as their head must be fully covered.

The Western Wall tunnel
Rarely can the opening of a new tourist attraction have caused so much controversy or left so many dead and injured. The **Western Wall excavation**,

running from the northern end of the Western Wall esplanade to the Via Dolorosa, passes right underneath the Muslim quarter as it follows the unexposed part of the Wall. It's a fascinating excavation, but one that the Palestinians feared would weaken the foundations of the Haram Al-Sharif. For this reason President Rabin, sensitive to the reactions of Palestinians, refused to open the tunnel in 1995, even though the digging had been completed some months before. President Netanyahu, however, had no such qualms, opening the tunnel to the public in 1996. The Palestinians responded in September of that year with protests, riots and pitched battles that left 94 people dead (all but 14 being Palestinians) and over a thousand wounded.

Despite the furore, it is possible to visit the tunnel today, though only as part of a tour group (tel: 02 6271333, the number of the **Western Wall Heritage Foundation**, for details). Inside the tunnel you'll find various passages and storage rooms from the Mamluke era, and an ancient **synagogue** from Ommayad times that was deliberately located on a site that lay close to the Holy of Holies, the inner sanctum of Solomon's Temple. Further north and down in the walk you'll see an impressive model of the city during the Second Temple period, and a **Hasmonean cistern** and **aqueduct**. The walk ends by the First Station of the Cross.

Ophel Archaelogical Garden
Sun–Thurs 09.00–17.00, Fri 09.00–15.00; NIS12/6
Also known as the **Temple Excavations**, this archaeological site beside the southern wall of the Temple Mount was first excavated by the fanatical Jewish historian Yigel Yadin with the intention of finding the ruins of the First and Second Temple. On his way down to this layer he unearthed ruins from almost every period of Jerusalem's history, from Fatimid towers to Ommayad Palaces.

The ruins are split into two sections by the Old City walls, and there are more excavations on the other side of the road. Unless you really know your archaeology, it's difficult to pick out the Crusader, Byzantine, Roman, Arab and Ottoman ruins from the dusty jumble of rubble scattered here, particularly as explanation boards are few. Joining one of the **guided tours** (English-language tours are held on Sun, Tues and Fri at 09.00) is therefore a good idea, assuming you can afford the extra NIS25. The highlight of the second section (reached by the small Excavation Gate) is the impressive **grand stairway** that led up to the Temple precinct's **Hulda Gates** (the outline of which you can still see in the wall), while amongst the best bits of the first section is a series of (now subterranean) **Byzantine houses**, complete with simple, patterned mosaic floors, and the **Crusader Tower** directly to the south of the Al-Aqsa mosque. From the top you have an unparalleled view of the Mount of Olives and southern Jerusalem; picture boards up here help you to get your bearings and point out the main sights.

Before you leave the Western Wall area altogether, take a look at the ledge sticking out of the southern corner of the Western Wall. This is all that remains of **Robinson's Arch**, a bridge that spanned the Tyropoeon Valley to connect the Temple precinct with residential Jerusalem. A second bridge, Wilson's arch, lay to the north where the Western Wall begins.

The Via Dolorosa – The Stations of the Cross and other sites
The 14 stations stretched along the Via Dolorosa from St Stephen's Gate to the Holy Sepulchre mark the last 14 significant events in the life, death and

resurrection of Christ, beginning with **His trial** in the Judgement Hall of Pontius Pilate, and ending with **His crucifixion** and **resurrection**. These stations have little basis in archaeology: while the Holy Sepulchre could well stand on the Hill of Golgotha where Jesus was crucified, most scholars now believe Jesus was tried in **Herod's Palace** which lay near the Jaffa Gate, not St Stephen's Gate. The Dominican Friars, however, are the only major denomination who begin their processions at Jaffa Gate, with almost every other order preferring to follow the route that was first established during the Byzantine era.

A procession along the Via Dolorosa ('Way of Sorrow') has become an act of devotion for many millions of pilgrims, some of whom carry wooden crosses the entire way in imitation of their Lord. If you'd care to join a group, the Franciscans meet in the courtyard of the Al-Umariyyah School, by Station I, every Friday at 16.00. Chapels now stand over the location of many of the stations, though you'll be lucky to get in and see them all. Apart from the stations, a number of other 'sights' surrounding Jesus' last days – His supposed prison cell, for example, and the Ecce Homo Arch – have grown up along the Via Dolorosa, and these are described below too. Stations X to XIV are in the **Holy Sepulchre**, which is described in detail at the end of this section.

Sights and stations on the Via Dolorosa

Beginning at St Stephen's Gate, the **Church of St Anne** (08.00–11.45, 14.00–17.00, closed Sundays; NIS6/4), is situated to the right of the road inside a large walled compound. The church, named after the mother of Mary who is said to have given birth to her daughter in the house next door, is built in a simple basilica style. There are almost no decorative embellishments on the exterior, save for an Arabic inscription above the main door telling us that this church was converted into a **madrassa** by Saladin in 1192, 52 years after its construction by the **Crusaders**. It remained in Muslim hands until 1856, when the Ottomans, grateful for the help given by the French during the Crimean War, donated it to the French Catholics. The inside of the church is as plain as the exterior; steps lead down to the **crypt** that supposedly marks the site of Mary's parents' house, which has a few mosaics and columns dating from an earlier, Byzantine church.

The overgrown ruins in the courtyard mark the site of the **Pools of Bethseda**, renowned since biblical times for their curative properties. It was here that Jesus cured a man who had been ill for 38 years (John 5), an act which, because it took place on the Sabbath, brought him into trouble with the Jewish authorities. Most of the ruins you see today date from Byzantine and Crusader times, including the impressive **Byzantine archway** at the northern end of the site and the large circular **Crusader chapel** in the centre. There are also the ruins of some **pagan baths** dedicated to the Egyptian bull-worshipping cult of Serapis, which date back to the 5th century AD. The noticeboards dotted around the site will help you decipher which building block belongs to which era.

Station I

Located in the **Al-Umariyyah Madrassa** (07.30–15.30 Mon–Thurs and Sat), Station I lies up the hill from St Anne's on the opposite side of the road; look for the ramp on your left with green railings. The Station marks the spot where Jesus was condemned to death by Pontius Pilate. Many believe this took place in Herod's Antonia Fortress, which later became Pilate's praetorium, and the madrassa does indeed lie over the location of this fortress. Saint Paul, incidentally, was also imprisoned here.

THE MUSLIM QUARTER

The Muslim quarter runs south from the Damascus Gate to the Temple Walls. It is packed with sights and some exquisite **Mamluke architecture**, though many of the best places are tucked away down dark alleys near the Temple Mount and are difficult to locate. Further north, the Muslim quarter is much more residential, and consequently quieter. You'll see a lot of houses daubed with red, black and green **graffiti** throughout the quarter; those with a picture of the black Kaba'a stone celebrate the resident's pilgrimage – the **Haj** – to Mecca and Medina.

The Muslim quarter is also something of a commercial centre, and home to the Old City's main shopping thoroughfare, **Souq Khan El-Zeit**. At its southern end the souq splits into three smaller roads; of these, **Souq Al-Lahamin**, the western of the three streets, is the Old City's meat market, and not a place to come if you're at all squeamish. The other main road running south from Damascus Gate is **Sharia Al-Wad** which heads off via a tunnel to the Western Wall esplanade. Between this road and the Temple Mount (to your left as you walk down Al-Wad) are some of the finest old buildings huddled around dimly-lit covered streets. Briefly: **Sharia Ala'eddin** is sometimes called the African Quarter because of the large numbers of Africans who set up home here during the Jordanian era, and plays host to two 13th-century buildings, **Ribat Al-Mansuri** and **Ribat Ala Al-Din Al Basir**, that were used as prisons during the Ottoman period. Al-Basir, the grimmer of the two, was for convicts sentenced to death. At the end of the street is Bab Al-Naazir, or Inspector's Gate, a Muslim-only entrance into the Haram Al-Sharif. The next street south, leading to and named after the **Bab Al-Hadid** (Iron Gate), also contains a wealth of Mamluke architecture, including the tomb of **Sharif Hussein Bin Ali**, the Sharif of Mecca during World War I and an ally of Lawrence of Arabia during the Arab Revolt. Continuing south we have the covered **Souq Al-Qattanin**, the Cotton Merchants' Market which is slowly being restored to its former glory after centuries of neglect. The road is lined with disused khans and dilapidated baths, the latter of which they hope to restore and open to the public again in the near future.

After the market, Al-Wad goes into the tunnel underneath **Wilson's Arch**, one of two Herodion arches built to span the Tyropoeon Valley between the Temple Mount and the residential quarters that lay to its west.

Station II

Antonia's Fortress stretched for quite some distance from the northern end of the Temple Mount, across the Via Dolorosa and up the hill. Station II, therefore, where Jesus was beaten and condemned to death, would also have lain inside the fortress. Today the Station is marked by two chapels lying opposite the madrassa, one of which, the **Chapel of the Flagellation** (Apr–Sept, 08.00–11.45, 16.00–18.00; Oct–Mar 08.00–11.45, 13.00–17.00; free), on the right as you enter, is simply exquisite. This church, designed by Antonio Barluzzi between 1927 and 1929, is constructed in a medieval style on the site of an earlier Crusader chapel. Inside, look up to the three wonderful stained-glass windows around the altar. Look at the expressions of the central characters in each of the windows. On the left, a demure Pilate washes his hands of the whole affair, as described in Matthew

(27: 24). In the centre, Jesus' face is contorted in agony as He is scourged; while on the right there's the ugly, almost demonic expression of Barabbas, the prisoner the public chose to set free instead of Jesus (Matthew 27: 15–26). As absorbing as these windows are, don't forget to look up to the mosaic dome, where the Crown of Thorns is exquisitely rendered in tiny gold, green and brown tiles.

The other chapel in this Franciscan compound is the **Chapel of the Condemnation**. Built by one of the Franciscan brothers in the first decade of the 20th century (1903–4), again on the ruins of a medieval structure, this chapel lacks the charm and finesse of its neighbour. It does, however, contain a reasonable **altar painting** of a diminutive Jesus looking suitably distraught as a Roman guard gestures to Him to take up the massive cross. The church also contains part of the pavement, or Lithostratos in Greek, that ran through the Fortress; according to John (19: 13), having taken Jesus outside, Pilate sat down on the so-called Seat of Judgement in a place called The Stone Pavement, which could be this Lithostratos.

CHRISTIAN QUARTER

Stretched between the Damascus and Jaffa Gates, the Christian Quarter is the second largest quarter in the Old City, though, like the Armenian Quarter to its south, much of it lies hidden behind the high stone walls of the hospices, monasteries and schools that take up most of the land. Though **Palestinian** and **Arabic** speaking, the quarter has a greater degree of ethnic variety than any other, thanks to the various monastic orders and churches from different nations that huddle around the quarter's main attraction, the **Holy Sepulchre**.

Parts of the Christian Quarter, particularly the area around the new Gate, are amongst the quietest in the Old City. In contrast, the stall-lined **Christian Quarter Road** and the Mauristan area immediately to the southwest of the Holy Sepulchre form something of a tourist trap, the streets lined with souvenir shops and restaurants that buzz throughout the day. The Mauristan, Persian for 'hospital' or 'hospice', was once filled with lodgings for pilgrims, hence the name. It was founded by Charlemagne in the 9th century, and plays host to the oldest church in the Old City, the **Church of St John the Baptist** in its southwest corner. Originally built in the 5th century, it has undergone a number of restorations since then, including the addition of a bright blue dome and a couple of bell towers. The church gave its name to the order of Crusader knights known as the Knights of St John, or simply the **Knights Hospitallers**, which in turn gave its name to the St John's Ambulance organisation in Great Britain. Unfortunately, the church is nearly always locked. Entry is through a small brown door on Christian Quarter Road, opposite Abu Khalaf Materials; your best chance of catching it open is between 07.00 and 09.00.

In the opposite, northeastern corner of the square is the **Lutheran Church Tower** (09.00–13.00; 13.30–17.00; NIS2.5/2), a 19th-century construction with a bell tower that affords magnificent views overlooking the Holy Sepulchre to the north and the Temple Mount and Mount of Olives to the south. Opposite, the **Alexander Hospice**, home of Russia's Orthodox community, stands over excavations (Mon-Fri 09.00–13.00 and 15.00–17.00; NIS3) of an old city wall, thereby providing proof that the site of the Holy Sepulchre would indeed once have stood outside the city walls, in agreement with the Bible's description of Calvary.

The Lithostratos continues west beyond the next street, Aqabat Rabat, and reappears in the basement of the **Ecce Homo Convent** (NIS6/4; 08.30–12.30, 14.00–17.00, Sunday closed). Excavations here have uncovered a wealth of architectural features from different eras, including the **Struthion**, or Little Cistern, a reservoir of water siphoned off from the moat that surrounded Herod's Fortress, and which marked the fortress's northwestern corner. The excavations here are not spectacular, but the lengthy and informative English explanations make this one of the more rewarding diversions on this, the first leg of the Via Dolorosa.

The convent is named after the **Ecce Homo arch** that spans the Via Dolorosa. Ecce Homo is Latin for 'Behold the man', the phrase uttered by Pilate when presenting Jesus to the crowd baying for His blood (John 19: 5). The arch we see today, however, post-dates Jesus' crucifixion by quite a few years, having been built during the reign of the Emperor Hadrian. While you're in the vicinity, you may as well have a quick 'ecce' at the cavernous basilica that adjoins it (Mon–Sat 08.00–12.30, 14.00–16.00).

The Via Dolorosa continues west for the next 200m with only **The Prison of Christ** (daily, 10.00–14.00, NIS4/2), now a shrine owned by the Greek Orthodox Church, to break up the walk. This place's claim to be the dungeon where Christ was held after His arrest seems highly dubious. Sure, this series of underground caves looks like a prison, but whether it really was one, whether it was one at the time of Christ, and whether it's the same one in which Christ was incarcerated seems distinctly improbable. Anyway, Christ's cell, according to the owners, is on the left of the entrance, while His fellow jailbird, Barabbas, had far roomier quarters downstairs. While this sight is both unexciting and unconvincing, the spectacular view up to the Sepulchre that you get by climbing the staircase to the roof makes a visit worthwhile.

At the end of the road the Way of the Cross kinks a little, turning left on to Sharia Al-Wad and then, fifty metres further on, right up the hill. There are two stations on Sharia Al-Wad.

Stations III and IV

Just by the entrance to the Armenian Patriarchate Hospice, opposite Bassti Pizzaria, is **Station III**, the spot where Jesus fell for the first time. A carved relief above the door of a small Polish chapel depicts this scene. Just a few metres on, above a pastel green door is a second relief marking **Station IV**, this time of a suffering Jesus encountering his mother in the crowd lining the road. Mary, having been barred from joining her son on His last journey, had no option but to join the rest of the onlookers en route. The chapel inside is usually locked, which is a pity as there's a splendid 5th-century mosaic inside, including an outline of a pair of sandals said to be Mary's footprints.

Station V and VI

Station V lies at the junction of Sharia Al-Wad and the second half of the Via Dolorosa, on your left. Worshippers touch a stone halfway up the wall where, so it is said, an exhausted Jesus placed His hand to lean and rest, prompting a Roman centurion to order a bystander, Symon the Cyrene, to help Jesus bear the weight of the cross (Mark 15: 21).

Marking the spot where Veronica wiped the brow of Jesus, a likeness of His face miraculously imprinting itself on the cloth, **Station VI** lies opposite Jelly Ibrahim's Silver Shop, and is marked by an ornate wooden door. The story of Veronica has no biblical basis, but is first recorded in the 14th century. The handkerchief in question was later said to have cured the Emperor Tiberias of sickness, and now resides in St Peter's in Rome.

Stations VII, VII and IX

At the top of the street, the Way of the Cross tends to meander a little. **Station VII** lies at the top of the hill on Souk Khan el-Zeit, and marks the spot where Jesus fell for the second time, while just around the corner on Aqabat Al-Khanqah is **Station VIII** where Jesus consoled the lamenting women of Jerusalem (Luke 23: 27–30). A small stone medallion in the wall with the Greek inscription 'NIKA' marks the exact place. From here you have to double back to the souq, take a right up Khan El-Zeit and a second right turn where you see a green metal sign for the Russian Archaeological Museum. Climb the ramp behind this sign towards the Ethiopian patriarchate; at the end of the road, right next to the door of the Latin Patriarchate, is a column embedded in the wall, with the figure '9' written on it in marker pen. This rather underwhelming sight is **Station IX**, the supposed site of Jesus' third fall.

By **Station IX** a door on the left leads into the **Ethiopian compound**. This slice of village Africa on the roof of Christianity's holiest building is the result of a fire in 1808, in which the papers pertaining to the Ethiopian ownership of part of the church were burnt. With the milk of human kindness obviously coursing through their veins, the other denominations in the church unceremoniously booted the Ethiopians out of the building altogether. Still, when one considers the two centuries of squabbling and carnage that have taken place underneath their feet, it looks as if the Ethiopians have had the last laugh.

Church of the Holy Sepulchre

07.00–20.00

This is Christianity's holiest site, the site of **Jesus' crucifixion**, His internment in the tomb and subsequent **resurrection** three days later (Matthew 27: 33–66 and 28: 1–9). It was designated as such by Helena, the Byzantine Emperor Constantine's mother, during her pilgrimage of AD326; the place where she is reputed to have found pieces of the **True Cross** lies at the eastern end of the church. At the time of her pilgrimage a temple to Aphrodite stood on the site, and the Romans' habit of building pagan temples over places sacred to other religions leads many to believe that there was a church here before the temple, possibly as early as AD60. This is just 30 years after Jesus' crucifixion, causing many to believe that this is indeed the Hill of Golgotha and Calvary, the site of Jesus' death and resurrection.

Save for a few capitals in the courtyard, the Rotunda wall and the front door (which now resides at the back of Zaltimo's Sweets, by the green metal sign to the Russian Archaeological Museum on Souq Khan El-Zeit), the church Helena's son built in AD348 did not survive the Persian invasion of AD614. Its replacement was torn down by the Fatimid Caliph Al-Hakim in 1099, so most of what you see today dates back to the 12th century and the **Crusaders**. Many famous knights, including Godfrey and Baldwin – the first ruler and first king respectively of the Kingdom of Jerusalem – lie buried inside.

Unfortunately, the feelings of visitors today are caught somewhere between reverence and revulsion. Cold and damp one expects in a church of this vintage; however, centuries of water damage staining the stones and weakening the foundations, soot on the walls from a 19th-century fire and whole portions of the building left in disrepair one does not, especially in a church of this importance.

The church has been allowed to sink to this state by the various Christian denominations who bicker constantly over its stewardship. The crux of the argument is this: an 18th-century agreement brokered by the Ottomans

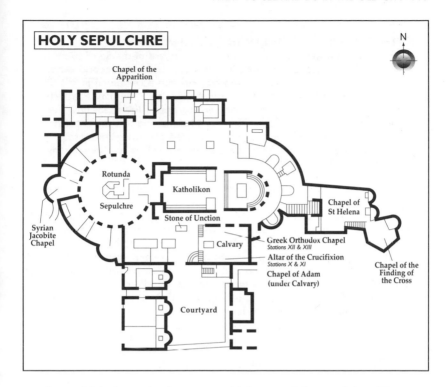

regulates which denomination owns which part of the sepulchre. However, one of the clauses states that whoever cleans or repairs part of the church can claim that section as their own. This has led to a war of attrition, as each denomination fights for the right to restore parts of the church. The results of this internecine battle: parts of the Sepulchre remain in a state of disrepair since the fire of 1809 (started, so it is said, by an inebriated monk and a votive candle); and the clean-up required following the earthquake of 1927 was eventually completed 32 years later, and only because of a Works Agreement the previous year. Larger structural repairs, some of which are now quite urgent, require a hitherto unheard-of level of cooperation between the churches. It's an unholy and shameful sectarian turf war that does no credit to anyone and disgraces the religion. It also makes for an unpleasant atmosphere within the Sepulchre, the tension permeating throughout the church. This, combined with the parlous state of much of the interior, makes the Holy Sepulchre something of a disappointment to many – although others find it spiritually moving despite its scars and shabbiness.

Inside the church

Though it's open all day every day, try to avoid visiting the church between 11.00 and 14.00; that's the busiest time, when you'll have to queue up to see parts of it and suffer the ear-bleeding racket caused by hollering tour groups that echoes throughout the building. If you can, try to visit twice: once for sightseeing, and once during prayer time when the Sepulchre is filled with the discordant noise from half a dozen services at the same time – rather appropriate when one considers the inharmonious relationships between its occupants.

THE MOSQUE OF OMAR IBN AL-KHATTAB

Right beside the southern entrance to the courtyard of the Sepulchre is a mosque that's closed to the public. It's dedicated to Islam's **second caliph** who conquered Palestine and to whom Jerusalem surrendered in AD637. Accompanying Ibn Al-Khattab to the Holy Sepulchre, the city Patriarch, **Sophronius**, asked him if he would care to pray. Al-Khattab, however, fearing that he might set a precedent for Muslims, and that the Sepulchre would then be converted into a mosque, declined, preferring instead to pray outside the Sepulchre. The mosque marks the spot where he chose to pray.

The building itself is a vast, cavernous, rambling, asymmetrical place that looks as if the architects added on bits as they went along without ever considering how their extensions would affect the whole. To the right, up the stone steps as you enter, are four of the last five Stations of the Cross. This is **Calvary**, divided into three sections. At the top of the stairs, the Roman Catholic **Altar of the Crucifixion** plays host to **Stations X**, where Jesus was stripped of his clothes, and **XI**, where Jesus was nailed to the cross. The other main altar on Calvary, the glittering Orthodox altar to the left, stands over a hole where the cross is supposed to have stood; this is **Station XII**. Nearby, two discs mark the spot where the crosses of the two thieves were positioned. To the right of the altar, under glass, is a fissure in the rock said to have been caused by the storms and earthquakes that occurred after Christ's death, while facing the pillar is Stabat Mater, where Mary is traditionally believed to have stood at the foot of the cross. Next to it, **Station XIII**, where Jesus was removed from the cross, faces the altar.

Descending the stairs we reach the **Stone of Unction**, the plinth where Jesus' body was supposedly anointed before burial. (The Greeks believe this to be Station XIII, where Jesus' body was removed from the cross.) Continuing round the church in a clockwise direction, soon you'll come to the **Holy Sepulchre** itself, **Station XIV**, Jesus' tomb. Queue up to visit the small antechamber where an angel told of the resurrection of Jesus, after which is the tomb itself. The marble bench is where His body is said to have been laid. Round the back of the Sepulchre is a **Coptic chapel**, opposite which, in the walls of the church, is a **Syrian Jacobite chapel** that stands in front of a Jewish burial chamber dating back to the first century AD.

This area of the church, the domed **Rotunda**, is the oldest part of the building; some of the walls date back to Constantine's original construction. The large rectangular area to the east was the main body of the Crusaders' church, the **Katholikon**, built and owned by the Greek Orthodox faith. The marble hemisphere under the cupola marks the so-called centre of the world according to Byzantine tradition. This section is usually roped off, so you'll have to head past the **Chapel of the Apparition,**where Jesus appeared to Mary Magdalene, and take the northern aisle, the area worst affected by the fire of 1808, to the Armenian **Chapel of St Helena**. This lies down the stairs at the eastern end of the church; note how its walls are covered with crosses carved by medieval pilgrims; the mosaic floor depicts various churches in Armenia. Beneath the chapel lies the **Chapel of the Finding of the Cross**, a disused quarry in Herod's time, where Queen Helena found what she maintained was the cross of Jesus, complete with nails, in an old cistern. A Jewish catacomb has been cut into the western wall.

The Mardigian Museum

Mon–Sat 9am–4.30pm; NIS3

This enlightening little museum, built round a courtyard of an old **theological seminary**, explores both the history of Armenia and the Armenian community in Jerusalem. Well-presented, with full explanations in English, the collection includes a **model of Jerusalem** as it would have looked in 1715, a fine collection of **Armenian mosaics** and tiles dating back to the 5th century AD, and a look at some of the characters in the history of Jerusalem's Armenian community, such as the patriarch Greg the Chain Bearer who, to raise enough money to pay off the Armenian monastery's outstanding debts, spent four years trussed up in chains begging outside a church in Istanbul.

St James' Cathedral

Mon–Fri 15.00, Sat & Sun 14.30; free

This fascinating little cathedral lies hidden behind the walls of the Armenian compound, but opens its doors to the public every day for just half an hour during the afternoon service. The monks and worshippers are still summoned in the traditional way by banging on hollow pieces of wood, a method that started in the 9th century after a ruling by the city's Muslim overlords prevented the ringing of bells. Inside, under the ribbed vaulting of the **cupola** and a plethora of **icons** all blackened by centuries of incense smoke, the priests chant the Armenian liturgy. The church is dedicated to **St James the Great**, the first martyred disciple (and, some say, the brother of Jesus). Originally a Georgian chapel dedicated to the same fellow, the church is built on the foundations of a 5th-century oratory dedicated to an obscure Egyptian martyr, St Menas. As a reward for supporting their campaign, the Armenians took over the site from the Crusaders in the 12th century.

The Tower of David

April–Oct, Sun–Thurs 09.00–17.00, Fri & Sat 09.00–14.00; Nov–Mar, 10.00–16.00, 10.00–14.00; NIS28/20)

Set in the Old City's restored **citadel**, the Tower of David provides an excellent introduction to Jerusalem. The Tower of David handle is actually a misnomer from the 5th century, when the Byzantines mistook the building for David's ancient palace. The citadel post-dates David's reign by about 800 years, and was probably built in the 2nd century BC, in the Hasmonean era. Herod built his palace, podium and three towers here (see page 88), one of which – Phasaelis – survived the Romans' destruction of the city in AD70. Most of what you see today, however, was built during the Crusader and Mamluke eras, including the large minaret, a 17th-century addition.

Running right round the citadel, the **history of Jerusalem** unfolds in a series of interactive displays, models, holograms and other assorted bells and whistles. Admittedly, the pro-Zionist viewpoint is little short of outrageous; nevertheless, it's obvious that a lot of thought has gone into this display, and it does provide a couple of hours of enlightening entertainment. The English-language labels are copious and well written, so there's really no need for the audio guide (NIS10) or for the free guided tours in English (Sun–Fri at 11.00). There's also a 15-minute cartoon of the city's history in the Phaeselis Tower, which some people have said they enjoyed, and the views from the top are stunning. There's also a **Sound and Light Show** (ask for times), and on Saturdays there's a **Murder Mystery**, where you have to work out who killed High Priest Aristobulus III.

Saint Mark's Church

09.00–12.00, 15.30–18.00

If it weren't for the large sign above the entrance, it would be easy to walk past this little gem of a church to the west of Habad Street, the last bastion of Christian humility in the supremely affluent Jewish Quarter. Its diminutive size has undoubtedly been a major factor in its survival over the last couple of millennia. While Persians and mad Egyptian caliphs were busy razing other, more ostentatious churches to the ground, the congregation at St Mark's merely had to take the sign down and their invisibility was virtually assured. That said, St Mark's didn't escape destruction by either the Persians (AD614) or the Fatimids under Caliph Al-Hakim (1009). But at least these invaders took less care in destroying St Mark's, and as a consequence the congregation managed to patch it up to look much as it had done previously.

As with most of these ancient buildings, a number of claims have been made about St Mark's that have yet to be proved. Some of these are dubious at best, such as the church's insistence that their icon of the Virgin Mary, now tucked away on the west wall, was painted from life by Saint Luke. But other claims bear further scrutiny: for example, the 6th-century **Syrian Aramaic inscription** on the pillar by the entrance, translates as:

> 'This is the house of Mary, mother of John, called Mark. Proclaimed a
> church by the holy apostles under the name of the Virgin Mary, mother
> of God, after the ascension of our Lord Jesus Christ into Heaven,
> Renewed after the destruction of Jerusalem by Titus in the year AD73'

This inscription lends much weight to the claim that this was indeed Mark's mother's house, to which, according to Acts 12, Peter ran following his angel-assisted escape from prison.

So is this the world's oldest church, used by the apostles as early as AD50? Possibly, though most of the upper room dates back only as far as the Crusaders. The cave below is much older, however, and has only recently been properly excavated. A few unidentified human bones were discovered in the cave, and are now preserved in the **reliquary** upstairs.

WHAT TO SEE AND DO IN EAST JERUSALEM

Walk for five minutes east from the quiet, leafy lanes surrounding the Russian Compound and immediately you'll find yourself back in the exotic atmosphere of the Orient. And not the quaint, tumbledown, frozen-in-time Orient of the Old City either, but the noisy, cars-revving, horns-blasting, radios-blaring, people-shouting frenzy of the modern Middle East. Arab East Jerusalem is really quite exhilarating once you have acclimatised to its pace. There are a number of sights here, some great shops and, at the top of the hill, a salubrious area of hotels and offices. It is this area that the PLO hope will form the centre of their national capital one day, and **Orient House**, the Jerusalem offices of the PLO, sits right at its centre. Here, and in the district known as Sheikh Jarrah to the north, you will also find plenty of foreign embassies from countries who refuse to recognise Israel's hegemony over the entire city.

Under the Jordanians, East Jerusalem became the administrative capital of the West Bank; these days, however, the two are separated by three rings of Israeli settlements and West Bank Palestinians require a permit to visit any part of the Holy City. Though *they* don't need a permit, the only Israelis brave enough to cross into East Jerusalem are heavily-armed soldiers. But, needless to say, East Jerusalem is perfectly safe for tourists. A tour around the centre of East Jerusalem should take a day or possibly a lot less, though you may want to do some shopping along the way. After that, you may want to explore the **Mount of Olives**, or the archaeological excavations in the **Kidron Valley** that runs beneath it.

Roman Plaza
Sat–Thurs 09.00–16.00, Friday 09.00–14.00; NIS6/3
The Damascus Gate is the only one of the seven gates to have been properly excavated, and the results can be seen by taking the steps to the west of the gate (left as you exit the Old City). Unfortunately, an eventful history doesn't necessarily translate into an exciting tourist attraction, and the inexpensive entrance fee reflects the fact that the Damascus Gate excavations are a little dull. The site is called the Roman Plaza because of the 20m stretch of Roman paving slabs which once formed part of the main plaza of the Roman city, **Aelia Capitolina**. As a sop to those who may feel ripped off at having paid money to look at paving slabs, a hologram of Hadrian's column, which originally adorned the plaza, stands in its middle. Lining the plaza is a series of photographs and drawings depicting the history of the Damascus Gate over the centuries – note how, even by 1860, there was no development outside the city walls.

To the left of the corridor, a small room, once a **Roman guardroom**, contains an oil press used during Arab times. A winding staircase leads up to the Ramparts Walk.

Zedekiah's Caves
Sat–Thurs 09.00–16.00, Fri 09.00–14.00, NIS9/4
Originally a small natural cave, the huge labyrinth that exists today is largely the work of the builders of the Second Temple, who came here on the hunt for some raw materials with which to rebuild the Old City. Legend has it that Solomon also used the stone from this quarry to build the First Temple, which is why it's sometimes known as **Solomon's Quarries**. The entrance to the caves lies in the city [...] amascus Gates.

[...] es, atmospherically illuminated by the ghostly
orai [...] retch for hundreds of metres beneath the Old
Cit [...] is **Freemasons' Hall**, so-called because the
Fre [...] ion as the founder of their order, have held
ann [...] the caves' rediscovery in 1854. The columns
sup [...] up an estimated half a million tonnes. There's
also [...] **h's tears**, the water supposedly formed from
the [...] destruction of the First Temple.

Rockefeller Museum
Sun–Thurs 10.00–17.00, Fri–Sat 10.00–14.00; NIS24/15
If you find the thought of traipsing all the way to, and then all the way round, the massive Israeli museum in West Jerusalem a daunting one, you could do worse than come to this little gem. Housed in a beautiful, fortress-style building built by the British in 1927, the Rockefeller Museum houses exhibits arranged in a clockwise, chronological order from prehistory to the Islamic era of the 7th century AD. Amongst the earliest exhibits are some rather well-preserved **skeletons**, including one which is over 100,000 years old, and a second that is in such a remarkable state of preservation that even its beaded headdress has survived intact. The highlights of the collection, however, are the statues and decorations from **Hisham's Palace** in Jericho. The **sculptures** of bare-breasted dancing women, and the **carved faces** that appear on the stucco walls and poke through the stucco icanthus leaves adorning the **Dome of the Diwan**, are simply

wonderful, and not a little surprising; clearly the palace's owner, Caliph Al-Walid Ibn Yazid, felt himself above the laws of iconoclasm that regulated the artistic creativity of his empire. Other items to look out for include the **clay coffins** from the Canaanite era, which resemble giant weebles, and the **Crusader lintels** that once surmounted the doorways of the Holy Sepulchre. Mention must also be made of the delightful arcaded central courtyard complete with fishpond, the perfect place for those who've overdosed on relics to sit and snooze.

Garden Tomb
Mon–Sat 08.30–12.00, 14.00–17.30; closed Sunday except for the 09.00 service
Of the possible locations of Christ's crucifixion, the Anglican-owned Garden Tomb is undoubtedly the most attractive. Despite its location overlooking the bus station, the Tomb and gardens are an oasis of peaceful greenery amid the hurly burly of East Jerusalem.

The site was first suggested as a possible location for Calvary by none other than **General Gordon** (of Khartoum fame). His reason for suggesting this hill is simple: Golgotha means **skull**, and the white chalky cliff-face at the back of the bus station did indeed, up until this century, resemble the face of a skull. For proof of this, go to the viewing platform at the end of the garden, where you can see a photograph taken in the 19th century in which the eyes and nostrils of the 'skull' can clearly be discerned.

Most of the evidence to back up this claim has since been refuted, to a point where even the Anglicans themselves now admit that this is unlikely to be the site of Calvary. But who cares, because this place is a wonderful little slice of rural England, only with added palm trees and sunshine. The gardens have an order about them that's rare in this part of the city, and when it comes to viewing the tomb (a modest two-chamber affair cut into the hillside) everyone waits in a queue. Even the people who run it seem quintessentially English, the bloke who took me round even wearing socks with his sandals. So while it may not be the site of Jesus' resurrection, the Tomb is the perfect place for those who need to escape Jerusalem for a little while.

St George's Cathedral and the Tomb of Kings
Built in 1890 during the episcopate of the splendidly named Bishop George Francis Popham Blyth (though it looks much older, thanks to its Crusader shape and gothic interior), **St George's** is the largest Anglican building in Jerusalem. The grounds of the cathedral include a school run along the lines of an English public school, a hostel (see page 95) and a bell tower, one of the most striking in the Holy City, built in memory of King Edward VII.

At the corner of Sharia Saladin and Sharia Nablus, the **Tomb of Kings** (Mon–Sat 08.00–12.00, 14.00–17.00; NIS3) was once thought to have been the last resting place of the kings of Judah – hence the name – though now it is thought that this is actually the royal cemetery of an obscure state within the Babylonian Empire, called Adiabene, whose royal family converted to Judaism. Rough steps lead down to a large square flanked by two submerged caves and, to the left, a huge quarry; the extensive catacombs lead off from the quarry through a hole in its western wall. A torch is essential if you wish to explore them thoroughly, though all eventually lead to a dead end (no pun intended).

Orient House and beyond
Opposite Orient House, the **Dar Al-Tifl** is a girls' school with a four-room **Folklore Museum** (Fri & Sun 08.00–14.30; donations). The highlight of the

collection is their Palestinian dress collection, with items from every Palestinian region. Behind Orient House, and accessible via the alleyway at the back, is the **Jerusalem Centre for Arabic Music** (see page 98). This recording-studio-cum-concert-hall is probably the most likely venue for hearing traditional Palestinian music in Jerusalem, though their public performances are seldom advertised, especially in the English press. Just beyond the recording studio, and sharing the same forecourt, is the **Palestinian National Theatre**, the Hakawati (see page 98). Further on along Sharia Nablus is the wonderful **American Colony Hotel** (see page 95) and, just below it, the **Sheikh Jarrah Mosque**, housing the body of a 12th-century saint.

The mosque gives its name to the affluent Palestinian suburb on the hill opposite. **Sheikh Jarrah** is home to most of East Jerusalem's embassies, a couple of hotels and the excellent **Palestinian Needlework Shop** (see page 99). Before heading up to it, however, take a left along Sharia Sama'an Al-Sadik (aka Sheikh Jarrah) and the **Al-Wasiti Art Gallery** (Mon–Sat 10.00–16.00; donations) at number 13. Named after an influential 13th-century Iraqi painter and housed in a restored 1920s Arabian villa, this small art gallery was founded in 1994 by four prominent Palestinian artists to foster the development, documentation and promotion of Palestinian arts throughout the world. As well as holding continuous temporary exhibitions, the gallery also has a small library of art books covering both Western and Islamic art, and an archive, the only one of its kind, dedicated to Palestinian art. All of these departments are open to the public, though for access to the library and archive they ask you to ring beforehand to let them know you're coming. It's well worth visiting, and afterwards you can call in to one of the upmarket **restaurants** along this stretch (see page 98).

Mount of Olives

During the life of Jesus, the Mount of Olives, separated from the Old City by the Kidron Valley, was the home of a large **Roman garrison**. As such, it would have provided a convenient refuge for Jesus away from the elders of the Temple, who saw him as a dangerous heretic (for their part, the Romans would have been largely uninterested in just another bearded religious fanatic, which their province of Philistina seemed to specialise in).

Whether Jesus actually did live on the Mount cannot be said for certain, but according to the gospels many of the last acts in His life were played out here. It was here that Jesus prayed while His followers slept; here that Judas betrayed Him with a kiss and here, in the **Garden of Gethsemane** at the foot of the hill, that He was arrested by the Roman guards (for the appropriate Bible references, see the descriptions below). Acts 1:12 also implies that this is the site of Jesus' ascension.

As you may expect, a number of chapels have been erected down the centuries over the spots where many of these events were supposed to have taken place. Thanks to some extensive archaeological work, we now know that there were at least 24 churches and chapels located here during the Byzantine era. However, with only one exception– the Tomb of the Virgin at the foot of the hill – none of the churches that you see today was built before the latter half of the 19th century. The Byzantine structures were pulled down during the Persian invasion of AD614, and the Fatimids under Caliph Al-Hakim did much the same in the 11th century. Earthquakes and neglect during the Mamluke and Ottoman periods did for the rest.

It was only during the late 1800s that Christians were finally allowed to own and build upon the mount again. The number of churches has increased steadily ever since, though available space on the western slopes is in short supply these days thanks to the ever expanding **Jewish cemetery**, the biggest and oldest in the

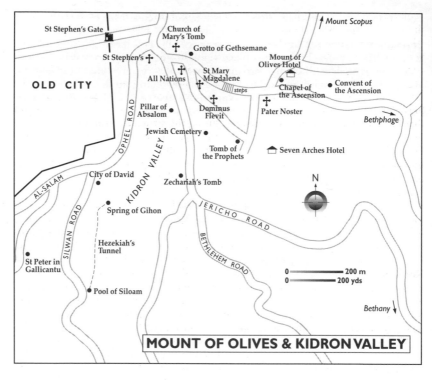

St Stephen's Gate

Church of
Mary's Tomb

Grotto of Gethsemane

Mount Scopus

St Stephen's

Mount of
Olives Hotel

OLD CITY

All Nations

St Mary
Magdalene

steps

Chapel of
the Ascension

Convent of
the Ascension

Pillar of
Absalom

Dominus
Flevit

Pater Noster

Bethphage

Jewish Cemetery

Tomb of
the Prophets

Seven Arches Hotel

City of David

Zechariah's Tomb

N

Spring of Gihon

JERICHO ROAD

Hezekiah's
Tunnel

BETHLEHEM ROAD

0 ——— 200 m
0 ——— 200 yds

St Peter in
Gallicantu

Pool of Siloam

Bethany

MOUNT OF OLIVES & KIDRON VALLEY

world. According to the prophet Zechariah (14:1–9), those buried on the Mount
of Olives will be the first to be resurrected on the Day of Judgement. Believers will
therefore pay handsomely to be buried there, to the extent that owning a burial plot
on it has become almost a status symbol. The disgraced British newspaper
magnate, Robert Maxwell, is one of the more infamous of recent arrivals.

At the foot of the mount

The best time to visit the Mount of Olives is in the morning (so the sun is on your
back when you're taking photos of the view over the Old City) and preferably on
Tuesday or Thursday morning when all the churches are open. Dress modestly (no
shorts) and bring a torch. If you don't fancy the 15-minute climb to the top, bus
number 75 from the Central Bus Station runs to Al-Tur, 400m north of the summit.

The mount is just a three-minute walk out and down the hill from the Lions'
Gate. The first sacred building you come to, on your left as you walk from the Old
City, is also the oldest, and is dedicated not to Jesus but to His mother. The
incense-infused **Tomb of the Virgin Mary** (Mon–Sat 06.00–11.00, 14.30–17.00),
built in 1130 by Benedictine monks and now shared between a number of
Christian denominations, is just one of many buildings that purports to house
Mary's grave. The tomb itself is a small stone affair protected behind glass.
(Incidentally, Mohammed was said to have seen a light over Mary's tomb as he
ascended to Heaven at the end of his Night Flight, and for this reason the tomb is
holy to Muslims too.) More impressive than the tomb, however, are the 12th-
century **marble steps** leading down to it, flanked by two semi-circular recesses
housing the tombs of Queen Melisande, to the left of the steps, and her son, the
Crusader king Baldwin II, to the right.

Emerging into the sunlight once more, on your immediate left before you leave the church compound is the **Grotto of Gethsemane** (daily 08.30–11.45 and 14.30–17.00). The name 'Gethsemane' is said to be derived from two Aramaic words: 'Gat', meaning oil, and 'Shemanim' meaning press. Significantly, an ancient oil press was found in this grotto in 1956, lending credence to its claim to be the cave used by Jesus when living on the mount – a claim also made by the much larger church over the road (see below). According to the Bible, Jesus prayed at Gethsemane while His disciples slept (Luke 22:39–45), and it was here that He was arrested (Matthew 26:49). During the struggle to capture Him, one of the disciples cut off the ear of a Jewish high priest who was present; Jesus healed the ear, so we can also say that this was the location of the last healing miracle performed by Christ. There's little to see in the grotto now save for traces of Byzantine mosaics in the floor, evidence that this grotto has been a place of veneration for over 1,500 years.

Directly across the road from the grotto, a small wooden door in the wall leads to the dazzling **Gethsemane Basilica of the Agony**. This basilica, built in 1924 by Antonio Barluzzi, supposedly marks the location of the Agony, where Jesus prayed and wept, frightened of the ordeal He knew He was to suffer while His disciples slept (Luke 22:39–45). The stone on which He knelt, the so-called **Rock of the Agony** on which His sweat, 'like drops of blood', fell as He prayed, lies exposed in the centre of the church, surrounded by a wrought-iron railing. As with all the churches on the Mount of Olives, the present Basilica has been built over the site of at least two previous churches, one Byzantine (built circa AD380 by Theodosius) and one Crusader, destroyed in circa AD1200.

This basilica, one of Barluzzi's first efforts, bears many of his trademarks, being rather austere and simple. The dark lighting, with little light filtering through the purple-stained windows, adds to the rather sombre mood, as befits a church commemorating one of the lowest points in the life of Jesus. It also, like all of Barluzzi's churches, contains some rather dazzling mosaics, including the beautiful design above the porch and the three mosaics on the back wall of the interior that depict, from left to right, the kiss of Judas, the Agony, and the 'Ego Sum' (see John 11.25). Over 15 different countries contributed towards the building of this church, hence the basilica's more common name: the **Church of all Nations**.

Before the church is the **Garden of Gethsemane**. What in biblical times was an olive grove is now a tidy flower garden of carnations, roses, daisies and pansies. However, there are eight **olive trees** still growing here, the roots of which, according to the monk who welcomes visitors at the gate, have been scientifically proved to be at least 2,000 years old. If only they could talk. . .

Climbing the Mount of Olives

Just above the church's entrance gate the road branches into three paths, all of which lead to the summit of the mount. The central one is the straightest of the three, while the right-hand track winds its way steadily up the hill, passing a number of important sites and churches on the way. The first of the latter is the Russian Orthodox **Church of St Mary Magdalene** (Tues & Thurs, 09.00–11.30), whose seven golden cupolas, currently shrouded in scaffolding as they undergo renovation, form one of the true landmarks of East Jerusalem. The church was built in 1888 by Tsar Alexander III and his brothers in memory of their mother, Empress Maria Alexandrovna, who is buried here. In the large mural by the Russian artist Ivanov above the marble and bronze iconostasis, Mary Magdalene (see page 154) is depicted holding a red egg, a symbol of the resurrection and eternal life, as she tells the Emperor Tiberias of the injustice of

Jesus' trial and death. According to Christian tradition, as a result of this meeting Pilate was deposed as governor of Judaea and sent into exile, though it's a scene without any biblical or archaeological foundation.

In front of the iconostasis sits the **Dogiditra** in a specially made wooden frame. This icon of Mary, originally from Lebanon, is supposed to possess special powers, having survived the burning of its original home, a church in Lebanon. It was also said to have cured people suffering from cholera during an epidemic in the 18th century.

The church of **Dominus flevit** (daily, 08.00–11.45, 14.30–17.00) is situated in some well-maintained gardens about 200m from the summit. The name of the church is Latin for 'The Lord Wept', referring to an incident described in Matthew 23 (37–39) and Luke 19 (41–44) when Jesus wept as He foresaw the bloody fate of Jerusalem. Appropriately, Antonio Barluzzi designed the chapel in 1955 in the shape of a tear. The interior of the chapel houses some fairly simple **mosaics** from a previous church dating back to the 7th century. By the entrance to the gardens are the excavations of four burial chambers from a 1st-century Judaeo-Christian cemetery, in which were found a number of **ossuaries** (bone boxes) decorated with the Star of David and the monogram of Constantine.

At the bottom of the small flight of steps leading up to the summit lies the **Tomb of the Prophets** (Mon–Fri 09.00–15.30), the prophets in this case being Haggai, Zechariah and Malachi. The tomb is often locked, but the Othman family who live in the house next door have the key, and also rent out torches at NIS5 a time. From the gate steps lead down to a semi-circular cave, from which exits lead off to a large, semi-circular corridor containing over fifty tombs.

The summit of the Mount

Having made it this far, it's time to relax and drink in the gorgeous panorama from below the Seven Arches Hotel. Those who haven't overloaded on churches may

THE ARCHITECT ANTONIO BARLUZZI

Visit any major 20th-century church in Palestine and the chances are that, if it is owned by the Roman Catholic church, it was built by the Italian architect Antonio Barluzzi. Chapels as miniscule as the **Altar of the Crucifixion** and the **Tomb of the Lord's Resurrection** in Jerusalem's Holy Sepulchre, and as magnificent as the **Chapel of the Flagellation** and the **Church of All Nations**, all bear the inimitable stamp of Barluzzi's imagination. His structures have earned praise from both the worshipping layman, who finds the atmosphere of his churches conducive to contemplation and prayer, and the architectural connoisseur, who marvels at the restrained originality of his designs. Barluzzi's churches have also earned him international awards. Made a knight of the Italian crown in 1922, the following year Barluzzi became a commander of the Equestrian Order of Knights of the Holy Sepulchre, and three years before his death in 1960, he was made Grand Officer of the Order of Merit of the Italian Republic, one of Italy's highest honours. Though undoubtedly deserved, these honours were something of an anathema for a man renowned for his uncomplicated, humble approach to life and his simple piety.

Antonio Barluzzi was born in 1884 in Rome, a city where he later studied for his degree in engineering. Unsure whether to follow in his elder brother's footsteps and become an architect, or to enter the service of the church, Barluzzi realised the possibility of combining both during his first trip to the Holy Land in 1913, where his brother was involved in the construction of a like to visit the cute little **Pater Noster Church** (09.05–11.30, 15.00–16.45), 150m north from the path on the bend in the road. This chapel is built round a small cave in the centre of the main courtyard, one of the three 'Mystical Grottoes' as designated by Constantine's mother Helena, a cave said to have been used by Jesus when fleeing from His persecutors. (The other grottoes can be found in the Holy Sepulchre, and at the Church of the Nativity in Bethlehem.) More importantly, this is also believed to be the spot where Jesus taught His disciples to pray, hence the 62 translations of the **Lord's Prayer** written on decorative, ceramic-tiled panels on the chapel walls.

The original Byzantine basilica, called the **Eleona Basilica** (Basilica of Olives), was destroyed during the Muslim invasion of 637, the grotto disappearing altogether under the ruins until its rediscovery in the late 19th century by Princess de La Tour d'Auvergne. The current building, including the simple chapel to the east of the grotto, dates from 1894.

One hundred metres further north lies the simplest of all the Christian shrines on the mount, the **Chapel of the Ascension** (08.00–17.30; NIS3), a rather unimpressive octagonal building that covers a rock marked, so it is said, by the last footprint Jesus imprinted on this Earth before He ascended to Heaven. The building was originally a 12th-century Crusader church, though it was converted into a mosque in 1198 by Saladin (Muslims also revering Jesus as a prophet), and remains an Islamic shrine to this day. The stone benches that stand in the courtyard are used as altars on Ascension Day, the one day that Christians are allowed to hold services at the site.

Heading north, behind the Mount of Olives Hotel is a **mosque** that's built over the cave of the 3rd-century monk Pelagia. Pelagia was not only a target of Christian persecutors but, as a woman, was subject to the rampant chauvanism of the time. For this reason, she spent her entire life disguised as a man called Pelagius, an

hospital. After World War I (in which he was rescued from a torpedoed ship near Malta, and went on to serve as sergeant for a detachment based at Rafah in the Gaza Strip) he decided to stay on in the Holy Land, and just one year after hostilities had ceased Barluzzi was given his first commission, the building of the **Church of All Nations** at Gethsemane. This was followed by the **Custodia di Terra Santa** and the **Hospice of the Good Shepherd** in Beit Sahour, both consecrated in 1925, then the wonderful **Church of the Flagellation** in Jerusalem and the two chapels in the Holy Sepulchre.

Wonderful as these structures are, Barluzzi's most productive and creative years still lay ahead of him. During the period 1949–55 he constructed many of of his most famous works, including the **Shrine of the Visitation** in Ein Karem, the friar's cloister by **St Catherine's Chapel** at Bethlehem (completed 1949), the **Shrine of St Lazarus** in Bethany (1953), the **Shrine of the Shepherds** in Beit Sahour (1954) and the **Dominus Flevit** on the Mount of Olives (1955). With each construction, his working methods were the same: for weeks beforehand he would live a life of rigorous austerity with the Franciscans in the Holy Land, meditating, praying, and scouring the gospels in search of inspiration for his buildings. His self-denial was such that on many occasions he is said to have collapsed through malnutrition; yet in spite of the hardships he often professed a desire to live and die in the company of his beloved Franciscans. That last wish was granted in December 1960, when Barluzzi, at the age of 76, passed serenely away in a small room of the Holy Land Delegation in Rome.

impersonation which proved so completely convincing that the other monks only found out about her deception whilst preparing her for burial.

The mosque is closed to the public, though the nuns from the nearby **Convent of the Ascension** are allowed to visit once a year. This church is another fascinating Russian Orthodox complex whose tower, 900m above sea level, is said to be the highest point in Jerusalem. Unfortunately, it operates the same restrictive opening hours as the Church of Mary Magdalene (Tues & Thurs 09.00–11.30). The convent, church and chapel are largely the result of the efforts of one man, a Russian priest named Antonine who established an ecumenical mission here in the latter half of the 19th century, at a time when Christians were forbidden from owning land on the Mount. By learning Arabic and riding around town on a donkey, Antonine managed to ingratiate himself with the locals who soon adopted him as one of their own. Eventually, he persuaded them to let him buy some land, and with the financial help of imperial Russia the church was built and consecrated in 1888. The nuns arrived soon after. Originally, most of the sisters were Russian, along with a few local ladies who had been abandoned as children at the gates by local families. Today there are over 50 sisters from over a dozen different countries, and the convent is one of the more successful in the Holy Land.

Having made your way past the blind and somewhat cranky guard (who may ask for a bribe before he lets you in), you find yourself in a pleasant garden with the wonderful little church to your left and, more often than not, the even more wonderful Mother Ksenia, your guide around the grounds, waiting outside. Engaging and knowledgeable, Mother Ksenia welcomes questions and will show you some or all of the features of the compound, depending on the level of interest you show – so pay attention!

The church is probably the third to have stood on this site, following one built on the orders of the tireless St Helena in the 4th century, and one built following that church's destruction by the Persians in the 7th. The bases of two **Byzantine pillars** can be seen in the church (a priest from the last century decided they were ugly and had the pillars themselves removed), and the smashed marble floor just before the altar also dates from this time. To your left as you face the altar is the grave of Antonine. The wooden picture-frame full of small **icons** that now rests on his grave originally hung in his room. At his feet, just outside the church, is his pupil and successor as head of the mission, Barthenius, who was brutally murdered in his library in 1909.

The real treasure of the convent, however, lies in the small chapel, built in 1922, to the rear of the church. According to the legend, it was here that two 4th-century Syrian monks discovered the **head of John the Baptist**, which was said to have been brought to the Holy City and buried by St Joanna. St Helena got to hear about this discovery, and decided to do what she always did in these situations: build a church. You can see the dip in the floor from where the head was supposedly recovered. Next to it, underneath the rugs covering the floor, is an astonishing mosaic, a series of birds, pigeons, dogs, cows, grapes and leaves, all painstakingly recreated from real life using tiny stone chips, or tesserae. No dyes were used to colour the stones, the workmen instead gathering different coloured stones from all corners of Palestine. Nobody is quite sure what this design symbolises. Nor do we know to whom the 7th-century **Armenian inscription** on the adjacent mosaic refers, when it says: 'This is the monument of Lord Bishop Jacov, built according to his instructions.' Nevertheless, we must be thankful that the ruins of the churches that once housed it have managed to keep it in such pristine condition.

Other features of the compound you may be shown include the **library of Barthenius**, a **locust tree** (when the Bible says John the Baptist ate locusts, it is

For details of the walk from Bethany via Bethphage to the Mount of Olives, please see page 156.

the fruit of this tree, rather than the insect, that it is referring to) and the entrance into a small cave used by hermits during the years of Islamic oppression.

Mount Scopus
The northern extension of the ridge that runs to the east of the Old City (and which includes the Mount of Olives) is known as Mount Scopus. It's a strategically vital hill, thanks to its unobstructed views over Jerusalem, and the Crusaders and the British have both camped here before taking the Holy City. Though geographically part of East Jerusalem, Mount Scopus is very much an Israeli enclave. It was the only part of East Jerusalem to remain in Israeli hands after 1948 (supplies were shipped in to the residents from West Jerusalem in convoys under UN protection), and it remains the only part, outside the modern settlements, that's predominantly Jewish today. The hill plays host to two significant Israeli institutions, the **Hebrew University** and **Hadassah Hospital**. Near to the hospital is a **World War I Commonwealth cemetery**, and a modern **amphitheatre**, while over to the south, on a part of the hill that was previously under Jordanian control, is the **Augusta Victoria Hospital**, built in 1910 and named after the wife of Kaiser Wilhelm. The tower is surely one of the most distinctive landmarks of outer Jerusalem, and gives its name to the local district, **Al-Tur**. The hospital, currently run by UNRWA, cares mainly for West Bank Palestinians. Bus number 4 from West Jerusalem runs to the mount.

The Kidron Valley
If, at the Greek Orthodox **Church of St Stephen** near the foot of the Mount of Olives, you take a right rather than a left, and then continue south along Sharia Ophel by the eastern walls of the Old City, you find yourself walking above the valley floor of the Kidron Valley. To your left as you walk you see the curious **Pillar of Absalom**, which, despite being named after David's incalcitrant son, is thought to date from the first century AD. Nearby is the grave of the Prophet Zechariah.

In biblical times, the Temple Mount was but the northern extremity of Jerusalem that stretched to the south in the shape of a windsock along **Mount Ophel** (the hill immediately to the south of the temple's Mount Moriah); the southern portion of Sharia Ophel thus cuts right across this ancient settlement. Excavations by Katherine Kenyon in the sixties and seventies on the southern slopes of Mount Ophel have uncovered some historically important ruins from this era, which have been fenced off from the rest of the valley and given the rather grandiose title the **City of David** (Sun–Thurs 09.00–17.00, Fri 09.00–13.00; officially NIS3, though this is rarely collected). The excavations have provided some valuable insights into ancient Jerusalem, including the discovery of no fewer than 25 different strata, each representing a different era in the city's history. Most of the excavations visible today actually pre-date David's city, including the giant **Jebusite Walls** that successfully repelled the attacks of Joshua, only to fall to David 200 years later. Signboards point out the important parts of the site, though they, like the rest of the site, appear to have been neglected, and now lie face down on the ground.

Steps from the southern end of the City of David excavations lead down the steep hill to the Kidron Valley floor and the **Spring of Gihon** (Sun–Thurs 09.00–16.00, Fri 09.00–14.00; NIS5). As far as anyone knows, this spring was probably the reason the Jebusites decided to settle here in the first place. The Judaean king Hezekiah recognised the importance of the spring, which is why he built a 512m-long tunnel between the spring and a pool inside the city walls, diverting the water from one to the other to ensure the city had a constant water supply throughout the Assyrian siege.

For another NIS5 you can walk through **Hezekiah's Tunnel**; bring a torch or hire candles from the shop by the entrance. For most of the way you'll be wading through shin- or knee-deep water, so this is one of the very few attractions in the Holy Land where it's actually advisable to wear shorts. The tunnel was originally dug by two teams of labourers working at either end who met in the middle, the exact spot where they met clearly shown by the differences in floor levels. The tunnel's destination, the **Pool of Shiloam**, features in John 9: 8 when a blind man, on the orders of Jesus, bathed here and was cured. (If you don't take the tunnel, entry into the pool is another NIS5.)

A second, vertical tunnel, known as **Warren's Shaft** (Sun–Thurs 09.00–17.00, Fri 09.00–13.00; NIS10/5) after its 19th-century discoverer, Charles Warren, also leads to the pool, though it's since been walled off. This shaft is even older than the tunnel, probably dating back to the Jebusites, though its original use is unknown. The other end of the shaft is housed in an old Ottoman building at the foot of the City of David; alongside the spiral staircase leading to the shaft is a small **museum** with pottery discovered during Warren's excavations.

Mount Zion

Lying immediately outside the Zion Gates, Mount Zion is never actually mentioned in the Bible, though the term 'Zion' as a pseudonym for both the city of Jerusalem and the Temple Mount occurs frequently throughout. However, the mount does have a place in Christian tradition, which not only holds that the Last Supper (Matthew 26: 26–30) took place here, but also that Mary, on the way to Egypt with Joseph and her infant Jesus, fell asleep on the mount, exhausted. Some also believe that this is where Mary lived and died after the crucifixion. A further tradition has it that the Council of Jerusalem in AD50 took place here, in which the apostles decided once and for all that Christianity was for everyone, Gentiles as well as Jews (Acts 15).

First inhabited in the 8th century BC and originally inside the city walls (as confirmed by the Madaba map, a 6th-century mosaic map of Palestine discovered in a church in Jordan), Mount Zion became separated after Suleyman's architects ran out of money. A further separation from the Old City occurred in 1948: while the Jordanians held the Old City, Mount Zion lay in Israeli territory. Officially, it still belongs to West Jerusalem.

Today, the mount is home to the Tomb of David, the Coenaculum, traditionally the site of the Last Supper, and, most prominently, the **Dormition Abbey** (daily, 08.00–12.00, 14.00–18.00). Built on the ruins of Byzantine and Crusader churches commemorating the death of Mary, the land was acquired by the German emperor in 1898, and subsequently handed over to the German Benedictine order who built the Romanesque-style basilica in 1906. In the apse is a large mosaic of Mary cradling the baby Jesus, who holds a book on which is written 'I am the Light of the World'. Beneath is a quotation from the prophet Isaiah, 'The virgin will be with child and will give birth to a son, and will call him Immanuel', and beneath that are portraits of the eight prophets who predicted the coming of the Messiah.

To the sides of the apse are **six small recesses**, or chapels, containing a total of five mosaics of various saints, and a wooden carving. From left to right, the altars are dedicated to: St Boniface surrounded by St Lioba and St Mauritius; St John the Baptist; Jesus' family tree; the Three Wise Kings; Mary, the patron saint of Bavaria; and St Benedict, here rendered in wood. The mosaic floor, completed by a local monk, includes, unusually for a Christian building, the twelve signs of the pagan **zodiac**, here representing the four corners of the world to which the Word of God has been taken. Downstairs in the **crypt** is a recumbent statue of Mary surrounded by pillars.

From the Dormition, turn right and walk for 50m, then take the first left through a door with an Ottoman inscription above it. Stairs on the left lead up to a second door, through which you reach the **Coenaculum** (08.30–17.00, closed Friday afternoon; free), from the Latin *Cenaca*, meaning dining-room. Almost certainly *not* the venue for the Last Supper, having been built during the Crusader era a thousand years after Jesus' death, it's nevertheless a reasonably peaceful, atmospheric spot. From here, head back to the courtyard entrance, then turn right down the stairs to the **Tomb of David**. Ascribed as David's final resting place in the 10th century, this rudimentary chamber contains a cloth-draped cenotaph. In an adjoining chamber, said to be directly beneath the Coenaculum, it is held that Jesus washed His disciples' feet at the end of the Last Supper.

Almost opposite the tomb, the **Chamber of the Holocaust** was Israel's first museum dedicated to those who died at the hands of the Nazis. Though smaller and less well-known than Yad Vashem (see below), the chamber still packs a huge emotional punch with its collection of items made of human remains – lampshades of human skin, soap made out of human fat – and its exhibition of contemporary anti-Semitism. Further down the hill, and across the main road, lies the **grave of Oskar Schindler**, one of the Righteous Gentiles who saved many of his largely Jewish workforce from the concentration camps of Nazi Germany. Still further, the **Church of Saint Peter in Gallicantu** (Mon–Sat 08.30–12.00, 14.00–17.00), supposedly marks the spot where Jesus was imprisoned by Caiaphas, the High Priest of the Temple, and where Peter three times denied knowing Him (Matthew 26:75).

WHAT TO SEE AND DO IN WEST JERUSALEM

The newest and most modern part of Jerusalem was first settled less than 150 years ago. It has everything you'd expect from a 20th-century Western town, such as bars, nightclubs and department stores, though the difference in prices between here and East Jerusalem is quite marked. Most of the attractions in this part of the city tend to be located in the outer suburbs, so you'll need to make use of the city's extensive bus service. Relevant transport details are given at the end of each section below.

The Israeli Museum
Sun, Mon, Wed, Thurs 10.00–17.00, Tues 10.00–22.00, Fri 10.00–14.00, Sat 10.00–16.00; NIS26/20; includes entry into the Rockefeller Museum within one week
This is one of the best museums of the entire Near East, a stylish, well-laid out and comprehensively-labelled collection that contains some of the greatest treasures of the Holy Land. Pride of place goes to the **Dead Sea Scrolls**, discovered in Qumran near the Dead Sea in Palestine (see page 174) and now housed in the **Shrine of the Book** (Mon–Thurs 10.00–22.00, Fri 10.00–14.00, Sat 10.00–16.00). The bulk of the museum, including the garden, is taken up with the **national art collection**, a curious pot-pourri of styles where the curators have apparently attempted to buy one work of art from every famous 20th-century artist. Nearby, the **Bible Lands Museum** is also worth a visit for those who haven't already overdosed on biblical stuff during their sojourn in Palestine.

Across the road is the Israeli parliament, or **Knesset**. Guided tours leave regularly from the foyer on Sundays and Thursdays or, to see the parliament in action, call in on Mondays, Tuesdays or Wednesdays. Bring your passport.

Catch bus numbers.9, 17, or 24 to reach these attractions.

Yad Vashem – the Holocaust Museum
Sun–Thurs 09.00–17.00, Fri 09.00–14.00; free

This place is a must. While the criticism levelled against the museum – that it is not so much a historical record as a cynical exploitation of human tragedy used to excuse subsequent Jewish atrocities in the Near East – may contain a kernel of truth, I defy anyone not to be moved by this absorbing and heartbreaking tribute to the victims of the Nazi holocaust. The museum, set in a pine forest, is split into many different sections; a free map provided at the entrance should ensure that you miss nothing. Alongside the displays recounting the history of the holocaust are a number of memorials to the victims. The **children's memorial** – one flame in a mirrored hall, with the names of the victims echoing in the background – is particularly moving. There is also a **train**, used in the transportation of the Jews to the concentration camps, and a **library** detailing the lives of those who perished. From Sunday to Wednesday you can catch a **guided tour** of the site, beginning at 10.00.

Catch bus 18 or 20 to reach the Yad Vashem, which lies 2km to the west of the Knesset.

Mea She'arim
Although not officially a tourist attraction, this Orthodox enclave to the north of the Jaffa Road entices many sightseers who come to observe the behaviour and customs of the **ultra-orthodox** *haredi* community. If it weren't for the incessant drone of distant traffic, a stroll in these streets could make you feel as if you've stepped back in time a couple of hundred years; the male residents with their beards, sidelocks and long black caftans emulating a style of dress conceived in 16th-century Poland. The locals don't take too kindly to tourists snooping around, especially if you're toting a camera, so be as discreet and polite as possible. Whilst it is unnecessary to adopt the local costume, make sure your arms and legs are covered. To reach here, walk to the junction of Jaffa Road and King George V Street, and then head north along the latter to Nathan Strauss; Mea She'arim is the compound on your right after HaNevi'im.

TRANSPORT DETAILS
Beit Jala bus 21 from Central Bus Station (NIS3)
Beit Sahour bus 47 from CBS (NIS3)
Bethany bus 36 from CBS (NIS1.5), or NIS2 by sherut
Bethlehem bus 124 from Damascus Gate (NIS2), or NIS2.5 by sherut from the Damascus Gate
Hebron bus 23 from Damascus Gate; alternatively, NIS2.5 by sherut to Bethlehem, then NIS4 to Hebron from there.
Abu Dees bus 63 from CBS (NIS1.5)
Al-Thouri bus 75 from CBS (NIS2)
Ramallah bus 18 from the Nablus Station (NIS2)

Ramallah, Nablus and the Northern West Bank

The region to the north of Jerusalem – known to the Israelis as Samaria after the ancient Israelite kingdom established here following the death of Solomon – is the least-visited part of the West Bank, probably because the northern towns lack the biblical resonance of those further south. This is a pity, because in **Nablus** the region has one of the prettiest **souqs**, while nearby **Sebastiye** can boast of the most complete **ruined city** in the Holy Land, and the hilltop town of **Ramallah**, the most modern city in Palestine, is a gourmand's delight – the perfect spot to escape from the ruins and wallow in houmous and cream cakes.

This chapter follows **Route 60** north via Ramallah to Nablus and beyond, a road that follows very closely the old Roman highway between Jerusalem and Nazareth. There are things to see all along the route as it wends its way through the Samarian hills, many of which are not accessible by public transport. The main sights, however, certainly are, and the transport details are given at the end of each section.

JERUSALEM TO RAMALLAH

Just outside Jerusalem, the four-lane Route 60 roars by the refugee camps of **Qalandia** and **Shufat** and the multiple rings of Jewish settlements that expand further into Palestinian territory with every passing year. Passing Mount Scopus (on your right), on your left you'll see a second hill surmounted by a mosque with a tall minaret. This is the hill the Crusaders christened **Mountjoy**, because it was from here in 1099 that they caught their first glimpse of Jerusalem. They later returned in 1157 to build a church, parts of which are now incorporated into the village mosque. In the Old Testament this village was known as Rama, though it's now called **Nabi Samwil** – 'The Tomb of Samuel' – after the cenotaph of the Old Testament's most famous judge that lies, draped with embroidered cloths, in the cellar underneath the mosque. There is no public transport to Nabi Samwil; catch bus number 74 to the village of Beit Hanina and walk up from there.

To the east of the road, 5km north of Jerusalem, lies **Tel Al-Faul**, the home of a ruined ancient fortress believed to be the palace of Saul, the first king of Israel. A stately but deserted pile stands nearby, built for the late King Hussein of Jordan but unfinished by the time the Israelis wrested control of the West Bank from his troops in 1967. Further on, the village of **Anata** was the birthplace of the prophet Jeremiah and contains a ruined Byzantine church.

Ten kilometres north of Jerusalem, a left turn leads past the village of Bir Nabala to **Al-Jib**. Archaeologists' suspicions that Al-Jib was in fact the Old Testament town of Gibeon – suspicions based initially on nothing more than a similarity in the names – were confirmed by the discovery of inscribed jar handles found on the tel. Gibeon became famous after the village elders managed to dupe the Israelite king Joshua into signing a peace treaty with them by pretending that their village lay well outside the Holy Land (Joshua 10). Bound by his word to defend the

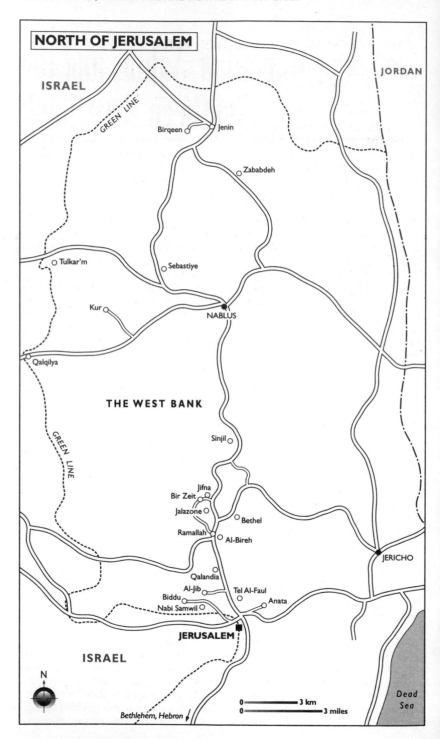

NORTH OF JERUSALEM

ISRAEL

JORDAN

GREEN LINE

Birqeen ○   ○ Jenin

○ Zababdeh

○ Tulkar'm   ○ Sebastiye

Kur ○

NABLUS ●

○ Qalqilya

THE WEST BANK

GREEN LINE

Sinjil ○

Jifna ○
Bir Zeit ○
Jalazone ○   ○ Bethel
Ramallah ○   ○ Al-Bireh

JERICHO ●

Qalandia ○
Al-Jib ○   ○ Tel Al-Faul
Biddu ○
Nabi Samwil ○   ○ Anata

JERUSALEM ■

ISRAEL

N

Bethlehem, Hebron ↓

0 ——— 3 km
0 ——— 3 miles

Dead
Sea

THE PALESTINIAN ASSOCIATION FOR CULTURAL EXCHANGE

About a squillion times better than anything else currently on offer, the Ramallah-based Palestinian Association for Cultural Exchange (PACE) is the best tour company in Palestine. Specialising in historical tours to every part of the country, the advantage PACE have over their rivals is their superior knowledge of the country (the founder, Dr Adel Yahya, is a professor at Bir Zeit), and the obvious love of their homeland, which does seem to be the main motivation behind their work. They also produce brochures and information booklets about Palestinian towns, and are in the process of producing a guide to the entire country. To find out more or book a place on one of their tours, either call in at their office on Ramallah's Nablus–Jerusalem Road or call on tel: 02 995 8825.

village against other attackers, Joshua fought a particularly bloody battle against the Amorites, during which he famously cried 'Sun, stand thou still upon Gibeon; and thou, Moon, in the Valley of Ayalon,' postponing dusk for a whole day to prolong the fighting (Joshua 10:12). The ruins of Gibeon lie on the Biddu road west of the village near a parking lot. The highlights include the town's very elaborate water system, including an impressively deep pool with a stone staircase cut into the walls, and a number of wine cellars.

Further north past the **Qalandia Airport** (known as Atarot Airport by the Israelis) and almost at the entrance to Al-Bireh, **Tel Al-Nasbah** is the site of the biblical village of Mizpeh. The location of Saul's victory over the Philistines (I Samuel 7: 5–11) and the place where eleven tribes of Israel congregated to declare civil war on the tribe of Benjamin for a gang rape perpetrated by the men of Gibeah (Judges 20:1), Mizpeh was excavated during the 1930s. The most prominent features on the site include a massive bronze-age wall (visible from the road), a gate from the 9th century BC, an Ottoman khan and the remains of a Byzantine church.

RAMALLAH رام الله AND AL-BIREH البيرة

Just 16km from Jerusalem, Ramallah is a Palestinian city without parallel. Lacking both the historical and religious significance of other West Bank towns, Ramallah has instead become the commercial, cosmopolitan heart of modern Palestine. If Gaza is Palestine's Canberra, this is Sydney: a brash, fun-loving, go-getting, caffeine-quaffing, lager-guzzling, disco-dancing town that's unique by the conservative standards of the country. This is the home of Palestine's only nightclub, its only brewery and many of its best restaurants. Walk along Sharia Rokab after 6pm and you'll find the pavements crammed with the young and beautiful of Ramallah's 213,000 population. So while there's nothing much to do in the daytime here, and the choice of hotels is rather meagre, tourists should try to spend one night, if only to see the city at its best: after dark.

Ramallah is much more than just Party Central. The city enjoys a reputation as a cultural and media capital – Palestinian TV has been broadcasting from here since 1994 – and an intellectual epicentre too, thanks to its proximity to **Bir Zeit University**. It is also possibly Palestine's most cosmopolitan metropolis, thanks to the large **American Quaker school** in the town centre that's been providing locals with a Western education – and an injection of Western culture into the bargain – since 1866. A number of foreign journalists have also chosen to make Ramallah their home, thus avoiding the violent clashes of culture (and exorbitant house prices) of

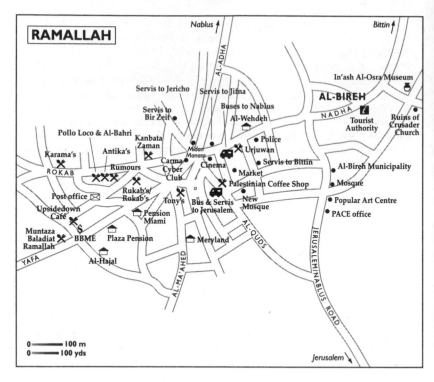

Jerusalem. Finally, there's Ramallah's traditional reputation as a holiday resort, its cool climate 860m above sea level providing Palestinians with a convenient escape from the blazing summer sun and the conservative attitudes of their home towns.

Next door, and almost swallowed up by the rampant expansion of its neighbour, **Al-Bireh** is a quieter, more unassuming place, an overgrown village that contains the only noteworthy site in the whole metropolis, the **Inash Al-Osra Museum**. If you're in Ramallah do pop along: for my money it's the best museum of its kind in Palestine.

Orientation and practicalities

When viewed from an aeroplane, Ramallah, whose name means **Height of God**, resembles (very loosely) a giant spider draped over a hill. Sitting on the summit and forming the body of the spider, **Midan Al-Manara** is the main roundabout, while extending down the slopes on every side are the spider's legs, the six main thoroughfares passing through the town. Most things of interest in Ramallah lie either within 150m or so of the roundabout – including the various **bus** and **servis stations** – or along Sharia Al-Nadha towards Al-Bireh.

The **Ministry of Tourism and Antiquities** is on the third floor of the Palestinian Investment Bank Building (08.30–14.00), on the way to Al-Bireh on Sharia Al-Nadha. They're not really a tourist office, but they do their best to help. There are a number of **money-changers** lining this road too, as well as the U\$AVE (02 401872) **car rental** company, with Opel Astras from US\$50 per day, US\$250 per week, or US\$900 per month. (Incidentally, if you have an account with HSBC or one of its subsidiaries, you can withdraw cash with no charge from the **cashpoint** at the British Bank of the Middle East, on Sharia Yafa. It also accepts Mastercard, Visa, Cirrus and Maestro.)

In the other direction, the **post office** lies on the steeply sloped Sharia Al-Muthaza, while there's an **internet café**, the Carma Cyber Club, on the 6th floor of the Al-Monarah Building (08.00–midnight, Friday 15.00–midnight). They charge NIS10 per hour (minimum one hour), with special deals for regular customers.

Accommodation

While Ramallah has a number of hotels, none caters for the budget traveller. The cheapest place, the Al-Wehdeh, still costs over US$20 per night. At the other end of the scale, Ramallah has Palestine's most expensive hotel, the Grand Park, a couple of kilometres from the centre to the west.

Al-Wehdeh Hotel Sharia Al-Nadha; tel: 02-9956422. Located on the third and fourth floors of an office block 100m off Midan Manara on the way to Al-Bireh, this is a bit of a travellers' haunt, at least by Ramallah's standards. Rooms are clean and spacious, and nearly all are en suite. Prices are approximately NIS100/150/180 sgl/dbl/tpl, including breakfast.
Grand Park Al-Masyoun Heights; tel: 02-9986194; fax: 02-9956950. Luxury hotel with everything you would expect for the price, including a pool and gym. Admittedly it's a bit far from the action, but if you're staying here, the facilities are so good there's no reason to step outside anyway. The restaurant is said to be truly superb.
Pension Miami Sharia Yafa; tel: 02-9956808; fax: 02-9955874. Small, 11-room hotel at bottom of the hill opposite the BBME building. All rooms come with shower and TV, and the prices (NIS130/170/200 sgl/dbl/tpl) include breakfast.
Meryland Hotel Sharia Al-Ma'ahed; tel: 02-998774; fax: 02-9987176. One of the cheaper establishments in town, this drab hotel is rather grim and completely lacking in atmosphere – though televisions, showers and teddy-bear lamp-stands feature in most rooms. Prices are NIS120/170/200 sgl/dbl/tpl.

Food
Cafés

Ramallah's café society is alive and percolating. Most of the traditional, spit-and-sawdust places, such as the popular **Palestine Coffee Shop**, reside at the top of Sharia Al-Quds, and though there are better and more atmospheric places in Palestine, these are handy if you're waiting for a servis to Jerusalem. As for the trendier, European-style cafés that Ramallah really excels in, Sharia Rokab is the first place to look. Check out any of the following: the **Kanbata Zaman**, just west of the Midan Manara along Sharia Rokab, is certainly the hippest place in town, with a gallery upstairs housing exhibitions by local artists and photographers; **Karama's**, further west, is a cute little chrome-filled café whose menu advertises 21 different sorts of tea, not to mention Black Forest Gâteau and other creamy delights (though beware: the chocolate is real, but the cream is rather too sweet and synthetic for many Westerners' tastes); the **Café Urjuwan**, part of the Balanda Cultural Centre on Sharia Nadha, is a Western-style snack bar offering a little bit of luxury, with freshly squeezed orange juices (NIS6) and carefully-prepared sandwiches and salads; and the **Upside Down Café** on Sharia Rashid is a reasonably priced (beer NIS8–10, juices NIS5, pizza and pasta NIS18–30) establishment with tables nailed to the ceiling and posters hung the wrong way up, thereby living up to its name.

Restaurants

Ramallah is the home of the zeppelin-shaped felafals, delicious home-made ice-cream and muntaza'at restaurants (large, al-fresco eateries stretching down Sharia

Yafa). Most places serve alcohol and, while the spirits are extortionate, the beer is cold and cheap (NIS8 for a Heineken; if they serve the local brew, Taybeh, don't miss the chance to try it). The following is just a tiny selection of the restaurants on offer.

Antika's is a wonderful little kebab shack on Sharia Rokab that stands out from the others because a) the salads and garnishes are superior to (and spicier than) the average kebab house, and b) you serve yourself, Nablus-style. At NIS3 for a felafal sandwich, it's good value too. Just round the corner down the alley, the **Al-Bahri** is Ramallah's finest fish restaurant, where the grilled sole with almonds (NIS30–40) is to be recommended. The Al-Bahri shares the building with **Pollo Loco**, a **Mexican** restaurant with adequate food – they make a pretty good fist of most of the dishes, particularly the fajitas (NIS30–40) – and surly staff. Heading south down Sharia Yafa, **Muntaza Baladiat Ramallah** is the largest **muntaza'at** in the city and is proving extremely popular with locals, especially the kids who enjoy the adventure playground next door. Their menu, filled with traditional Middle Eastern dishes and Western fast food, is all written in Arabic, though the helpful staff will gladly translate for you. Not cheap, though even those on a tight budget should consider coming here for an ice-cream and a beer. If you really want to splash out, however, try the **Al-Bayt Al-Falastini Restaurant**, on the fifth floor of the BBME building over the road. Palestinian cuisine doesn't come much more *haute* than the fare on offer at this place; try their Mulukhia with chicken (NIS26) or the stuffed neck of lamb (it's delicious, honest). Up the hill a little way, the **Plaza Restaurant** is probably the quietest of the three muntaza'at eateries along Sharia Yafa , though it can't be the food that keeps the crowds away – the masakhan (chicken and onions in bread) is exquisite. At the top of the hill, **Tony's Pizza** is a Western-style pizzeria on the seventh floor of the Al-Sa'a Tower Building, with pasta dishes for NIS20–26 and pizzas starting at NIS35. And last, but not least, no rundown of Ramallah's restaurants would be complete without mentioning **Rukab's**: in a town that's famed for its ice-cream, this parlour has become so popular the locals have named the street after it. And rightly so, for Rukab's ice-cream is delicious, particularly their pistachio flavour – the best in Palestine.

Entertainment

Ramallah loves neon. It's a little like Las Vegas after dark, only there are no casinos and definitely no showgirls. (Actually, that's not strictly true: some of the rooftop restaurants offer belly dancing as entertainment, though for fear of getting these establishments closed down for immoral activities, I won't mention them here.) Notice, too, how many of the cafés and bars in town have either upstairs or underground seating, so the Muslim patrons won't be caught drinking by people peering in from the street.

A night in Ramallah isn't cheap by Palestinian standards, but it certainly is by Western and Israeli ones; most drinks are reasonable, with beers between NIS8 and 12 and a G&T NIS15. Unfortunately, bars shut fairly early: by 01.00 everything has just about closed down. Ramallah's discos insist on couples only, though this rule is usually relaxed for Western visitors.

On the **bar** front, **Rumours**, recently opened, is already garnering a loyal following. Located four floors underground on Sharia Rokab, the Rumours complex includes a café, restaurant, well-stocked bar and live entertainment most evenings, including Thursday night's ever popular **oud nights**. The disco tends to kick off fairly late, allowing you to explore the rest of the 'scene' first. A second place, the Mexican bar/restaurant **Flamingo's**, holds a Blues Night every week, though sadly the locals tend to stay away; the recently inaugurated **jazz night** every Thursday does look like packing them in. The proprietor also hopes to open, soon, Ramallah's first 'proper' **nightclub** (as the manager put it). Other places to try out include the café **Kanbata Zaman** or, on Saturday nights, the disco at the **Black Horse Bar** (couples only), which is fast gaining popularity.

If all this drinking and dancing sounds a tad hectic, there are more sedentary entertainments on offer. The **cinema** on Sharia Nadha serves up a repetitive diet of action flicks and Arab comedies; for English language films, you're better off visiting the **Popular Art Centre** on Al-Moghtaribeen Street. This long-established arts centre, opposite the old mosque on the corner of the Jerusalem/Nablus Road, shows films every night, many in English. They also hold dance courses, and very occasionally small **concerts** and performances by a range of top Palestinian artists. Pick up their monthly programme from the lobby. The **Balanda Cultural Centre**, housed in a former school on Sharia Nahda, has plans to offer similar entertainment, though currently they tend to concentrate on workshops and courses. They also have a computer centre, which they hope to have connected to the internet soon. Once again, pick up a programme to see what's on.

What to see in Ramallah

As mentioned in the introduction, Ramallah has no major religious or historical sights. Though built on the site of a 4,000-year-old Canaanite village, modern Ramallah really only started in the late 15th century when, according to popular tradition, a Christian family fled to the well of Ramallah from Jordan to avoid having to marry their daughter off to a local Muslim chieftain.

Still, there are a couple of places in town that you should check out, including the local **vegetable market** behind the bus station. It lacks the picturesque setting of Nablus or Hebron, but it's pretty colourful, and the women traders who arrive by the score from the nearby villages sport all different types of traditional dress. It's certainly worth a photo or two.

Over in Al-Bireh, the **In'ash Al-Osra Society** is a women's organisation dedicated to improving the lot of Palestinian women in society. Formed in 1965, the society has grown to incorporate a nursery, an embroidery centre, a nursing school and other vocational training centres. Their **folklore museum** (08.00–14.00, closed Friday; NIS3) provides a comprehensive résumé of traditional Palestinian society. The English-language labels provide one-word descriptions only, but there's usually somebody on hand to answer your questions. The highlights include a four-foot-high model of a Palestinian hilltop village, looking like a giant worm cast and surrounded by photos from the '20s and '30s of Palestinian village life. There are also a number of ornate kohl pots, old passports from the British mandate, a display of traditional medicines, jewellery and a fine collection of **traditional costumes** from each of the Palestinian districts. The last couple of rooms have been given over to the reconstruction of a traditional village home and guesthouse.

The **Crusader church** marking the spot where Joseph and Mary are supposed to have rested lies across the road from the society. The couple were said to have stopped here on their way to Nazareth from Jerusalem after losing the 12-year-old Jesus in a crowd; they returned to the city later that day to find Him praying in the Temple. The story has no backing in the Bible, and the Crusader church marking the spot where they were supposed to have rested now lies in ruins. The **Mosque of Omar** next door is a modern building built on the site of an Ottoman mosque that was recently demolished.

Transport

Taxi companies stand near the Midan Manara, and it's possible to travel all the way to Sheikh Hussein Bridge for NIS50 (departure 08.30), or Allenby Bridge for NIS15 (leaving throughout the day). Phone 02 9956150 for a reservation.

The map on page 134 has all the various bus and servis stations marked on. **Bus** fares include: Jerusalem, NIS2 (bus number 18), and NIS6 to Nablus. Fares charged by the much-quicker servis taxis include: Jerusalem NIS3 (25min); Nablus NIS9; Jifna NIS2.5; and Jericho NIS8.

BETWEEN RAMALLAH AND NABLUS

After Ramallah the landscape changes. The earth seems to turn a darker shade of red, and the land folds into peaks and valleys like a crumpled duvet, each slope lined with mile after mile of olive groves. The road north from Ramallah is one of the most ancient in Palestine, following almost exactly the caravan route connecting Nazareth and Samaria with Jerusalem. Traditionally, it was also one of the most dangerous roads. The surrounding hills provided the perfect home for robbers and bandits, who preyed on the caravans that passed through the valley below. Fortunately, law and order have been restored to the region, though ruins from those early days can be seen all along the road.

Bittin بيتين

Amazingly, only Jerusalem and Hebron receive more mentions in the Bible than **Bittin**, a pretty village of 2,000 people and many more plum, olive, almond and fig trees. This is biblical Bethel where, amongst other episodes, Abraham built an altar to the Lord (Genesis 12: 8); his grandson Jacob had his famous 'ladder dream' (a sort of league table for angels, as described in Genesis 28: 10–19); and from where Samuel, the last of the great Judges, ruled over his subjects (I Samuel 7: 16). This was also the first capital of the northern kingdom of Israel, established by King Jeroboam as a rival to the Judaeans' Jerusalem (I Kings 12: 26–28). Later on, the city gained notoriety as a centre for pagan worship, a practice that brought condemnation from the prophets (Jeremiah: 48:12–14); when the region fell to Assyria, the Judaean king Josiah took the opportunity to pull down the cult temple that Jeroboam had installed (II Kings 23:15).

Archaeologists have been digging around Bethel since Edward Robinson first arrived in 1838, with the most important and extensive excavations carried out by the American W F Albright in 1927. Some massive **defensive walls**, a Roman cistern (the city was the last city to be captured by General Vespasian before he returned to Rome to become Emperor), a Byzantine pool and a Crusader church have all been found in or near the village. Unfortunately, these finds were either removed at the time or allowed to return to the earth, and as a consequence if I were to rate the ruins out of five today – with five being a must-see attraction and one being a sight that's worth visiting only if you have a day to spare and have done all your laundry – then Bittin's prehistoric rubble would struggle to reach one. The highlight is the ruined **Crusader tower**, Al-Burj, which stands on the site of the biblical cult centre on Rujm Abu Ammar, the hill facing the village across the valley. From the village mosque, head down that hill and up the other side to the school, then take the left where the road forks; if you're unsure of the way, ask the Brazilian shopkeeper who works just below the mosque. In the village itself there are the remains of the **Crusader church** that's since been converted into a women's mosque.

Bittin lies just 1km beyond Al-Bireh, within walking distance of the City Inn; servis taxis (NIS2) leave from behind Ramallah's municipality. Buses, from Sharia Al-Adha'a, are NIS1.5

Bir Zeit بيرزيت

The Byzantine town of Bir Zeit owes its fame to the massive **university** 2.5km to the south of town, 9km north of Ramallah. First established in the 1920s, it acquired university status only in 1976, yet in that short time has risen to earn a worldwide reputation for academic excellence. The university has long been a hotbed of political activism, standing at the forefront of protests against Israeli occupation. This militancy isn't confined just to the students: many of the professors and lecturers are experienced political campaigners, including such notable figures as Hanan Ashrawi, the spokeswoman for the PLO during the peace negotiations.

Today most of the lessons take place in the palatial campus on a hill to the south of town, built during the early eighties (a sherut from Ramallah costs NIS2.5). A visit is always worthwhile, if only to gauge which way the wind of political opinion is blowing in Palestine these days – the students are welcoming (once they've sussed you're not an Israeli spy) and will soon fill you in on any aspect of Palestinian life and politics you may care to ask about. Over the summer the university holds **classes in Arabic**, with subsidiary courses on Palestinian society, history and politics. For further information, visit their **website** at www.birzeit.edu.

Jalazone الجلزون and Jifna جفنا

The concrete refugee camp of Jalazone lies 8km to the north of Ramallah, overlooked by the Israeli settlement of Beth El. The camp, home to over 8,000 refugees, was formed in the wake of the war of 1948, yet still lacks many of the basic services – clean water, heating, a sewage system – that you'll find in other long-established camps. Like all other refugee camps, Jalazone is perfectly safe to visit, but to get a real insight into the living conditions of the inhabitants it's better to go on a tour: contact UNRWA or PACE (see page 133) for further details.

The village of Jifna lies just 1km north of Jalazone, on the old Roman road between Jerusalem and Nablus. Looking at this quaint little hillside village, it's hard to believe that during the Roman era this place was considered the second most important city after Jerusalem. The village has long been a Christian stronghold, though a third of its population is now Muslim and there are plans to build a mosque in town. The remaining Christian population is served by two **churches**: the 19th-century Orthodox **St George's**, to the right of the road behind the graveyard, and the Latin **St Joseph's**, part of the convent and monastery up the hill on the other side of the road. Opposite the entrance to this church, lying overgrown and neglected behind a wall, are the remains of a third church dating back to the Byzantine era.

Jifna is currently the subject of a massive renovation project to restore parts of the crumbling village to their former glory. As a result, it's well worth spending an hour or two just ambling around, for many of the houses are built into the ruins of old Crusader buildings. Jifna is renowned for its **restaurants**, the best of which is the excellent **Al-Burj Restaurant** in the restored Crusader citadel, **Burj Jifna** (Jifna Tower) below the Latin church. The restaurant serves traditional Arabic food (prices are about NIS35 for a main course) and alcohol, and you can either sit in one of the rocky alcoves inside or, if it's a nice night, climb the stairs to the roof overlooking the village. Should you wish to eat at the Al-Burj, consider spending the night at the delightful **Al-Morouge Pension** (tel/fax 02 9957881) at the opposite end of the village, though ring ahead to make sure it's open.

Servis taxis leave from opposite Ramallah's cinema to Jifna, Jalazone and back via Al-Bireh. If you're going to Jifna after 16.00, you may have to pay NIS5 extra as they usually don't bother visiting the village in the evening.

NABLUS نابلس

An hour's drive from Ramallah, Nablus nestles snugly in the valley between the steep-sided slopes of **Mounts Gerizim** and **Ebal**, the two holiest mountains of the **Samaritan faith**. This noisy, conservative yet laid-back metropolis is the West Bank's second largest city outside Jerusalem, with over 260,000 inhabitants. It is also Palestine's **secret treasure**, filled with attractions that amuse and amaze, from the adorable old city, known as the **casbah**, with its bustling, rough-and-ready souq, medieval architecture, dark, covered alleyways and restored **Turkish baths**, to the ancient cities of **Shechem** and **Sebastiye** lying in the surrounding countryside. Lacking the confrontational air of Hebron, the incinerating heat of Jericho and the rampant tourist overkill blighting parts of Jerusalem and Bethlehem, Nablus is both gorgeous and friendly; if it wasn't in Palestine, it would undoubtedly now be over-run with tourists.

What's more, Nablus is very cheap and the **food**, though lacking the variety of other towns, borders on the exceptional. Unfortunately, it does suffer from a lack of decent **accommodation**. Female visitors are restricted to just one, rather classy hotel, and though male travellers have a second and much cheaper option, it's nothing to write home about. However, do try and stay if you can: the sights both in town and in the countryside surrounding Nablus deserve a couple of days at least, and the city provides a comfortable base for exploring the northernmost reaches of the West Bank.

History

Though surrounded by ruins that comfortably pre-date the birth of Christ, the modern city of Nablus can trace its ancestry back only as far as the Roman city of **Neapolis**, founded near the ruins of the ancient biblical town of Shechem in AD72 (the Israelis still call Nablus by this name). The town has long been associated with the Samaritans (see page 146–7), whose holiest mountain, Gerizim, overlooks Nablus to the south, but since the ruthless crushing of the Samarian Revolt by the Byzantine Emperor Justinian in AD529, their presence in the town has numbered no more than a few hundred people.

Instead, conquered by the Arabs in AD637, Nablus has had a majority Muslim population for over 1,300 years, save for an 88-year tenure by the Crusaders (1099–1187). The ruins of Crusader churches and fortresses still lie in the vicinity, many built on the orders of Queen Melisande, widow of King Fulk of Anjou, who adopted Nablus as her home after her son, Baldwin III, had exiled her from Jerusalem in 1152. Not even a huge earthquake in 1927 could destroy these sturdy Crusader constructions, though much else was devastated at this time.

In the 20th century, Nablus has fostered a proud tradition of rebellion, a reputation given further lustre by events during the early 1900s. The focal point of anti-Zionist demonstrations in the 1930s, Nablus witnessed the establishment of the first Palestinian National Committee a few years later. The recent peace process has done little to quell the locals' ardour; the former mayor of Nablus, Bassam Shaka'a, a survivor of numerous assassination attempts by the Israelis (during one of which he lost both his legs), continues to speak out against the Oslo Accords, much to the embarrassment of the PNA. His stance is understandable: Nablus declined economically under the Israelis, and Jewish settlers still continue to build on the surrounding hills; both are problems that the peace accords have failed to properly address.

Practicalities

The centre of Nablus is a compact place, bounded to the south by the old city and Mount Gerizim, and to the north by **Sharia Feisal**, the main road leading to

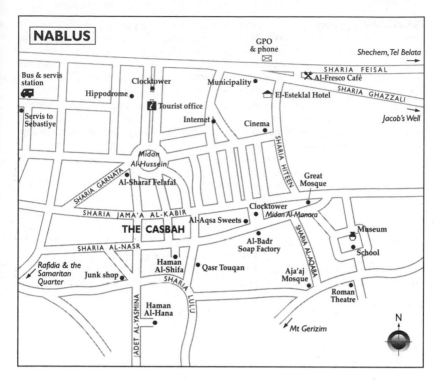

Ramallah in one direction and Jenin in the other. To the east and west the city atrophies into faceless suburbs that eventually peter out into countryside. Almost everything of interest to the tourist lies within a ten-minute walk of **Midan Al-Hussein**, the main roundabout in the centre of town. As a result, there's little call for a servis taxi, though if you do need one – for visiting the attractions around the suburb of Balata, for example – the charge is only NIS1.5.

Immediately to the north of Midan Al-Hussein is a clock tower, and beneath it the newly-opened **tourist office** (08.00–19.00, closed Friday). Run by the municipality, it's good to see at least one local authority is prepared to spend money on its tourist infrastructure. Unfortunately, currently there are no maps on offer, and the staff are not very knowledgeable, but I'm sure its performance will improve. Just round the corner and on Sharia Feisal, opposite the Municipality, is the **post office**; though these days Nablusians prefer electronic mail, for Nablus has embraced the internet revolution with a passion. There are now ten (!) **internet cafés** dotted around the city, mainly by the university in the west of town. The most convenient for the city centre is the **Net House** (Sat–Thurs, 09.00–midnight, Friday 15.00–midnight) in the Na'em Abdul Hadi Building on Omar Mokhtar Street. They charge NIS10 for one hour, and are scrupulously fair (they once refused to accept my payment because, thanks to a fault beyond their control, I couldn't log on to hotmail).

Strangely, for such a commercial centre, Nablus has just two **hotels**, and one of them is definitely not in the business class. The **El-Estateklal**, (09 2383618) the first house on the right as you head down Sharia Hiteen, is a large old house catering FOR MEN ONLY with rickety iron beds, large dorms and walls the colour of a badly-treated wound. That said, the non-English-speaking manager is kind and fair, and the price (NIS20) is cheap enough for even the most budget-conscious of backpackers. At the other end of the scale, the **Al Qas'r Hotel** on Sharia Omar Ben Al-Khatab (09 385444; fax: 09 385944) is a different proposition altogether. The rooms, all en suite and all with direct-dial telephone, satellite TV, shower, bath and bidet, aren't cheap at US$75/95+ 15% service charge (rising to US$200+15% for the penthouse) but are deliciously comfortable.

Food-wise, Nablus is the home of the do-it-yourself sandwich, where they put in the meat or felafal, and you select and put in the salads and sauces yourself from the wide selection of bowls on the counter. Most people prefer this way of doing things: you can make the sandwich to your own exacting specifications, and the prices happen to be very cheap too, with just NIS2 for felafal and NIS5 for shwaarma. Most of the better stalls are bunched around Midan Al-Hussein in the centre of town. My favourite is the **Al-Sharaf**, which has the biggest variety of curried sauces. Nablus' other culinary claim-to-fame is *kanafe*, a treacly concoction of white cheese sprinkled with a crunchy orange topping. The **Al-Aqsa** is an eatery renowned for its kanafe, though most baklava shops produce their own versions.

When it comes to **nightlife**, where Ramallah rocks, Nablus nods off. There are no bars or clubs here, and alcohol is difficult to find except in the tiny Samaritan quarter. The **cinema** is minuscule and tends to show Arabian action movies or Turkish skin flicks. There is a **pool hall** below the **internet café** on Omar Mukhtar, and the café itself stays open until midnight. It may also be worth checking out the Rafidia district near the university, the centre of Nablus' tiny café society. If anything is going on, it's probably going on here.

What to see in Nablus

Thanks to a massive restoration project, Nablus has the prettiest town centre of any Palestinian town. Its heart is dominated by the historical souq, or **casbah**, which lies at the very foot of Mount Gerizim. The market itself is fairly small and, thanks to the presence of **Sharia Jama'a Al-Kabir** and **Sharia Al-Nasr**, two parallel roads running east-west through the market, fairly easy to navigate too. Though largely Ottoman in origin, traces of Roman, Crusader and Mamluke architecture can be discerned in the buildings. The atmosphere is delightfully chaotic and distinctly Oriental, there are many historical ruins to check out, and the whole place deserves a morning of your time at the very, very least.

An ideal place to begin a tour of the town centre is at the eastern end of the Old City, where Sharia Jama'a Al-Kabir and Sharia Al-Nasr converge. At this junction you'll find the silver-topped Grand Mosque, or **Jame' Al-Kabir**. Originally a Byzantine Basilica stood on this spot, and later a Crusader Church, though following their defeat in 1187 the church was transformed into a mosque and the minaret added. Tradition has it that this is where Joseph's envious brothers showed their father, Jacob, Joseph's bloodstained coat of many colours, to fool him into thinking Joseph had been murdered (Genesis 37). As with all of Nablus' mosques, non-Muslims are forbidden to enter.

Twenty metres before the mosque, to the south of the street, stone steps lead up through a series of Mamluke arches to a boys' school, built on the lower slopes of Mount Gerizim. Underneath the school is a **museum** dedicated to the casbah (Sat–Mon, Wed and Thurs 09.00–16.00, Fri 13.00–16.00, Tues closed; NIS3/1). Opened in 1997 after funding by the French government, the museum's 700-plus objects are divided into ten showcases, each dealing with a different subject pertaining to the casbah, such as the soap factories, the houses, the Turkish baths and so on. Most visitors find it quite informative, and a good introduction to the origins and workings of the casbah.

PALESTINE'S TURKISH BATHS

If you've ever wanted to be pummelled into a pulp by a burly Palestinian (and let's face it, who hasn't), you have two choices: 1) declare your unfailing support for Jewish settlers, or 2) visit the restored hammams in Nablus. The second method has a number of advantages: not only will you be wallowing in history, but you'll also come out as clean and shiny as a new button, for which your room-mates will be exceedingly grateful.

My favourite of the two Nablusi baths, if only because it has one of those coloured glass roofs that allows light to filter through in a range of different hues, is the Hammam Al-Hana, and the description below pertains to that bath. The procedure, however, is roughly the same at both hammams. First, you walk into reception where a moustachioed fellow provides you with a **locker** for your valuables, a bar of Nablus soap, a kind of net flannel for washing yourself with, and a towel. He'll also provide you with a pair of shorts if you didn't bring your own, and show you through to a second room. This second chamber is a sort of relaxation room – the Romans, who knew a thing or two about baths, called it the **tepidarium**, or warm room – where you just lounge around and stare up at the glass ceiling. There are also a couple of cubicles for you to change in – leave your clothes on the stone benches or on the hooks.

A door by the entrance leads into the **caldarium** (hot room), dominated by what can best be described as a marble hotplate for humans, heated via underground pipes. The idea is to lie flat on top until you're literally basting in your own juices. I swear I smelt lemons when I was there, but I could have been delirious with the heat by this stage. If you happen to be made of asbestos and find the marble slab of an insufficient temperature to engender perspiration, haul yourself off to the **sauna** in the adjoining room. If, on the other hand, the heat becomes too much, the caldarium walls are lined with **basins**, with hot and cold taps and bowls which you use to pour the water over yourself. This is also where the soap and the net facecloth comes in.

If you asked for a **takee**, at some point during your time in the caldarium a guy with an abrasive glove will come in, flatten you out on the hotplate and proceed to roll cigars of dead skin from your back. I think the Roman's called this bit a strigil, which is probably Latin for 'excruciating'.

Now, five pounds lighter, you're ready for your pummelling; or at least, you're now in no state to resist. The firmness of the **massage**, of course, depends on the masseur, though if you're British or American you can expect him to be fairly violent thanks to your government's hostile foreign policy. After this, drag your limp, disorientated carcass to reception and treat yourself to a cup of **coffee**, which will not only revive but also remind you at which end of your body your mouth is.

The cost of this exquisite agony? NIS15 for a bath, NIS10 for a massage and NIS5 for a takee. Coffee's NIS1.5. Be certain to tell them exactly what you want before you begin, or they will assume you want everything.

Continuing up the slope behind the school, turn right along the main road, Sharia Ras Al-Ein, then take the first left. To your right at the top of the road lies an impressively large **Roman amphitheatre** in a terrible state of repair. The authorities are uncertain what to do with the site at the moment, though if they delay their decision much longer the stones will have all been nicked anyway, despite the high wire fence that surrounds it.

Returning to the main road, turn left then right before the **Aja'aj Mosque** down Sharia Al-Aqaba, the steep road leading back down to the Grand Mosque. At the bottom, turn left and continue west to Midan Al-Manara, the main square of the casbah. To the west of the square is the impressive entrance to the green-domed **Al-Nasr Mosque**, rebuilt in 1935 following the earthquake eight years earlier, while in the centre stands an Ottoman **clock tower**, built in 1895 on the orders of Sultan Abdul Hamid. Opposite, at number 20, is the Al-Badr (Full Moon) **Soap Factory**, one of the few soap factories still trading. Nablusi soap is renowned for its purity and its ability to lather, particularly the luxurious white version made with virgin oil; the second pressing of the olives gives the cheaper, green version.

There's no better place to test-drive the local soap than in one of the casbah's **Turkish baths**. The nearest, **Hammam Al-Shifa**, lies along Al-Nasr, 150m west of the soap factory up a stairway by number 68 (open daily; Tuesdays women-only, the rest of the week men-only); look for the banner written in English above the street. Built around 1840, this is the oldest working bath in Palestine. The second bath, **Hammam Al-Hana**, to the southwest of Al-Shifa, is just a few years younger, and on the way there you'll pass a number of **Qasrs**, or 'palaces' – large mansions once used by the city's powerful and most successful families. Unfortunately, two of them, Qasr Nablusi and Qasr Abdelhadi, are closed, but a third, **Qasr Touqan**, lies derelict and can be visited. Be careful, however, for the whole building is in a dangerously dilapidated state, and a ferocious feral dog lives in one of the rooms. Still, come here and dream of how it must have looked once, or how it could look now if fully renovated, and climb on to the roof for a close-up view of the dome of Al-Nasr Mosque.

From the Hammam Al-Hana, head back to the souq along Jadet Al-Yasmina, past the wonderful **antique-cum-junk shop** – selling everything from gramophones to ear trumpets – at the junction with Sharia Lulu and on to Sharia Jama'a Al-Kabir. You now have three choices: turn right and visit the other half of the souq; continue straight ahead through the modern centre of town and up to the fruit market, behind which you'll find another Roman ruin, this time a **hippodrome**, lying uncared for in the centre of town; or turn left, continue along Sharia Garnata and take another left until you're on the main road to Rafidia. About 400m along the road is the Samaritan quarter known as Haret Al-Samira. There are a couple of Samaritan synagogues here, and a **Samaritan Studies Centre** at 26 Sharia Omar Ibn Al-Khattab. For an insight into the world of the Samaritans, however, you're better off climbing up their holiest mountain, Mount Gerizim.

Nablus transport details

The bus station lies just 250m west of the Midan Al-Hussein. Currently there is nothing direct from Jerusalem to Nablus and travellers have to change in Ramallah, from where there are regular buses. Buses from the station cost NIS6 with the Tamimi company. Other fares include: Jenin NIS9 and Tulkarm NIS6 (both by sherut).

SITES IN THE NABLUS AREA
Mount Gerizim جبل جرزيم

It's a sweaty two-hour climb to the village of Gerizim, situated at the top of the mountain of the same name. There's no real fixed route; just follow any road that goes up the hill, as after a while they all join up and lead to the summit. A **taxi** will set you back about NIS20–25, one way.

The Samaritans believe this hill to be the oldest piece of land on earth (see box on page 146–7). This is where God took the soil to make Adam, and this, they believe, was the only piece of land on earth not covered by the Great Flood. As such, the Samaritans refer to this hill as **Har HaKadem**, 'The Early Mountain', and spend the entire Passover Week in the well-heeled village at the summit. In the centre of the village is a tiny **museum** dedicated to their history and culture (08.00–14.00, closed Sat; NIS4), which is mildly interesting, though all the labels are in Hebrew. Just beyond the village to the south is the altar where the Samaritans still conduct the week-long Passover celebrations, including the ritual sacrifice of lambs and male goats, following the precise orders given in Exodus 12.

Past the village and overlooking it to the east are the ruins of the **great temple**, built during the reign of Alexander the Great and destroyed by John Hyrcanus in 129BC. The ruins are currently closed for renovation, but are rather disappointing anyway, with the only building of note being Suleyman the Magnificent's **Ottoman fortress**, the small square building right in the heart of the site. To the north of here (and reachable by the white path from opposite the museum) is **Tel El-Ras**, where archaeologists discovered steps leading from the city to the temple after studying Roman coins of the time that clearly showed the staircase's exact location.

Shechem

Biblical Shechem lies about 1.5km east of Nablus near the suburb of Balata, home of the West Bank's largest refugee camp with over 18,000 inhabitants. There are a number of historical sites located here, including two which, between them, are sacred to all three major religions in Palestine. The sites take about an hour or two to cover in total, and you can either walk to them or catch a servis (NIS1.5 from the town centre).

Tel Balata (Shechem) and Khirbet Ashkar

First mentioned in ancient Egyptian texts, Shechem, meaning 'Shoulder' or 'High Place', was an important Canaanite city during the Middle Bronze Age Period (1900–1550BC), with evidence that its location had been settled up to 3,000 years before this, during the so-called Chaolithic period of the 5th millennium BC. There is no doubt, even from the sketchy ruins visible today, that Shechem was once a very powerful city. Unfortunately, however, most historical texts refer not to its past glories, but to the various destructions it suffered down the years at the hands of such forces as the Egyptians (1550BC), the 'Hapiru' (1360BC) – a mysterious Nomadic group whom some believe to be the Hebrews – and the Egyptians again under Pharaoh Shoshenq I (923BC). Though the town survived on each occasion, the construction of nearby Samaria in 876BC ensured Shechem would never again enjoy supremacy in the region. Its inhabitants were all deported during the 8th-century BC Assyrian conquest (thus forming part of the Ten Lost Tribes of Israel) and in their place a population loyal to Assyria was shipped in – ancestors, according to some, of the Samaritans who still live in Nablus (see box on page 146–7). The town enjoyed a brief renaissance during the Hellenistic period, but after yet another destruction, this time by **John Hyrcanus the Maccabee** in 117BC, Shechem was slowly abandoned, a process that was accelerated by the founding of nearby Nablus in AD72.

The site

Shechem, now more frequently called **Tel Balata** after the camp that lies nearby, was excavated for the first time earlier this century following the chance discovery of a cache of bronze weapons that are now housed in a museum in Berlin. As is normal, the ruins now lie below ground level, and thus you'll be looking down on to them from above. Most of the excavated ruins at Shechem date from the Canaanite period, including parts of the **city walls**, the largest ruins on the Tel. The best and easiest way to enter the site is through the defensive wall from the north via Sharia Amman. Study the site closely, and you should be able to make out two entrance gates, one in the northwestern corner (which you've just walked through) and a smaller one on the eastern side. There are also the remains of what the archaeologists have decided was a palace, complete with guard rooms and kitchens, immediately to the left (east) of the northwestern gate as you enter.

The importance to Jewish history of this small hillock sprinkled with fairly nondescript ruins should not be underestimated. Shechem was the first Palestinian city visited by Abraham following his migration from Mesopotamia, and the site of his first altar in the Holy Land (Genesis 12:6–7). His grandson Jacob followed suit, while Jacob's sons, Simeon and Levi, plundered the city in retaliation for the rape

WHO ARE THE SAMARITANS?

The Samaritans form one of the **oldest religious communities** in the world. Numbering fewer than 600, they are one of the smallest too, though this wasn't always the case: in their heyday in the 4th and 5th centuries BC their population touched 1.2 million. Since then their numbers have dwindled steadily, thanks largely to the political and religous upheavals of the last 2,500 years.

Though clearly part of the Judaic spectrum, the point in time at which they 'split' from the more conventional forms of Judaism is something of a mystery. The Samaritans themselves maintain that their break with Judaism pre-dates the establishment of the monarchy by Saul in 1100BC, and claim to be descended from Moses' brother Aaron through his son Itamar. The most commonly held belief, however, and one held by the rest of the Judaic world, is that the Samaritans are the descendants of those people shipped in to Palestine by the Assyrians from the far-flung corners of their empire to replace the 30,000 or so Israelites whom they had sent into exile following their victory in 721BC. Adopting the local religion and marrying into the Israelite families that hadn't been exiled, these new arrivals successfully integrated themselves into the local society. According to Jewish tradition this new, homogenised community of Israelites and Assyrians became known as the Samaritans after their capital, Samaria. Being of mixed parentage, the Samaritans are not regarded by the Jews as the true descendants of the Israelites, and thus refuse to regard them as cousins, (as made clear in II Kings 17: 24–41). As a result, the Jews refused the Samaritans' offer to help rebuild the Temple in Jerusalem after they had returned from exile in Babylon, and, with the backing of Alexander the Great, the Jewish community successfully barred the Samaritans from the Holy City altogether. Yet there is very little evidence to back up this hypothesis either, save for a few anecdotal references in the Old Testament which, it's important to remember, is written from a Judaic standpoint that is hostile to Samaritans. Indeed, there is nothing to suggest that the Samaritans have a link with the Assyrians or any other foreign group.

Persecution has played a large part in the decline of the Samaritans. They are in an unfortunate position: persecuted as Jewish by other faiths, yet persistently attacked by Jews for not being Jewish enough. Thus the Roman general Cerealis slaughtered 11,600 of them on Mount Gerizim in revenge for of their sister Dinah by Shechem, the son of Hamor (after whom, it is supposed, the city is named). But perhaps most importantly, it was here that Joshua renewed the Jewish covenant with God in a great ceremony (Joshua 24). After asking his subjects whether they wished to remain faithful to God, Joshua wrote a book of commands for his people to follow – a sort of updated edition of the Ten Commandments – and set up a stone against an oak tree, saying:

> 'Behold, this stone shall be a witness unto us; for it hath heard all the words of the Lord which He spake unto us: it shall be therefore a witness unto you, lest ye deny your God.'

The rectangular **El-Birith Temple**, easily distinguishable by the three pillars and the restored, semi-circular altar at its eastern end, is where the Book of Judges says this ceremony took place, and today they form the most impressive and distinctive set of ruins on the site. Incredibly, Ernest Sellin, a German scholar and the first man to excavate the site, did find a large standing stone nearby. Today it stands erect in the middle of the altar.

the Jewish Revolt of AD66, even though they'd taken no part, and the Byzantines attempted to suppress their religion throughout their long reign; when the Samaritans fought back they were massacred by the soldiers of the Emperor Justinian. The Muslims, too, persecuted them following the capture of their holy mountain, Gerizim, during the invasion of 637AD; the Samaritans only got it back in 1258 following the fall of the Abbassid caliphate to the Mongols.

Their treatment at the hands of their Jewish cousins has, if anything, been even worse, and the Bible is full of references to the bitter rivalry between the two. This hatred of each side for the other underpins the central theme of Jesus' famous **Parable of the Good Samaritan**, in which a Samaritan helps a Judaean who'd just been attacked on the highway by thieves, thus displaying a love for his fellow man that superseded sectarian divisions.

The **religion** of the Samaritans is essentially a conservative, old-school form of Judaism. Their holy book is the **Pentateuch**, or Torah, the first five books of the Bible as handed down by Moses, along with the Book of Joshua that describes the Jewish invasion of the Promised Land. They observe the **Sabbath** with a rigour that would make even the most Orthodox Jew blanch, foregoing all the devices used by Jews to facilitate normal life on that day, and they celebrate only the festivals described in the Torah, thus excluding the Jewish holidays of Hanukah and Purim. Their **language** is ancient Hebrew, the *lingua franca* of the Israelite kingdom, and they write using the ancient Hebrew script.

There is one other essential difference between the two. While Jews believe that Abraham tried to sacrifice Isaac (Genesis 22) on the Temple Mount in Jerusalem, the Samaritans maintain that it was Mount Gerizim. They also contest that Joshua built an altar here following the destruction of Ai, contradicting the book of Joshua which clearly states that Mount Ebal, opposite, was the site (Joshua 8).

The Samaritans have enjoyed something of a resurgence since their 1917 low of just 146 devotees. According to a census carried out in 1996, there are 583 Samaritans in Israel and Palestine: 286 on Mount Gerizim and Nablus, 297 in Neve Marka, in Holon near Tel Aviv. Most of the Samaritan community in Nablus spend only half the year on the mount, moving down to warmer climes in Nablus' tiny Samaritan quarter of **Haret Al-Samira** in winter.

Shechem was also the venue for most of the story of Abimalech, as told in the Book of Judges. Abimalech was the first to attempt to become king of the Israelites following their arrival in the Holy Land, ruthlessly killing his 70 brothers to prevent any rivals to his claims. He did achieve his ambition, though he was never popular, and was killed during a rebellion by the people of Shechem after just three years (Judges 9). In his attempts to quash the rebellion, the temple and much of the city was razed to the ground by fire. According to the American archaeologist George Ernest Wright, the discovery of a **second temple**, just to the northeast of El-Birith, seems to suggest that the first temple was destroyed, thus confirming the story of Abimalech. As is so often the case, however, the date of these ruins – circa 1500BC – doesn't tie in with the biblical account, being approximately 350 years too early. However, if David Rohl's theory on biblical chronology is to be believed, this date is consistent with the biblical story (see page 31).

From the northwestern entrance to the temple, cross over the road and adjacent to the second road on your left you'll see a litter-strewn field, in the far corner of which you'll find the remains of a 2nd-century AD Samarian tomb, known as **Khirbet Ashkar**. Returning to Sharia Amman, turn left, then right on the large straight road that leads on to Sharia Feisal. The next site, Jacob's Well, lies just 75m up the hill from the junction.

Jacob's Well بئر النبي يعقوب *and the Tomb of Joseph* قبر يوسف
Mon–Sat 08.00–12.00, 12.00–17.00; free

Currently surrounded by the scaffolding of a massive restoration project, this well is believed to lie in the centre of the 'parcel of land' brought by the Old Testament patriarch, Jacob, for 'one hundred pieces of money' as reported in Genesis (33:19). If this is true, and if we can trust St John's Gospel (4: 7–11), then it is also the spot where Jesus met a Samaritan woman on his return from Judaea. In Jesus' time, the Samaritans and Jews loathed each other with an intensity that often surpassed their mutual hatred for the Romans. Jews even refused to drink out of bowls used by Samaritans, which is why the Samaritan woman was puzzled by Jesus' request for a drink. Her curiosity was further aroused by Jesus' promise to provide her with 'life-giving water' in return, water which, in Jesus' words, 'whosoever shall drinketh…shall never thirst; but…shall be in him a well of water springing up into everlasting life.' Later, Jesus told the woman that He was the Messiah; she went and told all her friends, who persuaded Jesus to stay in town for a couple of days. Whilst there, it is said that He successfully converted many Samaritans.

The **Crusader church**, currently undergoing restoration following a particularly vicious earthquake in 1927, was built in the 12th century. Before that, a Byzantine chapel erected in AD380 had stood on this spot, until its destruction during the Samarian Revolt of AD529. Both churches were cruciform in shape, with the four arms aligned to the four cardinal points, and in both cases the well and crypt were situated directly beneath the altar. A small **museum** on the site houses various remnants from these two churches, including pottery shards, lamps and buckets used in the well.

It looks as if the church will be gorgeous when the restoration work is finally completed, but for the moment, whilst the church itself is hidden behind all the scaffolding, you'll have to make do with a quick glimpse of the well itself: one of the monks from the Greek Orthodox monastery will lead you down the steps and show you around the many icons that decorate the small interior of the cave. The well itself is 35m deep, and still contains fresh water.

Returning to Sharia Feisal, turn right up the hill, then take the first right down, then left at the end. At the junction, take a right and follow the road around to the heavily fortified **Tomb of Joseph**. Sacred to both sides, the tomb has been the venue of some pretty ghastly atrocities down the years. Like the Haram Al-Khalil in Hebron and the Haram Al-Sharif in Jerusalem, Jewish extremists claim the site as their own as it was once the property of their biblical ancestors, the Jewish patriarchs. It is still in the hands of the Israelis today, with a bunch of Israeli soldiers permanently garrisoned behind the reams of razor wire and high concrete walls. The building itself is distinctly Islamic, a plain white dome covering a Mamluke **sarcophagus**. All round the site, Palestinian soldiers keep guard. Back in 1996 the Palestinians opened fire on the Israeli soldiers following the opening of the Western Wall Tunnel in Jerusalem. The sight has been **closed to sightseers** ever since, and now only those who wish to pray at the tomb have the right to enter, having first obtained permission from the DCO (District Coordinator's office).

Sebastiye سبسطية and the ruins of Samaria
Open daily 08.00–16.00; NIS12/14
Lying approximately 13km northwest of Nablus, on the side of a hill cloaked with olive groves, is the pretty hillside village of Sebastiye. At the top of the village, covering the whole of the hilltop and interspersed by yet more olive groves, are possibly the most extensive set of ancient ruins in Palestine. This is ancient Samaria, or Sebastiye as it came to be known, the capital of the northern kingdom of Israel and a serious rival to the Judaeans' base at Jerusalem. Servis taxis from Nablus (NIS2) depart from the stop across the road from the bus/shcrut station; don't come on Friday, when servis taxis are rare.

The history of Sebastiye

> 'Therefore I will make Samaria as an heap of the field, as plantings of a
> vineyard: and I will pour down the stones into the valley, and I will
> discover the foundations thereof.' Micah 1: 6

Following the death of Solomon in 922BC, the Kingdom of the Israelites split into two. While the kings of Judah continued to rule from the traditional capital, Jerusalem, the breakaway northern kingdom of Israel (which was by far the larger, being made up of ten of the Israelites' original Twelve Tribes) were forced to look for a new base. Shechem (see page 145) and Tel Al-Farah (page 153) were both tried and rejected before, in 876BC, the Israelite authorities decided to move for a third time, on this occasion to a remote hill in the Samarian mountains. Under the guidance of the Israelite Kingdom's sixth monarch, Omri, a new capital slowly emerged, a city so huge and important that it would eventually give its name to the entire breakaway kingdom of Israel.

Built over a Canaanite village at the intersection of two major caravan routes, Samaria's location was ideal. It took advantage of this commercially strategic location, growing wealthy from the passing trade, enabling the king to finance the construction of mighty public buildings. Omri's son, Ahab, built a hugely impressive **Temple to Baal** for his Phoenician wife, Jezebel, while under the rule of Jeroboam II (784–748BC) the city became famous for its wealth and splendour, outshining even its Judaean counterpart and rival, Jerusalem. Thanks to its hilltop location, the city also enjoyed considerable natural defences to deter would-be invaders.

Not considerable enough, however, as it turned out. Old Testament prophets such as Amos, Micah and Hosea, horrified by the decadence and idolatry of the city, delighted in predicting Samaria's destruction (see the quote above), and there proved to be no shortage of armies willing to bring this about. The Assyrian king

Sargon II trounced the Samarian city in 721BC, expelling a third of the inhabitants (about 30,000 people) and replacing them with loyal settlers from far-flung places in the empire. Alexander the Great then stormed through in 331BC, rebuilding Samaria in Hellenistic style, vanquishing the inhabitants and displacing them to nearby Shechem, replacing them with Macedonian soldiers. They added a huge defensive wall and monumental watchtowers to strengthen the city's fortifications, but even these proved insufficient to prevent John Hyrcanus from destroying the city in 108BC during the Maccabean Revolt.

Then in 63BC, the Romans piled in. The Emperor Augustus bestowed it on his loyal vassal, Herod, who rebuilt the city once more, renaming it Sebastiye (Greek for 'Augustus') in the emperor's honour. Herod obviously liked the city: one of his many marriages took place here, and he executed two of his sons here too.

Herod's city was destroyed during the **First Jewish Revolt** (AD66–70), but flourished again soon after. While Sebastiye remained loyal to Rome, nearby Shechem showed signs of rebellion. As a result, the Roman governor of Palestine, Septimus Severus, rewarded Sebastiye, building temples, theatres, colonnades, hippodromes and so forth, while Shechem was neglected. Sebastiye's prosperity finally ended during the Byzantine era, and it was abandoned soon after.

The site

The servis will either drop you in the car park – once the **Roman forum** – by the ruins, or in the village square 100m below. The ticket kiosk stands on the opposite side of the car park to the ruins.

Sebastiye's last four historical eras (Hellenistic, Herodian, Roman and Byzantine) are all represented in the surviving ruins, with the majority dating from 1st-century Septimus Severus' reconstruction. These include the decorated masonry of what was obviously once a rather grand **portico**, in the shallow pit beyond the car park, which originally adjoined the **basilica** that lies behind and above it. The basilica was divided into three aisles by two neat rows of **columns**, some of which are still standing.

A path behind the café and souvenir shop to the right leads to the extensive remains of the **Roman theatre**. Here the path splits, with the lower trail leading round the hill to the Western gate, while a second path heads up behind the theatre and abutting Hellenistic tower (one of the finest examples of its kind, apparently) to the **acropolis**. The ruins of the **Temple of Augustus** – another fine piece of grovelling by Herod – mingle with the other blocks of masonry around here, while above, at the very summit of the hill, you'll find a platform that offers a 360° view of countryside.

Continuing anticlockwise around the hill, to the south of the summit is the small Byzantine **Church of John the Baptist**, where, so Christian tradition has it, Salome danced for Herod, and where John the Baptist's head was later discovered. The granite pillars here have been imported from Aswan in southern Egypt.

Below the path at the foot of the hill are a number of stone foundations, which together describe an outline of a series of small squares that were once shops. You can either attempt to scramble down the hillside, or, for the less nimble, walk to the end of the path and take a right past the Holy Land Souvenir Shop. This tarmac road, an impressively long track that gives some indication of just how big Sebastiye must have been, traces exactly the city's ancient colonnaded road. Roman pillars line the route on either side, and at the end you'll find the foundations of two huge Hellenistic watchtowers. From here, turn right into the field before the tower, and follow the contours of the hillside through the olive groves and back round to the car park.

THE AMAZING TRAVELS OF JOHN THE BAPTIST (DECEASED)

John the Baptist was renowned for his wilderness wanderings, but even they pale into insignificance when compared with the post-mortem peregrinations of his head. When Salome asked Herod for John's head on a plate as a reward for her dancing, she could have had no idea that it would continue its wandering sans corpse. According to Christian tradition, the head was first discovered in the small ruined church in the ruins of Sebastiye. From there it was taken to the village, and a much larger **Crusader church** was built around it. Apparently, after this a saint called Joanne rescued the head (from what, we do not know) and, unsure what to do with it, buried it on the Mount of Olives in Jerusalem. There's a dip in the floor of a small chapel in the **Monastery of Ascension** which marks the spot where Joanna buried it. There it remained until its rediscovery by two Syrian monks who dreamt about it one night, and dug it up. After that, the head goes missing again, and turns up next in the magnificent **Ommayad Mosque** in Damascus. The Ommayads, while converting this ex-church, discovered the head in the crypt, and placed it in a purpose-built shrine, where, in the absence of any further intelligence, we can only assume it remains today. His arm, incidentally, can be seen in the Museum of Relics at the Topkapi Palace, Istanbul.

The Mosque of Nabi Yaha

Lining one side of the village square, the mosque of Nabi Yaha, or **Tomb of John the Baptist**, supposedly marks the spot where the beheaded body of John the Baptist was buried. The mosque has clearly been converted from the ruins of a large Crusader chapel, built in 1160, that's entirely too big for the village that surrounds it. A Byzantine church had stood on the site before then. Most of the building you see before you today dates only from the 19th century, using the blueprint of Saladin's original from 1187. Apart from the body of John the Baptist, the cadavers of other biblical figures said to lie here include the prophet Elisha and Obadiah. According to popular tradition, the body of the butler of Ahab, the son of Sebastiye's founder, Omri, is also said to rest here. This anonymous butler is said to have hidden 100 prophets from his master's wife, Jezebel, in two caves here, feeding them on bread and scraps stolen from the palace (I Kings 18:1–4).

North of Nablus

Nablus is the southernmost of a triumvirate of cities forming the corners of an area of rich agricultural land known simply as the **Triangle**. The other two corners are **Jenin**, 27km north of Nablus, and **Tulkar'm**, 22km to the northwest. While Jenin has a minuscule old quarter, and a few minor sights in the villages nearby, Tulkar'm is bereft of any noteworthy attractions. Still, the undulating landscape of olive groves and fields of grain is, on occasion, quite splendid, and those with time on their hands or a real thirst for getting off the tourist trail might wish to explore.

Jenin جنين

Palestine's northernmost city lies on the main road between Jerusalem and Nazareth (NIS6 from Nablus bus station). Therefore, it is widely believed that Jesus would have passed through Jenin on His travels between the two, possibly even pausing for the night in the town. However, in this age of the diesel engine there is no need to pause and rest here any more, and most tourists, though they drive through in their air-con buses on their way to Nazareth from Jerusalem, have yet to venture out from behind their tinted-glass windows and see exactly what Jenin has to offer.

The answer is: not a lot, though the tiny **old quarter** is pretty in a higgledy-piggledy sort of way, and the **green-domed mosque** – which is Mamluke in origin, though it has undergone a number of restorations and renovations since then – provides a focal point to the town that's easy on the eye. The mosque lies one block south of the eastern end of Sharia Talal, the road running along the northern side of the servis station, while the old town lies one block east of the mosque (it's easy to recognise, as all the road signs have Old City in brackets on them). Little care has been taken to preserve the character of the facades, many of which have been plastered over with a layer of disfiguring concrete. Nevertheless, some retain their original 19th century details, particularly on their interiors, and as one of the few tourists intrepid enough to venture to Jenin, you'll doubtless be asked in for a cup of tea to appreciate them for yourself.

There is one accommodation option in town, the **Garden Hotel** (06 2436151), just to the west of the old mosque in the Al-Hasmeh fruit market. The area may look a little rough, but at least you're never far away from an orange. The hotel's exterior is rather grim, but the rooms are clean, fan-cooled, have en-suite bathrooms and are reasonably priced at NIS30 for a bed, NIS50 per room.

Birqeen برقين

Servis taxis (NIS1.5) leave from the main entrance of Jenin's main station to Birqeen, a pretty little village with a population of 5,000, only 200 of whom are Christian. Nevertheless, the flavour of the village centre, thanks to the presence of a couple of churches, remains distinctly Christian, and one of these churches is definitely worth investigating. The Orthodox **Church of St George** is built over a cave where, supposedly, Jesus cured ten lepers as He made His way from Nazareth to Jerusalem. Church services (conducted by a priest from Beit Sahour near Bethlehem) are held here only once a month; for the rest of the time the gate built into the church's high Crusader walls remains locked, though you can fetch the **key** from Yousef, the local schoolteacher, shopkeeper, and fount of all knowledge about the church.

Within the church is the **small cave** where the lepers lived. A hole in the roof (now blocked) is believed to have been their **food-hole**, with scraps dropped down by villagers too scared to touch them. The **tiny chapel** next to it probably served as the first church on this site; though its origins are unknown, it could be one of the oldest chapels in the world, pre-dating even the Byzantine era. A second, larger **cave** outside the church was used by villagers during the 1930s and 1940s as a school.

Tulkar'm طولكرم

Even Palestinians struggle to find something to say about Tulkar'm (NIS9 from Nablus), the West Bank's sixth biggest city. It's true that most Palestinians have been here, though more often than not they have merely passed through on their way to Netanya (the Palestinians' favourite beach), 18km to the west, or somewhere else in Israel. Given to the Palestinians by the Israelis in December 1995 as part of the second wave of handovers (following Jericho and Gaza the previous year), Tulkar'm has a population of 134,000, a figure augmented by two nearby **refugee camps,** Nur Shams and Tulkar'm, the latter of which, with a head count of over 14,000, is the second largest in the West Bank.

Servis taxis to Tulkar'm (NIS9 from Nablus) drop passengers by the roundabout in the centre of town, near the reconstructed mosque (the old one was destroyed earlier this century). A small **market**, neither colourful nor particularly vibrant, fills the street nearby. Down the hill from this roundabout lies a second, where you'll find the **municipality**, housed in an old Ottoman pile which is possibly Tulkar'm's most arresting building.

Other sites around Nablus

Kur is an enigmatic little village, where, so it is said, the inhabitants always marry within the village; to do otherwise is to risk exile. Situated on one of the hills to the west of Nablus, this was the seat of power for one of the many Sheikdoms that ruled over the land for the Ottoman empire in the 19th century. There is an entire complex of ancient palaces within the village, three in all, and each built by the powerful Jayousi family. Today, each of these stately piles has been abandoned, though you can visit all of them. As with the palaces at Nablus' casbah, however, take good care, particularly when climbing the steps (each of the palaces has three floors).

Tel El-Farah lies on the road to the Jordan Valley heading east of Nablus. Named after the local spring and valley, Tel El-Farah was first settled as early as 7000BC, a birthdate to rival Jericho's. This was also the first capital of the breakaway northern kingdom of Israel. **Tirza**, as the Bible calls Tel Al-Farah, was yet another victim of the 8th-century BC Assyrian invasion, as were Shechem and Samaria, the two cities that succeeded Tirza in becoming capitals of the northern Israelite kingdom.

It was eventually abandoned around 600BC. The ruins of the city today lie on the fringes of the Tel Al-Farah refugee camp, where you can just about make out the old city walls and defensive towers. The best thing about visiting the site, however, is the waterfall, **Wadi Al-Bathan**, which lies by the road on the way there.

MARY MAGDALENE – THE WIFE OF CHRIST?

Mary Magdalene is one of the more enigmatic characters of the New Testament. Often portrayed as a fallen woman, a prostitute who repented and was saved by the infinite mercy of Jesus, Mary Magdalene appears only briefly in the Bible (her name is mentioned eleven times altogether), but when she does it is often at crucial times. In particular, she is the person whom Christ chooses to appear to first following His resurrection. Such an honour would surely have been the privilege of one who was very close to the Lord, and this has led some to suggest sensationally that she was actually **Christ's wife**.

So what do we know about Mary Magdalene? Her name would suggest that she hailed from **Magdala**, a large city on the western shores of Galilee, while Luke (8:2) describes her as one of a group of women who had been 'healed of evil spirits and infirmities' who provided financial support for Jesus and his followers. Mary herself, according to Luke, had been purged of '**seven devils**' by Jesus, though it is unclear what is meant exactly by this phrase. Apart from this reference, and a walk-on part in John Chapter 19 (verse 25) as an onlooker at **Christ's crucifixion**, Mary appears in the Bible only in the post-resurrection scene. John (Chapter 20, verses 1–18) provides the most detailed account of this meeting. Mary had gone to anoint the body, but on arriving found the tomb open and two **angels** sitting where the body of Christ had lain. Jesus Himself was standing between them, but Mary failed to recognise Him. Indeed, at first she thought He was just a gardener, and asked Him where Jesus' body had been taken. It was only when Jesus spoke that she recognised Him for who He really was and, forbidden to touch Him, Mary hurried to the disciples to tell them what she'd seen.

All very interesting, but hardly proof that Mary was Jesus' spouse. But to further their claims, many have tried to identify Mary Magdalene with **Mary of Bethany** who, so the Bible seems to suggest, *did* enjoy a close relationship with Jesus. Indeed, at one point Mary's sister, Martha, complains that she has been left to do all the housework while Mary sits idly at His feet (Luke 10:38–41). Mary of Bethany is also the 'sinner' who anoints Jesus with precious oil, 'washing His feet with her hair' according to John's gospel.

It is perhaps this reference to her namesake being a sinner that led many to look upon Mary Magdalene as a prostitute. Yet there is no reason or evidence to assume that Mary Magdalene was a prostitute, nor that Mary Magdalene and Mary of Bethany are one and the same person, nor indeed to identify her with any of the other Marys who flit in and out of the gospels (of whom there are plenty, including the Virgin Mary, mother of Christ, Mary the wife of Peter, Mary the mother of John Mark and Mary the mother of James and Joseph). So in the absence of any further evidence, we must assume that if Jesus did take a wife, Mary of Bethany is more likely to have been the blushing bride than her namesake from Magdala.

Bethany to Jericho and Beyond

The main road east from Jerusalem passes near a number of sites and attractions as it wends its way to Jericho, 40km away. All can be seen as day trips from Jerusalem, though I'd advise that you see only Bethany and Bethphage in this manner; the rest are closer to Jericho, and best seen as day trips from there.

BETHANY (EL-AZARIYA) العيزرية

Situated 4km east of Jerusalem, and still officially part of the **Jerusalem Corridor**, Bethany is a largish Arab town clinging to the eastern slopes of the Mount of Olives along both sides of Route 417, the feeder road to Route One. Bus number 36 (NIS1.5) from East Jerusalem's Central Bus Station serves Bethany; jump out when, just after the road takes a sharp right, you see the Bethany Souvenirs Shop on your left.

The town features quite significantly in the life of Christ. It was here that Mary of Bethany anointed Him with precious oils (Mark 14:3–9), and here too that Jesus

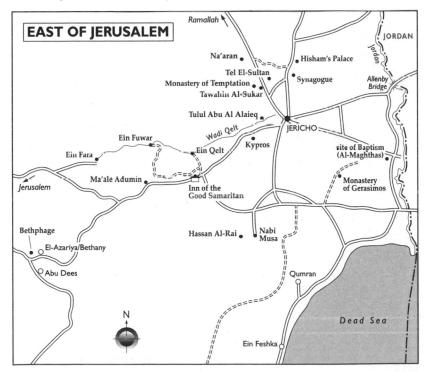

WALKING TO BETHANY AND BETHPHAGE FROM JERUSALEM

As an alternative to the number 36 bus, you may like to walk to Bethany via the Mount of Olives and Bethphage, calling in at some of the churches en route. See page 121 for details on climbing the Mount of Olives. From the entrance to the Pater Noster Church at the Mount's summit, turn right and follow the main road to the Franciscan monastery at Bethphage. From here, follow the track that runs by the side of the monastery to Bethany.

raised Mary's brother, Lazarus, from the dead (John 11). In this story, told with minor variations in each gospel, Lazarus and his family appear to have been old friends of Jesus. When news reached Him of Lazarus' demise, however, and for reasons best known to Himself, Jesus decided to wait for two days before visiting the family. Rebuked by Mary and her sister Martha for not visiting sooner, Jesus wept in shame and asked to be shown their brother's grave. Ignoring Martha's cautionary words, 'Lord, by this time he stinketh', Jesus ordered the tombstone to be moved, and shouted into the darkness within the words 'Lazarus come forth'. Sure enough, Lazarus emerged soon after, 'bound hand and foot with grave clothes', to the delight and wonder of all present.

The Arabic name for Bethany, Al-Azariya, translates as 'The Place of Lazarus' and on the hillside overlooking the main road you'll notice, rising above the village rooftops, an attractive and unusual sight: the slender white minaret of a

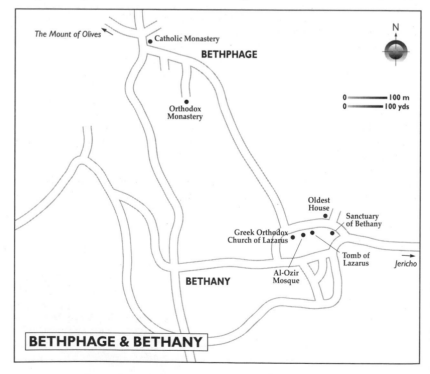

medium-sized **mosque** sandwiched between the domes and steeples of **two grand churches**, both of which commemorate Lazarus' resurrection. Unfortunately, the impressive **Greek Orthodox church** at the top of the hill, built in the 1960s, is only open to visitors during the Feast of Lazarus in April, and the 16th-century **Al-Ozir Mosque** below it is permanently closed to non-Muslims. Under the mosque, however, stone steps lead from the road to a dank, musty cavern split into two levels, known as the **Tomb of Lazarus** (daily, 08.00–17.30; NIS2.5). Other than its location in Bethany, there is little evidence to suggest that this was Lazarus' temporary grave, and to the secular sightseer the tomb will be of minimal interest, as will the so-called **oldest house in Bethany** that stands just down the hill on the opposite side of the road (daily, 07.30–17.30; donations extracted). The house, built round a 20m-deep well, does contain some features that were probably quite standard in a dwelling of 2,000 years ago, but to call it the oldest house in the village is probably stretching the truth a little, and the owner's boast that this is 'quite possibly the very home of Mary, Martha and Lazarus' is just outrageous.

Opposite the house, however, and just below the tomb, is a small gateway to a church that definitely *is* worth seeing. The **Sanctuary of Bethany** (April–Sept 08.00–11.45, 14.00–18.00, Oct–Mar 08.00–13.45, 14.00–17.00; free) is yet another masterpiece from the virtuoso Italian architect, Antonio Barluzzi. This Franciscan church was built in 1954, and stands on the ruins of two previous churches, one Byzantine and one Crusader. Traces of a **Byzantine mosaic floor** and, by the entrance gate, **buttresses** from the Crusader church are both on view in the modern church's courtyard. The wine and **oil presses** that also lie in the courtyard date back to the time of the Crusader Queen Melisande, who attached both a monastery and a convent to the church; these survived on the profits reaped from the presses. The ruins of the convent, built in 1138 by Melisande, lie next to the mosque on its eastern side, and are known locally as the Castle of Lazarus.

Barluzzi's modern church is built in a simple cruciform style, its central dome soaring up above the central aisle. More mosaics, this time from the Crusader church, lie beneath grilles just inside the church entrance, while to your left is a statue of Paul VI that commemorates his 1964 visit to the Holy Land – the first by a pope since Saint Peter. If you've already visited a Barluzzi building you'll be familiar with the simple, cool austerity of his interiors, and will also be delighted to see that once again the Italian Monticelli company were commissioned to decorate the upper walls of the church with their fantastic **mosaics**. These mosaics run in chronological order clockwise around the church, beginning with the one to your left as you enter which shows Mary sitting at Jesus' feet. The third figure in the mosaic is Mary's sister, Martha, who complains that she is left to do all the housework (Luke 10: 38–42) every time He visits, hinting, possibly, of a love affair between Christ and her sister. The **central mosaic**, above the altar, shows Jesus declaring 'I am the resurrection and the Life; he that believeth in me, though he were dead, yet shall he live', Jesus' reply to Martha after she'd accused Him of staying away and letting Lazarus die (John 11: 19–27). The raising of Lazarus from the tomb (John 11: 38–44) is depicted in the mosaic to your right, while finally, in the mosaic above the door, we find the anointing of Christ by Mary. This episode is dealt with slightly differently in all four gospels. In Matthew (Chapter 26) and Mark (Chapter 14) Mary anoints Jesus by pouring oil on His head at a supper given by Simon the Leper, an act that provokes anger among all the disciples who look on it as a needless waste of precious oil. In Chapter 12 of John, however, Mary anoints Jesus by washing not His hair, but His *feet* with *her* hair; furthermore, this takes place not at a supper given by Simon but by Lazarus, and the only disciple who actually complains is Judas. The mosaic portrays an amalgamation of both versions: the supper is given by Simon the Leper (the bald guy at the opposite end of the table), Mary anoints Jesus by pouring the oil on His head, while Judas alone, the standing figure in the centre, complains of the extravagance.

BETHPHAGE   بيت فاجي

From Bethany, opposite the Greek Church near the top of the hill, a track heads due west for 750m to Bethphage, the village with the greatest orthographic variability in Palestine (with Betphage, Bethfage and Bethphade being three of the more common spellings). According to the New Testament (Matthew 21:1), it was here that two disciples, under orders from Jesus, found the young colt (now more commonly translated as 'donkey') that Jesus rode on His triumphant procession into Jerusalem, a march celebrated in the Christian church during **Palm Sunday**.

Today there are two monasteries at Bethphage, one Greek and one Franciscan, both of which claim to have the stone which Christ used to climb on to His colt – though precisely why Jesus needed to stand on a stone to mount a beast that would have only come up to His waist is never explained. According to Anastasios, the gatekeeper of the **Greek monastery** that lies to your left as you walk from Bethany, during Easter week in 1999 their stone – which is now the centre-piece of a shrine – began mysteriously to leak water, a steady trickle that dried up once the Easter festivities had finished. The monastery is usually closed to foreigners; if you are allowed in, ask to see the small caves, probably disused hermitages, which lie in the surrounding fields of figs, olives, grapes and pomegranates. The monastery's founder, Gregorios, is buried to the east of the main chapel. A small, circular pagoda covers his grave, and the view from here towards Jericho and the Dead Sea is rather special.

The **Franciscan monastery** lies 150m further on, just round the corner on the main road. Only the monastery's church is open to the public (08.00–11.30, 14.00–17.00; pull the bell chain that hangs inside the gates to attract the attention of the one-legged, gold-toothed gatekeeper). A church has existed on this site, on and off, since Byzantine times. Two pilgrims – Bernard the Monk in his journals (AD870) and Theodore Libellus (1172) in his book *Holy Places*, mention visiting a church here. The current structure dates from 1883. Three of the four interior walls are decorated with sepia-toned **murals** depicting Jesus' journey to Jerusalem, including Zaccheus up a tree in Jericho (on the back wall), and the triumphal march into Jerusalem with the crowd waving palm leaves before Him. The stone from which Jesus mounted His donkey lies almost in the centre of the church; it too is painted with gospel scenes. From the church you can head up the hill to the Church of Ascension on the Mount of Olives, and then on to Jerusalem.

ROUTE ONE TO JERICHO

All along Route One, you'll notice **altitude markers**: to travel east along this highway is to descend 1,150m, from Jerusalem (800m above sea level) to Jericho (250m below). At **sea level**, there's usually a guy with a camel who charges for photos. Look out too for semi-permanent **Bedouin encampments** by the side of the road, though these days they're usually little more than collections of goat-hair tents, wooden shacks and rusty oil drums. Six kilometres from Jerusalem is the Inn of the Good Samaritan, or the **Al-Khan Al-Ahmar**, a 16th-century Ottoman structure standing across the road from the meagre ruins of the 5th-century church of **St Euthymius**. The church was built to commemorate Jesus' parable of the

Good Samaritan as recounted in Luke 10:33, and this is where the khan gets its nickname. The church was destroyed in the 13th century by the Mamluke sultan, **Baybars**, who was upset that it lay on the Islamic pilgrimage route to Nabi Musa. Today the khan is occupied by a **souvenir shop**, with a Bedouin tent serving refreshments nearby. Behind the khan is the Israeli settlement of **Ma'ale Adumin**, the largest in the West Bank, home to over 30,000 settlers, with plans to build homes for another 30,000 in the pipeline.

Maqam Al-Nabi Musa – the Tomb of the Prophet Moses
مقام النبي موسى

Daily, including Fridays, 08.00–sunset; free
The 13th-century Nabi Musa (or Nabi Moussa as it's sometimes spelt) is in many ways the archetypal Palestinian tourist attraction: it's ancient, it's sacred, it's controversial and its setting, in a barren **desert landscape** that's as harsh as it is beautiful, gives it an exotic, timeless atmosphere. The large, fortress-style construction (many buildings of this period, both secular and sacred, were heavily fortified against raids by passing Bedouins) is built around a tomb that supposedly contains the body of Moses. According to the Bible, 'And he (Moses) was buried in a valley in the land of Moab, over against Bethpeor: but no man knoweth of his sepulchre unto this day' (Deuteronomy 34:6). Final and incontestable proof, you may think, that the body inside Nabi Musa – if indeed there be one – is not that of the Islamic Prophet and Jewish Patriarch. Yet this hasn't prevented Palestine's Muslim population from venerating this site since its construction over 700 years ago.

Indeed, since the 12th century the *maqam* (tomb) has been the venue of a huge annual **pilgrimage festival**, or **mawsim**, attended by the devout from all over the Arab world. In all likelihood the festival is actually older than the building itself, dating back to Saladin's time when Muslims, banned from entering Jerusalem by the Crusaders, were forced to look for an alternative destination for their pilgrimages. The maqam was constructed soon after, and a set itinerary for the mawsim was established in the Mamluke period, kicking off with prayers at the Al-Aqsa mosque in Jerusalem, followed by a pilgrim's march to the maqam, and culminating in five days of prayers, celebrations, dances, feasts and even horse racing in the desert around the shrine. Down the centuries, a succession of local Muslim rulers recognised the value of the festival as a display of Islamic might and power, and encouraged the festivities as a result. During the Ottoman period one local pasha even changed the date of the festival so that it coincided with Easter, thus counterbalancing the influence of the waves of Christians arriving in the Holy Land.

Unfortunately, during the 20th century the festival began to develop a more overt political flavour, until in 1937 the British authorities, fed up with quelling anti-Zionist demonstrations year after year, banned the festivities altogether. For the next 50 years the maqam became a **military base**, first for the Jordanians and then for the Israelis. A brief revival of the mawsim in 1987, when over 50,000 people turned up, proved to be a false dawn, as the onset of the Intifada later that same year caused a suspension of festivities once more. Though the Oslo Accords of 1992 returned the maqam to the Palestinian authorities, the revived mawsim has failed to capture the Palestinians' imagination as it once did. Indeed, the only people you'll find at Nabi Musa these days are the guy who looks after the place, a couple of souvenir and drinks sellers, and the occasional day-tripping Palestinian family picnicking in the arcaded courtyard.

To be honest, I don't really care whether Moses' body rests here or not: Nabi Musa is exquisite and that, for the secular sightseer at least, should be all that matters. Entry is through the door in the western wall, above which an Ottoman inscription records their renovation of the site in 1820. Most of the buildings, however, including the unfussy **mosque** (on your left as you enter) and the **minaret** that stands in the northwestern corner of the complex (and which you can climb for a good view over the Dead Sea and beyond), are original features of the Mamluke building. So too is the **tomb** itself, covered with a heavily embroidered green cloth and located in a separate room just inside the mosque door. On a wall above the tomb is an inscription: 'The construction of this maqam over the grave of the Prophet who spoke with God, Moses, is ordered by his majesty, Sultan Thaher Abu Al-Fatah Baybars, in the year 688 hijra (1269/70).' Baybars also endowed the maqam with a large amount of agricultural land, including the Wadi Qelt, to finance its upkeep. Two hundred years later the **courtyard** was added, along with the 120 **cells** that line three of the four walls. These rooms were used to house the wealthier visitors; the less prosperous pilgrims were forced to sleep in tents outside the walls.

Adjacent to the maqam on two sides and stretching far into the desert is a large, dilapidated **graveyard**. The small **mausoleum** on the hill opposite the Nabi Musa is said to be that of A'isha, the favourite wife of Mohammed, though this too is unlikely (the scant evidence we have about her points to her being buried in Syria). A third tomb, about a kilometre further west along the road, is said to be that of Hassan al-Ra'i, the shepherd of Moses.

The maqam lies a couple of kilometres south of Route 1, the highway between Jerusalem and Jericho. Coming from Jericho, catch a Jerusalem or Abu Dees-bound servis taxi (NIS6), and ask to be dropped at the turn-off to Nabi Musa, a few hundred metres east of the sea-level marker. From there it's a pleasant stroll in the desert along a tarmac road, or you can try to hitch.

WALKING THE WADI QELT وادي القلط

The **hike** through the picturesque Wadi Qelt, a steep-sided waterway running all the way from the Jerusalem suburbs to Jericho, is enormous fun. The scenery is stunning, the ruins en route diverting, the wildlife plentiful (dozens of bird species including kingfishers, jays and doves, as well as marmots and mountain goats, have all made the wadi their home) and the shorter **one-day trek**, though arduous, is not exhausting. You can even go for a bathe in one of the pools near the torrential **Ein Qelt Spring** after which the wadi was named, and towards the end there's the most picturesque monastery in Palestine, the **Monastery of Saint George of Koziba** (see below), as a reward for all your exertions.

It is possible to hike the entire length of the wadi from Jerusalem to Jericho, a two-day trek (at least) of 40km. Most visitors, however, are happy to cover just the last 9km or so, from the turn-off on Route 1 to Jericho. This walk takes about four hours, though travelling to and from the end of the wadi takes time, and the whole enterprise usually takes a full day. For this reason, you'd be well advised to use Jericho as your base and travel by servis taxi to the start from there (NIS6 with an Abu Dees- or Jerusalem-bound taxi). Tell the driver you're going to Wadi Qelt and he should drop you off on Route 1 by a small road next to a bus stop, a couple of kilometres beyond the sea-level marker.

Despite warnings from the Israeli authorities – who'll insist you don't attempt this walk independently – the Wadi Qelt hike is actually fairly straightforward: apart from an initial downhill plunge, most of the path is fairly flat, and it's easy to follow thanks to some clear painted markings. That said, you'd be well advised *not* to try this trek on your own, just in case any misfortune should befall you on the way. You must also prepare yourself for a long day in harsh desert conditions. Though you'll be following an aqueduct for most of the way, the water inside is not fit to drink – as a quick glance at all the tin cans, fish and fungus at the bottom will testify – so bring plenty of your own. A sunhat, sunglasses, walking boots (or trainers) and loose-fitting clothes are also advisable, but make sure your clothes aren't too revealing or you'll offend the monks at the monastery (though they do provide some tatty rags for the skimpily-dressed).

The one-day walk

The small road where you'll be dropped off forks into two almost immediately, so take the path on your left that collides, after 500m or so, with a second, larger road. This is the old Roman road to Jericho, and for most of the last few kilometres it follows the wadi from above, along the clifftop. You, however, should cross straight over the road and clamber up the little hill opposite, from where you'll get a great panoramic view over the desert. To your left is a sheltered Israeli guard post; walking past it you'll notice beneath you an uncovered road that leads, after 30 minutes or so, down to the wadi itself. A **Herodian bridge** that at one time supported the aqueduct, possibly the most impressive of the ruins on the walk, lies at the bottom of some steps to your left, just before the wadi. The large building at the foot of the track, looking a little like a country manor transplanted to the middle of the Judean desert, is in fact a disused **flour mill**, now inhabited by a Bedouin family.

From the mill, scramble up to the aqueduct on the other side. You now have two choices: turn right and head straight for the monastery and Jericho, or turn left and make for the springs, **Ein Qelt** and (above Ein Qelt) **Ein Fara** and **Ein Fuwar**. The springs are fed by the winter rains of Jerusalem that collect in huge subterranean **aquifers** – a water-holding layer of rock or soil. The springs are merely faults in the rock that allow the water to gush out. Ein Qelt has a small **bathing pool**, but remember: don't drink the water. Continuing back to the mill, just beyond it to the east is a small **park** filled with bushes, benches and birdsong that's an ideal place to take your first recuperative break.

Throughout the wadi the cliffs are sprinkled with the remains of Hasmonean, Herodian, Roman, Ommayad and Ottoman **aqueducts**. However, for the next hour at least you'll be following the modern water channel that flows above the park and traces a course along the northern side of the wadi. It's a pleasant and peaceful amble, save for the odd excitable sheepdog carrying out its duties a little too enthusiastically. Don't worry, their bark is definitely worse than their bite. After about an hour the aqueduct follows the cliff as it takes a sharp left turn. A signpost here sums up your options: head down to the wadi floor, and either follow the **red painted markings** along the riverbed, or follow the **green markings** to continue walking alongside the aqueduct. I personally prefer the second option: the scenery is better, and both the hillside breeze and the sound of running water in the aqueduct provide some relief from the relentless heat.

After 45min or so, stone crosses begin to appear on the surrounding hilltops – a sure sign that you're getting close to the **Monastery of St George of Koziba**. Yet even these advance warnings can't fully prepare you for that first spectacular sight of the monastery, especially if you've taken the aqueduct path and are looking down on to it from above. It is simply magnificent.

The Monastery of Saint George of Koziba دير القديس جور

Sun–Fri, 08.00–noon, 15.00–17.00, Sat 08.00–noon, though visits may be possible outside these hours; free

The blue-domed Greek Orthodox monastery, situated just above the bed of the Wadi Qelt about 5km west of Jericho, has been providing hospitality for hermits and travellers since its creation 16 centuries ago. The monks originally lived in the **caves** that punctuate the cliffs on both sides of the wadi, and the original building here was not a monastery at all but a *laura*, a sort of spiritual retreat that specialised in the instruction of the divine liturgy. It was built next to a cave where Elijah was believed to have hidden from Jezebel, the Phoenician wife of the Israelite king, Ahab, a story recounted in Chapters 17 and 18 of the First Book of Kings. Jezebel had been promoting her native religion, the worship of Baal, ahead of that of the Israelite god Yahweh (Jehovah). To decide once and for all which God was superior, Elijah and the prophets of Baal met on the top of Mount Carmel. A pyre with a sacrificial bull on top was set up, but while the Baal prophets tried without success to kindle the fire, Elijah's exhortations to Jahweh worked and the pyre blazed furiously. On Elijah's order, the prophets of Baal were then rounded up and slaughtered. As Jezebel sought revenge Elijah was forced to flee to Mount Sinai; on the way there, he is supposed to have spent a night in this cave, where he survived on food brought to him by birds. (Curiously, visit the cave today and you'll often find a solitary black bird hanging around outside.) A further legend claims that in this same cave Saint Joachim was informed that his wife, Saint Anne, was pregnant with Mary, mother of Christ, though this episode has no biblical foundation.

The *laura* was eventually converted into a monastery in the 5th century under the guidance of John of Thebes, though it owes its name to a 6th-century monk who spent much of his life here, and did much to establish a permanent monastery on this site. Thereafter the history of the monastery is a familiar one, shared by nearly all the monasteries in the Holy Land: destroyed in AD614 by the Persians, restored by the Crusaders in 1179, restored again at the turn of this century (when the builders used the Crusader design as a blueprint), and now suffering a dramatic decline in the number of monks (only ten remain) that threatens its long-term future.

Walking up the hill into the **lobby**, on your right you'll find the beautiful **main chapel**, built in 1888 and home to a score of holy relics. The skull and bones of George of Koziba lie in a specially made casket on the far wall of the chapel, while in a smaller chapel at the back you'll discover the bearded John of Chozeva, a Romanian monk who died earlier this century, lying in state. Nearby, housed in two glass-fronted cabinets, are the bones of the martyrs of the 7th-century Persian invasion. The **6th-century mosaic** floor of this small chapel is the oldest part of the monastery.

Back in the lobby you'll see an even more beautiful sight: a free drinks centre, with three different types of squash, some coffee and a fountain for replenishing your water bottles. Stairs from here lead up to **Elijah's cave**, above the main chapel opposite the pretty **bell tower**.

Continuing on to Jericho from the Wadi

From the monastery the path continues along the northern cliffs of the wadi. It's a precipitous route that's not for vertigo sufferers, though the path is wide and the painted markings frequent so you shouldn't have a problem finding your way. Rock hyraxes are common along this stretch, particularly on the cliff-face opposite.

After an hour or so the path descends gradually to the wadi floor and the ruins of **Herod's Winter Palace**. On the southern side of the wadi is a pretty little café and the road to Jericho, a further 2km away. Traffic is infrequent along this stretch, particularly in the afternoons, so you may well find yourself walking all the way to Jericho.

Tulul Abu Al Alaieq – Herod's Winter Palace تل ابو العلايق

The Ommayads of Hisham's day (see the Jericho account below) were not the first to recognise Jericho as a perfect location for a winter retreat. Indeed, the builder-king himself, Herod, built no less than **three winter palaces** in the town – or rather, on the outskirts of the modern town by the entrance to Wadi Qelt. And one hundred years before him, the Hasmonean ruler John Hyrcanus (134–104BC) built a large palace on the north side of the Wadi Qelt. Traces of all of these palaces still litter the entrance to the wadi today and, while I don't recommend you make a special effort to visit the ruins, none of which are exactly scintillating, if you've been walking in the Wadi and still have some energy left you may like to check them out.

Herod's decision to build his **first palace** with mud bricks rather than masonry is undoubtedly one of the reasons why the ruins here are so unimpressive; the lack of any guards, protective fencing or entrance fee to protect the site today is undoubtedly another. The palace was built in 35BC, at the beginning of Cleopatra's five-year rule over the Jordan Valley. Humiliatingly, Herod thus had to rent his own estates in Jericho from the Egyptian queen, even though her lover, Mark Anthony, had originally handed control of them to him.

Herod spent little time at this palace, preferring instead the cut and thrust of political life in Jerusalem or the superior splendour of the Herodion, though he made good use of the swimming pool in 35 BC when he drowned his brother-in-law, Aristobulus III, one of his greatest rivals. Following Cleopatra's suicide in 31BC, Herod resumed control of the territory and added a **second palace** a year later, incorporating within it parts of the Hasmonean original. The construction of the third and largest palace, built around 10BC, followed a visit by the Roman general Agrippa. The general, full of admiration for Herod's grandiose architectural style, is said to have presented Herod with Roman workmen and materials with which to extend his palace. The palace was built on both sides of the valley, allowing Herod to enjoy the sight of the wadi's waters rushing through the palace's centre in winter. He also constructed a number of **fortresses** – Kypros, Nuseib and Dyok – on the hills around the wadi.

Herod spent his last painful days at the palace in the grip of arteriosclerosis, deranged and in considerable pain. According to the historian Josephus, Herod's slave Simeon then burnt the palace, but Herod's son, Archelaus, reconstructed it. The scant ruins that remain, however, have as yet yielded no proof to back up either of these stories.

Most of the ruins that remain lie on the low hills to the north of the wadi, and were part of the northern wing of the third palace. Potter around for long enough and you should be able to discern the outlines of a couple of colonnaded halls, the **Western Hall** and the smaller, neighbouring **Royal Court** to the east, about 100m north of the ruins of the first palace that lie next to the wadi to the north. Those columns that remain are made of mud, though they look as if they were hewn from marble. The **marble floor** of the Western Hall is still visible in places. To the northeast of the Royal Court are the well-preserved remains of the palace **bathhouse**, beyond which once stood the sprawling **royal gardens** and, to the northwest, the ruined **Hasmonean Palace**. The ruins continue further north of the gardens to the so-called '**industrial zone**', complete with wine presses, a sewage system, ovens and storage rooms. Before leaving the site, you may want to head back west along the road to the conical-shaped hill where you'll find the **Kypros fortress**, built by Herod and named after his mother.

JERICHO اريحا

> '..it will not be easy to light on any climate in the habitable earth that can
> well be compared to it. . . the warmth of the air calling forth the sprouts,
> and making them spread, and the moisture making every one of them take
> root firmly. . . The ambient air is here also of so good a temperature, that
> the people of the country are clothed in linen-only, even when snow
> covers the rest of Judea. But so much shall suffice to have said about
> Jericho, and of the great happiness of its situation.' Josephus, War.

Though little more than an overgrown village of just 33,000 people, Jericho's importance to historians, archaeologists and our understanding of society's development cannot be overestimated. As the world's oldest, continually inhabited city, evidence of almost every stage of man's civilisation, stretching way back into pre-history, can be gleaned from this small, unassuming desert oasis near the Jordanian border. It is in Jericho that we find evidence of mankind's switch, 10,000 years ago, from his nomadic, foraging ways to a settled, agrarian lifestyle; here too that we find the world's oldest fortified town, over 9,000 years old, complete with defensive walls and a tower; and here that we find some of man's earliest attempts at making pottery, dating back to 4500BC.

Situated at the foot of the western escarpment of the Jordan Valley that runs between the Sea of Galilee and the Dead Sea, Jericho, at 258m below sea level, is also the world's lowest city, ensuring that, in the height of summer, it can feel as if you're in an oven. Temperatures of 48°C are nothing unusual in the sweltering summer months. Indeed, in the heat of the day in summer, many shops and offices take an afternoon siesta rather than attempt to persevere in those sort of temperatures, and you'd be wise to follow suit.

While the ruins and excavations make up the backbone of Jericho's tourist industry, they form only part of Jericho's charms. It's a friendly, lush and laid-back place with a slow, dreamy pulse; a palm-dotted splash of green surrounded by the barren brown dust of the Jordan Valley. Most people choose to see the town as a day trip from Jerusalem, or, even more ridiculously, as part of a one-day organised tour that includes Masada, the Dead Sea and a whole slew of other places too. This is their loss. Jericho may be small, but its sights are many, and while the hotels may not be much to write home about and the nightlife non-existent, the food here is good and the small-town atmosphere provides a welcome change from city life.

History

The story of Jericho begins on the western outskirts of the modern town, at a hill called **Tel El-Sultan**. (Originally, there wouldn't have been a hill here at all, but the build-up of human settlements over time, one on top of the other, has led to the creation of a 30m-high mound.) The Tel's proximity to the gushing spring of **Ein El-Sultan** would have attracted hunters from the earliest times, and by 7500BC Mesolithic man had established a permanent settlement of some 2,000 people here. The earliest known building at the Tel, a rectangular construction, probably acted as some sort of shrine for these early settlers. The discovery of a defensive wall and tower built soon after this first settlement implies a high degree of social organisation, thus justifying Jericho's claim to be the oldest city in the world.

Another Neolithic people, who left behind them a curious series of skulls which had their owner's original features rendered in plaster upon them, displaced these original settlers in around 6800BC. Subsequent settlers on the site, probably living here around 4500BC, developed and manufactured pottery using the local clay.

From this date the Tel was under almost permanent occupation until its mysterious devastation in the **Middle Bronze Age** (1550BC). Many have tried to attribute this destruction to Joshua (see the next section, *Jericho in the Bible*), the leader of the Israelites following the death of Moses. Scholars have since cast doubt on this claim – ignoring Rohl's adaptations of the historical time line for the moment (see page 31), the destruction is at least 350 years too early – though in accordance with Joshua's curse, the Tel remained uninhabited for the next 900 years until the 7th century BC.

Following the exile of the Judeans to Babylon (604BC), the Tel was abandoned altogether, though an administrative centre was established during the Persian era (c550BC) in a different part of the oasis. The Tel was never the centre of the city again. The **Hasmoneans** extended the cultivated area by building an aqueduct from a second spring, Ein Qelt, 10km away in the Wadi Qelt, and around this time the city became a popular winter retreat for the rich and powerful who built palaces near the entrance to the wadi. For five years (34–30BC) Jericho even came under the rule of Cleopatra, after her lover Mark Anthony gave her the city as a gift.

The **Byzantines** shifted the town centre once more, this time eastwards to the site of the present town. The Ommayads revived the idea of Jericho as an exclusive winter resort when they built the spectacular Hisham's Palace, and though this was destroyed just four years later, Jericho has managed to cling on to its reputation as a popular winter holiday resort. Its agricultural fecundity has also provided the city with a stable economic base. The Crusaders developed Jericho's sugar industry, exporting it to Europe, while more recently the British during their mandate encouraged the cultivation of fruit; thanks to its year-round sunshine and plentiful water supply, Jericho's crops ripen two months before those in the rest of Palestine and the Near East.

This wealth has been somewhat dissipated recently by the influx of many **refugees** into the area. The first wave of approximately 70,000 arrived in the wake of the 1948 war, when Jericho came under Jordanian rule. Four major camps were set up on the outskirts of town at this time: **Aqbat Jaber**, **Ojah**, **Nue'meh** and **Ein El-Sultan**. Many of these refugees were displaced again following Israel's victory in 1967, with many fleeing east to Jordan.

Thankfully, Jericho has enjoyed better fortune recently. Following the Oslo Accords the town became the first in the West Bank to be handed over to the PNA (in 1994), encouraging businessmen both at home and abroad to look at the possibility of investing there. Though the turbulent political situation, and in particular the sporadic closure of the roads in and out of town by the Israelis, has put

JERICHO AND TOURISM

Unlike most Palestinian towns, Jericho is only too used to seeing **tourists**, and usually the worst kind of tourists at that: ignorant, beshorted, gum-chewing creatures wheeled in on luxury buses, who hop out of their air-conditioned, tinted-windowed sanctuaries just long enough to trot briskly around all the major sights, seeing everything and learning nothing, pausing only to have to have their photo taken on a camel in the Tel El-Sultan car park ˉbefore moving on to the duty-free souvenir stalls next door. Unfortunately, their presence in the town has resulted in **higher prices** for all foreigners. The basic foodstuffs for example (falafels, shwaarmas and even coffee and tea) often cost twice as much if it's a Westerner who's paying. Once your face becomes known around town you should be able to secure the proper price, but until then I'm afraid you'll have to pay the tourist rates.

off many, confidence in the local economy remains buoyant and a number of high-rise buildings are going up in town, including several new hotels. The refugee camps are gradually shrinking too; both Ojah and Nuemeh are today empty, while the total number of refugees in the other two camps is now below 7,000.

Jericho in the Bible

Considering its age and location, Jericho features surprisingly little in the Bible, and hardly at all in the New Testament. The most famous reference to the town concerns the destruction of the town by Joshua, the leader of the Israelites following the death of Moses, and the man who began the assault on the inhabitants of their 'Promised Land'. Thanks to its location, Jericho became the first Canaanite town to be captured by Joshua, a victory described in Chapter 6 of the book that bears his name. Having marched his men around the city for six days on God's orders, Joshua, on the seventh, again instructed by God, ordered his priests to march around the city seven times. As they went they were ordered to sound a loud, continuous note on their ram's-horn trumpets (the forerunner of the shofar). On the seventh lap the walls of Jericho 'fell down flat', and the city was captured before nightfall. Only the family of Rahab, a prostitute who had sheltered Joshua's spies a few days previously from the men of Jericho, survived the subsequent slaughter of the city's inhabitants.

At the end of the chapter, Joshua lays a curse on the city, warning that the person who attempts to rebuild the walls and gates will lose his eldest son. This fate eventually befell **Hiel**, an Israelite from Bethel, as described in the First Book of Kings (16:34). As with Joshua's battle, however, this 9th-century BC resettlement does not fit the archaeological evidence, which points to a resettlement of Jericho two centuries later, in the 7th century BC.

Later on in the Old Testament the prophet Elijah visited Jericho, shortly before he was swept up to Heaven in a Chariot of Fire (2 Kings 2:4–11). Not long after, his pupil and successor, Elisha, purified the water of the Ein El-Sultan (see page 173), which was causing miscarriages amongst the women of Jericho, by sprinkling salt into it (2 Kings 3:19–22).

References to Jericho in the New Testament are few, mainly because Jesus rarely visited the town except when travelling between the Sea of Galilee and Jerusalem (the more direct route through Samaria would have been considered too dangerous for a non-Samaritan). He kept Himself busy while in town, however. During one trip He cured Bartimaeus of his blindness (Mark 10:46), and on His final visit He stayed a night at the house of Zaccheus, a wealthy tax collector whom He had spotted climbing a tree as His procession passed (Luke 19:1–9).

Practicalities

For a place that insists on being called a city, Jericho is tiny. Most things of interest to the tourist – the **hotels**, the **servis taxis**, the **post office** and the **municipality** (where, in the absence of a tourist office, you can pick up a **map** of the town) – lie on or near the main square, where you'll undoubtedly be dropped off. There's also a local branch of the Arab Bank on the north side of the square, the only place where you can **change money**.

Walk a few hundred metres from the square in any direction, and you'll have virtually left civilisation behind. The sights all lie away from the town square, with the nearest, Tel El-Sultan, about 2km away. A **taxi** from the square to the Tel, or indeed to Hisham's Palace, shouldn't cost more than NIS5. A cheaper, healthier and more enjoyable option is to rent a bike from **Zaki's Cycles**, on the eastern side of the main square. A fixed rate of NIS3 per hour is charged.

After a full day of cycling or walking in the Wadi Qelt, heading back to Jerusalem is an absurd idea, so consider one of the three **accommodation** options in town. The venerable, crumbling 1920s **Hesham Palace Hotel** on Sharia Ein El-Sultan (tel: 02 2321282) could once boast of a guest list filled with the cream of Arabian society, and even the odd potentate or two: King Hussein, during his playboy years, was a regular visitor. Nowadays, however, it's in such a parlous state that the current king wouldn't even use it as a stable for his camels. Still, renovation is being undertaken (though when the manager says it will be in time for the millennium, I assume, judging by the work that still needs to be done, that he means the next but one). Double rooms in the renovated part cost NIS120; in the older section it's NIS40 per bed in a triple room (though you'll probably have the entire room to yourself).

Of better value – just – is the red-roofed **New Jericho Pension**, Al Quds Street (no phone), which moans and groans every time you walk inside and always feels like it's about to collapse. It's clean, however, and good value at about NIS30 per person. If there's nobody around when you call, the manager can usually be found in his brass souvenir shop opposite the driveway. The third option, the **Jerusalem Hotel & Restaurant** (tel: 02 9921329), 2km out of the centre on Amman Street, is by far and away the most upmarket, with the rooms (all different, as the manager was at great pains to point out) starting at NIS70. Unfortunately, it's also the least convenient for anything except buses to the border.

When it comes to eating, a visit to the open-air **restaurants** on Sharia Ein El-Sultan is as much a part of the Jericho Experience as a sunburned neck. On occasions, and particularly in winter, these eateries are alive with the buzz of chatter from the glitterati of Palestinian society. In the low season, however, you may well eat your food alone, with nothing but the sound of chirruping crickets and croaking bullfrogs to accompany your meal. Still, at least they all serve beer. Briefly: **Al-Khayyam** is the nearest, and the service goes some way to making up for the rather inadequate food; the **Seven Trees** and its neighbour, the **Green Valley**, are the swishest and currently the most popular on the street, while the **Na'ura** (aka the **Bedouin Tent**) serves the best food, especially the Arabian delicacy *shashlik* (lamb kebab on a bed of bread and onions). The old house here dates back to the 1920s, though the garden outside is a more pleasant place to dine.

The locals are fond of grumbling about the lack of **nightlife** in Jericho. The city does have a **cultural centre** on Sharia Jatta and, near the stadium, a **theatre**, but both are usually closed. Thus you'll usually find the locals, or at least the male half, hanging out at the **pool halls**. Foreigners, however, have it slightly better: the new **casino**, the *Oasis*, in the desert 3km to the south of Jericho, caters specifically to foreign gamblers (the local population, or at least the majority Muslim section, is forbidden to enter). A taxi from the square costs NIS8.

Transport details

There is no bus service to Jericho, but servis taxis travel to a couple of places, including Ramallah (NIS8) and, very occasionally, Jerusalem (NIS10). More often than not, however, you'll have to catch a servis to Abu Dees (NIS6) and change there. All servis taxis leave from the south side of the main square.

Getting to Jordan

The **Allenby Bridge** crossing to Jordan (aka King Hussein Bridge and Jeser Al-Karameh), spanning the Jordan River, lies about 16km east of Jericho. **Buses** to the bridge (NIS6) depart from a station near the Jerusalem Hotel, 2km from the city centre. A **taxi** to the bus station will set you back NIS10, while a taxi from the

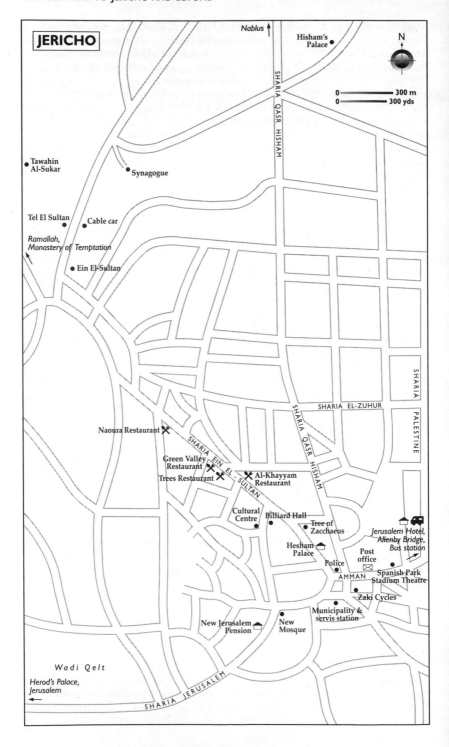

centre all the way to the bridge costs about NIS40. At the border you'll be asked to pay a departure tax of about NIS110. After the bridge (NIS10 on a bus), there are **servis taxis** from the foreigners' terminal to Amman (JD5), or **buses** from the locals' terminal (JD2).

What to see in Jericho town

The centre of town is not exactly chockablock with tourist attractions. The only one of any note is the **Tree of Zaccheus**, just north of the Hesham Palace Hotel on Sharia Ein El-Sultan, which, so it is said, Zaccheus climbed in order to get a better view of Jesus (Luke 19:4). Jesus ended up staying the night at Zaccheus's house, horrifying the locals who couldn't understand why Jesus would wish to fraternise with a tax collector. In the morning, however, Zaccheus gave away half his wealth to charity, so inspired had he been by the Holy Man in his house.

To the east of the town square, the **Spanish Park** is a neat recreational area of mowed lawns, fountains and cafés lying in the shadow of the local sports' stadium. Jericho Theatre lies opposite the entrance, though there haven't been any productions in a while.

Hisham's Palace – Khirbet al-Mafjar قصر هشام

Daily, 08.00–17.00; NIS10/7

Even though many of its greatest and most interesting treasures were carted off to Jerusalem years ago (where they now reside, cramped together in a small room at the back of the Rockefeller Museum), the surviving remains of the regal, 8th-century hunting-lodge-cum-winter-resort known as **Hisham's Palace** are still, without doubt, the most impressive sight in the Jericho municipality. Built in AD743 by the dissolute **Al-Walid Ibn Yazid**, the palace owes its name to his uncle, the Ommayad caliph Hisham Ibn Abd Al-Malik, to whom it was originally attributed. Yazid, described by a contemporary as 'a passionate aesthete and drinker, habitual companion of singers, himself the best poet and marksman of the Ommayads', was actually banished from the royal court of Damascus for 'wild living and scurrility'. He succeeded his uncle to the caliphate the following year, though he was to reign for less than a year before his death at the hands of an assassin. His demise signalled the end of the Ommayads' Golden Age, and construction work on the palace stopped soon after.

Though the seat of their power resided in Damascus, the Ommayad sultans were never keen on cities, preferring instead the wide open spaces of the desert, the natural abode of their forefathers. After the difficult and often joyless rigours of ruling an Islamic empire, Hisham's country pile would thus have been an ideal retreat: a pleasure palace filled with naked statues and naughty frescoes that would have had the po-faced iconoclasts in the capital shaking their head in disgust. As well as a swimming pool there were heated baths, a mosque in which to repent and salve the conscience, plenty of accommodation for friends and hangers-on, and all located in a desert setting that can't be beaten for either beauty or remoteness. Allah, however, clearly disapproved of the actions of his earthly representative, and just four years after building began (and possibly before it was even completed), the whole lot was shaken to smithereens by a huge earthquake (the same quake that destroyed the Holy Sepulchre). It is unknown whether the caliph ever actually spent any time here.

The site

If you've already marvelled at the originality and beauty of the palace's carved stucco decorations in the Rockefeller, the unadorned ruins from which they were brought may come as a bit of a disappointment. Though Saladin attempted some

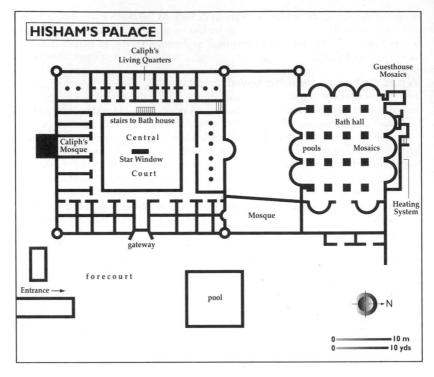

HISHAM'S PALACE

Caliph's
Living Quarters

Guesthouse
Mosaics

stairs to Bath house

Central

Caliph's
Mosque

Star Window

Court

Bath hall

pools   Mosaics

Mosque

Heating
System

gateway

forecourt

Entrance →

pool

N

0 ━━━━━ 10 m
0 ━━━━━ 10 yds

sort of renovation of the ruins in the 12th century, and some of his soldiers lived in the rooms for a short while, thereafter the entire site became a mere quarry from which locals would purloin stones and other materials for their own constructions. Indeed, it wasn't until the 1930s that the site was rediscovered. Enough remains, however, to get some idea of the palace's original splendour.

From the entrance a **gateway** on your left leads through to the **first courtyard**, in the centre of which is the famous carved stone window, star (literally) of hundreds of assorted postcards, tour brochures and other tourist paraphernalia. The original position of the window in the palace is unknown. Surrounding the courtyard are the household living quarters, that were originally two stories high. The caliph himself probably lived in the 12 slender rooms to the west of the courtyard. Look around the ruins today and you'll find some of the pillars have been inscribed with crosses; proof, possibly, that the caliph raided the ruins of the local churches for his building materials. A small **mosque**, possibly reserved for the private use of the caliph, lies due south of the stone window.

In the courtyard by the caliph's rooms, steps lead down to his private **bathhouse**, home of the first of the palace's collection of fine mosaics. The reception hall of the public baths, with its 16 large, rectangular pillars, many of which are modern reconstructions, lies adjacent to the courtyard to the north. The hall, its walls carved with geometric patterns, and its floor dotted here and there with a huge, so-so mosaic lying exposed to the elements, was probably the most elaborately decorated part of the palace. The niches in the walls used to house the scandalous statues of bare-breasted women and men in loin cloths that now reside in the Rockefeller, while many of the Rockefeller's plasterwork reliefs once decorated the bath hall roof.

The most valuable treasure of the palace, however, has survived *in situ*. Inside the small **guesthouse** to the northwest of the hall, and locked behind bars, is quite simply the most astonishing **mosaic** you'll see in the Near East. Its vibrant green and gold colours are just astounding. Its subject, the so-called **Tree of Human Cruelty**, is both highly unusual and enigmatic, while the artistry that's gone into producing such a detailed masterpiece – the tesserae are so small that the whole picture looks like a carpet rather than a mosaic – is just incredible. Doubtless you'll have seen the mosaic dozens of times on postcards and in brochures, but don't let that put you off visiting: it'll still take your breath away.

As well as being a work of art, the mosaic was also intended as a warning. In the symbolism of the picture, the lion is a metaphor for the caliph himself, while the gazelle that is being savaged represents any guest at the palace who wishes the caliph ill. The other two gazelles, by way of contrast, represent emissaries from kingdoms that are loyal to the caliph, and are thus allowed to graze unmolested. The allegory therefore acts as a warning to foreign emissaries staying at the palace of the consequences of upsetting the caliph. The symbolism of the mosaic even extends to the tree: each of the 15 pomegranates (or oranges) that hang from its branches represents a country ruled by the caliph, and the tree itself can therefore be seen to represent the Ommayad Empire.

Next to the guesthouse, the **heating system** of the baths has now been reduced to a series of crumbling canals and pits, though you can still see some of the original clay piping. Bathers would come and seat themselves directly over these pipes when requiring a sauna. From here, head back to the entrance through what were once the **palace gardens**. On the way you'll pass the **public mosque** (of which only the mihrab remains) on your right and, further on to your left, a **swimming pool** complete with diving platforms. Finally, before you leave the site, ask the guard to show you the small **museum** to the right of the entrance, which contains mainly pottery fragments collected on the site.

The Synagogue
Daily 08.00–17.00; NIS10/7
Housed inside a yeshiva (a Jewish seminary), about halfway between Hisham's place and the Tel El-Sultan, is Jericho's second breathtaking **mosaic** which, though somewhat cruder in execution than Hisham's masterpiece, is still mightily impressive. The bulk of the 6th-century mosaic consists of geometric **heart-shaped patterns**. In the centre, however, one finds a depiction of a **shofar** (the Jewish ceremonial horn), a **menorah** (the Jewish, seven-branched candelabra), an **olive branch** and, written underneath in Hebrew, the Jewish greeting **Shalom Al-Israel**, or 'Peace upon Israel'. Further proof that the mosaic once was on the floor of a synagogue is provided by the **Aramaic inscription** by the entrance:

> 'Reminder for Good be the memory of the entire Holy Community, the old and the young, whom the Lord of the Universe aided and were of strength and made the mosaic. He who knows their names and those of their children and of their families, may he inscribe them in the Book of Life together with all the pious friends of all Israel. Peace, Amen.'

Tel El-Sultan تل السلطان
Daily 08.00–17.00; NIS10/7
Huge and unsightly, the 30m-high dirt mound known as Tel El-Sultan may hold little for the layman to admire, but is of major interest to historians.

Following on from the first excavation in 1867, archaeologists, including such luminaries as the German scholar Ernst Sellin (1907), John Garstang of Liverpool University (1930) and, most famously, Dame Kathleen Kenyon, have been feverishly digging their trowels into the soil to unlock the Tel's prehistoric secrets. The **world's oldest staircase** and the **world's oldest wall** are just two of the features of the Tel, and though unimpressive physically, the importance of these structures to our understanding of prehistoric cultures has been profound.

Kenyon was the first to uncover and identify evidence of no fewer than **23 different settlements** stretching back over 9,000 years, from Neolithic to Byzantine. Together, stacked one on top of the other like layers in a cake, they form the Tel. (The city walls helped to keep the ruins of the different eras confined to the same area, so that the accumulated debris and ruins, instead of spreading outwards, was forced to grow upwards.) Most significantly of all, according to Kenyon the first settlement at Tel El-Sultan (ie: the settlement that today lies at the bottom of Tel El-Sultan, on which the other 22 have been built) represents the **transition** from nomadic to settled agricultural life. Excavating the Tel to its stone-age foundation she discovered grains of wheat and barley, crops which suggest that, by this time, man had forsaken his hunter-gatherer lifestyle for a more settled existence.

The site

Today, tourists are allowed to walk on the surface of the hill and look down into various excavation pits, all of which are roped off. The **sloping banks**, or *glacis*, that surround the site were actually once part of a fort dating back to the Middle Bronze Age. Great excitement erupted when this glacis was first discovered, for it appeared as if a **mud-brick wall** had tumbled down the sides of it, thus possibly providing evidence for the biblical story of Joshua's conquest. Unfortunately, the date given for this wall-tumbling is 1600BC, 350 years before the accepted date of Joshua's conquest. It is only if we use Rohl's chronological augmentation (see page 31) that the two dates can be reconciled.

From the entrance a path leads up to the top of the hill and a sheltered **observation point**. About halfway along the path a second track heads left, past a sculptured heap of mud and stones that's actually a section of the **city wall** dating from the 3rd millennium BC. Continuing down the hill we come to Kenyon's first major discovery on the Tel, a slightly bigger heap of mud and stones that's actually part of an **Early Bronze Age city wall** (c2600BC) that curves north from here round the Tel.

From these excavations, retrace your steps up the path and on to the observation point. Ahead of you on your right is a large square pit containing parts of wall discovered by John Garstang, while on your left is yet another exposed part of the Early Bronze Age wall, which I'm sure you'll all agree is a bigger pile of stones than the first pile, though it's not as big as pile number two. Separating these two excavations is the large **neolithic defensive tower**, the most impressive sight on the Tel, a 9,000-year-old, seven-metre-high conical structure made of stones and mud that knocks all the other piles of stones and mud into a cocked hat.

The world's oldest **staircase** resides inside this tower, invisible from the tourists' view. This tower, together with the evidence of an ancient Neolithic wall that ran alongside it, proves that Jericho was also the world's first fortified town. The earliest structure on the site, a small shrine, lay just to the north of this tower, though there seems to be nothing visible today.

Ein El-Sultan

The perennial **spring** of Ein El-Sultan, the prime reason why so many civilisations chose to build on nearby Tel El-Sultan and which even lent its name to the hill, is still a major source of water for the people of Jericho today, providing the city with over 700 cubic metres of water every hour. The spring derives its name from the legend that the Babylonians plucked out the eyes of the King of Jerusalem, or sultan, at this spot. It is also believed to be the spring that the prophet Elisha purified in the Bible (see page 166), hence its alternative moniker, **Elisha's Spring**. Unfortunately, as with the Tel, the history of the spring is more impressive than its appearance, unless you find the sight of a shed with a 'No Entry' sign outside somehow awe-inspiring.

The cable car

Daily, 08.00–20.00; NIS20/15 return trip).

The most visible manifestation of the boom in investment enjoyed by Jericho since the 1994 handover, the cable car provides both a decent bird's eye view of the city and the Tel, and a less exhausting way to reach the cliff-side Monastery of Temptation. Opened in 1999, the cable car forms the nucleus of a planned 'leisure complex' that will include, when completed, 16 souvenir shops, two outdoor terraces, a 55-room hotel and a French restaurant embedded into the mountains at the other end of the cable car. The cable cars, manufactured by an Austro/Swiss company, each take 5min 20sec to complete the 1,380m-journey up to the mountain.

The overland route to the Monastery of Temptation

Just 300m northwest of the Tel El-Sultan, **Tawahin Al-Sukar** is, as its name suggests, the ruins of a sugar factory founded by the Crusaders to export sugar to Europe. The remains of presses and an aqueduct leading from the spring, **Ain Al-Duyuk**, are still in place on the site. About 4km north of Jericho, beyond the turn-off to the monastery on the way to Ramallah, is **Na'aran** (daily, 08.00–17.00; NIS10/7), the Byzantine village of Jericho, built near the springs of **Al-Duyuk** and **Al-Nue'meh**. There's little to see here now, save for traces of an aqueduct heading from the springs to Hisham's Palace, and yet another beautiful mosaic from the floor of a synagogue. Filled with commemorative inscriptions, birds and animals, the highlight of the mosaic is the medallion in the centre showing two menorah flanking the **Ark of the Covenant**.

The Monastery of Temptation دير لتجرية

Daily, 09.00–15.00

Keeping watch over Jericho from its precariously lofty position halfway up the western cliffs of **Jabal Quruntul**, the Orthodox Monastery of Temptation is one of the most visited of Palestine's hermitages. The hill is supposedly the location of Jesus' **forty-day fast**, and His temptation by the Devil. Indeed, Jabal Quruntul is an Arabic translation of the Latin *Mons Quaranta*, the '**Mountain of the Forty**'.

Today's monastery is built round a cave 350m above sea level, where Jesus supposedly sat during the forty days. According to local legend it was yet another site identified by Queen Helena during her pilgrimage, though this is unproved. Despite this, the first church was built some 800 years later in the 12th century by the Crusaders. From the monastery, a path (usually barred by a gate) leads up to the foundations of a 19th-century church that was never actually finished. Remains of yet another fortress built to protect a winter palace, the Seleucid-built **Dyok** that was later used by the Hasmoneans, also lie scattered over the summit.

SITES EAST AND SOUTH OF JERICHO
The Dead Sea البحر الميت

The world's lowest body of water, the Dead Sea, measures approximately 80km by 18km, and averages 400m below sea level. It forms part of the Jordan Valley, which is really just a continuation of the **Rift Valley** that runs north under the Red Sea from East Africa. The waters are famously saline, with the upper waters rich in sulphates and bicarbonates and the deeper waters full of strong concentrations of magnesium, potassium, chlorine, bromine and hydrogen sulphide. As a result, plant and animal life finds it impossible to survive in the waters, though a few forms of bacteria thrive.

Currently some 25km of Dead Sea coastline lies within Palestinian territory. That's not much, though along this section there are a couple of sights of interest to the tourist: **Qumran**, home of the Essenes and the site of the discovery of the Dead Sea Scrolls, and the beautiful little resort of **Ein Feshka**. Unfortunately, though the Dead Sea lies just 10km south of Jericho, there is as yet **no public transport** between the two. Indeed, only Egged buses from Jerusalem (ten daily, usually running between Jerusalem and Eilat; NIS14) travel along this stretch of the Dead Sea coast. Thankfully, Qumran and Ein Feshka are only 3km apart, so it's possible to see both in one day.

Qumran قمران
Daily, winter 08.00–17.00, summer 08.00–18.00; NIS16/12
In 1947, a small shepherd boy was out looking for a lost sheep in the desert hills along the northern shores of the Dead Sea when he came across an **ancient cave**, high up in the cliffs, that he'd never seen before. Throwing a stone inside, the shepherd boy was surprised to hear it clatter into what sounded like pottery. Investigating further, he was amazed to discover no fewer than **50 storage jars**, each filled with leather scrolls. Excited, he did what any other shepherd boy would do in this situation – and used the scrolls to patch up the holes in his sandals.

Eventually, however, word got out about the shepherd boy's discovery. Further excavations in the 1950s revealed more scrolls hidden in other caves, including over 100,000 fragments of **biblical text** representing every Old Testament book except Esther, as well as a Revelations-style *apocrypha* on the end of the world and the Day of Judgement, called 'The War of the Sons of Light Against the Sons of Darkness'. The scrolls' copy of the Old Testament book of Leviticus predates any other existing copy by over 1,000 years. Today, the majority of these scrolls reside in a purpose-built room, The **Shrine of the Book**, in the Israeli Museum in Jerusalem, with a few stored in Amman in Jordan.

The Dead Sea Scrolls were written in the 1st century BC by the Essenes, a devout Jewish sect based in Qumran. Extremely strict in their adherence to Jewish law, the Essenes looked upon their Jewish Brethren in Jerusalem and elsewhere as corrupt and dissolute. For this reason, the harsh desert conditions of Qumran must have suited their simple, ascetic life perfectly. Details of the daily rituals and ceremonies of the Essenes are also documented in the scrolls. They remained in Qumran until AD68, when a Roman legion on the way to join the siege of Jerusalem destroyed the Essenes' home. The scrolls were probably hidden away in the cave just before the Romans attacked, presumably in the hope that they (the Essenes) would be able to return to the site later on. They never did.

Bereft of the scrolls, Qumran has little of interest for the layman visitor today. A map on the notice board points out various parts of the complex, including a **kitchen**, a **defensive tower** and, in the centre, the so-called **scriptorium**, where the scrolls were purported to have been written. You'll also find a large number of **cisterns** scattered around, presumably built to cope with life on a waterless hilltop.

Ein Feshka عين الفشخة

Daily, April–Oct 08.00–17.00; Nov–Mar 08.00–16.00; NIS25/22

The West Bank's only **seaside resort** lies just 3km south of Qumran, and is named after a **spring** that lies on the other side of the road from the sea. The spring attracts a wide variety of **wildlife** from all over the Dead Sea region – rock hyraxes and ibex included – and is now a nature reserve that's still run by the Israeli authorities. Apart from the reserve the resort is little more than a café by the sea, though the Palestinians do have big plans for the site.

Jesus' Baptism and the monastery of St Gerasimos
دير لقديس جر اسيموس

According to the Bible, Jesus was baptised in the Jordan River by John the Baptist. The exact location is, of course, unknown, but the Greek Orthodox church traditionally cite a section of the river just to the south of the Allenby Bridge, and to the north of the smaller King Abdullah Bridge. The site is called **Al-Maghtas**, and lies in an area closed off to tourists today for security reasons.

However, it is possible to visit the nearby monastery of **Mar Gerasimos**, 3km west of the Jordan. This Greek Orthodox monastery, also known as **Deir Hjleh** after a nearby spring, is named after a 5th-century monk whom Western artists have traditionally confused with Saint Jerome (see page 190). It was Saint Gerasimos, and not Saint Jerome, who, taking a leaf out of Androcles' book, pulled the thorn from the lion's paw, a service for which the lion was so grateful he never left the saint's side. In his book *The Spiritual Meadow*, the travelling monk John Moschos recounts a story concerning the saint and his pet. In the tale Gerasimos, as he did every day, handed over the monastery's donkey to the lion, who took it down to the river to drink. On one occasion, however, the donkey wandered too far away from the lion and was taken by thieves. The lion, downcast, returned to the monastery alone to face Gerasimos, who assumed that the lion had eaten the donkey. As punishment, Gerasimos ordered the lion (who was called Jordanes) to do the donkey's work, and carry food and water everywhere. Months passed, and then one day the thieves approached the monastery in the hope of selling some grain, which they had loaded on to the back of Gerasimos' donkey. Before they arrived, however, the lion recognised the donkey and chased the thieves, who fled in terror. The lion returned to the monastery with the donkey, as well as three camels that the thieves had also left behind in panic. Gerasimos, realising that the lion was not to blame for the donkey's disappearance after all, allowed the lion to stay with him in the hermitage, where he lived with the monk for five years, until Gerasimos passed away; it is said that the lion, on seeing his master's grave, lay down and died alongside it.

The monastery is difficult to visit. Thanks to its proximity to the border, the Israelis often close it off for security reasons. What's more, the monks aren't used to receiving visitors, though the monastery is advertised as an attraction in some tourist brochures. If you do manage to visit, ask to be shown the grave of Gerasimos, and the original cave in which he and the lion lived.

North to Galilee

Route 90 follows the Jordan Valley all the way to Tiberias, by the Sea of Galilee. It's a quiet, lonely road, with most of the traffic turning off to Ramallah and Nablus. There's only one sight of any note along the route, the castle of **Sartaba**, built by the Hasmonean king Alexander Jannaeus and rebuilt by Herod following its demolition by the Romans. There is no public transport to the site: Herodophiles will have to hire a special from Jericho to cover the 28km to the castle.

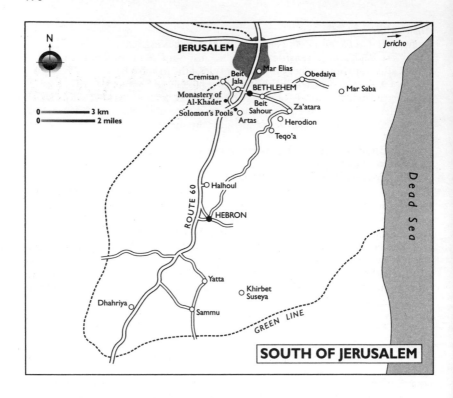

N

JERUSALEM

Jericho

Cremisan
Beit
Jala
Mar Elias
Obedaiya
BETHLEHEM
Mar Saba
Monastery of
Al-Khader
Beit
Sahour
Za'atara
Solomon's Pools
Artas
Herodion
Teqo'a

0 ———— 3 km
0 ———— 2 miles

Dead Sea

Halhoul

ROUTE 60

HEBRON

Yatta
Khirbet
Suseya

Dhahriya
Sammu

GREEN LINE

SOUTH OF JERUSALEM

The Southern West Bank

JERUSALEM TO BETHLEHEM

Twelve kilometres separate the two ancient cities of Jerusalem and Bethlehem, with half a dozen minor sights lying near the main road, Route 60, between the two. From Jerusalem, catch Bethlehem-bound bus number 124 (NIS2) from the Central Bus Station or a servis taxi from the Damascus Gates (NIS2.5). The **Monastery of Mar Elias** is the first and most visible of the sights. From here you can walk to a number of smaller places of interest, before flagging down a second servis taxi to take you either to **Rachel's Tomb** or straight on to Bethlehem (another NIS2/2.5). Sights beyond Bethlehem are dealt with later in the chapter.

Mar Elias دير مار إلباس

Daily, 08.00–11.00, 13.00–17.00; no entry fee

This 11th-century Greek Orthodox monastery stands on the apex of a hill by the side of the road just 5km from Jerusalem. According to tradition, the monastery is built on the spot where Elijah, weary and hungry, lay down under the shade of a juniper tree and prayed for death. Instead, an angel came down and fed him some cake and water (1 Kings 19:15), which isn't a bad substitute.

Today, the monastery is a popular resting point for pilgrims on the way to Bethlehem. During the Christmas Day procession the patriarchs call in to the monastery, where they are received by the local landowners and dignitaries. The monastery is named after **Mar** (Saint) **Elias**, the Greek bishop of Bethlehem who was interred in the monastery grounds here in 1345. Appropriately enough, given the monastery's hilltop location, Elias is the local patron saint of drivers. The age of the building is unknown, though it was restored by the Crusaders following a huge earthquake in 1160. Traces of these medieval renovations can still be discerned, though they're somewhat swamped by the building's more modern alterations.

Other sites near the monastery

Next door to the monastery, a stone bench inscribed with verses from the Bible in several languages commemorates the Pre-Raphaelite artist Holman Hunt, who spent many years in Palestine and painted two of his greatest pictures, *The Light of the World* and *The Scapegoat* near this spot.

Beyond the monastery to the northeast is a field full of small grey pebbles. This is known locally as the **Field of Grey Peas**, its name being derived from a local fable. According to the story, the Virgin Mary was walking past the field one day when she met the farmer out sowing seeds. 'What are you sowing?' Mary enquired, to which the farmer replied, sarcastically, 'Stones'. 'Fair enough,' said Mary, 'then stones are what you shall harvest.' Sure enough, when the time came to gather in the crop, all the farmer found were petrified peas – proof that even God hates a smart-aleck.

Over the road from the field, housed in a large 19th-century hospice, is the
Tantur Ecumenical Institute, an organisation that aims to promote peace and
understanding between the churches; if you've already visited the Holy Sepulchre
or Bethlehem's Church of the Nativity, you'll know that the institute still has a
long way to go to achieve its aim.

Rachel's tomb قبر رحيل / مسجد بلال

Sun–Thurs 07.30–16.00, Fri 07.30–13.30; free

Permanently under guard from a dozen or so heavily-armed Israeli guards, the
tomb of the matriarch Rachel is sacred to both Jews and Muslims. Whether this
really is Rachel's tomb is unknown, though it does fit in rather well with Genesis'
account of Rachel's demise (Genesis 35:16–19). Having fled from Mesopotamia
following an argument between her father, Laban, and her husband Jacob, a
quarrel in which she took her husband's part, Rachel died giving birth to her son
Benjamin, by the side of the road on the way to Jacob's hometown of Ephrath
(Bethlehem) in Canaan.

According to the Bible, a distraught Jacob 'set a pillar upon her grave'; since then
there have been a number of synagogues, and briefly a Crusader chapel, on the site.
The current building, however, is Ottoman, with the dome rebuilt by Sir Moses
Montefiore, the Jewish philanthropist, in 1860. Montefiore was also responsible
for the special vestibule, complete with mihrab, which he built for the exclusive
use of Muslim worshippers. The huge fortified walls that surround the tomb are a
modern, unsightly but necessary addition.

Pilgrims from all three religions regularly visit the site. One ancient Jewish
tradition dictates that pregnant women praying at the tomb will give birth to
healthy sons, and occasionally you may come across a group of expectant mothers
worshipping at the site, their arms tied to the cloth-draped tomb with threads. On
the wall above, a painting shows the spirit of Rachel rising from her grave to mourn
the Slaughter of the Innocents by Herod (see page 181), fulfilling the prophesy of
Jeremiah as quoted in Matthew (2:17): 'In Rama was there a voice heard,
lamentation and weeping, and great mourning, Rachel weeping for her children,
and would not be comforted, because they are not.'

RACHEL AND JACOB

The romance between Rachel and her husband Jacob is described in the book
of Genesis (Chapters 28–35). Instructed by his father Isaac to find himself a
wife, Jacob decided to visit his mother's home town in Mesopotamia, where
he stayed at his uncle Laban's house. Grateful for the help Jacob was giving
with the household chores, Laban offered Jacob a wage; but instead of
money, Jacob asked if he could take Laban's daughter, Rachel, as his bride.
Eventually, a deal was struck between the two: Jacob would work for seven
years for Laban, at the end of which he could take Rachel's hand in marriage.

Accordingly, at the end of the seven years a feast was prepared and
Jacob received his bride who, according to custom, was veiled. It was only
after the veil was removed that Jacob realised he had been tricked: instead
of finding the delectable face of Rachel beneath the veil, he discovered the
rather less appetising visage of Rachel's younger sister, Leah, grinning back
at him. Disappointed, but determined, Jacob grudgingly agreed to work for
another seven years for Laban in order to earn Rachel's hand in marriage.
And so it came to pass that 14 years after first setting his eyes on Rachel,
Jacob finally got his girl.

BETHLEHEM بيت لحم

As Palestine's third largest city, Bethlehem is no longer the 'Little Town' of Christmas carol fame. Instead, it's a sprawling, dusty, noisy, friendly metropolis of some thirty thousand souls, stretched across **two plateaux** between Beit Jala in the south and Beit Sahour in the east – both villages with which it now imperceptibly blends. It also enjoys a reputation as a booming **commercial centre**, and more recently – as the home of one of Palestine's largest universities – a prestigious seat of learning too.

Yet, no matter how much it continues to grow and prosper, Bethlehem will forever be associated, at least in Western minds, with events that may or may not have taken place in the heart of the town approximately 2,000 years ago. As the supposed birthplace of Christ, Bethlehem occupies a special place in the hearts of Christians worldwide. And though the city now has a majority Muslim population, the town is still the home to an incredible **54 churches**, and any number of Christian schools, hospitals, hospices and other ecumenical institutions. The random jumble of spires, steeples and minarets form a city skyline that is as pretty as it is distinctive. Inevitably, the city has also become a magnet for pilgrims who flock to the city all year round, not just at Christmas, giving Bethlehem the cosmopolitan air of a city twice its size.

Bethlehem is obviously rather proud of its biblical heritage. A quick scan of the street names, for example, throws up such gems as Manger Square, Manger Street, Shepherd Street, Star Street and King David Street. In fact, to be honest, the citizens milk the city's biblical connections for all they're worth. Every second shop in the centre sells souvenirs and icons, while its suburban craftsmen – the woodcarvers, stonemasons, glass blowers, rug weavers, goldsmiths and the workers of coral and mother-of-pearl – produce truckloads of mass-produced keepsakes for the hordes of visitors who swarm into the city day after day. Even the local municipality is getting in on the act. At the time of writing, Bethlehem resembled one massive building site with cranes now jostling the spires and steeples for supremacy in the sky. These are the most obvious manifestations of the authorities' attempts to titivate the city in time for the Millennium celebrations and the year 2000.

Fortunately, despite the hard sell of its heritage, the town has managed to avoid the worst excesses of the rampant commercialism that does so much to spoil Jerusalem's Old City. Hopefully, by the time you read this, all the building work will have been completed. The plan to pedestrianise the town centre is undoubtedly a good idea: until recently, **Manger Square** was little more than a *de facto* car park for the convoys of tour buses from Jerusalem. Some quarters, however, such as the souq and the charming ramshackle back streets leading off from Paul VI Street, derive much of their character from their scruffy and dilapidated state. Whether the 'improvements' will really improve these areas remains to be seen. But in spite of all these renovations, the billion-dollar investments and the big city pretensions, Bethlehem will always remains at heart just an overgrown, **typically Arab village**: a little scruffy, a tad grimy, usually chaotic and always friendly.

History

Bethlehem was a Canaanite settlement some 3,000 years before Mary and Joseph arrived to change the course of world history. The town was originally called Beit Lahama, literally 'House of (the God) Lahmo', though in the modern Arabic that has transmogrified into Beit Lahm ('House of Meat') and in the Hebrew, Bet Lehem ('House of Bread'). Possibly mentioned in the Amarna letters (a 14th-century BC correspondence between the Egyptian governor of Palestine and Pharaoh Amenhotep III, found in Al-Amarna, Egypt), the town was an important staging post for travellers between Syria and Egypt at this time.

Mary and Joseph probably arrived in the town in about 5BC, during the reign of Herod. Whether this is true or not, it is almost certain that Christians were worshipping at the cave, or 'stable', well before the end of the 1st century. Their freedom to worship was abruptly ended in AD135 by Emperor Hadrian who, in a bid to show the Christians who was boss, built a **Roman temple** over the cave and surrounded it with an olive grove, the **Grove of Thammuz**.

Although he didn't realise it at the time, by denying Christians the freedom to worship at one of their holiest shrines Hadrian had set a precedent that would be repeated again in later years by Saladin in 1187 (who expelled European Christians from Bethlehem in revenge for their mistreatment of Muslims in Jerusalem), the fanatical Mamluke sultan, Baybars, who went even further by banishing Christians completely from the town in 1263, and the Ottoman sultans from the 16th century onwards.

In between these periods of persecution the Christians have enjoyed moments of supremacy in Bethlehem, particularly during the Byzantine era when, following a visit by Queen Helena in AD326, the town became a major pilgrimage destination; later it grew to become a major monastic centre following the arrival of St Jerome in 384, and by 560 the town was large enough to feature on the **Madaba mosaic** (see page 128). A second era of Christian domination came with the Crusaders in 1099. Their arrival heralded a golden age of peace and prosperity for the town. Many Crusader kings chose to be crowned in the town rather than in Jerusalem, to avoid receiving a temporal crown in a city where their Lord had received his crown of thorns, and pilgrims flooded in from all over Europe and the Near East, reassured that, with Muslims banished from the town altogether, their safety in the town was guaranteed.

That's not to say that relations between Christians and Muslims have always been so sour. Soon after his conquest of Jerusalem in 637, the Muslim caliph Omar Ibn Al-Khattab visited Bethlehem, and relations between the local ecclesiastical authorities and Omar appear to have been good. A written agreement between the two allowed Muslims to pray within the church, but only as individuals without a muezzin, so as not to disrupt Christian worshippers, who were allowed to practise their faith unmolested. The mosque on the western side of Manger Square bears Omar's name to commemorate his enlightened tolerance.

Through all this religious upheaval, the town itself has continued to survive. Though hampered in its attempts at large-scale expansion by the lack of a fresh water supply (the population was still only 7,000 by the beginning of the 20th century), the town has grown in wealth and renown thanks to the steady stream of pilgrims. The most famous of these was Paul VI, whose visit in 1964 was the first by a pope since St Peter. Aghast at the plight of Palestinians, Paul called for the establishment of institutions to improve the quality of life for the locals. As a direct result, **Bethlehem University** was founded in 1973.

Thanks in part to an improved fresh-water supply, but mainly due to the influx of refugees from the wars of 1948 and '67, the population of Bethlehem has risen significantly over the last 50 years, to about 30,000, though this is stretching the town's infrastructure and natural resources to breaking point. The UN-backed programme to have the town looking shipshape as it enters the third millennium has thus arrived in the nick of time. Amongst the schemes of the **Bethlehem 2000 Project** is the construction of a huge cultural centre on the north side of Manger Square, and the re-paving of large sections of the old town. A whole programme of events running throughout the year, including festivals, parades, church services and concerts, have also been arranged to kick off the new millennium in style. For details, pick up a leaflet at the tourist office, or visit their website at www.bethlehem2000.org.

Bethlehem in the Bible

In the Old Testament Bethlehem is more commonly known by its former name, **Ephrathah** ('fertile' in Arabic), or **Ephrath**. It receives its first mention in Genesis (35:16–21) where, 'beside the road to Ephrath' Jacob's wife Rachel died giving birth to Benjamin. It was also the venue of much of the action in the Book of Ruth, and the home town of her mother-in-law, the Israelite Naomi. Ruth's great grandson, King David, also hailed from Bethlehem (Samuel 16), hence the Christmas carol's reference to Bethlehem as '**Royal David's City**'.

But it is as the venue for the **Nativity** that most people know Bethlehem, an episode recounted in the first chapters of the gospels of both Matthew and Luke. Recently, modern New Testament scholars have cast doubts on the veracity of this belief, citing Nazareth as a more likely location for the birth of Christ. They believe parts of the gospels are later accretions added to fulfill the Old Testament prophecy given in the Book of Micah (5:2): 'Bethlehem Ephrathah, though thou be a little among the thousands of Judah, yet out of thee shall he come forth that is to be ruler in Israel.'

The story of the nativity begins after the Emperor Augustus had ordered a census to be taken throughout the Roman Empire. Being of the house of David, Joseph was required to register in David's birthplace, Bethlehem. Mary, as his spouse, was required to go with him. I'll let Luke take over the story now (2:6–7): 'While they were there…she brought forth her first born son, and wrapped Him in swaddling clothes, and laid Him in a manger; because there was no room for them in the inn.'

In the days that followed, the family was visited by shepherds (according to Luke) and gift-bearing wise men (according to Matthew). The wise men's conversation with Herod (Matthew 2:1–12) has led them to be identified as three kings who, like the shepherds, had followed a bright star to the stable. After their departure, the holy family were eventually forced to flee to Egypt after Herod, who saw the infant Christ as a threat to his authority, issued a decree ordering the deaths of all boys under two years old in Bethlehem.

Orientation and practicalities

All of the major sights in town are located within a five-minute walk from Manger Square. Buses to Jerusalem and servis taxis terminate at the junction known locally as **Bab Al-Zqaq**, a 15-minute hike from Manger Square along **Paul VI Street**. If travelling by servis taxi, jump out at the corner of Paul VI and Amel Street to save yourself a little uphill walk. Alternatively, bus number 1 runs along Manger Street to the square (NIS1). As in many Palestinian towns, street numbers are rarely used, so in the text directions have been given instead.

A local **bus** and **servis stop** lies below Manger Square, at the top of Manger Street. Transport to most outlying villages, such as Beit Sahour, Obedaiya and Za'atara, can be caught from here. Incidentally, don't listen to the taxi drivers who'll try to persuade you that there's no bus to your destination: they're just lying, in the hope you'll hire them instead.

As with most Palestinian cities, there is no official **tourist office**, though the Palestinian Ministry of Tourism and Antiquities (Mon–Fri 08.00–14.30), above the Arab Bank on Manger Street, is more willing than most to deal with tourists.

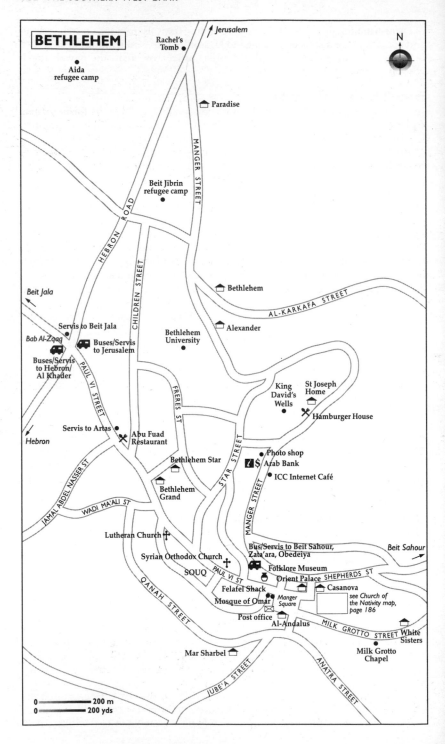

BETHLEHEM

N

↗ *Jerusalem*

Rachel's Tomb

Aida refugee camp

Paradise

MANGER STREET

Beit Jibrin refugee camp

HEBRON ROAD

CHILDREN STREET

Beit Jala

Bethlehem

AL-KARKAFA STREET

Alexander

Servis to Beit Jala

Bab Al-Zqaq

Buses/Servis to Jerusalem

Buses/Servis to Hebron/ Al Khader

Bethlehem University

FRERES ST

PAUL VI STREET

↙ *Hebron*

Servis to Artas

Abu Fuad Restaurant

King David's Wells

St Joseph Home

Hamburger House

STAR STREET

Photo shop

Arab Bank

ICC Internet Café

Bethlehem Star

MANGER STREET

Bethlehem Grand

JAMAL ABDEL NASSER ST

WADI MA'ALI ST

Lutheran Church ✝

Beit Sahour →

Bus/Servis to Beit Sahour, Zata'ara, Obedeiya

Syrian Orthodox Church ✝

SQUQ

PAUL VI ST

Folklore Museum

Orient Palace

SHEPHERDS ST

Casanova

QANAH STREET

Felafel Shack

Mosque of Omar

Manger Square

see Church of the Nativity map, page 186

Post office

Al-Andalus

MILK GROTTO STREET

White Sisters

Mar Sharbel

JUBE'A STREET

Milk Grotto Chapel

ANATRA STREET

0 ——— 200 m
0 ——— 200 yds

Previous page The Dome of the Rock, Jerusalem (HS)

Above Corner of Jericho (CO)

Below Main Square, Jericho (CO)

Above left Ruins at Jifna (HS)

Above right Carved window of Hisham's Palace, Jericho (HS)

Below Monastery of St George of Koziba, Wadi Qelt (HS)

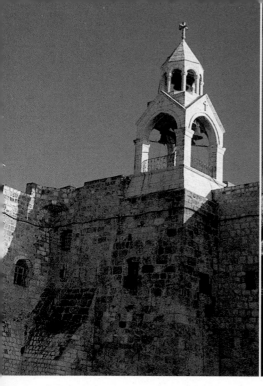

Above left and right Church of the Nativity, Bethlehem (CO)
Below Church of All Nations, Mount of Olives (HS)

In the future one floor of the building will be set aside to deal with tourist enquiries, though as they've only just moved to these apartments, exactly which floor that will be has yet to be decided. Next door you'll find an **Agfa photographic shop**, a reliable place to buy film, while over the road is the **ICC Internet Café**, which charges just NIS7 for 30 minutes. Johny Skafi is your helpful host, and the speed of the machines is excellent. Back on the main square you'll find the **tourist police**, on the southern side of Manger Square below the Al-Andalus Hotel, and on the western side, under the Municipality building, is the **post office**.

This guidebook should provide you with enough information on the sights. If, however, you need to hire a guide, a number of licensed **guides** hang around the popular tourist spots. Most are pretty competent, though I can personally recommend Walid Kunmah; his English is excellent (he has a master's degree in the subject), and his knowledge of the area pretty encyclopaedic. He's usually to be found at the top of Manger Street by the local bus stop.

Transport details

At the Bab Al-Zqaq junction, buses and servis taxis heading for the same destinations leave from the same place. Details of where you should wait for your transport are shown on the map on page 182. Buses and servis taxis to **Hebron** (bus number 23 for NIS4, servis taxis NIS5), **El-Khader** (NIS2), **Beit Jala** (NIS1) all pull up at the Bab Al-Zqaq junction, as does bus number 124 (NIS2) to **Jerusalem**, and servis taxis for NIS2.5.

From Manger Street you can catch buses to **Beit Sahour** (NIS1), **Obedaiya** (by green-and-white bus number 60 for NIS2.5), and minivan servis taxis to **Za'atara** (NIS2.5).

Accommodation

There's no shortage of hotels in Bethlehem, and a dozen more will doubtless have been built by the millennium. Finding a room, therefore, is not a problem except at peak times, by which I mean Christmas and Easter. Mary and Joseph couldn't find anywhere to stay, but then they should have known better than to turn up over the Christmas period without booking in advance.

If you're on a very tight budget things could be a little difficult: hotels in Bethlehem tend to cater for kings rather than shepherds, and those counting every agorat are advised to stay in Jerusalem and commute from there. Only a couple of places offer rooms for less than US$20, and there is only one (overpriced) **dormitory** in the whole town. At Christmas and Easter, as you'd expect, the picture is even grimmer. Most hotels double their prices, while those that don't are booked up at least six months in advance.

That said, there are some terrific bargains to be had in the **low season** (three-star double rooms with breakfast for as little as $35, for example) as managers are forced to resort to all sorts of desperate tactics to fill their rooms. Bargain hard for the best deals: they're unlikely to turn you away.

The prices given below are low-season prices, and include breakfast unless stated:

Alexander Hotel Manger St; tel: 02 2770780; fax: 02 2770782. This is a nice family-run place, with an excellent view over the valley and some very tidy, air-conditioned rooms. But what really makes the hotel special is the manager, Joseph, an opinionated, and occasionally very funny, pot-bellied Palestinian. Rooms, all en-suite and with TV and mini-bar, range from $35/45 (sgl/bl) including breakfast – great value.

Al-Andalus Guest House Manger Sq; tel: 02 2743519; fax: 02 2742280. Hostel in a perfect location, and, ermm... that's it. The square can be noisy after dark; rent a room at the back to ensure you have a Silent Night. At $25 per person, you pay for the location.
Bethlehem Hotel Al Madbassah St; tel: 02 2770702; fax: 02 2770706. Massive three-star hotel with a facade like a Christmas tree, catering mainly to tour groups and particularly Americans. All mod-cons in the rooms; $45/70 sgl/dbl.
Bethlehem Grand Hotel Freres St; tel: 02 741440; fax: 02 741602. Good value, if impersonal hotel with huge clean rooms (with the emphasis on huge), all with satellite TV and shower ($45/70 sgl/dbl). Also boasts a fine Mexican Restaurant, the Mariachi.
Bethlehem Star Hotel Freres St; tel: 02 2743249; fax: 02 2741494. Friendly hotel that's popular with local businessmen (always a good sign) and with a great rooftop restaurant. Rooms come with all the usual facilities (TV, phone, shower, air-conditioning), and are good value at $35/60 sgl/dbl.
Casanova Manger Sq; tel: 02 2743981/2/3; fax: 02 743540. Right next to the Church of St Catherine, this spotless hotel is in fact a pilgrims' refuge run by Franciscan monks, and has been since 1347 – though the buildings date only from the beginning of this century. It's the best-value accommodation on the square. Prices remain fixed throughout the year at $33/$40 sgl/dbl including breakfast, $43/$60 full board.
Mar Sharbel House Qanah St; tel: 02 2742155; fax: 02 2777321. Quiet, unassuming little hospice in good location just to the south of Manger Square. Usually for pilgrims only, the attached chapel gives guests the chance to witness a Maronite prayer service. Nice rooms, excellent food. US$35/55 sgl/dbl.
Orient Palace Hotel Manger Sq; tel: 02 2742798; fax: 02 2741562. Flash-looking luxury hotel to the north of the square decorated in a sort of quasi-Arabesque style that's not unpleasant. Rooms en-suite with cable TV, mini bar and telephones ($80/100 sgl/dbl).
Paradise Hotel Manger St; tel: 02 744542/3; fax: 02 744544. Large but unexceptional hotel at the western end of Manger Street, over 2km from Manger Square.
St Joseph Home Manger St; tel: 02 2770155; fax: 02 2770334. Pleasant hospice built around a 19th-century Syrian Catholic chapel. Caters mainly to groups, but may have the odd bed free occasionally.
The White Sisters Milk Grotto St; tel: 02 2742441. Charming little hospice lying virtually opposite the Milk Grotto (look for double gates and ring the bell) run by the French order of nuns, the White Sisters. The hospice has some basic rooms with shared bathroom for $12–14 – the cheapest in town – with some en-suite doubles for $25 per person, including a bread-and-cheese breakfast. Prices are roughly the same at Christmas, but phone at least six months in advance for a reservation.

Food and restaurants

Of the felafal shacks, **Abu Fuad**, five minutes up the hill from Bab Al-Zqaq, is the best; a normal felafal will set you back NIS2.5; a larger one in a sesame seed roll is NIS3. The anonymous little **felafal restaurant**, on the left-hand side just 20m up from Manger Square on Paul VI Street, is the best of those near the square. The **Hamburger House**, open in the evenings only, serves ice-cold beer alongside its greasy fast food, and the **St George** makes a decent stab at cooking Western food, though they charge too much. In my opinion, however, the best food in the area is to be found not in overpriced Bethlehem, but in neighbouring Beit Jala (see page 198). The **Syrian Orthodox Club**, 200m up from the Lutheran church, serves up some fantastic Arabian dishes, including *musakhan taboun* (chicken with onions, NIS6) and the hard-to-refuse sheep's head soup (NIS12); they also make valiant attempts at Western fare. The **Barbara Restaurant**, down the hill from the Everest Hotel, is also highly recommended.

WHAT TO SEE IN BETHLEHEM
The Church of the Nativity كنيسة المهد

Daily,05.30–18.30; dress conservatively; admission free

A colossal stone edifice completely dominates the eastern side of Manger Square, looking for all the world like the façade of a Crusader fortress – undecorated, secular, imposing. Only the twin bell towers and small crosses poking up above the huge walls give any indication that this is actually one of Christianity's oldest and most sacred buildings. What was once a lowly cattle shed is now the centre of a huge **ecclesiastical complex** containing two churches, a labyrinthine series of underground chapels and no fewer than three monasteries. Over 12,000m² of classy Christian constructions, and all encased behind one huge, 14m-tall wall.

At the centre of the complex lies the **Grotto of the Nativity**, the traditional site of Jesus' birth. Ironically, it was the Roman emperor Hadrian's attempts to stamp out Christianity that led Helena to identify the cave in AD326 as the location for the birth of Christ. In AD135 Hadrian built a number of temples to Roman gods (in Bethlehem's case, Adonis) on sites that had previously been used by the local people to worship their own god. Not only did this policy prevent the locals from continuing with their ceremonies, but it also acted as a metaphor for the superiority of Rome above all other civilisations. However, it also enabled Helena to deduce that the cave in Bethlehem on which the temple had been built had previously been venerated by the local Christians in the first century AD, less than 100 years after the nativity. This cave was therefore the likeliest location for the birth of Jesus Christ.

Another reason for believing that Helena was correct in her choice of location is that the church has, by the standards of Palestine, led a pretty charmed life. Only once has it been destroyed (during the Samarian Revolt of AD529), and on that occasion the ambitious Byzantine emperor Justinian (527–565) gave orders for a new one to be built that would outdo the original in both size and beauty. Even the Persians, whose devastating progress through the Holy Land in AD614 had left almost every other sacred building in ruins, felt compelled to leave the Church of the Nativity unharmed after one of their sharp-eyed soldiers spotted a mosaic of the three wise men (re-discovered in 1933 on the gable above the narthex), in which each was wearing traditional Persian clothes. Out of respect to their forefathers, the Persians decided to wreak their havoc elsewhere. The Muslim invaders of 637 left the building unscathed too. Their leader, Omar Ibn Al-Khattab, recognised the importance of Jesus as an Islamic prophet, and prayed in the southern apse of the church (which is conveniently orientated towards Mecca). His agreement with the local ecclesiastical authorities made provision for both faiths to pray in the church for the first time. Even that arch-destroyer of all things Christian, the 11th-century Egyptian caliph, Al-Hakim, decided against demolition, believing this would have jeopardised the substantial amount of tax he received from the churchgoers.

The Crusaders carried out the first major restoration of the church. The exhausted marble floor was replaced, the wooden roof lined with lead and new mosaics shimmered above the nave and on the walls of the grotto. Save for a 52-year hiatus beginning in 1187, the Crusaders remained in control of the church and the town until 1291, when the Mamlukes assumed power. Thereafter the church suffered centuries of neglect. Later, during the Ottoman period the church was also subjected to routine pilfering. Yet throughout these years the church's importance to Christians from all over the world never faded, and the question of its ownership inflamed passions throughout Europe. Napoleon's arbitrary decision to declare the entire complex as French property in 1852 angered the Russians and

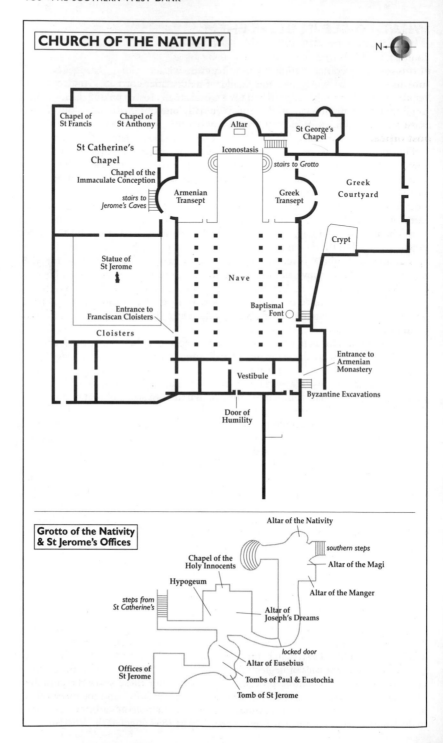

CHURCH OF THE NATIVITY

N

Chapel of St Francis

Chapel of St Anthony

St Catherine's Chapel

Chapel of the Immaculate Conception

Altar

Iconostasis

St George's Chapel

stairs to Grotto

stairs to Jerome's Caves

Armenian Transept

Greek Transept

Greek Courtyard

Crypt

Statue of St Jerome

Nave

Baptismal Font

Entrance to Franciscan Cloisters

Cloisters

Entrance to Armenian Monastery

Vestibule

Byzantine Excavations

Door of Humility

Grotto of the Nativity & St Jerome's Offices

Altar of the Nativity

southern steps

Chapel of the Holy Innocents

Altar of the Magi

Hypogeum

Altar of the Manger

steps from St Catherine's

Altar of Joseph's Dreams

locked door

Offices of St Jerome

Altar of Eusebius

Tombs of Paul & Eustochia

Tomb of St Jerome

led, indirectly, to the Crimean War of 1853, pitting the might of imperial Russia and Ottoman Turkey against the West European superpowers, France and Britain.

Today, alas, the arguments continue to rage, and only an uneasy truce between the Franciscans, Orthodox and Armenians – backed up by an elaborate schedule of services designed to prevent the denominations from praying in the church at the same time – prevents further animosity. It also means that Christmas Day is celebrated three times in the church: on December 25 by the Catholics and Western Churches, on January 6 by the Eastern Orthodox Church and on January 19 by the Armenians.

The church

Entrance to the church is through the tiny door in the western wall. What was once a suitably grand doorway was shortened by the Ottomans to prevent mounted horsemen from entering, although you can still see the outline of the original. Such was the extent of the reduction that it's now totally out of proportion to the rest of the church, and anyone over five feet tall will have to stoop to enter – hence its nickname as the **Door of Humility**.

Ducking down inside, you'll find yourself under the wooden roof of the vestibule. This small antechamber was originally part of the narthex of Justinian's church that stretched along the whole of the basilica's western end. A second tiny door leads into the main body of the church that looks so empty and undecorated, like a big, disused warehouse. There are no pews and the church's decorations have either faded away, or are tucked away high up under the roof or beneath the floor. The body of the hall is divided into four side aisles and a main central **nave** by four rows of ten 6m-high pillars, two on each side of the nave. The pillars were once painted with **frescos** of saints, including St George and St Canute (yes, *that* Canute, the Danish king who tried to turn back the sea), though they have virtually all faded away now. The 6th-century **baptismal font**, behind the pillars by the right hand wall, is the only permanent piece of furniture in this entire hall.

The nave's decorations which have survived, such as they are, lie mainly underneath the trapdoors in the 19th-century floor, where you'll find remnants of the original **Byzantine floor**. The mosaics are fairly patchy and, restricted in scope and subject by the rules of iconoclasm, rather bland, though they do give an indication of just how wonderful the original church must have been. Of more interest, perhaps – though in a terrible state of repair – are the mosaics above the main central aisle, just below the windows, where a series of green and gold half-figures representing the earthly ancestors of Christ emerge from the whitewashed walls. Above them, the roof itself is made of sturdy English oak, and was a gift of England's King Edward IV. The roof's original lead covering was used by the Ottomans to make bullets, and the current covering was supplied by the Greeks, who restored the church following a huge earthquake in 1834. The glittering **iconostasis**, a cacophony of saints and scenes from the gospels roped off at the eastern end of the central nave, also dates from this time.

The grotto

Two sets of steps, one on either side of the iconostasis, lead down into the church's *raison d'être*, the cave, or stable, where Jesus was supposedly born. Blackened down the centuries by incense and candle smoke, for all its religious importance the rectangular grotto is a somewhat gloomy, poky shrine. Examine the walls closely and you'll notice that they're covered with 19th-century **tapestries** depicting the childhood of Jesus.

A **silver star** to the right of the southern staircase, fixed to the floor in a small alcove known as the **Altar of the Nativity**, marks the exact spot of Jesus' birth. The star was installed by the Catholics in 1717, removed by the Greeks in 1847 and replaced by the Ottomans in 1852 during the Crimean disagreements. Like the lamps above the stone of unction in the Holy Sepulchre, the ones dangling above the star are each owned by different denominations, with the Greeks owning six, the Armenians five and the Catholics four. On the other side of the staircase is a second recess containing the **Altar of the Manger**. This altar is the one used by Catholics to celebrate Christmas mass; the Armenians and Greeks use the Nativity altar. The marble manger replaces a silver one dating from the Byzantine era, which since the 12th century has resided in the Basilica of Maria Maggiore in Rome. This in turn replaced a clay manger found by Helena, which was supposedly the one in which the infant Jesus lay. Facing the manger in the same alcove is a third **altar** dedicated to the three Wise Men, and marking the spot where they knelt before the manger in supplication and offered their gifts of gold, frankincense and myrrh. A painting of the scene by the Italian artist Maello stands above the altar.

St Catherine's Chapel and the cloister of St Jerome
Back in the main hall of the church, a small door in the northwest corner leads off to a pleasant sunlit courtyard, in the centre of which is a **statue of St Jerome**, the 4th-century monk whose translation of the Bible into Latin was of vital importance in the dissemination of Christianity in Europe. The courtyard forms the centre-piece of the **Franciscan monastery**, the oldest in the complex, dating back at least as far as the Crusaders and built over a 5th-century convent established by St Paula. **Medieval cloisters**, designed by the Crusaders and restored in 1947 by Antonio Barluzzi, surround the courtyard on three sides.

St Jerome's study now forms part of an underground **cave complex**, the entrance to which lies in the cool and pleasant **Church of St Catherine of Alexandria** that stands on the eastern side of the courtyard. St Catherine was a 4th-century martyr who, according to popular legend, converted the wife of the Roman emperor Maxentius. Sentenced to death for her beliefs, the spiked wheel on which she was meant to be killed split in two; fed up with these new-fangled gadgets, the executioner resorted to the trusty sword and beheaded her instead. (According to the legend that grew up around her after her death, milk rather than blood gushed forth from the wound on her neck. And centuries later her body was discovered, uncorrupted by time, on the top of a mountain in the Sinai desert where it had been taken by angels.)

The 19th-century church will be familiar to many people as the church in which the televised midnight mass is held. Two chapels flank the central apse, dedicated to St Francis (north) and St Anthony (south). A third shrine, the **Altar of the Immaculate Conception**, stands in the southern wall. The model of the baby Jesus which, every Christmas, is taken down in a procession to the Grotto of the Nativity and placed in the manger, lies behind glass in the altar. A daily procession (at noon, or 1pm in winter) conducted by the Franciscan fathers leads from the church to the basilica; it is one of the few occasions when a reverent hush fills Manger Square.

Stairs next to the altar lead down to the subterranean complex. The first chamber we enter is the 4th-century **Hypogeum** (underground chamber). A door at the far end of the room leads through to the Grotto of the Nativity, though it's permanently locked these days. The altar standing on a higher level ahead of you commemorates Joseph's Dream, in which he was told by God to flee with his family to Egypt (Matthew 2:13) to avoid the slaughter of the children ordered by Herod (Matthew 2:16–17). The small, trisected alcove to the left is a shrine dedicated to those children, known as the **Holy Innocents**, who didn't escape the slaughter. As the first people to shed their blood for Christ, they occupy a special place in Christian tradition.

To the west of the hypogeum, a doorway leads through to the **offices of St Jerome**. The first chamber has been divided into two halves, each with its own chapel dedicated to a follower or pupil of St Jerome: the first is dedicated to St Eusebius, while beyond is an altar dedicated to the female saints Paula and her daughter Eustochius. The cell used by St Jerome is now a small chapel, the mosaic behind the altar depicting St Jerome and these three followers. The Latin quotation is taken from the opening lines of St John's gospel: 'In the beginning was the word, and the word was with God'.

The Armenian and Greek monasteries

A door on the southern side of the narthex – to your right as you enter the Church of the Nativity – leads to the **Armenian monastery**. At the moment, the three monks who still live here are very reluctant to allow visitors inside, particularly as major renovations and excavations are taking place. It is hoped, however, that the monastery will open properly again in the new millennium. Inside, you can view the ongoing archaeological excavations taking place underneath the monks' living quarters. A 6th-century Byzantine construction, possibly part of **Justinian's atrium** – a colonnaded quadrangle that preceded the entrance into the church – is slowly emerging after centuries beneath the soil. So far 13 Byzantine pillars have been unearthed, as well as a vaulted, sky-blue ceiling. At the moment, you can only view all this through a gate at the western end of the courtyard, though there are plans to build a sort of museum based around these discoveries.

Immediately to the east lies the **Greek monastery**, reached via a door in the southern apse of the Church of the Nativity to the south of the iconostasis. It may surprise you to know that Arafat has stayed at this convent on a number of occasions when visiting Bethlehem. A door in the courtyard's eastern wall leads to the **Church of St George**, used by the Anglicans for their Christmas Eve carol service, though usually closed to the public for the rest of the year. Opposite the church entrance, steps lead down to the **crypt**, a series of grisly chambers where one can see the **skeletal remains** of the interred pushing up through the soil. According to the monks, many of these bones belong to the children slaughtered by Herod in the Massacre of the Innocents.

Back above ground, if you plead with one of the monks they may allow you to climb the **bell tower**, which sounds only once, at 4am, to summon the monks to prayer.

Milk Grotto مغارة الحليب

Daily, 08.00–11.00, 14.00–18.00; free

Southeast of the Armenian monastery, the Milk Grotto, or *Magharet Sitti Mariam* (**Grotto of the Lady Mary**), is located along a souvenir-shop-lined street to which it has given its name. Though it has no biblical basis, the story behind the Milk Grotto is a popular and enduring one, having been around since at least the 4th century. In it Joseph, having been told in a dream to escape to Egypt, orders Mary to prepare for the journey ahead. Mary, who was breastfeeding the infant Jesus at the time, spilt some milk on to a rock as she moved, turning it from red to white in an instant.

ST JEROME

Visit any exhibition of Italian Renaissance art and the chances are you'll come across at least one, and probably several, powerful portraits of St Jerome, or Eusebius Hieronymous to give him his full Latin title. Most of these pictures convey the impression that Jerome was some sort of wild-eyed, long-haired religious fanatic, a **wilderness wanderer** who spent his days deep in contemplation and prayer, breaking off only to beat his breast with rocks until he bled whenever wicked thoughts suddenly entered his head. Undoubtedly, somewhere in the picture you'll also find a **lion** – or at least the medieval artist's interpretation of what a lion should look like, as very few of them would have seen a lion in the fur before.

So who was Jerome, and are these depictions of him accurate?

Born in AD342, Jerome hailed from **Dalmatia**, in modern-day Croatia. Baptised at 18, he already had a reputation as a man with a sharp intellect and a volatile temper, both of which had been honed during eight years of schooling in Rome. Following a brief sojourn amongst the desert hermits of Syria, Jerome returned to Rome to serve as **secretary to Pope Damasus I**. Such a lofty position gave him unprecedented access into the very highest echelons of Roman society, and it was here that he met, and became mentor to, a number of pious upper-class women. These unlikely friendships, combined with his acerbic style and ultra-ascetic sermons on the evils of money and power, aroused envy and hatred among the husbands. When Damasus died, Jerome feared for his life, and in 386 he fled to Bethlehem.

With cash donated by his female followers back in Rome, Jerome founded a religious academy. But his ambitions lay in other directions. In particular, Jerome wanted to write a **definitive Bible** in the common tongue of Latin. He wasn't the first to try, for Bibles in Latin had been in existence for at least 100 years before Jerome started his work, but by common consent these versions were either incomplete, inelegant or unreliable. And so, in AD387, having left the academy in the charge of Paula (one of his admirers from Rome, who had decided to emigrate to Palestine following the death of her Roman-senator husband), Jerome began to translate the Bible into Latin from the Hebrew and Greek originals.

This rock (which is now most definitely black, thanks to the smoke from 15 centuries-worth of votive candles) lies inside a small cave reached by a **mother-of-pearl staircase**. The current chapel dates from 1872, though it's believed that there may have been a church here as early as the 5th century. As is typical of a Catholic building, the chapel is stuffed with **religious statuary**. The rock itself, tucked away in a quiet corner, is an object of veneration for both Muslims and Jews. It is said that the rock can restore barren women to fertility, and you'll often find young women praying by the shrine. Mothers, too, come to the shrine when they have trouble producing a sufficient amount of milk for their child: a lump of the white rock, when ground into powder and mixed with water, is supposed to provide a failsafe cure, though naturally the authorities would prefer it if the mothers didn't chip away at the rock, and are trying to discourage them from doing so.

David's Wells بير النبي داو ود

Daily, 07.00–noon, 14.00–19.00

Inside the premises of the Catholic Action Club stand three wells, supposedly the same cisterns mentioned in the Second Book of Samuel (23:15–17). According to

Initially, Jerome had even loftier ambitions for his version of the Bible. His great dream, he confessed, was to provide a piece of Christian literature to rank alongside the pagan works of the great Roman writers Virgil, Cicero and Horace. But, following a dream in which God accused him of being a Ciceronian (a follower of the 1st-century BC philosopher), Jerome decided that the meaning of the Bible had to take priority over any considerations of style.

Already fluent in Greek, widely acknowledged as a master of Hebrew and a student of Aramaic, Jerome had all the intellectual equipment necessary to undertake such a mammoth task. Yet he also had to decide which books warranted inclusion in his Bible, and which were superfluous. (For example, there were around two dozen different gospels produced in the early days of Christianity, which Jerome whittled down to the four we know today. The books which didn't make it into Jerome's version, but which are regarded by some as part of the sacred canon, are known as **Apochryphal texts**, or simply *Apocrypha*).

Though the Old Testament alone took 15 years, during which time Rome (and, by extension, Jerome's funding) were under constant threat from the Barbarians, Jerome finally completed his work in AD405. The public was quick to embrace his version of the Bible which he called the **Vulgate**, from the Latin *Versio Vulgata*, or 'common language'. Armed with such a consistent and reliable text, the missionaries of the Catholic church found it much easier to convert the pagans of Western Europe. It's for this reason that Jerome is revered as one of the fathers of the Latin Church, and his portraits crop up so regularly in Catholic art. Following his death in AD420, his body was removed from its tomb in Bethlehem to Rome, and Jerome, his eccentricities forgiven, was canonised soon after.

And the pet lion? Well, Jerome never mentions a lion in any of his writings. However, **St Gerasimos** is said to have befriended one by pulling a thorn out of its paw (see page 175). Therefore, one can only assume that the Latin translators mistranslated Gerasimos as Jerome, and the misattribution has survived to this day.

the story, David was camped in the Valley of Rephraim overlooking Bethlehem, which at the time was occupied by the **Philistines**. Frustrated by his inability to visit his home town, he muttered to himself, 'Oh that one would give me drink of the water of the well of Bethlehem, which is by the gate.' Unbeknown to him, he was overheard by three of his men, who broke through the Philistinian ranks that same night and snatched some water for their master. Their actions were in vain, however: drinking the water that they had risked their lives for, David explained, would be akin to drinking their blood. Instead he poured 'it out unto the Lord', on to the floor in front of him.

Today there are two approaches to the wells. The first and simplest is to walk north from the centre along King David Street until you come to the Catholic Action Club (a large concrete building on your right with 'Jesus' written in bold black letters on it). The more difficult approach is to climb the **zigzag steps** from Manger Street. Halfway along is a locked gate: you'll have to call in on the elderly couple living beneath the steps to ask them to unlock it for you. Given the wells' biblical connections, it seems quite curious that the small shrine by the three cisterns is dedicated not to David, but to the Virgin Mary. A second statue, of

Mary Magdalene, kneels in supplication beside her. As you can probably tell from my account, this site is a little disappointing, and isn't redeemed by the insubstantial ruins of a **5th-century convent** and **church** founded by St Paula that lies nearby.

Bethlehem Museum
Mon–Sat 10.00–17.00; NIS8
Possibly the best, and certainly the oldest, of the plethora of museums dedicated to the traditional culture and lifestyle of Palestine, the Bethlehem Folklore Museum lies down an alley to the north of Paul VI Street, just to the west of the steps leading down to Manger Square. Established in 1970 by the local **Women's Union**, the museum occupies a 17th-century house appropriately called the **Old Bethlehem Home**. As well as displaying a variety of exhibits, all donated by local families, the museum also runs a small shop selling hand-embroidered items such as cushions, waistcoats, tablecloths and so on.

The first room in the museum, housing **jewellery**, traditional Palestinian **dresses** and ceremonial items such as the *shatweh* head-dresses – headscarves decorated with a 'veil' of silver and copper coins or coral beads – is the most interesting. The rest of the museum is given over to a reconstruction of a traditional **Palestinian home** including the living room (complete with icon-filled altar), bedroom and, round the back, the big kitchen with its large collection of wooden and brass utensils. Perhaps the most absorbing section of the museum, however, is the collection on the stairs of old black-and-white **photos** of Palestine during the twenties and thirties.

AROUND BETHLEHEM
Sights around Bethlehem range from the must-see (Herod's winter palace, the **Herodion**, and the desert monastery of **Mar Saba**) to the missable. If you have time, I strongly recommend that you do the **walk through Artas Valley** as described on page 201, as it takes in a number of these attractions in one go. If you don't fancy walking, details of how to get to all of these sights are given in the accounts.

Beit Sahour بيت ساحور and the Shepherds' Fields حقل الرعاة
Just one kilometre north of Bethlehem, at the foot of a precipitous drop from Manger Square, sits the village of Beit Sahour. It's possible to walk to Beit Sahour from Bethlehem, or you can catch a bus from Manger Square (NIS1). This village with a large Christian majority (whose name translates as 'The House of Vigilance') is pleasant enough in a genteel sort of way. It has a pretty town centre with some fine churches (including one, the Latin **Church of Our Lady of Fatima**, designed by the Italian architect Antonio Barluzzi) and a reputation as a high-tech manufacturing centre – Palestine's own Silicon Valley.

But few visitors would bother making the steep descent from Bethlehem if it were not for the groves and meadows that lie ten minutes to the east of the centre. The so-called **Shepherds' Fields** are traditionally held to be the site where the shepherds were visited by the Angel Gabriel, who told them of the birth of Jesus in nearby Bethlehem. As we all know, rather than contemplate the steep uphill climb and decide against it, the shepherds chose to make the effort (Luke 2: 8–14), writing themselves into the Gospels as they did so.

Two possible sites, 600m apart, have been put forward as the exact location of this divine visitation. The first and most popular (at least with the tour buses), is the **Der El-Siar** ('The Sheepfold'), run by the Franciscan order (08.00–11.30, 14.00–17.00). It lies about 1.5km from the bus station. Head east from the bus station, turn right by the shops, then take a left at the end and follow this road as it continues past the Shepherds' Fields Restaurant; on your right, in the distance, you should see the bright, glittering **dome** of a decagonal chapel emerging from amongst the conifers. (Incidentally, the watchtower that you can also see poking up above the walls is known as the **Tower of the Flocks**, and is said to be built on the site of an older tower mentioned in Genesis 35:21; today the tower forms part of the Franciscan hospice.)

The **chapel**, the work of Antonio Barluzzi, was built in 1954. Appropriately, both the laying of the foundation stone and the dedication of the chapel took place on a Christmas day. Gabriel, etched on to the bronze door, welcomes visitors into the interior of the circular body of the church. Three recesses punctuate the walls, each containing a large shepherd-themed mural, recounting their involvement in the Nativity story. The two grottoes behind the chapel were probably used by shepherds for shelter during Jesus' time. The Byzantine floor mosaics found inside these grottoes, combined with the excavations on the far side of the garden, prove that the site has been venerated by Christians since at least the 4th century, thus lending further credence to the Franciscans' claim that this was the spot where the shepherds were visited by Gabriel.

Such a claim is hotly contested by the Greek Orthodox Church, however, who have their own location, **Der El-Rawat** (Convent of the Shepherds), 1km to the south. From the monastery gates, turn left and keep straight on down the slope; the red domes of the Greek Orthodox church (daily, 08.00–11.00, 13.00–17.00; free) soon appear in the fields straight ahead.

The **subterranean chapel** in the church grounds, originally built on Helena's orders, once again contains the remnants of an ancient Byzantine church, including floor mosaics and murals on the ceiling – though the latter are incredibly difficult to discern through the blue paint that covers them. The chapel, as one would expect of a Greek Orthodox building, is filled with painted icons, and the iconostasis in the eastern wall, with portraits of the 12 disciples on the top row, is particularly fine. The shepherds themselves are supposedly buried just to the west of the chapel, and you can still see some tombs there today.

The large modern church next door was originally meant to stand over the underground chapel, though as they were preparing the ground they discovered the remains of three other churches dating back to the 5th, 6th and 7th centuries. Rather than destroy the lot, they decided to build the new church next to the grotto rather than over it. The **murals** in this new church (it was built in 1982) are quite startling. It has thus far taken ten years to paint the walls and roof, and the monks estimate that they'll need at least one more year before the work is complete. Scenes from the last days of Christ – the agony in the Garden, the betrayal by Judas and subsequent arrest, the condemnation by Pilate and the Crucifixion – fill one side of the ceiling. Don't miss the large portrait of **Christ Pantocrator** inside the main dome too. The three altars are dedicated, from left to right, to the archangels Michael and Gabriel, the Virgin Mary, and, on the right, St Panteleimon, a Greek martyr and healer. Incidentally, the field to the west of Der El-Rawat is known as the **Field of Ruth**, and is traditionally held to be the site where Ruth worked for Boaz, a wealthy landowner who later became her husband (Ruth chapters 2–4).

Mar Theodosius دير مار ثيودوسيوس and Mar Saba دير مار سابا
The village of **Obedaiya**, 8km to the east of Bethlehem, lies on the edge of the biblical *locus horrendae et vastae solitudinis*, the **Judaean wilderness** that stretches east from Bethlehem towards the Jordan Valley. The village dribbles on over three hills and is overlooked by Mar Theodosius, one of the most intriguing monasteries

in the Holy Land. It is also the nearest source of civilisation for Mar Saba, possibly the most famous, and certainly one of the most picturesque, of all the desert monasteries in Palestine.

Mar Theodosius is named after a 5th-century monk from Cappadocia (in Central Turkey). Theodosius, a friend of Saint Saba (see below) and a one-time pupil of Simon the Stylite (page 195), began his monastic career as a novice in Jerusalem, in a monastery that once lay near St David's Tower. From there he moved to 'the old place' as he called it (probably the monastery of Mar Elias, see page 177) after which he decided to indulge in a bit of wilderness wandering. It was during this time that he discovered a cave in which, he believed, the **three wise men** stayed for a night during their return journey from Bethlehem. So convinced was Theodosius of this cave's heritage that in 476 he decided to settle and spend the rest of his life here, dying at the age of 105 on January 11 AD529.

The monastic village that grew up around the cave continued to prosper after his death. During its heyday over 690 monks lived here, and the compound they built contained no fewer than four churches, each holding services in a different language to cater for the many pilgrims who passed through the area. Though it was sacked in AD614 by the Persians and again in 808, on each occasion the monks were able to pick up the pieces and continue the tradition of monasticism at the site. But, eventually, the pressures of maintaining a life of Christian monasticism under the Islamic Mamluke and Ottoman empires took their toll: by 1620, the monastery had been abandoned, and lay in ruins until its reclamation by the Greek Orthodox church in 1899.

This **monastery** is well worth visiting, though whether you'll get the chance is debatable. As I write, only one monk lives in it, and when he goes the future of the place is uncertain. The monastery has no set opening hours either – though Monday and Thursday mornings are the best time – and more people get refused admittance than are allowed to enter. The secret is to be persistent: ring the bell (tug on the chord poking through the gate of the main entrance), and keep on ringing every 30 seconds or so until someone answers.

Inside, separated from the door by a courtyard of **Crusader pillars** and paving slabs, is a bright and shiny new **church**, consecrated in 1955. Its interior is simple by Orthodox standards, with plain green walls and simple, monochromatic stained-glass windows. A painting of Mar Theodosius on his death-bed hangs from one wall.

Of more interest, at least to the ghoulish amongst us, is the monastery's collection of skulls from the Persian massacre of 614, each with a cross painted slap bang in the middle of its forehead. Look closely and you may be able to discern the neat gashes cleaved by Persian swords in the top of the skulls. The skulls are stored in **Theodosius' cave** under the courtyard, in a recess to the left of the stone steps. At the bottom of the steps is a large cave where the three magi were supposed to have rested, after being warned by God in a dream not to visit Herod, but to return 'into their country by another way' (Matthew 2:12). Today the cave contains the grave of **Mar Theodosius**, whose body was brought back by the Greeks on their return in 1899, as well as those of the travelling monks John Moschos and his pupil Sophronius the Sophist. In AD587 these two monks set off on a journey that would take in the entire Byzantine Empire, staying in caves, monasteries and remote hermitages, collecting and recording the wisdom of the monks and holy men they met upon the way. John Moschos eventually turned his jottings into a book, *The Spiritual Meadow*, which became a huge bestseller. John Moschos died in Constantinople in 619, just a few months after the end of his journey. His body was brought back to Mar Theodosius (where he

DESERT MONASTICISM

It would appear that nothing thrives in the desert like a monastery. In the monastic movement's heyday in the 6th century there were over 150 monasteries in the Holy Land alone, inhabited in some cases by as many as 5,000 monks. The reason why monks and deserts go together is a simple one: deserts can provide one of the main essentials of monasticism, namely isolation. Isolation allows monks the chance to indulge in a life of austerity and spiritual contemplation away from the temptations and distractions of normal life. Indeed, the word 'monk' comes from the Greek 'monos', meaning alone.

Deserts have the added advantage of being inhospitable, deterring would-be invaders from attacking the monastery. Mar Saba is a typical example of a monastery that thrived because it was all but invisible to the outside world, as is St Catherine's in the Sinai. And just in case they were discovered, monks built their own fortifications to ward off invaders; many monasteries, including **Mar Theodosius**, look more like fortresses than places of worship.

Though Palestine seems the logical home of monasticism, the first monastery was actually born a few hundred miles to the southwest, in the hostile deserts of Egypt. Furthermore its founder, **Saint Anthony**, fled to the desert to escape not his enemies, but his admirers. Obviously a painfully shy fellow, Anthony first tried to hide from his fans (made up largely of the intelligentsia of Alexandria, for whom he had become something of a hero) towards the end of the 3rd century AD. No matter how far he retreated, however, people would always track him down. Eventually, after reaching the most inhospitable part of the Egyptian desert, 300 miles from Cairo and 350 from the Red Sea, Anthony gave up his quest for solitude. Instead, he organised his followers into a community. That way they would be happy, and he, by living in a cave on nearby **Mount Kolzim**, could both keep watch over his community, and keep his distance.

By the end of the next century monasticism had reached Europe. Several breakaway orders emerged at this time as monks sought ever more excruciating ways of living. Thus we encounter the **Stylites in Syria**, who spent their entire monastic lives on top of pillars praying under the desert sun. The most famous stylite and founder of the order, **Simon the Stylite**, sat on top of his 60ft pillar for 37 years. In Palestine there emerged the cult of the **wandering monks**, who would literally roam the desert feeding on nothing but insects and plant roots, grazing the floor like goats. It seems incredible today that people would do such a thing, sustained only by the promise of the afterlife. Nor can we put down such actions to sheer desperation or stupidity: most monks were well educated and came from privileged, middle-class backgrounds.

Today, the fashion for desert monasticism has largely faded. The rise of Islam, the return of Judaism and the friction between these two heavyweights has left the Christian population in Palestine in serious decline. In such unhelpful conditions, monasticism doesn't stand a chance. The wandering monks have disappeared, as have the Stylites, and while a handful of the 150 monasteries still operate in the Holy Land, they hang on by a thread, often with just one or two monks in each.

had been educated and tonsured) by Sophronius. (Incidentally, Sophronius eventually rose to become the patriarch of Jerusalem in AD631, and therefore had the unenviable task of defending the Holy City from the invading Muslim hordes that were sweeping up from Arabia, conquering all before them. It was Sophronius who reluctantly surrendered the keys of Jerusalem to the Muslim leader, Caliph Omar Ibn Al-Khattab, in AD637.)

Bus number 60 to Obedaiya (NIS2.5) leaves from below Manger Square; ask the driver to stop by the monastery.

Monastery of Mar Saba

Sun–Thurs 08.00–16.00; free. Men only; dress conservatively
The honey-coloured monastery of Mar Saba (or Sabbas) lies in the lee of a sheer canyon wall overlooking the **Kidron Valley**, 8km to the northeast of Theodosius. It was one of 14 monasteries – together with four hospices – founded by St Saba, a 5th-century holy man from Cappadocia, and it was here that Saba died, aged 94, in AD533. Fifteen years later his body was dug up by the Byzantines and whisked off to their capital at Constantinople. Miraculously, instead of the expected odour of rotting flesh, the Byzantines noticed a sweet, perfumed aroma emanating from the corpse. Saba was declared a saint (Mar) soon after.

In the centuries following its founder's death, Mar Saba became one of the largest monastic communities in the Holy Land, with a population approaching 5,000. The monastery soon earned a reputation for scholarly excellence too, and the writings of St John Damascene, an 8th-century monk of Mar Saba, were instrumental in smashing the tyranny of iconoclasm that threatened to strangle the creativity – and fun – out of Christianity.

Today Mar Saba has just a dozen or so monks left, yet, such is the current parlous state of monasticism in the Holy Land, this place still ranks as one of the more populous and successful of Palestine's ancient monasteries. It is also the one with the strictest regime. The day begins at 2am, when the monks rise and sing the office continuously for five hours. A short rest follows during which they eat their only meal of the day. This is always bread – made once a week and stale by the third day – and boiled vegetables, together with a watery soup and cheese. Fish is allowed on Sundays, with oil for a dressing. The monks then return to their cells for the rest of the day, returning only to sing vespers at the appointed hour.

This kind of severe routine has remained largely unaltered since the monastery's inception in the 5th century, the only serious interruption occurring in AD614 when the Persian army ransacked the monastery and slaughtered the monks (about 400 of them all told). Such a devastating misfortune necessitated a two-week break in the monastery's schedule while new monks were recruited.

The collected bones of these martyrs line the apse at the back of the **cave church**, founded by Mar Saba himself. Dedicated to Saint Nicholas, the cave still lies at the monastery's heart, though these days most of the services are held in the larger, **free-standing church** nearby; at a mere 1,500 years old, this church quite a recent addition.

Under the church's elaborately decorated roof (the paintings, incidentally, are mainly modern additions) is yet another part of the monastery that's changed little down the centuries: the **body of Mar Saba** himself, which lies behind glass opposite the entrance. Snatched by the Byzantine authorities from his original resting place in the small (and now restored) kiosk in the monastery courtyard, then moved again from Constantinople to St Mark's in Venice in 1256 by the Crusaders, the cadaver of Mar Saba was finally returned to the monastery he founded in 1965. Considering he was 94 when he died, and has had about 1,500 years to rot away since then, Mar Saba looks remarkably well, and can still boast his own teeth, nails and skin. He is also fairly flexible, according to the monks who dressed him in the fine raiment that he wears today.

The cliff face on the opposite side of the valley is punctured with hundreds of small caves or **hermitages**. During the Byzantine era, the monks would retreat to these caves from Sunday to Friday, only crossing to the other side of the valley on Saturday to attend church and eat together. Each of the caves has a **prayer niche**, much like the mihrab in a mosque, showing the correct direction for praying. One cave, marked with a cross and the letters 'AC', was for five years Saba's own hermitage. Don't forget to visit this side of the ravine: though the caves are all empty, they provide the best and most complete view of the monastery opposite. It's only from here that you realise how huge the place is. The **river** below the monastery is the Kidron that runs from East Jerusalem to the Dead Sea. It's now used as a sewage carrier – as you'll notice if you go near it – so monks are forced to rely on rainwater and a small spring for their freshwater supply.

The monastery has a well-deserved reputation for hospitality to strangers. One of the monks will doubtless show you around the monastery, and will leave you in

TRAVELLING BETWEEN THEODOSIUS AND SABA

The walk from Theodosius to Saba is a pleasant 7.5km stroll: 5km ambling along a pleasantly undulating ridge, most of it still in Obedaiya, followed by a steep 2.5km descent through the desert to the monastery. Unfortunately, the walk in reverse is a lot tougher, as that steep 2.5km descent becomes an extremely steep 2.5km ascent. For this reason, most people choose to take a special to Mar Saba: expect to pay about $20–25 return from Bethlehem, including a stop at Mar Theodosius and waiting time at Saba.

If you do want to walk, but aren't too keen on tackling the entire 7.5km, **bus** number 60 from Bethlehem to Mar Theododius continues on to the eastern extremity of Obedaiya, about 1,500m before the start of the steep descent to the monastery. Of course, that still leaves you with the task of climbing the steep 2.5km on the return journey, but at least you should have conserved enough energy by this method to tackle it successfully.

If, on the other hand, you feel fit enough to **walk the whole way**, the road is fairly easy to follow. Simply turn left as you leave Mar Theodosius and follow the main road as it winds its way down and up, past and behind the mosque on the hill opposite, from where it continues on to the next hill. Near the summit of this second hill the road forks by a 50km/h sign: take the left track, then another left by the 'grosary' store 200m further on. The village finally peters out about 1km further on, while the road continues east to a **rubbish tip** on top of yet another hill, from where you should be able to see the twin towers of Mar Saba in the desert below. Just look how isolated it is. In the entire **60km panorama**, apart from the occasional temporary Bedouin camp, the towers of the monastery are the only man-made structures.

Whether you walk the whole way or not, it goes without saying that trekking in this climate is very dangerous, and you should prepare yourself accordingly: bring a sunhat, sun cream, sunglasses and lots and lots of water.

·the small **dining room** where you can fill out the guest book and drink water, ouzo, coffee and eat sweets (which is a far more appetising spread than the one the monks have to survive on). Unfortunately, this hospitality doesn't extend to women, who are barred from entering the monastery and have to make do with a distant view from the nearby **Women's Tower**.

South of Bethlehem: Beit Jala, Cremisan, El-Khader, Artas
Beit Jala   بيت جالا
Now relegated to a suburb of Bethlehem, and lying just 3km from Manger Square, **Beit Jala** is a medium-sized, Christian-dominated town huddled on a hill around four churches. Despite its proximity to the city of the nativity, Beit Jala (whose name translates, intriguingly, as 'Grass Carpet'), features but seldom in the Bible, though some have identified the town with the biblical **Giloh**, the birthplace of David's adviser, Ahitophel. Today, the town is famed for its apricots, which flourish in the temperate climate here, its stonemasons, whose work decorates many of the churches in Bethlehem, and the embroidered dresses of its women, though these seem to be less in evidence than the brochures would have you believe.

Servis taxis from Bab Al-Zqaq (NIS1.5) drop you off in the centre of town at Municipality Square. Of the churches, it is the two owned by the Greek Orthodox Church – **Saint Nicholas** and **Santa Maria** – that are the most interesting. With its silver dome that glistens in the midday sun, **Mar Nicholas**, to the west of Municipality Square, is certainly the most striking of the two; and though it is the younger (having been built in 1932), it stands on the ruins of a 4th-century Byzantine church dedicated to St George. You can see the remains of this earlier building by taking the stairs to the basement of the new church (the family behind the blue door opposite the church entrance have the key to the front door). It is said that Saint Nicholas, who hailed from Cappadocia in Central Turkey, inhabited this subterranean cave.

Santa Maria, or the **Church of the Virgin**, lies on the main road about 150m up from Municipality Square. It too is usually locked, but Father Jacob, whose offices are just inside the upper entrance gate on the bend in the road, will gladly show you round. It's the oldest church in town, having been consecrated in 1862.

Accommodation in Beit Jala
There are just two choices of accommodation in Beit Jala, at either end of the town. The first is the **Nativity Hotel** on Al-Sahel St (tel: 02 6470650; fax: 02 744083), a large business-class hotel with a nativity theme (show me a hotel round here that hasn't). Prices aren't cheap, ($40/60), but it's reasonable value. The second option is the **Everest Hotel**, beyond the town on top of Ras Beit Jala (tel: 02 742604). Built in 1922, the hotel is currently closed for renovation, though I was informed that when it does finally reopen, in late 1999, it will be one of the cheapest in the region (probably because the 27 rooms have just four bathrooms between them). Open or not, make the effort to get here to admire the **panoramic view** that encompasses Jerusalem, Bethlehem and even Hebron, in the far distance to the south.

The Cremisan   كريمزان
Mon–Fri 08.30–11.30, 13.30–17.00, Sat 08.30–17.00, Sun closed
At the top end of Sharia Al-Sharafa, the road running through Beit Jala, lies a crossroads. The road to the left runs to the western end of **El-Khader** and the Monastery of St George (see below); straight ahead leads to Jerusalem, while the

road to the right (signposted Har Gillo) quickly splits into two. The left-hand branch winds up to the Everest Hotel, while the right-hand fork in the road heads down past Barbara's Restaurant to the **Bethlehem Arab Society for Rehabilitation**, founded in 1960 as a home for the disabled. At the bottom of the hill by the Centre, a road continues west (left) past fields of apricots, vineyards and olive groves to the **Cremisan Monastery**, on the very outskirts of metropolitan Jerusalem. Founded by the Salesian Father Belloni in 1882, the monastery is one of the more prosperous in Palestine, thanks to its renowned wine cellar. For over a century now the monks of Cremisan have been concocting their own wine, using grapes from the vineyards below the monastery. The **cellars**, 500m from the entrance gate, are open to the public, while a small **shop** by the entrance allows you to sample the results and buy a bottle or two.

El-Khader الخضر

El-Khader is an elongated village of 5,000 inhabitants, stretching for over 1.5km due east of the Jerusalem Tunnel. From Bethlehem, catch a Hebron-bound servis (NIS2) and jump out when you see a stone arch fenced off in the middle of the road. This arch is one of the few surviving examples of a monumental village entrance that used to be very popular in Palestine.

The two main attractions of El-Khader lie at either end of the village; a taxi between the two should cost no more than NIS1. The **Monastery of El-Khader**, also known as the Monastery of Saint George, at the western end of the village near the Jerusalem Tunnel, has become a place of pilgrimage for Muslims and Christians alike. El-Khader (literally, the 'Green One') is something of a magical figure in Islamic folklore, a benevolent spirit who travels the world dispensing justice and good advice. St George is merely one human manifestation of El-Khader (the Old Testament prophet Elijah is another), and St George's defeat of the dragon and the rescue of the damsel in distress are typical of El-Khader's style. For this reason, all Christian churches dedicated to St George (and all sites associated with Elijah) are also venerated by Muslims as sites associated with El-Khader.

There are three entrances into the monastery (daily, 08.00–noon, 15.00–19.00), usually all locked; hammer on the small metal door to be let in. The present church, constructed in 1912, is built over the ruins of a **16th-century chapel**, located on a spot where St George was supposed to have lived for part of his life. Little of this original has survived. The modern edifice has a typically Orthodox Greek interior, with a highly decorated ceiling and walls and a portrait of **Christ Pantocrator** in the dome. St George, in the process of killing the dragon, appears twice in the murals on the left hand wall, and again in the large icon to the right. In both Christian and Muslim traditions St George is associated with healing the sick, and **during** the Ottoman era some of the rooms in the convent were used to house the mentally ill. St George is also famed for his protective powers, and for this reason you will see a lot of Christian houses with a stone carving of St George, in the process of killing the dragon, above the door.

The second and more worthwhile attraction of El-Khader, **Solomon's pools**, lies just 200m east of the arch. Unfortunately, following years of neglect, they're not quite the spectacular sight they once were. Of the three pools, the middle one contains a murky dribble of unsanitary water, while the other two are both dry, and currently undergoing some much-needed renovation. A few locals still attempt to go for a swim in the mucus-coloured soup of the second pool; join them at your peril. The large, rusting pile of car chassis at the western end of the third pool are proof that the locals regarded the pools as a convenient rubbish dump.

The attribution to Solomon stems from a quote in the Book of Ecclesiastes (2:6): 'I made me pools of water, to water therewith the wood that bringeth forth trees'. The pools were once part of an ancient water system, and were designed to collect rainwater. The first, or upper, pool is the largest, measuring just under 180m long by 64m wide. It is also the deepest, at over 15m. As well as an essential reservoir of precious water, it's also said that Solomon built the pools as **swimming baths** for his wives; and as he had over 1,000 wives to cater for, it's just as well the pools were huge.

Whether Solomon actually did build the pools is unknown. What is certain is that Pontius Pilate repaired them, Herod the great built the **aqueducts** to take the water to the Herodion, and the Ottomans built a further set of pipes from the pools to Jerusalem.

Next to the first pool by the road is what looks like a mini-castle, but is in fact a fortified khan known locally as **Burak Castle**. It was built on the orders of Suleyman the Magnificent in 1617 to provide protection and accommodation for commercial travellers, though later it became a barracks for the Ottoman troops charged with protecting the pools. Push open the rusty metal door and you'll find a couple of dilapidated rooms, including a mosque and some stables, and the remains of four square towers at each corner.

Artas ارطاس

The gorgeous village of Artas, the biblical **Ethan**, stands on a near-vertical slope 1.5km south of Bethlehem. (Catch a servis taxi for NIS1.5 from opposite the Abu Fuad Restaurant.) The name of the village is an Arabic corruption of the Latin for garden, 'Hortus', and the agricultural fecundity of the village and the valley in which it sits contrasts sharply with the bare hills that surround it. The name is a reference to Solomon's **Hortus Conclusus**, a metaphor for virginity used in the Song of Solomon (4:12–13) which, according to tradition, was inspired by this valley: 'A garden enclosed is my sister, my spouse; a spring shut up, a fountain sealed.' According to the historian, Josephus, Solomon regularly visited the valley to enjoy the fragrant and plentiful waters of the gardens, so its identification with the biblical Ethan may not be so far-fetched.

The spectacular **convent** and **church of Hortus Conclusus** stand opposite the village on the southern side of the valley. The convent was founded at the beginning of this century by the Archbishop of Montevideo (in Uruguay). The building was designed by local architects, though a close inspection is forbidden as the chapel and convent are closed to the public. Sometimes you can cross the bridge above the valley floor, though often even this approach is barred. Still, the view from the bridge back towards the village, with the houses looking as if they've been stacked one on top of the other, is pretty spectacular.

Unfortunately, the serenity of Artas masks some serious, longstanding problems. The boundary between zones A and B, as defined by the Oslo Accords, runs right through the village, bringing confusion and tension over which authority controls which part of the village. What's more, predatory **Jewish settlers** have bought the hills behind the convent and have plans to develop them, sparking considerable anger amongst the residents of Artas, particularly as the hills are strategically very important: as well as overlooking Artas, one can see both Jerusalem and Bethlehem from the summit.

Gorgeous though it is, Artas would normally be considered too small to feature on any tourist itineraries. That it does so is largely due to one man: Musa Sanad. Not only is Musa responsible for the day-to-day running of the **Palestinian Ethnographic Museum** (Wed–Mon 09.00–18.00; free), just up from the village mosque, but he is also its founder. The museum was established in 1993 as a way of celebrating the traditional lifestyle of the Palestinians. As with many of these museums, while the exhibits are rather unspectacular, the place is not without a homely, parochial charm and has a few mildly interesting exhibits, including a radio dating back to the World War I, and some ancient Canaanite caves that lie beneath the museum.

He is also the man behind the **Artas Folklore Centre** (tel: 02 274 4046), which currently resides just up the hill from the museum's office. The centre houses art exhibitions as well as a small shop selling local craft, though you'll probably have to call in at the office to fetch the key. Whilst there, ask one of the staff to point out the **Mamluke prison** behind the **Mosque of Omar**, and the **House of Luisa Baldensperger**, a local missionary who lived in the town for most of her life and produced a number of books about the Palestinians. The house, some of which is in ruins, lies up the hill from the local **spring**, 50m below the museum on the same side of the road.

The revival of the **Artas Lettuce Festival**, a celebration of traditional Palestinian music and dancing centred around a huge, week-long fruit and

WALKING THE WADI ARTAS – EL-KHADER TO THE HERODION

April to June, when the scenery is lush and the sun not too wilting, is the best season for walking in the Wadi Artas. Don't forget to take plenty of water and wear sunscreen, sunglasses and walking shoes.

At the moment the paths have no signposts – though they should be installed pretty soon – and finding the correct route can be a little tricky, though there's usually somebody around to ask if you lose your way. The Artas Folklore Centre (see above) organises **thrice-weekly walks** during the spring season for about $30 a time (including food and entertainment in the evening): reservations must be made at least one week beforehand.

The shortest walk goes from **El-Khader** via **Solomon's Pools** to Artas, an easy jaunt of 3km. From the **stone archway** in El-Khader, head east for 250m towards the three pools. A path running between the second and third pools continues east into the Artas Valley past old German and British **pumping stations**. Continuing southeast along the path that runs parallel to the road, after a kilometre or so you'll see, a little way away to the north, the bare face of an open **quarry**, a bit of an eyesore in this part of the world. The road splits soon after as it goes around the hill. At the top of the hill is the **Khirbet Al-Khokh**, the Roman ruins of a village that some have identified as the original settlement of Etam. The paths rejoin to the northeast of the hill, and continue on to **Artas**.

If you want to make a day of it, you can continue on to the **Herodion**, a total distance of 12km. Speak to Musa or anybody in the Ethnographic Museum/Folklore Centre in Artas about the correct route to take. The path follows the Artas Valley for much of the next couple of kilometres, then joins up with a long-established trail originally built by the Israeli authorities. The Herodion springs into view soon after you've left the valley. Please note that the last bus service to Bethlehem from Za'atara, 2km on from the Herodion, is at 15.30, so try to complete your sightseeing before then.

vegetable market, is another Musa Sanad initiative. Apparently Artas is famous for the size and quality of its lettuces, hence the name. The festival takes place every April, with a second festival of **Palestinian music and dance** taking place every July near Solomon's Pools.

The Herodion هيروديون
Daily,08.00–17.30; NIS18/15.30

King Herod, the so-called Builder King, constructed a number of palaces and pleasure houses in the desert around Jerusalem. The Herodion, 6km to the south of Bethlehem, is undoubtedly the most impressive of these, its ruins far more complete than similar sites near Jericho (see page 163) and Masada in Israel, near the Dead Sea.

The history behind the Herodion is very similar to that of the complex at Masada. Both were built by Herod as pleasure palaces for use in the summer months, both later found use as bolt-holes for Jewish insurgents during the First Revolt (AD66–70) against the Romans and again in the Bar Kochba Revolt (page 32) – the latter culminating in the mass-suicide of all the rebels encamped in both palaces – and both were later used as retreats by early Byzantine monks. In addition, the Crusaders used the Herodion as a lookout post, and made their last stand in the Holy Land there before being ousted by Saladin's troops in the latter half of the 12th century. For this reason, the hill is sometimes known as the **Mountain of the Franks**. Traces of all these periods can be found amongst the ruins both on top of the hill and to the north by the road.

There is every reason to believe that the Herodion, built to commemorate Herod's victory over his rival Antigonus in 42BC, was Herod's favourite palace. According to the historian, Josephus, Herod was buried here too, as was his dying wish, his body being borne in a great procession for 39km from his deathbed in Jericho. His tomb, however, has yet to be discovered.

The Herodion is built on an almost-perfectly symmetrical hill in the desert between Bethlehem and the Dead Sea. Originally, there were two identical hills – 'like a woman's breasts' as Josephus puts it – standing next to each other in the desert. Herod ordered one to be demolished and the earth piled on to the other to make one big hill. The top of this was then levelled off, and the palace was built on top. With the passing of the years, the palace ruins have now sunk beneath the summit, giving the rather weird impression that they now lie within the mouth of a symmetrical volcano.

Sheruts usually disgorge passengers at the foot of the hill by the remains of a Herodian or Roman **garden**, a large, sunken square lined on two sides with pillars. Aqueducts from Solomon's pools, about 8km away, fed the garden and the adjacent Herodian **baths**, the partially reconstructed ruins of which now separate the gardens from the tarmac road that leads up to the ticket office. From the ticket office it's a ten-minute walk to the summit. This winding path is new: originally, visitors to the Herodion would have climbed a monumental **marble stairway** on the northeastern slopes of the hill, traces of which can still be seen by looking down from the small wooden bridge at the top of the hill by the eastern tower.

At the summit a path circles the ruins, affording great views over Jerusalem and Bethlehem to the north and the Dead Sea to the south. It's a peaceful spot, the stillness broken only occasionally by the sonic boom of Israeli jets on manoeuvres. **Four defensive towers** – the large circular eastern tower and three semi-circular towers to the north, south and west – would have protected the palace in Herod's day, and their ruins are still clearly visible today. Descending into the excavations via the steps near the Western Tower, you find yourself in the centre of Herod's

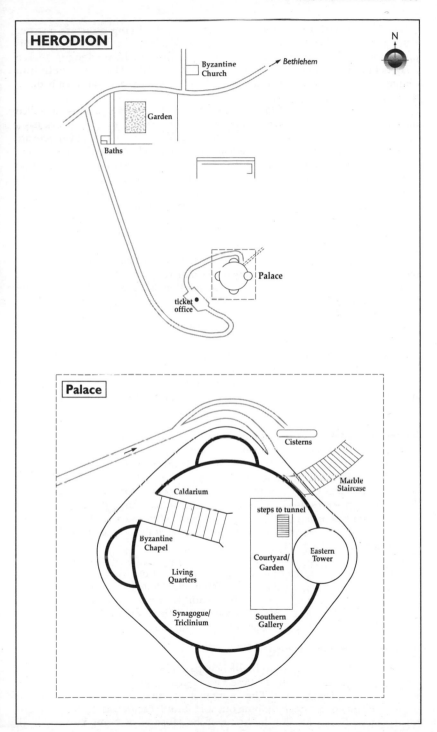

palace. The **caldarium**, or hot bath, to your left, the **living quarters** on your right, and the **garden** that once grew at the foot of the steps, all date from this time. Amongst the ruins that post-date Herod's palace are the **synagogue**, tucked away behind the living quarters in what used to be the Herodian **triclinium** (dining-room), the Byzantine **church** to the west of there and the ritual baths to the east of the synagogue.

A second flight of steps from the garden lead into a series of smooth-walled tunnels penetrating deep down inside the hill. This subterranean network has a history every bit as rich as the palace itself. Basically, what we have down here are **three cisterns** – the first, or intermediate, cistern just below the palace floor at the foot of the steps, and two others at the end of the tunnel network leading out to the northern side of the hill. In Herod's time water would have been carried from these lower cisterns (which collected rainwater streaming down the hill) up the monumental stairway to the intermediate cistern, and from there it would have been drawn up through the hole in the roof to the palace itself. During the First Revolt, however, a tunnel was built by the rebels, enabling them to siphon off some water from these lower cisterns without being seen by the Romans who watched the hill from beneath. Later, during the Bar Kochba Revolt (AD132–135), the underground system was enlarged, the cisterns emptied of water, and the tunnels used to launch surprise attacks on any Romans brave enough to attempt invasion. From the western cistern a path leads round the hill, joining up with the main path by the shelter dedicated to David Rosenfeld, an Israeli guard who was brutally stabbed to death by terrorists here in 1982.

To reach the Herodion from Bethlehem, catch a yellow minivan servis (NIS2.5) to Za'atara, the nearest village. The sheruts often continue on to the Herodian baths when looking for passengers, from where it's a 15-minute walk up to the ticket office. Alternatively, you can hire a taxi in Bethlehem, though expect to pay at least US$15 for the return journey plus waiting time. Bring some water, as the fountain by the ticket office is often dry.

Khureitun خريطون and Tequ'a تقوع

Just 2km or so on from the Herodian to the southeast, on the way to the Dead Sea, lies the **monastery of St Chariton** in the **Khureitun** ravine. St Chariton, a troglodytic monk who founded the monastery in 330, is buried within the labyrinthine cave complex. There are seven chambers in total, each connected to the others by passages. It's good fun exploring, but take care: it's very easy to get completely lost, so bring some string to mark the way, and a torch and plenty of water are absolutely essential too. Alternatively, one of the local Bedouin boys may volunteer himself as a guide.

Three kilometres further on to the southwest lies the Canaanite village of **Tequ'a**. An outpost in the desert, Tequ'a features on the Madaba map (see page 128) and remains a largish village of 6,000 people. Dotted throughout the village are a number of ruins from various eras – with Byzantine and Crusader remnants predominant – but most people will probably get a buzz out of the view from this hilltop village of the Dead Sea, Hebron and Bethlehem.

SOUTH TO HEBRON

The road south to Hebron from Bethlehem passes by some of the greenest hills in Palestine – a sharp contrast to the desert wastes that lie just a few kilometres to the west. So green in fact, that you'll just want to jump out of the taxi and go hiking in the hills. If you do, consider jumping out at **Halhoul**: not only is the town famous for its vineyards, but it's also the home of the **Mosque of Nabi Yunus** which, according to Muslim tradition, is built over the grave of the Old Testament prophet – and regurgitated fish food – Jonah. From Halhoul, it's another 8km on to Hebron.

HEBRON, AL-KHALIL الخليل

Hebron is scary and exhilarating at the same time. As one of the oldest cities in the world, with a deliciously labyrinthine **souq** crammed with sumptuous **Mamluke architecture**, it is without any shadow of a doubt one of the most absorbing places anywhere in the Near East. Its people provide a wonderfully warm welcome to tourists, the surrounding hills are beautifully bucolic and, in the **Haram Al-Khalil**, the city can boast Palestine's holiest site outside Jerusalem. As a very conservative town that would rather cling to tradition than embrace the new-fangled, Hebron is full of all those photogenic Palestinian clichés too: the over-laden donkey struggling with its burden, the elderly tattoo-faced lady in the fine embroidered dress, the *nargileh*-sucking Bedouin, the backdrop of tumbledown buildings and the claustrophobic bedlam of the bazaar, crammed with noise and vitality.

But, unhappily, Hebron happens to be the one city where the clash between Palestinian and Israeli is at its most profound, and often its most violent too. Elsewhere in Palestine, Jewish settlers sensibly keep a respectful distance from the Palestinian cities and towns, preferring instead to establish their own villages some distance away on neighbouring hills. But not in Hebron, Palestine's most populous city with over 400,000 residents, where **Jewish settlements** have sprouted right in the centre of the city, separated from their Arab neighbours only by colossal brick walls, electrified wire fencing, closed-circuit security cameras and reams and reams of razor wire.

It is Hebron's unusually holy status that lies behind much of the troubles. Indeed, the full Arabic name of the town, **Al-Khalil Al-Rahman**, translates as 'The beloved of God the Merciful'. As the last resting place of the patriarchs Abraham, Isaac and Jacob, and the first capital of the Israelite King David, it ranks as one of the four sacred cities of Judaism (along with Safed, Tiberias and Jerusalem). But Abraham is also revered by Muslims as the founder of monotheism, the father of Ismael (from whom all Arabs are said to be descended) and a precursor of Mohammed, so they too regard the city as holy. As a result, both sides want it for themselves, and neither seems willing to share it.

The antagonism between the locals, or **Khalilia**, and the Jewish settlers who live in their midst can flare up at any time. Those dreamers labouring under the illusion that peace is imminent in the Holy Land because Arafat and Rabin appended their signature to a piece of paper in Oslo in 1993 should visit Hebron to disabuse themselves of such notions. Of all the cities in the West Bank, this is the only one that has had to be officially divided into two parts, 80% Muslim under the control of the PNA, and 20% in the hands of the Israelis, with the border running north-south through the heart of town. Ludicrously, the Israeli quarter, known as **H2**, includes the market area and centre of Hebron which, despite the presence of two large Israeli settlements, is patently predominantly Arab. It's an anomaly that serves only to aggravate the situation.

That said, don't let the tension in Hebron deter you from visiting. Unused to seeing tourists, the local people may initially regard you with some suspicion, at least until they know where you're from. But it never feels threatening. Indeed, the Arabs of Hebron are just as open and friendly as their brothers in other parts of Palestine – possibly more so, because they're so keen to dispel their undeserved reputation for hostility towards outsiders.

JEWISH SETTLEMENTS

Since Israel's capture of the West Bank and Gaza Strip in 1967, the encroachment into the Occupied Territories by Jewish settlers has grown steadily, in strict violation of both the Geneva Convention and Resolution 242. At first, the settlers were almost exclusively right-wing religious fanatics in pursuit of ideological convictions. At their head was the fanatical organisation known as the **Gush Emumin** ('Block of the Faithful'), a group of rabbis and activists who viewed the policy of establishing settlements as a first step on the road to capturing the whole of '**Eretz Yisrael**' – literally 'The Land of Israel', their term for the combined territory of Israel and Palestine. At first their actions found little favour with an Israeli government still wary of provoking the Palestinians. The settlers who tried to set up a Jewish compound in Hebron, for example, had to wait four years before receiving official sanction. But later on, projects such as the **three-tier settlements** encircling East Jerusalem enjoyed government sponsorship, not least because it promoted the Israeli's claims of sovereignty over the entire metropolis by cutting off the Holy City from the rest of the West Bank.

By the late seventies the radical fanatics had been joined by a more moderate, secular, apolitical sort of settler. The zealous Likud government of **Menachem Begin**, keen to appropriate as much Palestinian territory as possible, invested heavily in the settlements' infrastructure and offered subsidised housing to all new residents, tempting those whose prime motivation was not religious conviction, but financial concern. The policy worked. By 1992, a total of **144 settlements** (128 in the West Bank, 16 in the Gaza Strip), each one illegal according to international law, had sprouted up on Palestinian territory, housing a total of 101,000 settlers. Another 150,000 lived in the settlements around East Jerusalem. Many of these settlements overlook Arab villages and towns from lofty hilltop positions, much as the castles of the Crusaders had done several centuries before.

The contrast between the living conditions of settlers and the local Palestinian villagers is marked. One group lives in modern, comfortable housing, enjoys cheap rent and other financial benefits, has a reliable power source, priority access to the limited freshwater supply of the region, and their own immaculately-maintained road and transport network to link them with Israel and Jerusalem. The other group, to put it simply, does not. And while one group has been allowed to have guns, vote in Israeli elections and enjoy civil justice for some years now, the Palestinians have had to remain defenceless and, up until the recent handover of territory to the PNA, could not vote in elections, and were subject to the arbitrary judgments of Israel's military courts.

Unfortunately, since 1993 the situation has, if anything, worsened. While the **Oslo Accords** ordered a halt to all new settlements in the West Bank and Gaza Strip, their failure to address the future status of Jerusalem enabled Israeli prime minister **Binyamin Netanyahu** to expand the settlements in and around the metropolis, despite protests from Palestinians, the UN and even the Israelis' old ally, the United States. Following the acquisition of Arab houses in Silwan (to the south of the Old City) by Jewish radicals in 1991, the government consolidated

History

Hebron's past can boast a degree of turbulence that's remarkable even by the standards of Palestine. Its early origins are obscure. In the book of Numbers the Israelis' stranglehold on the whole of Jerusalem by giving permission for a new Jewish suburb at Abu Ghoneim in February 1997. Though the Israeli government insisted that the houses in this suburb would be available to all, including Palestinians, the cost of buying a house in the suburb is likely to be beyond the reach of most Palestinians. Furthermore, the suburb completes the encirclement of East Jerusalem, cutting it off from the West Bank for good. The attempt by Jewish extremists later that same year to take over the Arab suburb of Ras Al-Amud, after American millionaire **Irving Moscovitz** bought a bus parking lot in the district's centre, served to increase the tension.

The question of the future status of the Jewish settlements remains a large and painful stone in the shoe of the peace process. A lot depends now on the policies of incoming prime minister **Ehud Barak**. So far his proclamations have been ambiguous: whilst Barak was ordering a halt to the construction of one major settlement, the head of the right-wing National Religious Party, Yitzhak Levy, said in an interview with Reuter that Barak had promised him that he will not block the extension of existing Jewish settlements, though he was opposed to new settlements being constructed.

Visiting a settlement

For all the ideological bombast surrounding them, the settlements are, aesthetically at least, really dull. The layout of each settlement is pretty much the same: row after row of identical whitewashed concrete housing, topped with red-tile roofs and solar panels glinting in sunlight. William Dalrymple, in his book *From the Holy Mountain*, describes the largest settlement of them all, **Ma'ale Adumin**, as 'Milton Keynes transported into the landscape of a Mediaeval Italian fresco'. It's a pretty accurate description.

But like it or not, the Jewish settlements remain an important feature of the West Bank, and a visit to one may further your understanding of the settlers' motives and the Arab-Israeli tensions. All the settlements have bus connections with the Egged Station in West Jerusalem. The best one to visit, in my opinion, is **Kfar Etzion**, one of 17 settlements gathered in a block known as **Gush Etzion**, 13km to the south of Bethlehem. This settlement is one of the oldest in the West Bank, and its history is one of the most eventful. Abandoned in the face of Arab hostility just one year after its foundation in 1935, and again in 1948 with the arrival of the Jordanians, it was the first to be re-established in the West Bank following the Israeli victory in 1967. The settlement's history is recounted in the local museum which, though unsurprisingly one-sided, is at least thorough, and offers an entertaining audiovisual presentation of the events of 1910.

Some travellers have recommended the tour around **Jewish Hebron** offered by the settlers, which you can book in advance on tel: 02 996 2323. Of course the settlement is one of the most interesting, partly because it's one of the most controversial, but bear in mind that by taking this tour you are financially supporting the settlers. Do not think either that, at the end of the tour, you are free to walk out of the gates and look around the rest of Hebron: Khalilians will look upon your visit to the settlement as tacit support for the inhabitants' ambitions, and won't be best pleased.

(13:22), it states that it was settled seven years before Zoan in Egypt, which would date it to about 1710–20BC. Muslim tradition, on the other hand, believes it to be much older: Adam and Eve are said to have lived out their final years here

SAFETY IN HEBRON

Unsurprisingly, the Khalilians' warmth and hospitality towards visitors does not extend to the Jewish settlers or their supporters. For this reason, it's advisable to break one of the golden rules of travelling and try to look as much like a tourist as possible. Keep up with the latest bulletins, too, and postpone your visit during times of unrest. It's also a good idea to carry your passport with you – a legal requirement in any case – and if things really do get hairy, remember the phrase *Mish Jehud* ('Not Jewish'); I've never had to use it, but it could come in useful.

following their exile from the garden of Eden. Archaeological excavations support neither hypothesis, having found evidence of a Canaanite village that existed here about 4,000 years ago.

The town's other Old Testament name, and now the name of one of the largest Jewish settlements in Hebron, is **Qiryat Arba**, or the Village of the Four. This may be a reference to the four Canaanite tribes who lived in the city at the time of Joshua's conquest, or to the four biblical couples (Adam, Abraham, Isaac and Jacob and their wives) who are supposed to have lived here.

Prosperity arrived in Hebron with the anointing of David as King of Judah within the town. The city later became part of the Edomite kingdom (the Edomites were a Semitic tribe based largely to the east of the Jordan). One of their number, Herod, built the walls of the Haram, but most of the architecture in the city today dates back to the Mamlukes and Ottomans during 1,281 years of Islamic rule (637–1917) broken only by the Crusaders in the 12th century.

Hebron has long had a reputation for insurgency, with the current bout of unrest dating back to 1929. Taking exception to British rule and the influx of Jewish immigrants into the Holy Land, the Arabs in Hebron responded by slaughtering 67 Jews, part of a 2,000-strong minority that had lived peaceably in the city for centuries. It was a sign of the troubles to come.

The surviving Jews fled in fear of their lives in 1929; though some returned later on, they were re-evacuated by the British following further riots in 1936. Barred by the Jordanians during their tenure (1948–67) from living in the city altogether, Jewish settlers tried to re-establish a community in Hebron following the Israelis' victory in the Six-Day War. Initially the Israeli government, wary of causing further trouble, banned them. But in 1967 Rabbi Moshe Levinger booked a room in Hebron's Park Hotel and, safely ensconced inside, staged a four-year 'sit-in' in protest at the government's stance. In 1970 the government caved in, giving the settlers official sanction to build a settlement on the outskirts of the city. The first settlement started at **Qiryat Arba**, just 1km to the north of the Haram. The rabbi's tactics were then copied by Miriam Levinger who, together with a group of women and children from Qiryat Arba, occupied the Daboyah Building, a disused hospital in the heart of town. After seven months they too were granted permission to settle permanently. In each case the Jewish settlers argued that they were merely resetting areas stolen by Arabs following the 1929 massacre, and it's true that **Bet Hadassah** (as the compound round the Daboyah Building has been renamed) does lie near the old Jewish quarter. The purchase of property to build a second compound, **Bet Romano**, right above the market, with Palestinian merchants continuing to trade in the shops below, only serves to heighten the tension between the two sides.

The Palestinians' frustration at the Israeli government's policies towards the settlers spilled over into violence again in 1980, when six yeshiva students were killed in a grenade attack as they were leaving the Haram, the terrorists firing from the rooftops opposite the Hadassah building. Jewish extremists organised revenge killings; their subsequent arrest caused further controversy amongst their supporters. To even things up, the Israeli authorities then banished the mayors of Hebron and Halhoul in 1983, replacing the former with a junior officer of the Israeli army. In order to quell the growing violence and safeguard the Jewish compounds, extra troops were sent to patrol the city where they've remained ever since. Their all-too-obtrusive presence and their heavy-handed methods of dealing with the locals only aggravate the current tensions, endangering the peace that they're employed to maintain.

Hebron in the Bible

Hebron first crops up in Genesis (23:2–20, 25:7–8 and 35:27) as a burial site for the patriarchs. Abraham started the trend by burying his wife, Sarah, in the Cave of Machpelah, and he in turn was buried there by his two sons, Isaac and Ishmael, on his death at the ripe old age of 175. Isaac follows him into the cave a few decades later, at the even riper age of 180.

A few centuries and books further on, in Numbers (13:21–23), Moses sent spies to Hebron to check out the land, at the end of their 40-year journey from Egypt. As proof of its fertility, the spies brought back a bunch of grapes so huge that two men had to carry it on a pole between them (you'll see this image time and again in the Holy Land, for it's the emblem of the Israeli Tourist Authority). At the time, Hebron was under the rule of an Amorite king. Joshua (10:36–38) led his troops to the city and 'took it and smote it with the edge of the sword, and the king thereof, and all the souls that were therein; he left none remaining…but destroyed it utterly…'. Soon after, the town became part of Judah, and according to Joshua (20:6–8) later became, on God's designation, a **City of Refuge**, where people who had accidentally killed someone could come to hide from those seeking revenge, and live safely in exile. (Pre-meditated murderers were returned to their home town for execution.)

However, it is as **David's first capital** that the city is probably most famous (2 Samuel 2:14) After consulting with God, David and his wives Ahinoam and Abigail settled in the town. A little while later, David was anointed **King of Judah** by the locals. He ruled from Hebron for seven-and-a-half years, during which time the Israelite tribes visited him and swore their allegiance. Later, after David had moved his capital to Jerusalem, his son Absalom, in a rather good impersonation of his father, moved to Hebron and declared himself king. His actions set off a wave of rebellions that had David fleeing for his life from Jerusalem. Absalom was eventually defeated by his dad in some woods in Ephraim, and was killed, against his father's wishes, by the commander of David's forces, Joab.

Hebron is mentioned on a couple of occasions after this in the apocryphal book of Maccabees, that describes the events of the inter-testamental period (ie: the period between the Old and New Testaments). Hebron was by this time part of Edom (a kingdom whose capital lay to the east of the Jordan) and became the venue for a battle between the Edomites and Judas Maccabeus (Maccabees 5:65). These books, however, are not included in most modern editions of the Bible; and after this mention, Hebron slips into obscurity, and isn't mentioned once in the New Testament.

Practicalities

Most people see Hebron as a day trip from Jerusalem or Bethlehem, though trying to see everything in one day is a bit of a struggle and you may find yourself coming

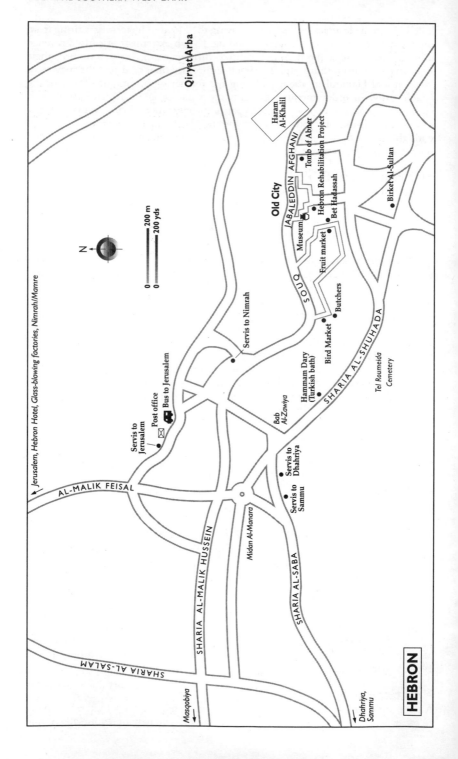

HEBRON

back a second time. Alternatively, you can stay in Hebron: the **Hebron Tourist Hotel** (tel: 02 2254240; fax: 02 2226760) lies round the back of the Al-Amanah Supermarket on Sharia Al-Malik Feisal. Coming from Jerusalem, look out for the UGU (University Graduates Union) on your right as you head downhill into town; the steps by the side of this building lead up to this clean and spacious hotel, where every room has satellite TV and shower and every member of staff wears a smile. Rooms are $35/45/55 sgl/dbl/tpl, including breakfast. A second hotel, the Mizan, is currently under construction to the north of here, though we have no information about it at the present time.

Servis taxis and **buses** from Jerusalem and Bethlehem pull in at the town centre, at the busy junction known as Bab Al-Zawiya. A couple of hundred metres east of here is the Old City and its **market**. The **post office** is at the southern end of Sharia Al-Malik Feisal. There are no outstanding **restaurants**, though you can fill your face with felafal or shwaarma very cheaply from one of the myriad of food stalls near the centre. Most of the jewellers double as **money-changers**, and there are a couple on the north side of Bab Al-Zawiya.

Transport details
Bus number 23 to **Jerusalem** (NIS5) via **Bethlehem**, Beit Sahour, Obedaiya and Bethany leaves from the eastern end of Sharia al-Malik Feisal, while Jerusalem sheruts park a few hundred metres further on (NIS7); the last one leaves about 19.00. Servis minivans to local villages leave from the Bab Al-Zawiya junction.

Hebron's Old City
Though fairly small, the old city of Hebron consists of so many different quarters, each with its own individual character, that it's hard to find suitable adjectives that adequately describe the whole. The souq occupies most of the old city, though even here there are significant variations in atmosphere. Immediately to the west of the Haram al-Khalil, for example, many of the traders have been forcibly removed, and the district where they and their families have traded for centuries is now eerily quiet. By contrast, towards the western end of the souq the atmosphere is alive with the chattering, clattering pandemonium of shoppers and traders. Shafts of light penetrate through tears in the canopy roof of the fruit and vegetable section, steam rises from the carcasses of freshly-slaughtered animals in the butchers' quarter, and in the household goods market the din and hurly-burly continues unabated throughout the day. It's quite intoxicating. This is Palestine at its most raw, its most enigmatic, and its most disorientating.

Unlike the fully renovated old cities of Nablus or Jerusalem, Hebron remains in a fairly knackered state. One of the problems is that so many of the beautiful, huge **old houses** have been abandoned. Nowadays the younger generation places a greater emphasis on privacy, and the huge open houses of the old city, where entire extended families used to live under one roof, are simply unsuitable for this modern lifestyle.

Nevertheless, there is a huge renovation programme currently under way, organised by the **Hebron Rehabilitation Centre**, which hopes to have the old city looking shipshape by 2002. Their office lies near the centre of the souq behind the Jewish compound near the **museum**. Currently the museum is still in the process of moving the exhibits from its old home in the Municipal Office; when completed, expect a pretty thorough rundown of Hebron's history, including some particularly fine gravestones and cenotaphs. The museum's new home is in a renovated **Turkish bath**, restored to its former glory, but alas not in working order. To compensate, the rehabilitation centre has renovated a second bath, the

Hammam Dary, which should be open to the public by the time you read this. The centre claims that this will be the most authentic bath in Palestine: even the heating system, using underground pipes and wood for fuel, is authentically Ottoman. A little to the east behind a fence is the **Birket Al-Sultan**, a huge rectangular reservoir-cum-rubbish-dump, traditionally the site where David hanged the murderers of his son Ishbosheth (2 Samuel: 4:12).

Other things to look out for in the old city include the **Tomb of Abner**, at the eastern entrance to the souq opposite the Haram, wherein (according to my sources) lies the body of a Jewish man, who converted to Islam and fought as a commander in Saladin's army. Then there's the **butchers' section** where camels, their throats cut and stripped bare of skin (though still wearing the same disdainful expression), hang from meat hooks, while goats' heads – or maybe a cow's face – stare out through the shop windows. And before you go, don't miss the hill above the souq to the north. With its hushed back streets and tumbledown buildings it's a charming mix of the dilapidated, derelict and delightful. The **green-domed mosque** at the western end, north of Bab Al-Zawiya, is the oldest in the city apparently, pre-dating even the mosque at the Haram al Khalil.

Haram Al-Khalil – the Tombs of the Patriarchs   حرم الخليل

Sun–Thurs 08.00–16.00; bring your passport, and wear suitably conservative clothing; free
The Haram Al-Khalil is a microcosm of the city itself: fascinating, ancient, controversial and divided. The reason for the controversy is clear: in the Machpelah **cave** underneath the Haram, or sanctuary, lie the tombs of the patriarchs Abraham, his son Isaac and grandson Jacob and their wives, the matriarchs Sarah, Rebecca and Leah – figures revered by all three monotheistic faiths. And they may not be the only Old Testament figures buried here. According to tradition, Abraham is said to have chosen the cave as a tomb for his wife after learning through divine inspiration that Adam and Eve were buried in the cave. Furthermore, Muslims believe that a fourth patriarch, Joseph, son of Jacob and Rachel, is interred underneath the sanctuary, and that Mohammed rested at the Haram briefly during his famous night flight to Jerusalem (see page 103).

With such a roll call of venerated prophets and patriarchs (only Jacob's second wife Rachel is missing from the hierarchy; her tomb lies near Bethlehem, see page 178), it's small wonder that the Haram arouses such strong and often violent emotions. Only Jerusalem's Western Wall is more sacred to Jews, while to Muslims it ranks second in Palestine only to the Dome of the Rock, and fourth in the entire world (behind Mecca and Medina). And whereas in Jerusalem the two faiths are divided by a huge stone wall, here the junction between the two is much more intimate as they share the same building, with only some heavy wooden shutters separating the two.

Windowless, monolithic and austere, as are so many sacred buildings in Palestine (the Church of the Nativity and Nabi Musa spring to mind) the Haram Al-Khalil looks more like a military compound than a place for contemplation and prayer. The two sets of armed Israeli soldiers guarding each entrance only add to this impression. Their presence is necessary to prevent the sort of atrocity that occurred in 1994, when a Jewish zealot named Barukh Goldstein opened fire in the mosque during Friday prayers, killing 29 people. The horror was compounded by the Israeli troops outside the Haram who, believing the people fleeing the mosque were in fact rioting, began to open fire. The Haram was closed for six months following the shooting, and when it was re-opened it was divided into two, one half for the Jewish worshippers, and one half for the Muslims. It has remained divided ever since.

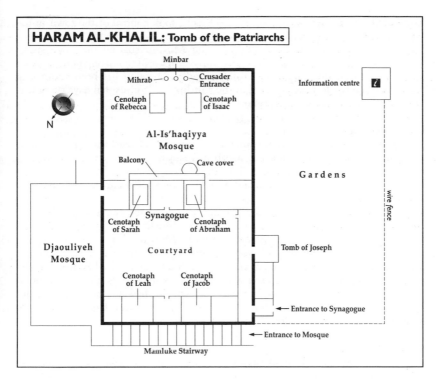

HARAM AL-KHALIL: Tomb of the Patriarchs

Minbar

Mihrab — ○ ○ ○ — Crusader Entrance

Information centre

Cenotaph of Rebecca

Cenotaph of Isaac

N

Al-Is'haqiyya Mosque

Balcony

Cave cover

Gardens

wire fence

Synagogue

Cenotaph of Sarah

Cenotaph of Abraham

Djaouliyeh Mosque

Courtyard

Tomb of Joseph

Cenotaph of Leah

Cenotaph of Jacob

Entrance to Synagogue

Entrance to Mosque

Mamluke Stairway

According to Chapter 23 of Genesis, Abraham bought the Machpelah cave and surrounding land from Ephron, a Hittite. Whether the cave under the Haram is actually the Machpelah Cave is open to debate, as is much of the later history of the sanctuary. The massive stones, or **ashlars**, of the enclosing wall are obviously Herodian, though many argue that the site is much older than that. The last of the patriarchs possibly buried here, Joseph, died about 1600BC, (according to best estimates), so a Haram of sorts could have existed here as early as then. Another Arab tradition attributes the construction of the walls to King Solomon, who built them with the help of Jinns, or benevolent elf-like spirits.

Herod's building was probably a roofless hall, with the entrance to the cave sealed: a **Herodian rain gutter** runs along the stone floor by the southwestern wall of the mosque. The Byzantines appropriated the hall to build a **church** and a roof, allowing the Jews to build a **synagogue**, probably where the current synagogue stands. This church was in turn converted into a mosque after the Arab conquest of AD637, though the Christians exacted a bloody revenge five centuries later in 1100 when the Crusaders re-converted the mosque into a church, destroyed the synagogue and massacred both Muslims and Jews. They also made an exploration of the Machpelah cave, the last time anybody did so.

The pendulum of power swung once more in 1187 with the victory of Saladin. Yet again, the church became a mosque. The Mamlukes expanded and prettified the building, adding the **Djaouliya Mosque**, four minarets (of which two remain), the **Mosque of Joseph** and five of the seven **cenotaphs**. (These cenotaphs, incidentally, merely provide a focus for prayers; the actual tombs are in the cave below the floor of the Haram.) They also barred the Jews from the Haram, permitting them only to climb up to the seventh step. This situation continued for exactly 700 years until the Israelis took control of the town in the Six-Day War of '67. For 27 years, until the massacre of 1994, the Haram was a model for religious tolerance, with Jew and Muslim sharing the same space, scheduling their prayers for different times to avoid confrontation. Barukh Goldstein ruined this happy compromise, and the tension has been simmering ever since. Today, Jews are allowed in the Muslim half for just ten days every year to pray at the cenotaphs of Isaac and Rebecca.

The building

The Haram is a rectangle, approximately 64m long and 35m wide. A secondary building, housing the **mosque** and **tomb of Joseph**, lies adjacent to the western wall by the Jewish entrance. The walls of the Haram, 15m high, are constructed of long ashlars (square-hewn stones) and topped off by a set of curvaceous Mamluke crenellations.

There are two entrances into the Haram: the traditional one, up the Mamluke stairway adjacent to the north wall, leads into the Muslims' share of the sanctuary, while a second leads through the old Mamluke Mosque of Joseph and into the **synagogue**. Either way, you'll have to go through two security checks and two metal detectors. (You may object to their treatment of local Muslims, but the soldiers are usually politeness itself when dealing with tourists. Be nice to them: it'll certainly make things easier for you.) You will also have to state your religion: Muslims are allowed only on the Muslim side, Jews on the Jewish side, while Christians and others are allowed into both.

The Muslim section

At the top of the Mamluke stairway a corridor leads past the Mamlukes' Djaouliya Mosque whose two minarets rise above the walls of the Haram to a small door in the wall on your right. Before 1994, this small vestibule formed the northeastern corner of the courtyard, but it is now sectioned off by wooden shutters. Removing your shoes and passing through a door in the southern wall, you find yourself in the Al-Is'haqyya, or **Grand Mosque**. Formerly Herod's roofless hall, and later a Byzantine and Crusader church, the mosque is quite beautiful. The ceiling in particular, painted with blue and brown *trompe-l'oeil* patterns, is splendid. Look too for the inscribed frieze that runs unbroken along the four walls.

The interior is divided by two rows of columns into a main nave and two side aisles. The 14th-century cenotaphs of Isaac, to the right as you enter the mosque, with that of his wife, Rebecca next door, stand in the nave. Between the two, at the end of the room against the wall, is the intricately carved **wooden minbar**. Made in 1091 for a mosque in Ashkelon, the minbar was presented to the Haram exactly 100 years later by Saladin. To the left of the minbar is the **mihrab**, while to the right (southwest) is the entrance dug by the Crusaders down to the cave, now sealed and covered by a petite, open-sided **kiosk**. A second tunnel leading straight down into the cave lies at the opposite end of the nave, under the balcony on the northern wall. The local imam often sits nearby, receiving the salutations of his congregation. Just to the left, a second entrance in the north wall leads into a small room, from where you can see the **Cenotaph of Abraham** through the grille on your right – the only cenotaph shared by Jews and Muslims.

The synagogue

A monumental stairway leads up to the synagogue through the **Mosque of Joseph** which, before the Haram was divided, used to serve as the **women's mosque**. Collect a yarmulka from the box just inside the door then continue along the corridor, past **Joseph's Cenotaph** on your right. As Muslims aren't allowed here, and the Jews prefer to believe that he's buried in Shekhem, as written in the book of Joshua (24:32), this cenotaph is largely ignored these days. Opposite the tomb is the entrance to the **courtyard**, now the synagogue; on your right as you enter are the 9th-century cenotaphs of Abraham and, opposite, his first wife Sarah. Two more cenotaphs, dedicated to Jacob and his first wife, Leah, stand in the alcove on the other side of the courtyard.

Mamre مامره and Masqobiya المسكوبية

> Then Abram removed his tent, and came and dwelt in the plain of Mamre, which is in Hebron, and built there an altar unto the Lord.
> Genesis 13:18

The biblical village of Mamre appears fairly regularly in the book of Genesis, mainly because Abram dwelt here for a few years (this was before he changed his name to Abraham on God's orders). Indeed, it was here that he was visited by three angels who told him that Sarah, his wife, though 'well-stricken with age and ceased to be...after the manner of women' (ie: was past child-bearing age) would bear him a son (Genesis 18:18). Unfortunately, nobody knows exactly where Mamre is today: the only clue the Bible gives is that the Cave of Macpelah – now supposedly under the Haram al-Khalil – lies 'before Mamre', so we can assume that Mamre is somewhere in the vicinity.

Two possible sites have been put forward, one on the ouskirts of town to the west and one to the north. The first is now called **Masqobiya**, and lies about 2km west of the town centre. As you're heading up Sharia Al-Masqobiya you'll notice, in gardens to your right, a withered old **oak tree**. This, supposedly, was the oak that Abram and Sarah rested under during their stay. By my reckoning that makes the oak about 4,000 old; hardly surprising, therefore, that it needs the support of huge iron calipers to keep it erect.

The Russian church built a small monastery at **Masqobiya** in the 19th century, though it's usually closed to the public. It's a long and sweaty walk from town and, to be honest, the monastery, even if you do manage to gain entrance, is not sufficiently interesting to justify the effort expended in reaching it. The **tower** in the garden outside, however, with views as far as the Dead Sea, provides partial compensation.

The other possible site for Mamre is known locally as **Nimrah**, and lies just a couple of hundred metres east of the road to Jerusalem, about 3km north of the town centre. A servis taxi from just outside the souq costs NIS1.5. Below the local school here you'll find a raised platform, formerly part of a Byzantine church. The church was large enough to feature on the Madaba mosaic (see page 128). Apart from Abram, the **Holy family** (Mary and Joseph, and the infant Jesus) were also supposed to have rested here on their return from Egypt; the church was probably built to commemorate their stay.

Glass-blowing factory

Hebron is famous for its glassware, which comes in all shapes and colours (though the deep **cobalt blue** is the most ubiquitous and popular). Apparently, the skills were imported by Spanish and Venetian Jews fleeing persecution in their native lands in the 15th century. The methods have changed little since then. You can see the glass being blown and manipulated into shape at a couple of factories on the main road into town. Opposite the road to Nimrah is the **Hebron Glass and Ceramics factory**, and 200m before it, towards Jerusalem, is the **Al-Salam Glass and Pottery factory**. In both cases you're free to wander around and take photos, and, refreshingly, you're unlikely to be subjected to any hard sell by the owners.

SOUTH OF HEBRON
Dhahriya الظاهرية

Just 7km from the Green Line, the lively market town of Dhahriya couldn't be further removed from its Israeli neighbours, in character at least, if it tried. This dusty town is the Wild West of Palestine, a place where outsiders are treated with suspicion, women are nowhere to be seen and the menfolk, mostly Bedouin tribesmen, sit outside the town's murky **cafés** drinking Turkish coffee and smoking joints. Nobody seems to speak more than a few words of English and – almost uniquely in Palestine – nobody seems to want to speak to you.

If that description makes Dhahriya sound intimidating then you're right, it is – at least at first. But if you fire off enough 'Marhabas' at everyone, eventually somebody will pluck up the courage to respond and before you know it you're up to your neck in glasses of tea and invitations to people's houses.

The reason the locals are so suspicious of foreigners is because so few tourists get here, for the simple reason that there's very little to attract them. A couple of kilometres back along the road to Hebron, however, there's a little slice of Bedouin life that is worth seeing. The **livestock market** that takes place by the side of the road every Wednesday morning was once a grand affair, perhaps the biggest in Palestine, with tribesmen from all over southern Palestine flocking (no pun intended) to Dhahriya to trade their camels, goats, donkeys, sheep, chickens and other assorted beasts. Nowadays, alas, the market is much reduced in size, with often only a few tatty-fleeced sheep and a bored-looking mule or two up for grabs. Nevertheless, it's one of the few traditional markets of this type still operating in Palestine, and is reasonably photogenic. The market takes place early in the morning – by 10.00 it's all but finished – so turn up as early as you can.

Sheruts leave regularly from Hebron's Sharia Al-Saba, costing NIS3.5.

Sammu سموع

Also written as Sumo'a, Sammu is an ancient village and the site of the biblical **Eshtemoa**, one of the places that received a share of the spoils of David's victory over the Amalekites (I Samuel 30:26). According to Jewish tradition, this treasure lies buried beneath the remains of the 4th-century **synagogue**, next to the village mosque. Excavations in the sixties did indeed uncover a pot of silver treasure, though it post-dated David by a good few centuries. Peer over the fence at the ruins and you may just be able to make out traces of the synagogue's mosaic floor, and three niches in the north wall which would have held the ritual scrolls such as the Torah. This is just one of a number of ancient synagogues that lie in the vicinity (including **Yatta**, 6km to the north of Sammu and served by servis taxi from the village, and the best, **Khirbet Suseya** to the northeast, which isn't), though Sammu's is the easiest to reach – and the only one with buried treasure.

Curiously, Sammu has also achieved a certain level of fame as a **carpet-weaving town**. I say curiously not because the carpets of Sammu are in any way bad – in fact, they're superb – but merely because almost every village in this area practises carpet weaving, so why Sammu has been singled out is a mystery. The carpets are superb quality and very durable; rugs, camel bags and prayer mats are also available. You may also be able to pick up one of the elaborately embroidered traditional **dresses** worn by the Palestinian women. The prices aren't rock bottom (depending on your bargaining skills) but the quality is top rate. Most of the carpet shops aren't signposted. The best is the green-doored **cooperative**, 200m past the mosque at the bottom of the big dip in the road, on the left-hand side.

Servis taxis to Sammu run throughout the day from Sharia Al-Saba in Hebron, with the last one back at about 16.00.

Appendix 1

VOCABULARY
Useful words

English	Arabic	Transliteration
aeroplane	طائرة	*tayara*
airport	مطار	*mataar*
bank	بنك	*bank*
baths	حمام	*hammam*
beach	شط	*shatt*
bicycle	دراجة هوائية	*bisklatt*
bus	باص	*baas*
café	مقهى	*mak-hah*
church	كنيسة	*kaniisa*
clock tower	برج الساعة	*burj as-sa'a*
embassy	سفارة	*sifaara*
good		*tayeb*
hill	تل	*jabal, tel*
hospital	مستشفى	*mustashfa*
hotel	فندق	*funduk*
laundry	مصبغة	*masbagha*
market	سوق	*souq*
mausoleum		*dariha*
monastery	دير	*der*
mosque	مسجد	*masjid*
museum	منحف	*madhaf*
passport	جواز سفر	*jawaaz safar*
police	شرطة	*buliis*
post office	مكتب البريد	*maktab al-bariid*
restaurant	مطعم	*mata'am*
room	غرفة	*ghurfa*
servis (taxi)		*servees*
shower		*duush*
station	محطة	*mahataat*
street	شارع	*sharia*
taxi	تكسي	*taksi, special*
telephone	تلفون	*talifawn*
temple	كنيس	*kanis*
ticket	تذكرة	*tadhkara*
toilet	حمام	*bayt mayy*
tourist office	مكتب استعلامات	*saayih maktab*
tower	برج	*majdal, burj*

Food and drink

beer	بيرة	biira
bread	خبز	khubz
breakfast	فطور	futu'ur
cheese	جبنه	jibneh
chicken	دجاج	djaj
coffee	قهوة	qahwa
fish	سمك	samaka
fruit	فاكهة	fa'akiha
ice-cream	بوظة	buuza, dondurma
juice	عصير	a'asiir
lamb	خروف	saru'uf
pork	لحم خنزير	lahm khanziir
salad	سلطة	salata
soup	شوربة	behar
spicy	بهار	behar
tea	شاي	chai
vegetarian	نباتي	nabati
water	ماء	mayy

Numbers

Unlike the written language, Arabic numerals run from left to right.

1	واحد	wahid
2	اثنين	ithnayn
3	ثلاثة	tala'ata
4	اربعة	arba'a
5	خمسة	khamsa
6	ستة	sita'a
7	سبعة	saba'a
8	ثمانية	tamanya
9	تسعة	tissa'a
10	عشرة	a'ashra
11	احدى عشر	ihdashr
12	اثنى عشر	itnaysh
13	ثلاثة عشر	tala'atash
14	اربعة عشر	arba'ata'ash
20	عشرين	ishri'in
21	واحد و عشرون	wahid wa'ishri'in
30	ثلاثين	talathi'in
40	اربعين	arba'ati'in
50	خمسين	khamsi'in
60	ستين	sitti'in
70	سبعين	saba'i'in
80	ثمانين	tamaani'in
90	تسعين	tis'i'in
100	مائة	miyya
200	مائتين	mittayn
1,000	الف	elf
2,000	الفين	alfayn
3,000	ثلاثة الف	tala'athat aalaaf
1,000,000	مليون	malaayin

Days of the week

Monday	يوم الاثنين	*Yawm al-Ithnayn*
Tuesday	يوم الثلاثاء	*Yawm al-Tala'ata*
Wednesday	يوم الاربعاء	*Yawm al-Arbaa*
Thursday	يوم الخميس	*Yawm al-Kamis*
Friday	يوم الجمعة	*Yawm al-Jumba'a*
Saturday	يوم السبت	*Yawm al-Ahad*
Sunday	يوم الاحد	*Yawm al-Sabt*

Conversation

hello	مرحبا	*maharba* (formal: *salaam wa'aleikhoom*)
goodbye	مع السلامة	*ma asala'am* (to a man), *ma asala'meh* (to a woman)
yes	نعم	*na'am, aywa*
no	لا	*la*
please	من فضلك	*min fadlak*
sorry	سامحني	*smahini*
thank you	شكرا	*shukran*
what is your name?	ما اسمك	*ma asmak*
you are welcome	اهلا و سهلا	*hlan wasahlan*
I would like..	من فضلك	*min fadlak*
how much?	كم	*kam?*
cheap	رخيص	*rashi'is*
expensive	غالي	*ghaali*
how long (time)?	كم	*gaddaysh*

Appendix 2

GLOSSARY

Abbassids Sunni Islamic caliphate dynasty (749–1258) based in Baghdad that superceded the Ommayads as the major power in the region

Abu Father (Arabic)

Aid/Eid Muslim festival (see page 58)

Apocrypha Old Testament books included in the Latin version of the Bible, but not the Hebrew Bible or most modern editions

Argila Also called the *sheesha*, *nargileh* or hookah pipe, a large water-filled device used for smoking tobacco

Ayyubids Sunni Islamic dynasty of Sultans (1171–1250) founded by Saladin who ruled Egypt and Palestine from his base in Cairo

Bab Gate or door (Arabic)

Borj/Biurj Tower or fort (Arabic)

Caliph Spiritual leader of Islam and the successor to Mohammed

Caravanserai Inn for travellers and traders often found attached to the town market

Dar House (Arabic)

Deir Convent (Arabic)

DFLP Acronym of the Democratic Front for the Liberation of Palestine, a PFLP splinter-group

Eid *see* Aid

Emir Prince

Fatah The Palestinian Liberation Movement, founded by a young Yasser Arafat in 1959

Fatimids Shi'ite Islamic dynasty (968–1175), originating in northern Africa, which fought with the Abbassids for control of the Levant from their capital in Cairo

Felahin Farmers, rural Palestinians (Arabic)

Green Line Hotly disputed border between Israel and the Palestinian-controlled West Bank

Haj Pilgrimage to Mecca

Halal Allowable under Islamic law; usually used in reference to the preparation of Islamically-acceptable food

Hajira/Hejira/Hijra Flight by Mohammed from Mecca to Medina in AD622 – which became the year zero in the Islamic calendar

Hamas Arabic acronym of Islamic Resistance Movement, a fundamentalist organisation founded in 1987 with the aim of turning the whole of Israel and Palestine into an Islamic state

Hammam Bath (Arabic)

Iconoclasm A religious movement common to all three monotheistic faiths that opposes the use of religious images, particularly of humans or God, in worship.

Very prevalent in the 8th and 9th centuries in Christianity

Iconostasis Screen bearing icons and separating the sanctuary from the nave in Orthodox churches

Intifada A Palestinian campaign of civil disobedience, protests and strikes, 1987–93, against the Israeli occupation of Palestine

Jabal/Jebel Hill or mountain (Arabic)

Jama'a Mosque

Judaea and Samaria The Israeli name for the West Bank

Kala'a/Kala'at Fortress (Arabic)

Keffiyah Arabian headscarf

Khan Caravanserai

Koran The holy book of Islam, dictated by Mohammed to his followers in the years before his death

Levant Geographical term, originally used by the Crusaders and referring to the countries of the eastern Mediterranean, comprising Syria, Lebanon, Jordan, Palestine and Israel

Madrassa Islamic school, usually attached to a mosque, which originally only taught religious studies but now has a wider remit

Mamlukes Warrior slaves under the Ayyubid Empire who eventually usurped their masters and established an empire over much of the Near East (1250–1517)

Mar Saint (Arabic)

Maristan Hospital or hospice

Midan Square (Arabic)

Mihrab Niche in the qibla wall indicating the direction of Mecca

Minbar/Minber The pulpit of a mosque

Monotheism Belief in one God only

Muezzin The man who calls the Muslims to prayer five times a day

Mufti Expounder of Islamic law and leader of an Islamic community, usually used in reference to the Grand Mufti of Jerusalem

Nakba Palestinian term for the loss and dispossession of 1948

Nargileh *see* Argila

Narthex Railed-off western porch etc in early Christian church, used mainly by women

Nave Main body of church, usually separated from aisles by pillars

Ommayads First Islamic caliphate dynasty, who ruled over the Levant from their capital in Damascus (AD661–750)

PFLP Popular Front for the Liberation of Palestine, a radical left-wing PLO organisation

PLO Palestine Liberation Organisation, the umbrella name for all Palestinian resistance organisations, founded in 1964

PA/PNA Palestinian National Authority, the ruling body of autonomous Palestine

PNC Palestinian National Council, the ruling body of the PLO

Pasha The local representative of the Ottoman Empire

Pogroms Anti-Jewish campaigns organised in Eastern Europe and particularly Russia at the turn of the century

Qala'a Fortress (Arabic)

Qasr Palace or castle (Arabic)

Qibla Direction of prayer for Muslims

Ramadan Islamic holy month of fasting

Servis A shared taxi, known in Israel as a *sherut*

Sharia Street (Arabic)

Shariy'a Mulim law
Sheesha *see* Argila
Sheikh Respectful term for old man
Sheikha Respectful term for old woman
Shi'a/Shia/Shi'ites Islamic faction, the followers of the descendants of Ali (Mohammed's son-in-law) who believe that the caliphate should be hereditary
Shofar Ceremonial Jewish horn
Souk/Souq Market (Arabic)
Sufi Follower of mystical form of Islam
Sultan King or ruler
Sunni Orthodox Muslim
Sura/Sure A chapter of the Koran
Talmud Sacred Jewish text concerning the oral law of Moses, written between the 2nd and 6th centuries AD
Tel Hill or mound formed from layers of ancient settlements
Torah Sacred Jewish scriptures equivalent to the Pentateuch, or the first five books of the Old Testament
Ummayads *see* Ommayads
Vespers Evensong
Vestibule Antechamber or porch of a church
Wadi Valley (Arabic)
Yarmulka Jewish head-covering or skullcap
Zionism Jewish nationalism, the driving force behind the creation of the state of Israel

Appendix 3

FURTHER INFORMATION
History, the Bible and archaeology

The Lebanese journalist Amin Maalouf's *The Crusades through Arab Eyes* is one of the most fascinating **historical accounts** I have ever read, providing an alternative view of a European movement based upon accounts written by Arab chroniclers of the time. Not far behind is P J Newby's *Saladin in his Time* (Faber and Faber), a thoroughly readable study of the man behind the myth. Read it to see what all the fuss was about. *Byzantine Civilisation* is an enormous two-volume opus by A Vasiliev (University of Wisconsin Press). It's really only for the very enthusiastic, or those with a lot of time on their hands. Similarly, *Soldiers of Fortune - the story of the Mamlukes* is an exceptionally well-researched book concerning this oft-ignored empire by J B Glubb (Glubb Pasha), the leader of the Arab Legion protecting Jordan following its independence in 1923. Reading it can be a little wearisome at times, but it is useful to dip into now and again when one wishes to know the chronological order of their empire. *The Ottomans* by Andrew Wheatcroft (Viking) is not a complete history, but is the most readable, least academic of all the studies of the Turkish empire.

One of the most fascinating **biblical studies** that I dipped into often while researching this book is the *Oxford Companion to the Bible*, a massive reference work full of interesting little snippets of information; it's the kind of absorbing book that you delve into time and again just for pleasure.

On the **archaeological** front, Kathleen Kenyon's *Digging up Jericho* and *The Bible and Recent Archaeology* are the first two books you should read on excavations in Israel and Palestine, written by the Dame who has done more digging in the Holy Land, and made more important discoveries, than anyone else. After those two, try to track down a copy of David Rohl's *A Test of Time*, in which the author expounds on his controversial theory on the chronology of the Bible (see page 31).

Modern history

If it's an analysis of the Palestinian affair you're after you have plenty of choices, although most are polemics rather than straightforward historical accounts. If you read only one book on the subject, track down *Arab and Jew: Wounded Spirits in a Promised Land* (Bloomsbury) by David K Shipler. Perceptive, accurate and well-balanced, it offers a very precise description of the troubles. For a simplified account, *O Jerusalem* by Larry Collins and Dominic Lapierre retells the story of the 1948 War of Independence and the birth of Israel.

Edward Said's *The Question of Palestine* (Vintage) is perhaps the most eloquent account of the Arab-Israeli conflict written from a Palestinian perspective. To gain a better understanding of the plight of the Palestinians, read *Gaza, Legacy of Occupation - a Photographer's Journey*, by Dick Doughty and his Palestinian friend, Mohammed el-Aydi (Kumarian Press), which is a photo-journal of Doughty's time in the Canada refugee camp near Rafah. Entertaining and distressing in equal measures.

This, of course, is not the only work on the rough treatment of Palestinians at the hands of their Israeli overlords. The title of Walid Khalidi's *Before their Diaspora – A photographic history of Palestine 1867–1948*, published by the Institute of Palestinian Studies, is pretty self-explanatory. Poignant though this book is, I preferred Nur Masalha's *Expulsion of the Palestinians – The concept of 'transfer' in Zionist political thought 1882–1948*, which attempts to explain the thought processes behind the policy of land confiscation and dispossession carried out by the Israelis since 1948, and the grim reality for many Palestinians that resulted from these policies. Walid Khalidi's *All that Remains* (Institute of Palestinian Studies) is an encyclopaedic reference work detailing the four hundred Palestinian villages that now lie within the borders of Israel, most of which are now deserted, while Robinson's *Building a Palestinian State – the incomplete revolution* (Indiana press) discusses the emergence of Palestine as an independent nation, and finishes with a rather pessimistic discourse on the prospects of the survival of the state.

Students of the Palestinian struggle will also find Walid Khalidi's *From Haren to Conquest – Readings in Zionism and the Palestinian problem*, a chronological anthology of British policy reports and other official documentation, as well as eyewitness accounts and newspaper reports of the troubles in the Holy Land, absolutely invaluable. If you think the British were guilty of mere incompetence – rather than any malicious intent – during their mandate over Palestine, this book should prove enlightening. Finally, Sami Hadawi's *Bitter Harvest – a modern history of Palestine* (Scorpion Press) is detailed and thorough, and offers a number of thought-provoking insights, though it's a little outdated too, covering the period up to and including 1967 only.

Jerusalem

While K J Asali's *Jerusalem in History* (Olive Branch Press) provides a standard account of the history of the Holy City that will be of interest to first-time visitors, Meron Benvenisti's *City of Stone – the hidden history of Jerusalem* (University of California Press) explores, as the title suggests, the side of the city's history that doesn't usually make it into the tourist brochures. On occasions, this book can be fascinating.

As well as its past, Jerusalem's imminent fate also comes under scrutiny in *Scenarios on the Future of Jerusalem*, edited by Mohammed Shtayyed (PCRS), where contributors from both sides of the political fence – Arab and Israeli – propose their own solutions to the seemingly intractable problem of the future status of Jerusalem. Though often a little too academic in style and content, this book does at least propose some clever and practical ways in which to overcome the biggest obstacle on the path to peace.

A Jerusalem of Peace, written by the Gershon Baskin and published by the Israeli/Palestinian Centre for Research and Information, provides a similar exploration of the issues surrounding the future status of Jerusalem, and comes up with solutions similar to many of those detailed in Scenarios. Finally, honourable mentions must also go to Karen Armstrong's *A History of Jerusalem – one city, three faiths* (Harper Collins), and Michael Dumper's *The Politics of Jerusalem Since 1967* (Columbia), both of which explore the intractable problem of the ownership of Jerusalem.

The Palestinian people

While the turbulent political situation they have been forced to endure has been documented in a thousand different ways by a thousand different authors in ten thousand different books, the Palestinian people themselves, their roots, culture and traditions, have as yet received little attention. *The Folk Heritage of Palestine* by Sharif Kanaana, published by the Research Centre for Arab Heritage, is the glossiest and most colourful and, indeed, best of the few books that have attempted to capture the flavour of Palestinian culture. While this book is an unashamed celebration of Palestine and its people, *Palestinian Women of Gaza and the West Bank*, edited by Suha Sabbagh, explores a less savoury aspect of Palestinian life, namely the continued oppression of women and their rights. The book provides a thorough discourse on the role of Palestinian women in society, the part they have already played in the fight for independence, the Intifada and emergence of the Palestinian state, and the (bleak) prospects of the women's rights movement in Palestine.

Biographies

A couple of biographies about the Palestinian leader, Yasser Arafat, have been gracing the bookshelves for a couple of years now, both of them well worth buying or (as they're both available in expensive hardback only) borrowing from the local library. The first, *In the Eye of the Beholder* by Janet and John Wallash (Lyle Stuart Publishers), provides an accurate and honest assessment of Arafat's rise from freedom fighter to ruler. This portrayal is unflattering, but not half as unflattering as Said K Aburish's *Arafat, from Defender to Dictator* (Bloomsbury), a condemning indictment of both the man and the corrupt regime that he leads.

Hanan Ashrawi's *This Side of Peace – a personal account* is the autobiography of the Christian, mother, founder of the Palestinian Independent Committee for Citizens' Rights and professor at Bir Zeit University, who also happened to be the spokeswoman for the Palestinians in the Occupied Territories.

Travelogues

Many famous authors have travelled through Palestine, recording their opinions (not always favourable) and experiences (not always pleasant) for the enjoyment of others. Mark Twain's *The Innocents Abroad* is my favourite, being a very personal account of a cruise taken in 1867 with a band of pilgrims to the Holy Land, written with Twain's typically jaundiced, sarcastic pen. It is often very funny. It's now out of print, but see if you can track down a second-hand copy. *Holidays in Hell* (Picador) is P J O'Rourke's irreverent account of his experiences in some of the world's troubled hotspots. As you may expect, Israel and Palestine feature prominently. William Dalrymple's *From the Holy Mountain* (Harper Collins) describes the author's attempts to follow in the footsteps of the 6th-century monks John Moschos and his apprentice Sophronius, who journeyed between Greece and Egypt, stopping at a couple of the monasteries featured in this book. Exquisitely written, this book is particularly strong on highlighting the demise of monasticism in the Near East and the reasons behind it.

Guides

There are numerous guides to the Holy Land, and all without exception concentrate on Israel at the expense of Palestine – which is, of course, their loss. The best of this bunch is the *Rough Guide to Israel and the Palestinian Territories*, which is quite detailed in its summary of sights in Jerusalem and the West Bank, though less thorough in its treatment of the Gaza Strip. Pilgrims to the Holy Land may be interested in *Living Stories: A Pilgrimage with Christians of the Holy Land – a guide* by Alison Hilliard and Betty Jane Bailey (published by Cassell), which is good on description, but a bit of a lightweight when it comes to practical information.

Websites

Bir Zeit University www.birzeit.edu
Website of Palestine's largest university, comprehensive summary of Palestinian life, culture etc, and good guide to Ramallah city
Centre for Palestinian Research and Studies www.cprs-palestine.org/
Webpage of organisation devoted to scholarly research on issues related to Palestine. Good for political and economic insights into the country
Palestine Airlines www.palestinianair.com
Includes flights, timetables etc
Passia www.passia.org
PASSIA is an Arab non-profit institution located in Jerusalem/Al-Quds with a financially and legally independent status. It is not affiliated with any government, political party or organisation, which, like the PCRS above, seeks to investigate the Palestinian question through academic research and dialogue.
   This site can be a little too academic at times, but is good on statistics and current state of play in the peace process.
Taybeh www.taybehbeer.com
Site dedicated to the Ramallah-based brewery.
Palestine.net www.palestine-net.com
Contains everything to do with the country, from the economy to the latest news bulletins; indeed, everything you need to know about Palestine, including the geography, history, politics, culture, education, business, etc
P.A.C.E. www.planet.edu/~pace/
Website of the number one organisation in Palestine for tours, historical and archaeological research. Includes list of publications, photos of historical sights.
British consulate in Jerusalem www.britishconsulate.org/
Best of the consulate's websites, and a good place to pick up the latest news and travel advice
Baraka www.baraka.org/
Details of Palestinian NGOs and their websites, including PCRF and Inash El-Usra
PCRF www.wolfenet.com/~pcrf/
Webpage of the children's charity (see page 37)
Bethlehem 2000 www.bethlehem2000.org/
Website devoted to events surrounding the Millennium celebrations
Islamic Association for Palestine www.iap.org/
Founded in 1981, the Islamic Association for Palestine is a non-profit organization based in Dallas dedicated to working towards a fair, just and comprehensive solution to the problem of Palestine. Site includes political maps, excerpts from newspapers etc
Arab hotels association www.palestinehotels.com/
Website of the Palestinian-based hotel association
Palestinian Refugee Researchnet www.arts.mcgill.ca/MEPP/PRRN/prfront.html
A Canadian address, and the most comprehensive site dedicated to Palestinian refugees

The Bradt Story

In 1974, my former husband George Bradt and I spent three days sitting on a river barge in Bolivia writing our first guide for like-minded travellers: *Backpacking along Ancient Ways in Peru and Bolivia*. The 'little yellow book', as it became known, is now in its seventh edition and continues to sell to travellers throughout the world.

Since 1980, with the establishment of Bradt Publications, I have continued to publish guides for the discerning traveller, covering more than 100 countries and all six continents; in 1997 we won *The Sunday Times* Small Publisher of the Year Award. Palestine is the 164th Bradt title or new edition to be published.

The company continues to develop new titles and new series, but in the forefront of my mind there remains our original ethos – responsible travel with an emphasis on the culture and natural history of the region. I hope that you will get the most out of your trip, and perhaps have the opportunity to give something in return.

Travel guides are by their nature continuously evolving. If you experience anything which you would like to share with us, or if you have any amendments to make to this guide, please write; all your letters are read and passed on to the author. Most importantly, do remember to travel with an open mind and to respect the customs of your hosts – it will add immeasurably to your enjoyment.

Happy travelling!

Hilary Bradt

Hilary Bradt

19 High Street, Chalfont St Peter, Bucks SL9 9QE, England
Tel: 01494 873478 Fax: 01753 892333
Email: bradtpublications@compuserve.com www.bradt-travelguides.com

Index

When sorting this index into alphabetical order, the Arabic prefixes Al- and El-
have been ignored; thus El-Khader, for example, is listed under 'K' and not 'E'.
Page references in bold indicate main entries; those in italics indicate maps.